HANDBOOK OF GYMNASTICS
IN THE SCHOOLS

Instructional, Exhibitional, and
Competitive Gymnastics
For Men and Women

JAMES A. BALEY

Professor and Chairman of Physical Education
Jersey City State College

ALLYN AND BACON
Boston

This book is dedicated to my wife,
who is always so nice to come home to.

CONTENTS

Contents

8. SKILLS FOR SENIOR HIGH AND COLLEGE MEN AND WOMEN

190

9. INTERNATIONAL LEVEL SKILLS FOR MEN

257

10. INTERNATIONAL LEVEL SKILLS FOR WOMEN

271

11. PUBLICITY AND PUBLIC RELATIONS TO ENLARGE THE EDUCATIONAL ARENA

277

12. JUDGING AND OFFICIATING

281

PREFACE

This book has been written to help the practicing physical educator and the physical educator in training to teach gymnastics, tumbling skills, and related activities with greater skill, confidence, and efficiency. It is also hoped that many readers will become sufficiently interested in the sport of gymnastics to initiate exhibition and competitive programs in their schools. That there are many physical educators who would like to learn more about this sport has been indicated by the increasing number of people attending gymnastic clinics, exhibitions, and meets.

Gymnastics is a sport on the move! More schools, colleges, Y.M.C.A.s, and Y.W.C.A.s are starting gymnastic teams. States are organizing for gymnastic competition. More gymnastic equipment is being sold. More films on gymnastics are being produced. More articles and books on gymnastics are being written. While every physical educator cannot be an expert on gymnastics, every physical educator should be able to teach gymnastics and tumbling in his physical education classes.

Principles drawn from the disciplines of anatomy, physiology, psychology, kinesiology, and sociology are applied to the teaching of gymnastics and tumbling in this book. The use of gymnastics and tumbling as a modality to achieve the larger educational goals is discussed. Methods of class organization and safety procedures are thoroughly presented. Spotting procedures are described for almost all skills.

Undoubtedly, the biggest deterrent to success in learning gymnastic skills is inadequate strength and flexibility. When students improve these qualities, they learn much more rapidly and, consequently, with greater joy and satisfaction. For this reason, thirty self-testing activities, eight animal relays, and ten partner and group relays are presented. These have been selected because they will develop the specific muscle groups and the specific skills necessary for success in gymnastics and tumbling. Furthermore, they are fun for the students. In addition, exercise programs to improve the flexibility, strength, power, and endurance of competitive gymnasts are thoroughly described.

Since the support and growth of any activity depends upon public acceptance and recognition, publicity and public relations are also discussed. Suggestions are made for the use of such publicity media as television, radio, newspapers, posters, newsletters, and announcements. The demonstration and exhibition troupe is recognized as one publicity medium, although the troupe itself has educational objectives of much greater importance.

Competitive gymnastics is also discussed in depth. Methods for initiating a competitive program, organizing and conducting gymnastic competition, coaching techniques, composing routines, taking care of the hands (a problem common to all competitors in gymnastics), and judging are discussed.

Preface

Chapters 6 (Skills for Elementary School Boys and Girls) and 7 (Skills for Junior High School Boys and Girls) and 8 (Skills for Senior High School and College Men and Women) are organized to present a challenge to physical educators and to the profession. Some child of the appropriate school age has done each move described in Chapters 6 and 7; however, no child has done them all. Yet, it is probable that if a school system had a complete gymnastic program in the elementary schools of the type presented in this textbook, many students in physical education classes in the junior and senior high schools would be able to perform the skills described in Chapters 7 and 8. Until elementary schools present students with a thorough program in gymnastics and tumbling, physical educators in the junior and senior high schools and in the colleges will have to draw heavily from Chapter 6 for suggestions for class work. Those who are coaching gymnastic teams or directing exhibition troupes will need to draw from Chapters 7 and 8 and material in the appendixes. It is hoped that school administrators and physical educators, particularly in the elementary schools, will accept the challenge issued throughout Chapters 6, 7, and 8.

J. A. B.

HANDBOOK OF
GYMNASTICS IN THE SCHOOLS

1

VALUES IN GYMNASTICS

Before initiating any undertaking it is wise to ask: "What is the value of this activity? Is its value adequate to justify the necessary expenditure of time, energy, and money? Of what benefit is it to me? To society?" The boy or girl or young man or woman about to join a gymnastics team or club, and the Chairman of Physical Education or the Athletic Director must ask themselves these questions before adding gymnastics to their program.

In writing this book, the author must answer these questions for his readers—and for himself. Fortunately, this is not a difficult task, for gymnastics contributes to the physiological, psychological, and sociological objectives common to all physical education activities. It can also be justified from the anthropological, cultural, and economic points of view.

FROM AN ANTHROPOLOGICAL PERSPECTIVE

Man has been on this earth for approximately two million years. The Industrial Revolution was ushered in only a little over two hundred years ago with the invention of the flying shuttle for the hand loom. Then came the steam engine and the gasoline motor to substitute for muscle power and man no longer found it necessary to become physically exhausted in order to survive. For the approximately 1,999,880 years previous to the machine age man had to depend entirely upon his muscles for survival. He did have hoes, shovels, and picks, but he had to move these with his muscles. Physical fatigue was a normal part of life. Earlier, as a hunter, man had to hike great distances in stalking game, run for his life, move with great agility to avoid being impaled on an animal's horns, and throw a spear with sufficient power to pierce a tough hide. For roughly 9,999/10,000 of his time on earth, man has led an extremely vigorous life. During this long time his body systems and organs grew to depend upon large, regular, and continuous doses of vigorous physical activity. He has been unable to adapt in such a short time as 200 years to his present sedentary life. When he does not utilize invented and artificial forms of exercise such as games, sports, dance, calisthenics, or gymnastics, he becomes obese, or at least fat, because if he takes in so few calories as to avoid the accumulation of fat he suffers vitamin and mineral deficiencies; his heart muscle becomes weak and flabby; cholesterol accumulates in his arteries to make them narrow and brittle; he becomes constipated; and his respiratory system becomes so inefficient that he wheezes when he walks up a flight of more than five steps. Those who participate in gymnastics regularly do not suffer from these physical anomalies which are some of the penalties of a highly developed technology. People who lead a vigorous life live in harmony with nature. Nature demands regular exercise and imposes harsh penalties upon those who do not observe her laws. Regular participation in strenuous exercise is as much an ecological desideratum as is avoidance of polluting our air and water. The sedentary man violates the laws of nature just as do those who dump chemicals and other pollutants into our air and our rivers.

Our common ancestry with the simians leads us naturally to gymnastics and tumbling. The instinctive drive of children to climb over and on top of, to swing, to roll, to twist, and to turn is an indication of this calling. Children enjoy these activities—unless they are overweight or otherwise physically unfit, or unless the activities are presented in a stilted, formalized, or unchallenging manner.

During apparatus work, muscle insertions become origins with a considerably greater resistance offered against the muscle (the body) than is offered in most team and dual games (the ball, racket, or bat). This accounts for the well-developed musculature of the experienced gymnast. Gymnastics particularly develops the muscles of the thorax, shoulder girdle, and arms. These are the very muscle groups which are neglected in the most popular spectator sports in the United States.

FROM A SOCIOLOGICAL PERSPECTIVE

Gymnastics, when properly taught and coached, can make substantial contributions to societal objectives. One way in which gymnastics contributes to social objectives is by providing people an opportunity to use their increased leisure in a manner constructive for themselves and their society. The great English historian, Arnold Toynbee, has pointed out that of 21 great civilizations which have collapsed, 19 have collapsed from within as a result of a slow rot of the moral and physical fiber of the people, rather than as a result of conquest from without. How people of a society use their leisure is perhaps even more important than how they use their working time, because it is during their leisure that they can choose either to engage in activities which make them better people or to engage in those which are debilitating. Not all leisure activities have the same value. Some are more valuable than others. A hierarchy of leisure activities could be established as follows:

1. At the highest level would be such *creative* activities as writing, composing music, painting, or designing.
2. At the next level would be those activities in which one *participates,* such as dramatics, athletics, singing, or dancing.
3. The next level would include all *spectator* activities such as watching and listening to dramatics, television, music, or athletics.
4. At the next level would be activities which are *harmful to self* such as drinking, staying up all night, smoking, or overeating.
5. At the lowest level would be those activities which are *harmful to others,* such as juvenile delinquency, crime, or driving at excessive speeds.

The gymnast usually operates at level 2, but very often he operates at the highest level (level 1) when he designs routines or creates new moves or unusual combinations.

Gymnastics, when properly taught, can improve qualities of social fitness such as cooperation, conservation, tolerance, courtesy, leadership and followership, helpfulness, appreciation for the abilities of others, and fair play.

Members of gymnastics classes, teams, and exhibition troupes must work together cooperatively in setting up and returning equipment, in spotting one another, in pyramid building, and in preparing for and presenting exhibitions and demonstrations. When students are told: "Today Johnny Jones, Sam Smith, and Bill Brown will set up and return the equipment," it is teacher rather than group pressure which is being utilized. This procedure may ensure return of the equipment, but it does not develop a spirit of cooperation. It develops response to command. Cooperativeness is an attitude. It is not a response to a command. The wise and able teacher will seize upon teachable moments not only to teach the advisability of cooperative endeavor to meet the specific objectives of a particular class, but also to effect a "transfer of training" of this quality to general life situations. This is most effectively accomplished during the elementary and junior high grades. Teachers at these school levels have a tremendously important job.

Students learn to conserve equipment by refraining from dragging mats or bouncing on the trampoline with their shoes on, and by participating in such repair and maintenance activities as saddle-soaping the side horse, and oiling and greasing adjustable or moving parts of other equipment. Obviously, these learning situations will not occur spontaneously. Constant efforts to educate, but not to compel, must be made. When children endeavor to conserve equipment when the teacher is not present, we have an indication that the teacher has been successful in instilling this quality.

Gymnasts soon learn to empathize with fellow gymnasts who are experiencing difficulty in learning a specific move because they, too, have probably had a similar experience with another move. With proper leadership, they will learn tolerance for the slow learners because they will observe that some slow learners have become champions as a result of determined and persevering effort. They will learn, too, that popularity among their fellow gymnasts results from appreciation and praise, not from an attitude of superiority or scorn.

Among members of the champion gymnastic teams and in the most productive gymnastics classes there exist attitudes of both competitiveness and helpfulness. Members coach one another, pass on pointers, spot for one another, and assist each other in setting up, returning, and moving equipment. While they compete with one another to see who will be first to learn a new move or combination, they sense that when one makes progress, he makes it a little easier for the others to follow.

Gymnasts learn to appreciate the abilities of others because they know, quite accurately, how difficult the skills are which others have mastered. After the conclusion of gymnastic meets, the winners can often be seen coaching their opponents of a few moments ago in a skill which helped them to win. The gymnast learns to appreciate movement as an art form because the sport is not directly competitive. He can express this appreciation whether the movement was executed by a teammate or an opponent.

Exhibition and demonstration groups—because of their numerous committees, officers, captains, and squad leaders, and because of the many tasks to be executed—provide opportunities to develop leadership and followership. Inherent in them are opportunities for students with all kinds of skills to contribute to the production. Sign painters, carpenters, musicians, jugglers, unicycle riders, script writers, ad writers, production managers, seamstresses, electricians, publicity men, and artists can all provide their special skills and leadership and thereby contribute to the effectiveness of the production.

FROM A PSYCHOLOGICAL PERSPECTIVE

Gymnastics contributes to many of the psychological objectives of physical education. A baby is not born with such qualities as physical courage, determination, perseverance, self-respect, self-reliance, and empathy. These qualities are acquired and learned through life experiences. A physical educator can utilize gymnastics to help develop these qualities in his students.

Self-reliance Gymnastics, like all individual sports, develops self-reliance. The gymnast cannot blame another player for his failure. This characteristic of gymnastics encourages *realistic self-appraisal*, particularly during competition.

Empathy When a gymnast notices another gymnast experiencing difficulty in learning a move, he will recall his own difficulty in learning that skill or another skill. He realizes that not all people learn with the same facility. Some students will find it necessary to work on a particular skill longer than most other students, but will learn other skills more quickly. This understanding will enable gymnasts to feel empathy toward one another. In spotting and coaching one another and in cooperatively setting up and replacing equipment, students learn to cooperate in order to achieve common goals.

Self-realization Undoubtedly, the greatest value of gymnastics lies in the self-realization, ego satisfaction, or gain in self-esteem which comes from learning a new skill, improving the performance of a skill, or putting moves together into a new and more difficult routine. One can see college students hop up and down with unrestrained joy after doing a new skill for the first time. Every gymnast can have this experience *many* times.

Adaptive Reactions A gymnast learns to make adaptive reactions quickly and accurately as he hurtles, spins, twists, and turns through the air. Because gymnastics is a highly individualized sport and no one, including the teacher or coach, knows his abilities and potential better than he, the gymnast must make a realistic appraisal of his present and potential abilities and must then plan his practice sessions intelligently, with determination and self-control.

FROM A PHYSIOLOGICAL PERSPECTIVE

Participation in gymnastics will improve the participants' strength, power, flexibility, agility, and muscular endurance. Some improvement in cardiovascular-respiratory efficiency can be accomplished, but not so much as in activities such as swimming, track, soccer, and basketball, which require sustained effort in which many repetitions of a movement are performed against a small resistance.

People who have participated extensively in gymnastics invariably possess surprising *strength* relative to their body weight. This is because they must move their bodies while hanging from or supported on their hands. Their muscles are consequently required to overcome a considerably greater resistance than when throwing a ball or swinging a bat or racquet. Their own body is obviously heavier than any of the usual sports paraphernalia.

Because of the explosive movements called for in gymnastics (vaults over the long horse, mounts onto the parallel bars, uprises, kip-ups, and dismounts) and because improvement in strength will produce improvement in *power*, experienced gymnasts score well in measures of power.

Flexibility is constantly being tested—and consequently developed—in a number of gymnastic events. In the floor exercise event, the gymnast is challenged to execute splits, back bends, needles, and scales, all of which require extreme flexibility. Eagle giant swings, stoop vaults, straight arm-straight leg press-ups, and many other moves require flexibility as well as strength, power, balance, and agility.

Agility, the ability to make quick and adaptive movements, is obviously a quality developed through gymnastics. One need only watch a gymnast perform to be convinced of this. The tumbler executing a round-off into two back handsprings into a double full twisting back somersault into a front salto has obviously demonstrated a high degree of agility. A gymnast on the horizontal bar doing a shoot into a giant swing has also demonstrated agility.

In executing the scale, handstand, and one-arm half lever, and in performing on the balance beam, the gymnast demonstrates a high level of *static balance*. While executing tumbling, trampoline, horizontal bar, parallel bar, ring, and side horse routines, he demonstrates *dynamic balance*. While learning and practicing these moves and routines, he is improving both his static and his dynamic balance.

While executing routines on the various pieces of gymnastic equipment and while repeatedly attempting moves, the gymnast is demonstrating and improving his *cardiovascular-respiratory endurance*. This facet of physical fitness is developed most effectively while practicing routines in tumbling and in rebound tumbling.

The great contributions of gymnastics to the biophysical objectives of physical education are unquestioned. This is so because gymnastics stresses muscles, ligaments, tendons, and the cardio-respiratory system. It is a fundamental law of nature that most living things adapt to the stresses to which they are subjected. The camel has adapted to the arid climate of the Sahara. The whale, which has lungs like those of other mammals, can hold his breath for long periods. Man has adapted to life in the heat of the equator and in the cold of Alaska; to the humid climate of the jungle and to the arid climate of the desert; to the rarified air in Mexico City and to denser air in Salt Lake City; to great varieties of diet; and to the stresses imposed in conditioning for competition in sports.

Regular participation in progressively increased doses of exercise has beneficial effects upon most of the body systems. Muscle size and strength increases. The number of capillaries increases to facilitate bringing of oxygen and nutrients to and taking away of carbon dioxide and waste products from muscle cells. Cholesterol, which is responsible for making arteries more brittle and increasing blood pressure and the probability of suffering a cerebrovascular accident or myocardial infarction, is metabolized. Exercise has been found more effective than diet in controlling cholesterol. Exercise increases the number of erythrocytes or red blood cells. Red blood cells carry oxygen to the body cells. The greater the number of erythrocytes, the more oxygen the blood can carry to other body cells. This delays the onset of fatigue. Regular participation in vigorous exercise increases both the vertical and the horizontal diameter of the thorax during inspiration, thereby facilitating a greater volume of air exchanged. This is made possible because the muscles of the thorax and the diaphragm, a broad sheath-like muscle stretching across the lower end of the rib cage, become stronger. The excursions of the diaphragm become greater. The alveoli, or air sacs, which make up the lungs and through whose walls the exchange of oxygen and carbon dioxide occurs, are increased in size and number. This facilitates greater utilization of inspired air. The heart muscle becomes stronger and more efficient so that it can pump out a greater volume of blood with each stroke. This is why the resting pulse rate of well-conditioned athletes is so much slower at rest than that of people who do not exercise. The athlete's heart can meet the needs of the body at rest with fewer beats per minute and enjoy a longer resting period.

The athlete's heart can beat as rapidly as the heart of the nonathlete; however, considerably more physical stress is required to cause it to accelerate as much as the heart of the nonathlete. The athlete's heart can keep pace with the demands of the body under physical stress whereas the nonathlete's heart cannot. This is why the athlete does not become fatigued as quickly—and why those who continue to exercise regularly throughout their lifetime are less likely to suffer a cardiac malfunction, and if they do, are more likely to recover. People should not avoid physical activity; they should seek it out, as Ponce de Leon sought out "the fountain of youth." Gymnastics is one of the best forms of physical activity.

Physical Courage A gymnast develops physical courage without foolhardiness because, if the gymnast is to succeed, he must learn skills in their progressive order of difficulty and must use proper safety and spotting procedures. The gymnast should learn early that the practice of proper safety procedures not only will enable him to continue to enjoy the activity by avoiding injury but also to learn the skills more quickly. Courage is required to do the back handspring, but before attempting this move, the gymnast should master the elementary skills, such as varieties of forward and backward rolls, all the springs and their varieties, cartwheels, round-offs, and backbends. During his first attempts on the back handspring, he should have two spotters holding the ropes of a safety belt. After he has mastered this step, he should have one spotter hold one rope of the safety belt. Having mastered the second step, he should call for two hand spotters, and then one hand spotter. He should master each of the four steps before attempting the skill without assistance. During this learning process, he will very likely develop physical courage without foolhardiness, and he is not likely to suffer an injury that would delay his progress or shake his confidence.

Determination and Perseverance Gymnastics develops determination and perseverance because skills are seldom mastered in a few attempts. Mastery of some skills requires a year or more of regular daily practice. Every aspiring gymnast, however, if he continues his efforts, can master the next hardest skill. Having observed that repeated efforts ultimately bring the satisfaction of success, the gymnast learns to respect effort and perseverance.

Self-respect When a gymnast has mastered a challenging and difficult move or combination, he gains in self-respect. The satisfaction, joy, and sense of achievement in having conquered space, time, and gravity after having executed a straight body vault over the long horse for the first time is incomparable. This feeling is experienced almost every time the gymnast learns a new skill. It is a feeling of power and strength—a feeling of self-mastery. When he performs a move or a routine well before a few other gymnasts or before an auditorium filled with spectators, he feels as satisfied and fulfilled as the author who sees his article or book in print for the first time, the architect who sees his plans materialize, or the lecturer who feels his audience has responded as he had hoped they would.

BIBLIOGRAPHY

Baley, James A., and Childs, Harold. "The Appeal of Gymnastics." *Journal of the American Association for Health, Physical Education, and Recreation*, February, 1956.

Baley, James A. "Some Contributions of Gymnastics." *The Physical Educator*, December, 1956.

————. "Gymkana—A Superb Educational Tool." *New York State Journal of Health, Physical Education, and Recreation*, October, 1957.

————. "Physical Education and Gymnastics, an Integral Part of the Educational Process." *The Southern Amateur Athlete*, April, 1959.

————. "Are Gymnastics and Tumbling Essential?" *The Physical Educator*, May, 1961.

————. "Any School Can Have a Complete Gymnastics Program." *The Mentor*, December, 1961.

————. "Any School Can Have a Complete Gymnastics Program." *The Texas Coach*, March, 1963.

————. "Establishing Gymnastics as a School Sport." *School Activities*, February, 1964.

Frederick, Bruce A. *212 Ideas for Making Low-Cost Physical Education Equipment*. Englewood Cliffs, N.J.: Prentice-Hall, Inc., 1963.

2

HISTORICAL DEVELOPMENT OF GYMNASTICS

The beginnings of gymnastics and tumbling are lost in antiquity. Very likely, early man was skilled in arboreal activities and delighted in climbing and swinging on vines and on branches. He invented different moves and combinations of moves and challenged his peers to accomplish them. These activities have culminated in the modern events known as the rope climb, swinging and still rings, trapeze, and horizontal bar.

PRIMITIVE MAN

Primitive man included movements in his dances that were similar to those seen in today's tumbling and floor exercise routines. Very likely he included cartwheels, handsprings, and even somersaults in his vigorous and expressive dances.

THE EGYPTIANS

We know that in Egypt, as early as 1500 B.C., acrobatic movements were included in the dances. Inscriptions left by these early Egyptians on vases, mosaics, reliefs, and paintings indicate that the older children tumbled, turned somersaults, and did other gymnastic moves. Pictures in stone prove that the Egyptians participated in pyramid building and balancing as long ago as 2100 B.C. The Chinese engaged in tumbling even before this time.

THE PERSIANS

The vigorous and warlike Persians of 558–331 B.C. may have initiated moves on the side horse. In their practice for combat, they mounted and dismounted their horses in a variety of styles while traveling at a full gallop. Many of these skills were similar to those performed on the side horse today. It is interesting to note that early side horses not only had one end raised and tapered like a horse's neck but also had a tail attached to the opposite end. Today, since horses are mounted from the horse's left side, the part to the left is called the "neck," the part to the right is called the "croup," and the center part between the pommels is called the "saddle."

THE GREEKS

While the early Greeks worked with apparatus rather than upon it, they did establish the word "gymnastics" which meant "naked art." It was the early Greeks who glorified the human body participating in sports and athletics. They symbolized this concept through their beautiful statues, demonstrating their recognition of the unity of man's body, mind, and emotions. Greek gymnasia served as meeting places both for intellectual discussions by philosophers, scholars, and politicians and for participation in track and field events, wrestling, chariot racing, and boxing. The early Greeks developed the most wholesome physical education and sports programs of all times. They erred, however, near the end of their period of supremacy, by allowing the majority of Greek citizens to secure their satisfactions in athletics vicariously by identifying with and cheering for their athletic champions rather than through their own participation. Increasingly, valuable rewards were given to their victorious athletes and increasing numbers of people became merely spectators. The citizens became indolent and soft and were ultimately conquered by the vigorous and warlike Romans.

THE ROMANS

The early Romans kept themselves strong, vigorous, and agile by constant practice at war games. They were ambitious for world conquest and they did, in time, conquer all of their known world. In order to practice mounting and dismounting from a horse they invented and made use of the wooden horse which has been modified through the years to the piece of equipment we see in today's gymnasia. The seed of error, however, was present in the Romans' physical training program from its beginning. This error was in their use of athletics and sports as a means of conditioning for war and conquest. As soon as they had conquered the surrounding nations, they had no further reason for undergoing the unpleasantness of war games and tough physical conditioning. They forced their captives to do all the manual work and to entertain them with displays of their athletic prowess. They luxuriated and dissipated and became an easy target for the rugged, strong, tough barbarians who swept down from the north.

THE DARK AGES

The fall of Rome was followed by five centuries of political disorganization known as the Dark Ages. This was a period of rape, slaughter, and fear. However, while there was little time for athletics and games as a diversion, a powerful vigorous body was necessary for survival. The Teutonic people secured their exercise through armed combat, hand-to-hand combat, running, and weight casting. The religious leaders of this time were the sole intellectual leaders. They wished to avoid the errors of the decadent Romans and, believing that the Romans' indulgence in wine, food, sex, and things bringing pleasure to the body led to their downfall, extolled the soul and condemned athletics and sports as being of the body. To demonstrate their disdain for the body, which they regarded as only a cage for the soul, some adopted the practice of inflicting pain upon themselves in various ways. Neglect or mortification of the body were marks of otherworldliness. Even bathing was banned; the "odor of sanctity" was not just a phrase. Unfortunately, the idea that mind and body are separate entities has persisted in some quarters to this day.

The knights were probably the only men participating in organized physical activity during this era. Their activities included climbing, vaulting, swimming, riding, archery, tilting and jousting, wrestling, fencing, jumping, dancing, and climbing on ropes, poles, and ladders. Pyramid building and acrobatics were presented at fairs and other public gatherings to entertain the public. While the churchmen of these times decried participation in sports as frivolous and vain, they did succeed in preserving the learnings of the ancients.

THE AGE OF RECOVERY

The Dark Ages were followed by the "Age of Recovery." Peoples grouped themselves to form the beginnings of nations, and on a smaller scale, their desire for security and protection was satisfied through feudalism. This was a system of government based upon ownership of land and the ability to fight. The status of those who were not landowners was little better than that of slaves or work animals. However, among the feudal aristocracy, the cultural embellishments became desired. As a result, rules of conduct evolved into the institution we know as chivalry, which became the code of the knights. Chivalry's code of conduct introduced elements of courtesy, fidelity, mercy, and justice into the pattern of men's behavior. During his training for knighthood, a young nobleman was tutored in the social graces, received religious instruction, learned to dance, participated in sports and games, hunted, and assisted in battle. A rigorous program of physical conditioning was among the most important facets of his training program.

Chivalry affected only a small eligible minority. Most of the people continued to lead a life both harsh and precarious. Yet their lot had improved enough that they found some opportunities for play in the form of mock jousts and tournaments. They fought with a staff or rod in place of real weapons. They competed in running, wrestling, weight throwing, and in several kinds of ball games. Toward the end of this period universities became established, some of which centered in existing clerical institutions, while some were more independent of the church. Because instruction was often pedantic and boring and because students were left to their own devices outside the classroom, students' leisure hours were often devoted to pranks, brawling, and riotous living. Educators had no desire to channel the students' energies into wholesome recreational activities, nor were they concerned with their health or aware of its relationship to academic performance.

During the Crusades, those traveling to the lands of the "infidels" had contact with ideas and opinions different from their own. These stimulated men to question and reflect—eventually even to question their own established ideas, mores, and customs. The period known as the Renaissance began, and men studied man instead of the divine. They studied his origin and destiny, his nature and his anatomy, his environment, and his universe. It was during this period that physical education came to be recognized again as a definite and neces-

sary part of the educational process. Educational leaders of this period such as Michel de Montaigne, Richard Mulcaster, and John Amos Comenius emphasized the unity of mind and body and stressed that education was concerned with the whole man rather than just a part of him. Comenius advocated the inclusion of vigorous athletic activities in the school program. However, few schools had physical education programs by the end of the sixteenth century, although many people participated in exercises, sports, and games.

From the fifteenth century on, all aspects of civilization in Europe grew rapidly in sophistication and complexity. More democratic forms of government pointed up the need for cooperation and for greater educational opportunities for all. The foundations of modern educational procedures were laid during this time by such men as Rousseau, Basedow, Pestalozzi, Froebel, and Spencer. All of these accepted physical education as a fundamental part of the educational process. Through the leadership of physical educators such as Guts Muths, Jahn, Spiess, Nachtegall, Ling, Maclaren, Beck, and Catherine Beecher, physical education entered a period of rapid development and expansion. These physical educators and others established the form and content of gymnastics.

THE EIGHTEENTH AND NINETEENTH CENTURIES

Scientists of the eighteenth century demonstrated that nature could be better understood and controlled to prevent disease and to increase productivity through observation and study. This led other men to wonder whether man's social structures could not be similarly improved through objective observation and study. Jean-Jacques Rousseau (1712–1778) was one of those who thoroughly examined governmental and educational institutions. Rousseau's studies led him to the conclusion that not only should children learn about their environment primarily through their senses, but also that they should be free of any authority, including that of the Bible and of society, to develop their personality fully. Children, he believed, should develop according to the laws of nature. This was the major thesis of *educational naturalism* to which Rousseau had given birth. The naturalists, believing that youth was the time to build a strong and skillful physical organism, gave to physical education a central role in the educational process. Basedow's Philanthropinium was the first school organized according to a naturalistic philosophy. Students in this school spent three hours each day in physical activity and another two hours at manual labor. Basedow's school had balance beams, high jumping pits, seesaws, hoops, tennis courts, and badminton courts. Skating, marching, and posture exercises were also included among the activities. The posture exercises were the forerunners of today's floor exercises performed in competitive gymnastics.

The nineteenth century witnessed the rise of a nationalistic spirit in the countries of Western Europe. This trend resulted not only from the Crusades and the Christian-Moslem wars of earlier years, but from contemporary technological advances. The Industrial Revolution created a demand for raw material from foreign lands and for foreign markets for manufactured goods. The printing press, by providing for mass dissemination of ideas and information on a national scale, encouraged the breakdown of provincialism. People began to understand the relationships between their own welfare and that of the nation.

This nationalistic spirit infused a number of educators who saw in physical education a means for nurturing this spirit in others. Education under nationalism promotes civic ideals, social and political homogeneity, and patriotism. Physical education used to develop physical fitness enables citizens to become maximally productive and better able to defend their country.

Frederick Ludwig Jahn (1778–1852), who was the physical education leader of this era, possessed both a great love of liberty and pride in Germany. He utilized physical education to develop people's physical powers for national defense, to instill a love of country, and to promote a sense of individualism and freedom. Jahn's interest in physical education developed when, as a teacher, he took his students on biweekly hikes into the country. On these hikes, he encouraged such big muscle activities as running, jumping, wrestling, climbing, swimming, and stunts. He led the children in patriotic songs, told them of Germany's history, and urged them to work for liberty and for their country. He im-

provised horizontal bars (a horizontal oak limb), javelins (straight sticks), and jumping standards. In 1811, he opened his first Turnplatz outside Berlin. Patterned after the Greek Palaestra, it consisted of a fenced-in rectangular area enclosing homemade inclined and horizontal ladders, jumping standards, horizontal bars, climbing poles, balance beams, climbing ropes, pole vaulting equipment, broad jumping pits, a running track, a wrestling ring, and a hut for dressing. The following year more diverse and better equipment was added. In 1813 the War of Liberation from the French broke out and Jahn and his Turner members joined in the battle. The great surge in patriotism which followed the victorious efforts caused a rapid growth in the Turner clubs, and Jahn became a national hero. However, Jahn's effectiveness was relatively short-lived because in 1818 the Turner organization was outlawed by most of the German states since the authorities feared the liberal teachings of the organization. Jahn was arrested the following year for allegedly inciting revolutionary practices.

A few Turners met secretly during the time the organization was outlawed, but it did not enjoy a true revival until 1860 when members decided to avoid all political activity. After this, the organization grew to number many thousands of clubs all over the world and many more thousands of members. Until the early 1940's many of the outstanding U. S. gymnasts had received a good part of their training in the Turner clubs in this country.

Adolph Spiess (1810–1855) was responsible for bringing gymnastics and physical education into the schools of Switzerland and Germany and consequently became known as the "Father of School Gymnastics." Spiess was concerned with gymnastics as an important part of the educational curriculum, while Jahn viewed it in nationalistic terms and as an out-of-school activity for both adults and students. Jahn emphasized freedom and liberty, while Spiess believed that physical fitness could be most effectively improved through quick and accurate response to commands. He believed in order and precision. He preferred activities and methods which would enable one instructor to lead large groups exercising simultaneously and in unison. Consequently, he stressed marching and calisthenics. Since he was gifted musically, he arranged many of the exercises and marching drills so that they could be done to music. In most of his drills, the students stood in circles or rows and performed the exercises to count. The Spiess system was adopted by most of the German schools, although later it was modified through inclusion of some aspects of Swedish gymnastics.

Per Henrik Ling (1776–1839), who came to be called the "Father of Swedish Gymastics," became interested in physical education when he noted improvement in an afflicted arm during a course of lessons in fencing. He taught Norse mythology, poetry, and history and served as fencing master. He became a literary leader who incited patriotic feelings through his poems and plays. He saw in physical education a means for strenghtening the people of Sweden so that they could recapture their former glory, which had been lost to Finland and Russia. Ling believed that physical education should develop endurance, agility, and power; that it should always be conducted according to the known facts of the human organism; and that the military, medical, pedagogical, and aesthetic goals of physical education are a unity which should be pursued simultaneously. He evolved a program which consisted of fencing, vaulting, free exercises, and light apparatus work making use of stall bars, booms, saddles, window ladders, vaulting boxes, climbing poles, and horizontal, vertical, and oblique ropes. After he became director of the Royal Central Institute of Gymnastics in Stockholm, he enlarged upon his study of and experimentation in the use of physical activities as a modality for the amelioration of physical anomalies.

Franz Nachtegall (1777–1847) was the leader in physical education in Denmark during the turbulent years of the Industrial Revolution, French Revolution, and the Napoleonic Wars. He held the title "Director of Gymnastics." Although he believed in a broadly based program, the Napoleonic Wars forced him to conduct physical education in such a manner as to achieve military goals. Consequently, he advocated activities on hanging ladders, climbing poles, rope ladders, and wooden horses. Jumping, running, vaulting, balancing, swimming, and military drills were included. His writings are the first to mention the use of mats as a safety procedure.

A Spaniard, Colonel Francisco Amoras (1770–1848), established the foundations of the French military and school physical education programs. Amoras, like Prokion Clias who established the elementary school program in France, directed his program primarily toward the achievement of military objectives. Amoras's program utilized progression in stretching exercises accompanied by singing or a metronome and followed by more vigorous activities such as apparatus work, balancing, marching, leaping, climbing, vaulting, and jumping. Amoras was one of the first to use rings, the trapeze, inclined boards and ladders, rope ladders, the giant stride, and a machine to measure strength.

While the French had to call on the Spaniard Amoras and the Swiss Clias to establish patterns for their military and school physical education programs, it was one of their own, Baron Pierre de Coubertin, who made the greatest contribution to athletics, when his efforts to revive the Olympic Games finally came to fruition. The first modern Olympic Games were held in Athens, Greece in 1896.

There are several other European pioneers in gymnastics with whom gymnasts and teachers of gymnastics should be familiar. One of the most important is Johann Guts Muths (1759–1839), who is known as the "Great-grandfather of Gymnastics," since he published the first book on gymnastics, *Gymnastics for Youth*. Gerhard Vieth (1763–1836) published an encyclopedia of exercises in which he described a number of vaults over the side and long horse and over a horizontal pole (a forerunner of the parallel bars and the horizontal bar). He also described balance beams, jumping ropes, climbing ropes and poles, the vaulting table, and the buck. He emphasized the mental and moral values of physical activity in addition to its physical values.

Archibald Maclaren (1820–1884), an English educator, wrote a military manual in which he advocated the use of Jahn's apparatus activities to supplement games and sports.

Early settlers in the United States came principally from England; consequently, they preferred the games and sports of England to the gymnastics of central Europe. Most of the early settlers left their native land to escape political and religious persecution. This, plus the ruggedly independent lives they were forced to lead in the Colonies, made it difficult for them to accept rules, regulations, regimentation, and authority. These factors discouraged the ready acceptance of the regimented, military, formal gymnastics programs practiced throughout central Europe. Yet, early physical education programs in this country were patterned after those of central Europe. They were doomed to failure because they were not indigenous to this country. These programs reflected the customs, values, way of life, and aspirations of the people of the countries of their origin—not those of the people of the United States. It wasn't until the early 1940's that gymnastic leaders in the United States began to interject into gymnastics the elements of freedom and self-expression which made the sport more palatable in our culture. Today gymnastics is one of the fastest growing sports, but it has received some shattering setbacks after an initial flying start.

In 1825, the Round Hill School of Northampton, Massachusetts, appointed Dr. Charles Beck, a former student of Jahn, to direct its physical education program. At the same time, another advocate of Jahn gymnastics, Dr. Charles Follen, was appointed to establish a gymnastic program at Harvard University. German gymnastics flourished for a few years in areas of New England and New York that had large numbers of German immigrants. By 1860, there were over 150 German Turnvereins in this country. In 1865 the American Turners organized the Normal College of the American Gymnastic Union. Today this college is affiliated with Indiana University. At the Chicago World's Fair of 1893, 4,000 Turners participated.

The American Sokol, which had been founded by Dr. Miroslav Tyrs in Prague, Czechoslovakia in 1862, was initiated in St. Louis in 1865. Branches were established in Chicago in 1866 and in New York City in 1867. Other clubs were organized in major cities throughout the country until the membership totaled over 100,000.

The Y.M.C.A., founded by George Williams, a salesman, in England in 1841, has been instrumental in fostering the growth of gymnastics ever since the Y.M.C.A.s decided to add gymnasia to their facilities in 1856.

Starting in 1920 and continuing until about 1950, a decreasing number of schools provided instruction in gymnastics, an increasing number of Turnvereins and Sokol Clubs closed their doors, and fewer Y.M.C.A.s sponsored gymnas-

tic groups. The major reasons for this decline in participation were probably the following:

1. Administrators made an erroneous application to physical education of John Dewey's philosophic statements which seemed to recommend free play. At the same time teachers of gymnastics continued the use of distasteful highly formal procedures in the teaching of gymnastics.

2. A decrease in the average person's strength, power, and endurance resulted from the decreased need for physical labor, making success in gymnastic skills harder to achieve. Hence fewer participants experienced the joy of success.

3. Physical educators began to teach less strenuous activities because these contained a smaller element of hazard and because through them the physically unfit could experience a modicum of success.

4. The growth in popularity of team sports (and the accompanying false stimuli of marching bands, cheer leaders, pep rallies, and large amounts of publicity) caused students and the community to regard these games as a measure of school and community loyalty, social status, and virility. This led to an increase in the facilities for spectators and a corresponding decrease in the facilities for participation. The great amount of attention given team sports caused many unthinking physical educators to believe that they were the most important physical education activities and led many of them to teach team sports exclusively while they completely neglected individual and dual activities.

Physical educators must always take cognizance of the political, social, and economic milieu in which they are teaching. It was unfortunate that many of the early physical educators in this country failed to recognize this important principle. They persisted in teaching gymnastics in a highly formalized manner quite out of keeping with our democratic and flexible way of life. Students stood in line at "parade rest" while waiting their turns. The instructor then often read from a card the directions for a skill. Each student, in his turn, "popped" to attention, marched stiffly forward in right-angled turns and attempted to execute the described routine. These highly formal procedures were not much fun for the students. However, it was not the activity which was formal; it was the method of teaching.

Today, gymnasts design their own skills, combinations, and routines. The coach is regarded as a resource person, not a dictator. There are a great many opportunities for creative self-expression in gymnastics when it is properly taught. The words "formal" and "gymnastics" have no inherent relation. Gymnastics should never be taught in a manner which causes people to speak of "formal" gymnastics.

Highly competitive football is taught in a very formal manner. There are prescribed manners of blocking, tackling, passing, and kicking. Players are instructed when to start running, at what angle to run, how fast to run, whether to hit high or low, and when to arrive at a designated spot. Football, as currently taught in many places, should perhaps be called "formal football." It is not the activity which is formal. It is the method of teaching. *Any* activity could be taught in a highly formal manner.

The teaching of team sports is less demanding than is the teaching of gymnastics. Gymnastics requires individual instruction, analysis, and spotting. Team sports lend themselves more readily to mass teaching. It was an easy rationalization for instructors of physical education to discard gymnastics in order to devote their entire attentions to the team sports on the basis of the supposededly greater worth in a democratic society. The rationalization was made even easier when writers began to claim that participation in team sports developed such qualities of sportsmanship as cooperation, a sense of fair play, and consideration for others. It is not primarily the activity which determines the amount and quality of social behavior developed—it is the way in which the activity is taught. Any sport can be taught in such a manner as to develop consideration for others, respect for the spirit as well as the letter of the law, modesty in victory, and grace in defeat.

People enjoy doing that which they do well. A boy who plays baseball most skillfully will enjoy baseball more than he will other sports and will therefore participate in baseball most frequently. The same is true of any sport.

Any boy, regardless of how low his level of physical fitness, can, after a large enough number of trials, experience success in foul shooting, golf, archery, horseshoes, and similar activities which do not demand a high level of strength, endurance, or agility. In gymnastics the student will never experience success in a skill until he develops the requisite strength through repeated practice.

Records kept at Harvard University, for example, indicate that although today's college men are bigger and better nourished than ever, they are not able to do as many chin-ups, push-ups, and dips on the parallel bars as students in former years.

Because of deficient strength, fewer boys enjoy success in gymnastics. Furthermore, a lack of strength increases the probability of a fall. Statistics show that gymnastics is one of the safest of activities, ranking just behind swimming in the incidence of injuries. Yet many believe it to be hazardous. One reason for this is that a fall from the trampoline or flying rings is spectacular. Another is that we have grown to accept injuries in certain sports as part of the game.

For all of the foregoing reasons, gymnastics almost disappeared from the American sport scene until recent years. It has made a phenomenal comeback, however, for several reasons:

1. The U.S. has suffered humiliating defeats in the Olympic Games.
2. Gymnastic meets and exhibitions performed by the touring teams of foreign countries have been televised, bringing the beautiful movements of gymnastics before millions of people who had never seen them.
3. Dedicated men have struggled against discouraging obstacles to keep the sport alive during its "lean" years.
4. There has been renewed emphasis upon physical fitness as a major objective of physical education and a recognition of the great value of gymnastics as a means for achieving this objective.

While the Olympics is a contest between individuals of different nations and there is no official team score, sportswriters of all nations cannot resist the temptation to compute and publish unofficial team scores. Gymnastics, which, like track and swimming, has many individual events, counts heavily in the unofficial scoring. Furthermore, gymnastic events have always been scheduled during the final days of competition. Invariably it has appeared that the United States amassed the largest unofficial team score until the gymnastic events began. At that point, Russia and other countries began pulling ahead. American gymnasts and their coaches were blamed for the loss, and, during the "finger pointing" by the sportswriters (especially in 1956), gymnastics received more publicity in the few weeks following the Olympics than it had received during the previous four years. While the publicity was unfavorable, it did bring attention to the sport and consequently brought increased budgets, better equipment, better schedules, increased use of gymnasia, and other administrative contributions to improved performance.

The Olympic gymnastic teams of Russia, Japan, Sweden, and Finland have toured the United States, performing in major cities from coast to coast before packed houses. An increasing number of gymnastic meets have been televised. A television program, "The Wide World of Sports," has shown movies of the gymnastic events in the Olympic Games. This has brought gymnastics into the homes of millions of people.

THE TWENTIETH CENTURY

Gymnastics was kept alive during its lean years by the unselfish and untiring work of dedicated leaders. Leslie Judd, Professor Emeritus at Springfield College, presented demonstrations with his gymnastic teams throughout the northeast. Dr. Hartley Price accomplished the same objective in the midwest with his famed Gymkana Troupe, organized to develop creativity and skill in democratic processes. Hundreds of former members of Rene Kern's Brooklyn Central Y.M.C.A. Gymnastic Team have continued to promote gymnastics in many sections of the United States.

After World War II gymnastics began to grow through the efforts of coaches of gymnastics throughout the United States. The late Roy Moore, who served as chairman of the National American Athletic Union (A.A.U.) Gymnastic Committee in the years immediately following World War II, directed the revitalization of gymnastics with vigor and enthusiasm. Gymnastics re-

ceived a tremendous impetus with the initiation of the National Gymnastics Clinic in Sarasota, Florida, in 1951. The name has been changed to the Eastern Gymnastics Clinic because so many others have been initiated, all attracting several hundred gymnasts, men and women of all ages, their coaches, and their parents. Two of the larger clinics are the Western Gymnastics Clinic in Tucson, Arizona, and the New England Clinic, which rotates among several New England cities. Hundreds of local gymnastics clinics are being sponsored by high school and college physical education and athletic departments. Numerous gymnastic camps operate during the summer. Hundreds of gymnastic meets are held throughout the country for both boys and girls of all ages and for college men and women at all levels of skill. The high level of skill demonstrated by the competitors at even local meets is surprising to one who has not coached for several years. There can be no doubt that gymnastics is a sport on the move. When our students and adults become more sophisticated and learn to appreciate the aesthetic aspects of sports as well as the competitive aspects, the popularity of gymnastics will grow even more rapidly.

At the first modern Olympic Games in 1896, gymnasts competed on the side horse, parallel bars, flying rings, long horse, horizontal bar, and in tumbling and the rope climb. Since that time, still rings have been substituted for the flying rings and the rope climb has been eliminated. Gymnastics for girls and women experienced a great surge in popularity when the floor exercise rules were changed, uneven parallel bars substituted for the even bars, and the balance beam added. Today, girls' gymnastics is probably growing in popularity more rapidly than is gymnastics for boys.

The painful conflict between the A.A.U. and the United States Gymnastics Federation (U.S.G.F.) has finally been resolved through the formation of the National Gymnastic Commission. Each of the two groups will have five representatives entitled to a vote. They will also provide a nonvoting, rotating president on an annual basis. Jerry F. Hardy, U.S. Representative to the *Federation Internationale de Gymnastics*, has been the principle promoter of this commission.

Alfred Jochim of the Hudson County (New

Jersey) Turnverein, probably the most famous gymnast the United States has produced, won the National A.A.U. All-around Championship seven times between 1925 and 1933. George Wheeler won in 1937, 1938, 1939, 1940, and 1941. Frank Kriz of the New York Sokol, won the long horse event in the 1924 Olympic Games. One of the most famous of women gymnasts was Clara Schroth, a six-time winner of the National A.A.U. All-around Championship for Women. These four gymnasts were among the first great gymnasts in the United States.

Tumbling has been an event in only one modern Olympic Games, the Tenth Olympiad held in 1932 at Los Angeles. The event was won by Rowland Wolfe of the United States. The United States has always been strong in tumbling, and many coaches and leaders in gymnastics in the United States would like to see tumbling re-introduced in the games.

The United States has been successful in winning the unofficial team title in gymnastics in the Olympic Games only once since the inception of the modern games. This occurred at St. Louis in 1904, when the U.S. team was led by Anton Heida, who won the Individual All-around, the horizontal bar, and the side horse events, and tied with George Eyser in the long horse event. In that year, Eyser also won the parallel bar event, while Herman Glass won the flying rings event. In the six Olympiads of 1904, 1908, 1912, 1920, 1924, and 1928, the U.S. managed to win only one first-place medal. This country did not field a strong team until 1932, when the U.S. gymnastic team won five first-place medals. The teams which represented the United States in the 1936, 1948, 1952, 1956, and 1960 Olympiads were unable to capture any first-place medals. However, the 1960 team placed fifth out of 33 teams entered. The 1964 team placed seventh.

UNITED STATES PERFORMANCE IN RECENT OLYMPIC GAMES

Although Olympic gymnastic teams representing nations with smaller populations than that of the United States placed ahead of the United States in the 1968 and 1972 Olympic Games, it is remarkable that U.S. teams did as well as they did in view of the small amount of attention given gymnastics by the media, particularly the sports pages of newspapers, and the meager financial support given gymnastics by high schools, colleges and universities.

Team scores and places for the first six places in Women's Gymnastics in the 1968 Olympic Games follow:

> 1st U.S.S.R.—382.85 points
> 2nd Czechoslovakia—382.20 points
> 3d East Germany—379.10 points
> 4th Japan—375.45 points
> 5th Hungary—369.80 points
> 6th United States—369.79 points

Although there were 110 competitors in the women's competition, the members of the U.S.A. Women's Gymnastic Team placed in respectable positions. The six members of the women's team placed as follows in the 1968 Olympic Games:

> 16th Cathy Rigby—74.95
> 28th Linda Metheny—74.00
> 30th Joyce Tanac—73.65
> 31st Kathy Gleason—73.60
> 34th Colleen Mulvihill—73.05
> 39th Wendy Cluff—71.08

The team standings in the men's competition were as follows in the 1968 Olympic Games:

> 1st Japan—575.90 points
> 2nd U.S.S.R.—571.10 points
> 3d East Germany—557.10 points
> 4th Czechoslovakia—557.10 points
> 5th Poland—555.40 points
> 6th Yugoslavia—550.40 points
> 7th United States—548.90 points

The members of the U.S.A. Men's Gymnastic Team placed and scored as follows in the 1968 Olympic Games:

> 24th Dave Thor—110.60 points
> 34th F. Roethlesberger—109.70 points
> 36th Steve Hug—109.60 points
> 57th Sam Freustein—108.00 points
> 80th J.K. Allen—105.45 points

In the 1972 Olympic Games, women's gymnastic teams placed as follows:

> 1st U.S.S.R.—380.50 points
> 2nd East Germany—376.55 points
> 3d Hungary—368.25 points
> 4th United States—365.90 points
> 5th Czechoslovakia—365.00 points
> 6th Romania—360.70 points

The members of the U.S.A. Women's Gymnastic Team of 1972 placed as follows:

10th Kathy Rigby
28th Kimberly Cace
33d Roxanne Pierce
36th Linda Metheny
(Joan Moore and Nancy Thies placed lower than 36th)

The members of the 1972 U.S.A. Olympic Gymnastic Team were Steve Hug, Makato Sokomoto, John Cosby, Marshall Avener, Jim Culhane and George Greenfield. This team placed 10th with 533.85 points, being led by Japan (571.25), Russia (564.05), East Germany (559.70), Poland (551.10), West Germany (546.40), Korea (545.05), Romania (538.90), Hungary (538.60), and Czechoslovakia (538.35).

BIBLIOGRAPHY

Van Dalen, Deobold B., and Bennett, Bruce L. *A World History of Physical Education.* 2nd ed. Englewood Cliffs, N.J.: Prentice-Hall, Inc., 1971.

Weston, Arthur. *The Making of American Physical Education.* New York: Appleton-Century Crofts, 1962.

3

PRINCIPLES FOR TEACHING AND COACHING GYMNASTICS

As he prepares to build a house, a worker can learn the characteristics, strengths, and limitations of the materials he will use and may, with justification, expect them to perform in the customary manner. Consequently, he can establish specific procedures for the construction of his house with some assurance of success. This is not true when one works with people, and particular with children.

No two children are alike physically, mentally, emotionally, or socially. They differ from one another in strength, power, flexibility, agility, endurance, balance, courage, intelligence, enthusiasm, discipline, cooperativeness, weight, ability to perceive spatial relationships, and in many other ways. Still, the task of teaching children is not insurmountable, for there are many ways in which children are similar, and there are certain principles which can serve as guides in the conduct of classes in gymnastics.

The common characteristics of children; teaching principles; anatomical, physiological, psychological, and kinesiological principles; and methods of class organization will be discussed in this chapter. Though there is no substitute for experience, the principles should provide a helpful frame of reference for the beginning teacher and enable him to enjoy a satisfying measure of success. The beginning teacher may gain courage from the knowledge that there have been many outstanding teachers and coaches of gymnastics who have never competed in gymnastics. The willing and enthusiastic teacher will not refuse to teach gymnastics simply because he does not possess gymnastic skill. He will read, study, attend clinics, and attempt to learn the fundamental skills and to understand the mechanics of those skills which he is unable to demonstrate so that he can teach them to the children in his charge.

An understanding of the principles presented in this chapter will greatly facilitate the learning, teaching, and coaching process, inasmuch as the reader will then better understand the potentialities and limitations of his body; he will understand why his body reacts in certain ways when he executes certain movements and why skills should be done in prescribed manners; he will be better able to deduce the movements necessary for proper execution of skills; he will be a more effective spotter; probability of injury will be decreased; if he is a teacher or coach, his students will progress more rapidly; and if he is a performer, he will progress more rapidly. It is because physical education incorporates the knowledge arising from other disciplines and because it has itself contributed to human knowledge that it is regarded as a profession rather than a trade.

PRINCIPLES FROM ANATOMY AND PHYSIOLOGY

1. *Center of gravity:* The center of gravity has been defined as "an imaginary point representing the weight center of an object" or as "that point in a body about which all the parts exactly balance each other." In men, the center of gravity is located about 56 percent of the height while in women it is at about 55 percent of the height. The lower center of gravity, along with the anatomic and structural differences which do not permit as great development of the musculature of the upper trunk, shoulder girdle, and arms in girls, mandates that equipment and rules in gymnastics competition for girls and women differ from those for boys and men. The best women gymnasts could never equal the performance of proficient male gymnasts on the parallel bars, side horse, or still rings because these events require powerful arms and shoulders relative to total body weight. When the rules of women's gymnastics were modified and adapted to the unique physical and psychological characteristics and sociological roles of women, the popularity of the sport surged. Their lower center of gravity gives girls and women an advantage over men in work on the balance beam and uneven bars. Vaulting over the side horse does not place as much stress on the shoulder girdle as does vaulting over the long horse. The patterns of movement in the floor exercise event are designed to accentuate the greater beauty and grace of the female.

In the normal standing position with the arms at the sides, the center of gravity is located in the pelvis in front of the upper part of the sacrum. The three planes of the body (anteroposterior or sagittal, frontal or lateral, and horizontal or transverse) bisect the body, pass through the center of gravity, and are at right angles to one

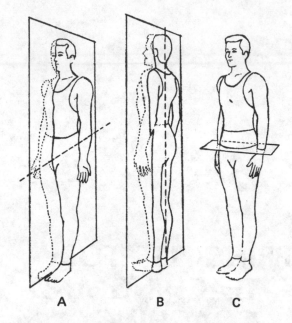

Planes and axes of the body: A, sagittal or anteroposterior plane and anteroposterior axis; B, frontal or lateral plane and vertical axis; C, horizontal or transverse plane and lateral horizontal axis

another. The body revolves around three axes (vertical, lateral horizontal, and anteroposterior horizontal), all of which intersect at the center of gravity. In twisting moves the body rotates around the vertical axis. It rotates around the lateral horizontal axis in forward and backward rolls, hip circles, and somersaults. It rotates around the anteroposterior horizontal axis in cartwheels and side somersaults. The axes and the center of gravity change location with different positionings of the body. The vertical and lateral horizontal axes move forward during a tuck or pike, and backward when the back is hyperextended or arched. The anteroposterior horizontal and vertical axes move sideward when the trunk is bent to the side.

Hip circles are easier to execute when the lateral horizontal axis of the body is brought as close to the bar as possible. This is why free hip circles rate higher in difficulty than do regular hip circles. The center of rotation should be as nearly between the points of support as possible. This makes it easier to maintain stability. In the front and back handsprings, the body rotates around the lateral horizontal axis. The points of

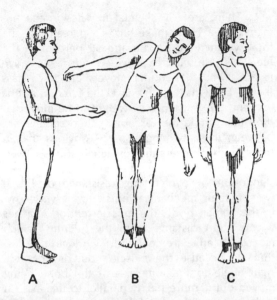

Movements of the body in three planes and around three axes: A, forearm moving in the sagittal or anteroposterior plane around the lateral horizontal axis; B, trunk moving in the frontal or lateral plane around the anteroposterior horizontal axis; C, head moving in the horizontal plane around the vertical axis. (Adapted from Katherine F. Wells, Kinesiology, 5th edition, W. B. Saunders Co., 1971, p. 10.)

support are the hands. Therefore, in these two moves, the hips should be moved to a point directly above the hands as soon as possible and remain there as long as possible. In side horse work, the performer carries his trunk backward as his legs swing forward, and forward as his legs swing backward. This keeps his center of gravity between his hands, which are his points of support.

2. *Stability:* Stability is enhanced when the *line of gravity* (a perpendicular line from the center of gravity to the floor or other base) is *between the points of support.* The wider the base of support, the greater the stability. From a kinesiological point of view, the practice of landing after a dismount with the feet together is not sound. In gymnastics, this is done to demonstrate control. In order to prevent injury to ankles or knees, it would be well to advise beginners to land with feet shoulder width apart until they have acquired good control. When doing stationary skills such as the headstand, scale, handstand, one-hand handstand, one-arm half lever, or moving skills such as double-leg circles on the

side horse, scissors, or swinging on the parallel bars, the gymnast will find he can execute the move with less effort if he keeps the line of gravity between the points of support. In doubles, triples, and quadruples balancing, the center of gravity must always be between the points of support.

3. *Flexibility:* Gymnastics require a high degree of flexibility. Practice on front and back handsprings, straddle and stoop vaults, front and back walkovers, and side and front splits will help to develop flexibility. However, the gymnast who does exercises which will increase the range of motion through stretching the ligaments, tendons, and fascia of the ankle, knee, hip, shoulder joints, and back will learn many gymnastic skills more quickly, because lack of flexibility will not be a deterent to his learning. Such exercises include the "inchworm," "back breaker," "backbend," "quadriceps stretcher," "bouncer," and others which are described further in this textbook. Because of the phenomenon known as the stretch reflex, these exercises should be done slowly with a strong, steady pull to the point of some discomfort. The stretched position should be sustained for several seconds. These exercises should not be done forcefully, fast, or in a bobbing manner. It should be realized that flexibility is developed slowly over a period of several weeks or months. The stretch reflex is a proprioceptor reflex, which arises from within the muscle. When the tendon of a muscle is stretched as the result of the contraction of an antagonistic muscle, the pull of gravity, or some other force, impulses are carried to the spinal cord and to the motor neurons which send impulses back to the muscle being stretched, instructing it to contract. This mechanism exists to facilitate ballistic-type movements and to protect the joint fascia, ligaments, and tendons. The stretch reflex mandates against doing stretching exercises in a jerky or bobbing manner.

The shoulder joint possesses remarkable flexibility. This flexibility is made possible by the looseness of the capsule which permits one to two inches of separation and the shallowness of the glenoid fossa. The head of the humerus rests against the glenoid fossa (its socket) as would a softball in a saucer. It is obvious that this joint would be easily disclocated were it not for the muscles of the shoulder girdle, arms, chest, and back. This points up why diving forward rolls, long horse vaulting, and certain other skills are contraindicated for most girls and some young men who have poor shoulder girdle development.

4. *Strength:* Perhaps the outstanding characteristic of champion gymnasts is their unusual strength and power relative to their body weight. The gymnast must manipulate a fairly heavy tool (his body) as compared to those used in most sports (rackets, bats, balls). It is for this reason that gymnasts become strong. As in developing flexibility or endurance, stress must be provided to increase strength. However, each of these qualities is a specific. Flexibility is increased by providing stress in the form of stretching. Endurance is enhanced by stressing the cardiovascular-respiratory system by doing many repetitions of an activity against little resistance as in running, rope skipping, or swimming. Strength is developed by stressing muscle fibers through demanding that they overcome great resistance. Strength is developed most effectively not by doing a large number of foot pounds of work (curling 10 pounds a distance of 2 feet 100 times = 10 lb. × 2 ft. × 100 rep. = 2,000 ft. lb. of work), but by lifting a weight as great as can be lifted (or greater than can be lifted—an isometric contraction) a few times (curling 150 pounds a distance of 2 feet once = 150 lb. × 2 ft. × 1 rep. = 300 ft. lb. of work).

Possession of strength is important for success in all sports but particularly for the gymnast. Lack of the strength necessary for the execution of a skill has prevented many aspiring gymnasts from progressing as rapidly as they might have. Through repeated unsuccessful attempts at a skill they may have developed the strength necessary for success, but in the process have experienced many bruises and much frustration. Progressive resistance exercises are strongly recommended for all gymnasts to hasten the learning process, to minimize the probability of injury, and to enable "saving" of a skill. Exercises such as the front and reverse "curl," "military press," "supine press," "pullover," "dead lift," "bent over rowing exercises," and front and lateral dumbbell raises are especially recommended. Isometric exercises have been found just as effective as progressive resistance exercises with barbells for increasing strength, and they present the advantage of a considerable saving in time.

There are 656 skeletal muscles in the human body. They make up 42 percent of the total weight in the male and 36 percent in the female. These muscles provide the force to move levers. Almost all human levers are third-class levers. Third-class levers have the fulcrum at one end and the resistance or weight to be moved at the other, while the force is applied somewhere between these two points. It is obvious that in these kinds of levers the resistance arm is always longer than the force arm and that, from the standpoint of overcoming resistance or lifting weight, their mechanical efficiency is very low. In the human body, the muscle tendon attaches a very short distance from the fulcrum, which makes for an extremely short work arm. Additionally, because the muscle's pull is not at a right angle to the long axis of the bone being moved but is more nearly parallel to this axis (in order to provide a stabilizing force by pulling the ends of the two bones toward one another), the true work arm is even shorter than it appears. Obviously, the muscles must generate great force to move the body, particularly against resistance or to lift a weight. Rasch and Burke[1] point out that the deltoid muscle must generate 300 pounds of force to enable it to raise the extended arm 80° when a ten-pound weight is held in the hand. Imagine the force that must be generated by the involved muscles when pulling from a hang into a crucifix! If the tendon from the triceps passed over a tuberosity twelve inches high and inserted just above the wrist, we would not look very attractive, but everyone could press up into a handstand with ease.

Human levers favor speed, but since power is necessary for speed and power is in large part a function of strength, an increase in strength will produce an increase in speed. Strength is necessary not only for the planche, crucifix, and the several press-ups, but also for casts, back uprises into a handstand, pirouettes, and many other skills. It has been well established that when strength increases power increases. It also has been established that when strength is increased, muscular endurance increases. The strong gymnast uses a smaller proportion of his

[1] Philip J. Rasch and Roger K. Burke, *Kinesiology and Applied Anatomy*, 2nd ed. (Philadelphia: Lea and Febiger, 1963), p. 158.

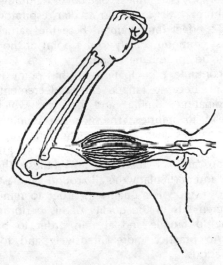

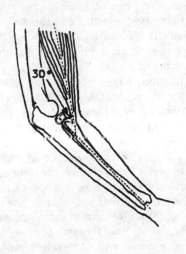

The biceps muscle pulling at an angle greater than a right angle

The biceps muscle pulling at a 30° angle to the mechanical axis of the radius

First Class:

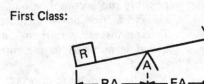

Axis is between resistance and force.

Second Class:

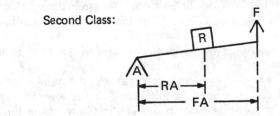

Resistance is between axis and force.

Resistance arm is always shorter than force arm; consequently, force is favored rather than speed.

Third Class:

A = Axis of rotation
F = Force
R = Resistance or weight to be moved
RA = Resistance arm
FA = Force arm

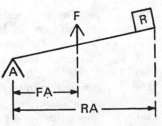

Force is between axis and resistance.

Force arm is always shorter than resistance arm; consequently, speed is favored rather than force.

The three classes of levers

total strength to accomplish a given task; consequently, some of his muscle fibers can rest while a skill is being performed. Even the single event gymnast needs muscular endurance. The all-around gymnast needs great muscular endurance.

An explanation of the physiology of muscular contraction makes obvious the advisability of isometric or progressive resistance exercises for development of strength. Muscle fibers are grouped together to form a motor unit. A motor unit may consist of as few as three muscle fibers (extrinsic muscles of the eyes) or as many as a hundred or more (muscles of the thighs). Each motor unit contracts as a unit since all its fibers are innervated simultaneously by one motor nerve. Where precise and delicate movements are needed, as in the fingers, tongue, lips, or eyes, a motor nerve will innervate a motor unit with only a few fibers. Where gross movements are called for, as in the thighs, back, or abdomen, a motor nerve innervates a motor unit with many muscle fibers. Some muscle fibers are very seldom used in routine daily activities, consequently they atrophy.

It is only during intensive muscular contraction that all the muscle fibers responsible for moving a part of the body are brought into play. The reason for this is that each motor unit requires a different minimal stimulus to produce contraction. This is known as the threshold stimulus. A minimal stimulus will bring into play only those motor units with the lowest threshold. Stronger stimuli will cause more and more motor units to contract. A maximal stimulus will excite all the motor units. The muscle fibers of each motor unit contract maximally if they contract at all, but the whole muscle does not unless the effort is maximal. This explains why maximal contractions, as done in isometric exercises or in progressive resistance exercises, are so effective in increasing strength and muscle size. It also explains why light calisthenic movements or other activities done against little resistance will never be effective in producing great strength. However, if light exercises are sustained until thorough fatigue is produced, they will improve both blood supply to the exercised area and muscular endurance.

5. *Cardiovascular-respiratory condition:* Gymnastics has been rated by physical educators as the activity making the greatest contribution to overall physical fitness objectives, although it contributes little to cardiovascular-respiratory fitness. To effect improvement here the participant must continue activity to the point of thorough fatigue, producing respiratory stress. One cannot continue participation to this point in gymnastics, because fatigue causes decrements in coordination, timing, and balance, which could lead to injuries. The gymnast employs other modalities such as running, jogging, rope skipping, swimming, handball, soccer, or squash to develop cardiovascular-respiratory fitness. The gymnast, and particularly the all-around gymnast, needs to develop this quality in order to minimize decrements in the quality of his performance due to fatigue and also in order to be enabled to practice more intensively and for longer periods.

The onset of fatigue in the gymnast who spends some time in endurance activities will be delayed for several reasons:

a. Hypertrophy of the heart muscle makes possible more complete emptying of the ventricle and a consequent increase in stroke volume. This means more oxygen- and nutrient-carrying blood is pumped to the muscle cells where it is used.

b. Hemoglobin, which carries oxygen, is increased, permitting the conveyance of a greater supply of oxygen to the muscle cells.

c. Blood flow through the muscles will be increased up to three times. This results, in part, from an increase in the number of capillaries. Increases as great as 45 percent have been noted in the muscles of guinea pigs after a program of exercise.

d. An increase in the number of alveoli (air sacs), a thickening of the alveolar septa, an increase in the elastic fibers in the lungs, and an increase in the excursions of the diaphragm all result in the inhalation of a greater volume of air. The end result is that a greater amount of oxygen can be brought to the muscle cells.

6. *Function of the brain in learning skills:* Intense concentration is required when learning a new skill, but after the skill has been mastered through many repetitions, some gymnasts can think about the succeeding move or their evening date. Some can even carry on a conversation while doing a series of back handsprings or double leg circles. When a new skill is being learned

and when constant monitoring is necessary, the motor area of the brain is primarily involved, but as the skill is being mastered, the premotor area of the brain takes increasing responsibility for initiating and controlling the movement. However, at all times, the strength, duration, and range of movements are being coordinated by the cerebellum through its connections with the motor area of the cortex and with the proprioceptors of the muscles and joints. However, the gymnast should not think of this process nor of which muscles are involved, for he may suffer "paralysis by analysis" or, like the centipede when asked how he walks, be unable to move. It is well for the gymnast to mentally reconstruct the movements of a skill or a routine. This author has learned several skills while sitting on a bus on the way to the Turnverein. A similar process occurs when a gymnast, watching another perform or while watching a move or loop film, acquires an insight into a skill and can sometimes kinesthetically "feel" the move while sitting. Exteroceptive stimuli have activated the proprioceptors to simulate a muscular response. A gymnast should try to "project" himself into the body of the performer he is watching. This empathy, though not yet understood, is a valuable learning technique.

Coordination varies with each activity. It is doubtful that general coordination can be improved. Effective explanations, demonstrations, use of visual aids, ability to interpret the laws of physics and of motion and to relate their application to movement are things the teacher can do to improve children's coordination. A photographic mind with respect to movement; ability to understand the teacher's explanations and demonstrations; ability to understand the laws of motion; and adequate strength, power, agility, and muscular and cardiovascular-respiratory endurance are things the child can gain or learn which will improve his coordination.

7. *Bone damage:* Since most of the major epiphyses of the long bones do not close until age seventeen to nineteen, many orthopedists think that football, wrestling, and pyramid building are undesirable for younger people. It may also be true that jarring dismounts are harmful. However, there is no current experimental evidence to indicate that any child has inflicted damage to the epiphyseal ends of his bones as a result of participation in these activities. On the other hand, so much good has been proven to result that there should be little question about their continuance.

8. *Femininity:* Girls do not become less feminine in appearance as a result of participation in gymnastics or in any other vigorous sports activity. All people genetically possess varying amounts of feminine and masculine physical characteristics. Participation in sports or other activities will not change this balance. Girls and women can become quite strong and not lose one iota of their femininity. In fact, a girl's practice in gymnastics can do much to improve her coordination and grace of movement—thereby contributing to her femininity.

9. *Individual differences:* Because of the many differences among individuals, instructors and coaches should not have the same expectations for all participants. Nor should they expect them to learn specific skills with the same facility. Individual differences do not present a problem in gymnastics since there is a great variety of skills, each adapted to certain combinations of characteristics, so instructors and coaches can present a great variety of skills and permit students to select those best suited to their abilities. It is a mistake to evaluate all students in a class on one routine which has been designed by the instructor. Instead, each student should be permitted to design his own routine in order to accommodate individual differences and also to experience the joy and satisfaction of creative effort. This principle is in keeping with those democratic ideals which encourage differences.

10. *Mind and body:* There is no dichotomy between mind and body. Each is dependent upon the well-being of the other for maximum efficiency. Students cannot learn gymnastic skills (or any other physical skills) when they are angry, frustrated, or unhappy. They cannot comprehend readily or succeed fully in academic areas when they are ill or physically unfit. It is a mistake to classify some activities as mental and some as physical, for all of man's activities combine elements of both. The physical education teacher must constantly remind himself that he is working with the whole child. The child's physical, emotional, mental, and social facets are all being influenced for good or ill by the physical education teacher or coach. The classroom teacher

must also remind himself that he is working with the whole child and not with just his intellect.

PRINCIPLES FROM PSYCHOLOGY

The mind and body are but parts of one entity—the human being. Whatever influences the mind influences the body, and whatever influences the body influences the mind. Studies have shown that mental information can produce effects upon involuntary processes. When a woman was told she was to begin exercising, her blood pressure went up and her heart rate increased even before she did any exercise. People under emotional stress have accomplished Herculian feats of strength and endurance. Highly motivated "underdog" teams have upset the favored team. The coach or teacher of gymnastics cannot ignore the psychological aspects of motivation, teaching procedures, individual counseling, and group dynamics if he is to become maximally effective.

1. *Self-realization, ego-satisfaction, a pleasing self-image, and prestige* are all related. All people, including children, will struggle in different ways to achieve them. There are numerous opportunities in the teaching of gymnastics to give each child a moment of self-realization, of recognition, of ego-satisfaction. Following are several techniques which the teacher can use:

a. He can present to the class a number of very easy skills so that a greater percentage of students will experience success.

b. He can present skills in their progressive order of difficulty to increase the probability that students will continue to experience success. When students master fundamentals, they learn more advanced skills with greater ease and also are less likely to become injured.

c. He can present a wide variety of skills and permit students to select those best adapted to their own unique physical and emotional characteristics. Some skills require greater power, others greater flexibility, and so forth.

e. He can designate the heavier-boned or obese students, who may have difficulty performing the moves well, as spotters, and make sure

they are complimented for doing this important job well and conscientiously.

f. He can arrange demonstrations, exhibitions, and intramural and interscholastic competition to provide greater opportunities for self-realization for more students.

g. The instructor can put up a wall chart listing students' names and a variety of skills for them to achieve. The chart will provide a daily form of recognition as well as motivation. Each time a student learns a skill, a gold star or check mark can be placed alongside his name in the proper column.

EXAMPLE OF WALL CHART

| Name | Tumbling | | P. Bars | | |
	Front Roll	Side Roll	Back Roll, (etc.)	Straight Seat	Uprise
Joe B.	x	x	x		
Jim J.	x	x		x	
Jack S.	x	x	x	x	x

2. *Challenge* stimulates almost everyone, and all students in a gymnastics class can and should be constantly challenged to exceed their present level of ability. Those students who learn quickly can be challenged to perfect their form, to learn variations of individual skills, and to attempt various combinations of skills.

3. *The need to create* is a basic need common to all people. There are many opportunities in gymnastics to give expression to this need. Students can create routines and even new skills. (They should be required to describe any new skill to the instructor before attempting it because they sometimes get some bizarre and even dangerous ideas.) In presenting exhibitions, there are many opportunities to be creative—designing routines, numbers, and properties; art work on posters, programs, and tickets; planning the theme, continuity, musical background, and lighting effects are only a few of the many opportunities to create which exhibitions present.

4. *Beauty* is inherent in gymnastics at its best— "a poetry of motion." Students should be helped to develop an understanding and an appreciation of beauty in form and movement

visually when seeing others perform and kinesthetically when feeling themselves perform. When there are no outstanding gymnasts in the area, students can develop an appreciation of the aesthetic qualities of gymnastics through movies or demonstrations by touring groups such as those of the Finnish, Russian, or Swiss Olympic teams, the University of Maryland and the Florida State University Gymkana Troupes, or the Springfield College Gymnastics Team.

5. Fear is not something students should be ashamed of. Intelligent people have fear because they are capable of visualizing the possible outcomes of error. Only extremely stupid people have no fear. But students should also learn that fear can be overcome through applying the principles of progressive learning. For example, the student wishing to learn the front somersault on the trampoline should first master the lead-up skills in their progressive order of difficulty and then have four or more alert spotters when he finally attempts it. He need have no fear of the skill because he will have worked up to it in safety and yet have been challenged to overcome his fear. The laws of progression will have been observed in both his learning of the skill and in the development of his courage.

INDIVIDUAL DIFFERENCES

Dr. Joseph L. Massimo, Clinical Professor of Psychiatry at the Boston University School of Medicine and a gymnast himself, points out that individual differences dictate that different gymnasts must be taught and coached in somewhat different manners. Some like long explanations of procedures for executing skills, while some prefer a minimum of verbiage. Some fear a specific skill or aspect of a skill while others have a generalized anxiety ("I'm afraid of slipping off" vs. "I'm psyched out"). Some like a rigid schedule, while others enjoy greater freedom and individual choice. Some need to be "scolded" at times, while others require more gentle rebukes. They react differently to frustration, failure, and pain. Some have compulsions. They relate differently to members of the team. While the coach cannot become a clinical psychologist,

he must give these matters some thought and study if he wishes to help all of his pupils.

MOTOR LEARNING

Scott[2] has summarized the findings from studies of the effectiveness of learning based on kinesthesis. Since success in gymnastics, more than in most sports, is based on kinesthetic awareness of the beauty of execution rather than on achievement of a specific goal (putting the ball through the hoop, kicking a goal, or driving the ball onto the green) these conclusions would seem to have special import for gymnastics:

1. "New skills should be built on known ones if possible. This will avoid some of the beginner's tension. It will permit performance of the general pattern so that attention may be devoted to new aspects." This implies that related skills (skills made up of similar movements) such as neck-, head-, and handsprings or kips on the parallel bars, horizontal bar and rings, or circling moves should be presented for learning in sequence. Some textbooks on gymnastics are organized in this way. The author believes the reader is capable of doing this himself and has organized his material by age and event for easy reference.

2. "The skill should be learned as a whole rather than in its component parts. This will permit the establishment of the chain of proprioceptive stimuli and responses, and avoid relearning through annexation of parts. Progressive part learning would also appear to be better than distinct part learning where the total whole is not feasible."

3. "Learning should start with general form and rhythm of the action rather than with details and emphasizing accuracy. This will provide for better feeling of action and serve as a base on which precision may be controlled." There is much to think about in learning most gymnastic skills. Form, height, and elegance should be emphasized after the basic movements are learned.

[2] M. Gladys Scott, *Analysis of Human Motion*, 2nd ed. (New York: Appleton-Century-Crofts, 1963), pp. 382–383. Copyright © 1942 by F. S. Crofts & Co., Inc. Copyright © 1963 by Meredith Publishing Company.

4. "Learning should proceed at nearly a normal tempo for the skill as soon as possible. This does not mean starting with maximum speed. Such emphasis usually leads to tension and interferes with perceptions necessary for accuracy. However, a slow-motion style of execution differs too much mechanically and it is too hard to adjust to a faster rate later. A compromise on a more moderate speed would seem best." Adequate momentum is necessary for execution of almost all gymnastic skills. Consequently, gymnasts learn early that they have to "go" for most moves. Use of a safety belt and spotters will alleviate anxiety which sometimes causes gymnasts to restrict their speed when attempting a new move.

5. "Individual tempo should be established rather than imposing a fixed one on the entire class. This is desirable because of individual differences in length and weight of levers and in strength."

6. "Skills should always be performed in optimum equilibrium for that skill so as to free the attention for details of hand or foot action."

7. "Practice should be carried out with proper equipment and the same equipment each practice period." The amount of force needed to execute a back uprise into a handstand on springy parallel bars will not be the same as the amount of force needed to execute this move on stiff parallel bars. The whip and pull needed to do a rear vault catch on a six-foot horizontal bar will be greater than that needed to do this move on an eight-foot horizontal bar.

8. "Players of all levels should be taught to note differences in degree of effort at different points in the skill or game and to use the opportunities for relaxation to the maximum." Teachers and coaches of gymnastics soon learn to shout "pull" or "push" at key points during a gymnast's movement through a skill.

9. "In the early stages the learner should not work past the point of mild fatigue when interference with movement sensations appears to begin."

The gymnast must develop the ability to make an accurate appraisal of the amount of force being exerted. He must be able to recognize the differences in the kinesthetic feeling of different attempts at a skill. He must develop a good sense of balance.

PRINCIPLES FROM SOCIOLOGY

The teaching of gymnastics and tumbling provides a great many opportunities to direct students' attitudes and behaviors into socially acceptable paterns. The major prerequisites to the achievement of this goal are that the teacher consider it an important responsibility and that he conscientiously search out opportunities for effecting learning in this area (or set them up).

Although there is no conclusive evidence that a transfer of training from the sports arena to the larger socioeconomic-political arena occurs, there is no excuse for failing to make efforts in this direction. Of what practical use is it for skilled individuals to be outstanding in various important accomplishments—athletic, scientific, humanitarian, or whatever—if as a group they are unable to work together harmoniously toward common goals? Sociological problems, from failures in marriage to world tensions, destroy man's productivity and satisfactions, and man himself. Undoubtedly, improvement of students' social behaviors is the most important objective of physical educators from a long-range point of view.

Coaches and physical educators have a unique opportunity to effect improvement in the social behaviors of their students. They are in a favorable position because:

1. The younger students often regard the coach or physical educator as a person they would like to emulate.

2. The coach or physical educator can establish rapport with his students more easily than can most other teachers because his subject matter (skills and the human body) is more elemental than are most subjects. Students are interested in their own bodies and in learning what they can do with them.

3. The subject matter is interesting and challenging to most students, and it is personally applicable.

4. The coach works with students in a highly emotion-charged situation, where there is for the moment a greatly desired goal—victory. This goal is often achieved more easily by bending, ignoring, or circumventing rules. However, achievement of the goal does not bring material rewards; it brings primarily ego satisfaction as a result of proving oneself better in an activity

than another person or team. If rules, whose purpose is to ensure equality, are circumvented, no superiority has been proven by the "victory." Where the desire to win does not achieve ridiculous proportions and where the coach regards himself as an educator rather than a trainer, sports provide an outstanding tool for teaching social behaviors. Lecturing about sportsmanship can never be as effective as can practical experience during the excitement and sweat of actual participation in the emotionally charged situations that occur in sports and games.

Cooperation One of education's most important goals is to develop the ability to work cooperatively with others. Gymnasts soon learn that when they offer to spot others and to coach others, the favor will be returned. The coach or teacher can facilitate this learning in several ways:

1. He can have students work in pairs (similar to the "buddy system" used in swimming) to coach and spot one another.

2. He should publicly compliment evidences of effective or courageous spotting. (Spotting often calls for greater courage than does trying a difficult move.)

3. He should reprimand failure to spot or to ask for spotters. This reprimand may be in verbal form or by subtracting points in the point system used to determine the course grade.

4. He can reward for spotting, for coaching others, for maintaining equipment, and for regularly assisting in the setup and return of equipment by evaluating these items as objectively as possible in order to give credit for them in the grading plan.

5. In skills performed by more than one person, each participant should be reminded that his failure to perform his assigned task will result in failure for the entire group and possibly injury to others.

6. In exhibition and demonstration groups there are unparalleled opportunities to teach the values of cooperative efforts. A number of committees, such as program, ticket, publicity, theme, costumes, music, equipment, and stage, are needed. Cooperative efforts are required in long-range preparations for the show and also immediately preceding, during, and after the show in the form of loading, unloading, and setting up equipment. Music, lights, background,

equipment, and costumes must be readied on time and returned after the show.

7. The author has devised a self-rating sheet for use by his students. Students are asked to rate themselves as honestly as they are able. The instructor then reviews each self-evaluation and, if he deems it necessary, adjusts each rating upward or downward. The author has seldom found it necessary to change the scores because most students are surprisingly honest when they know that they are trusted. Results of this self-evaluation should make up 5 to 10 percent of the students' grades. Distribution of the sheet presents an opportunity to make comments on the importance of sportsmanship and desirable patterns of social behavior. One class period can be devoted to a lecture on this topic. (The self-rating sheet is included in Appendix B.)

Leadership and Followership Another social goal is the ability to lead and follow. There are opportunities for followership and leadership experiences in gymnastics through the formation of squads with squad leaders and in the many committees needed for exhibitions and demonstrations. The opportunities inherent in exhibition troupes for these kinds of experiences will become apparent to the reader after reviewing the section on exhibition and demonstration troupes.

Courage While we no longer have to fear attack by wild animals or savage tribes, courage is as necessary as it ever was. Moral, rather than physical, courage is most often demanded in today's world, but the development of moral courage is facilitated by the development of physical courage. In gymnastics, physical courage, like skill, is developed progressively, while at the same time the student is kept as safe as possible. Physical courage is not developed when students are injured. The spotting and safety procedures in learning many gymnastic stunts illustrate this progressive process of developing courage. As a student's skill in executing a new skill increases, his need for extra safety precautions and spotters decreases, and his courage about the skill is reinforced with each degree of success.

Students should be prohibited from taking unnecessary chances and every precaution should be taken to prevent a bump or a bruise. However, instructors should know that some students can become overly dependent upon the safety belt. Students who develop the habit of almost never "coming out of the belt" are more likely to be handicapped by fear when they finally do away with the belt, with a resulting increase in the probability of falling. This type of student should be urged by the instructors to proceed to the next step in the learning process as soon as he has mastered the preceding step. Students should not be allowed to believe they have learned the move until they can do it without assistance. In gymnastics, as in swimming, lack of confidence and fear can cause accidents.

Through these processes, gymnasts will soon learn the difference between courage and foolhardiness. They will learn that fear can be overcome by making adequate preparations through learning skills in their progressive order of difficulty and by utilizing spotters and other safety procedures as needed.

PRINCIPLES FROM KINESIOLOGY

There are a number of mechanical principles that all high school students learn in physics class which have special application to gymnastics. A thorough understanding of these principles will help the physical educator or coach to analyze any gymnastic skill and will make him a more effective teacher. Some of these follow:

1. *When a body attains a given speed, it tends to maintain that speed until it is stopped.* In all skills, the gymnast must first overcome standing inertia. After achieving the desired speed, this speed tends to be maintained until it is stopped by another force. To slow this speed or to stop it, another force must be applied. For example, in a front flyaway from the horizontal bar, the gymnast should release the bar when he is about 105° to 115° from the vertical. At the moment of release, the gymnast's body has established an upward-forward speed and has established a trajectory. At the same time, it is rotating around its center of gravity. The upward-forward movement and rotary momentum established previous to the release of the bar will continue after the release at the speed developed. When the release is made at the proper moment

and if the speed or rotation is correct, the gymnast will rotate just enough to land on his feet. When his feet contact the mat, a force (friction) is applied to stop his rotation. The force of gravity will ensure his return to the mat.

2. *There are three types of motion in gymnastics—linear motion (movement in a straight line), angular or circular motion (movement around a central point), and a combination of these two.* A thief vault over the side horse is primarily an example of linear motion. A hip circle on the horizontal bar is an example of angular motion. A front salto (somersault) in which the horizontal axis of the body moves forward while the body rotates around this axis is an example of combined linear and angular motion.

3. *Momentum has been developed when inertia has been overcome and the body is moving at a given speed.* Gymnasts utilize momentum in many ways. A tumbler builds up the momentum necessary to execute a back somersault in layout position by first doing a round-off and a series of back handsprings. These give him linear momentum. To do the front uprise on the parallel bars, the gymnast swings his legs forward and upward, which gives him momentum in a forward-upward direction, enabling him to extend his arms easily under his rising body.

4. *The momentum of a part of the body may be transferred to the whole.* In the upper arm (top) kip on the parallel bars, this principle is well illustrated. When the legs are extended forward-upward at the hips, they generate momentum in the same direction. When this extension is checked, the momentum of the legs is transferred to the trunk, causing it to move forward-upward over the hands and enabling the gymnast to extend his arms easily. A great many skills, such as the front and back uprise on the parallel bars and rings, the backward roll on the mats and parallel bars, the glide kip on the parallel bars, and the kip on the horizontal bar, to mention only a few, necessitate application of this principle.

5. *A shortening of the radius accelerates the speed of rotation, while a lengthening of the radius decreases the speed of rotation.* In executing a flying front somersault, a trampolinist goes into a swan position, somersaulting slowly as his feet move over his head. He then shortens his radius of rotation by suddenly flexing at his

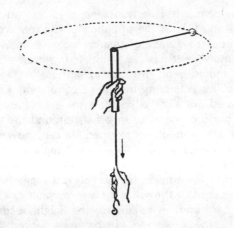

Shortening the radius of rotation accelerates the speed of rotation

hips and knees, which increases his angular velocity and enables him to complete the somersault very quickly. In executing a shoulder roll on the parallel bars, the gymnast shortens his radius by flexing at the hips as his body swings upward. This accelerates his speed of rotation, enabling him to bring his feet over his head. As his feet come up over his head, he extends at the hips to slow down his rotation.

This principle can be dramatically illustrated by tying a weight to one end of a string, then passing the string through a hollow cylinder, giving the weight a spin, and pulling down on the opposite end of the string. This shortening of the radius of rotation will accelerate the speed of rotation.

Let us assume that the radius of the circle being made by the weight is five feet and that the weight makes one revolution per second. It is therefore traveling at the rate of 31.4 feet per second. (Circumference = pi × 2R or C = 3.14 × (2 × 5) = 3.14 × 10 = 31.4.) If we now pull on the string so that the radius becomes 2.5 feet, the weight will continue to move at the rate of 3.14 feet per second, but the new circle will have a circumference of only 15.7 feet, or half that of the previous circle. The weight will therefore make two revolutions per second.

6. *The longer the lever, the greater will be the force required to move it, but also the greater will be its angular movement of momentum and its angular reaction.* When the gymnast wishes

to generate momentum, as in a giant swing on the horizontal bar, he extends his body to lengthen his radius on the downward swing. Since his head and feet make the same number of revolutions in a unit of time, and since his feet describe a circle of greater circumference than does his head, his feet must be traveling faster than his head. If he moves his feet closer to his head during the downward swing by bending at the hips, knees, or shoulders, he will cause his feet to travel at a slower rate of speed and therefore will not generate the momentum necessary to complete the giant swing. This principle is applied in many gymnastic skills, particularly on the horizontal bar and rings. The principle explains why good form demands straight legs; longer levers provide greater momentum and consequently greater angular reaction. The principle also explains why it is more difficult for tall gymnasts to do skills such as the planche and other lever skills and why tall gymnasts can generate so much momentum on the horizontal bar.

7. *Action and reaction are equal and in opposite directions.* In leaping into the air to gain height for the back salto, the trampolinist or tumbler first pushes against the bed or mat with his feet by extending his legs. This is the action. The bed or mat then pushes against his feet to lift him. This is the reaction. In doing a peach basket on the parallel bars, the gymnast drops downward (while at the same time rotating). This action is downward. He then rebounds upward (while continuing to rotate) to rise above the bar. This is reaction. Springy bars provide greater reaction. Skilled gymnasts secure maximum reaction.

8. *In many tumbling skills, efforts should be made to bring the center of weight as high above the mat as possible.* This will give the tumbler more time in which to bring his feet under his center of weight. The need for doing this is quite obvious with regard to front and back saltos (somersaults) and their variations. It may be less obvious with regard to neck-, head-, and handsprings. When the tumbler lifts his hips high on the springs, he can more easily whip his feet under his hips. In the neckspring and headspring, this implies that he should extend his hips when his back is at approximately a 50°–60° angle to the floor. In the handspring, this implies the advantage of keeping the arms perpendicu-

lar to the floor and extending at the shoulders as he passes through the handstand.

9. *In many swinging exercises, at the critical part of the swing, a force should be applied to bring the center of weight closer to the point of support.* That is, the center of weight should approach the axis, center of rotation, or point of support. This principle is clearly illustrated in the front uprise on the rings. In this skill, there is a quick flexion of the hips just before the end of the forward swing is reached. At the same time, the extended arms pull downward. This action brings the center of weight, the hips, up between the rings. During the move there are three centers of rotation—at the attachment of the rings' cables to the ceiling, at the shoulder joint, and at the hips. A few of the other skills in which this principle is illustrated are the front and back uprise on the parallel bars, the kip and back uprise on the horizontal bar, and the reverse kip and back uprise on the rings.

10. *There are two critical points in almost all timing on the apparatus.* These are:

a. *In circling movements with a fixed support (such as on the horizontal or parallel bars), one critical point occurs just as the center of weight passes a point directly under the hands.* This, for example, is the moment when the hips are flexed slightly during giant swings.

b. *In free-swinging movements, such as those done on the rings, horizontal bar, and parallel bars, the critical point occurs right at the end of the swing, when the momentum resulting from the swing and the pull of gravity are exactly equal.* (At this moment the body is weightless.) This is the moment when almost all swinging skills are executed, either on the forward or the backward swing. Initiating skills before this point is reached causes the hands to be pulled away due to centrifugal force, while initiating the move after this point is reached results in too great a downward pull due to gravity.

11. *To initiate rotation around any of the three axes, force must be applied at an angle to the axis.* Everything else being equal, the greater this force, the greater will be the speed of rotation. Everything else being equal, the longer the force arm in relation to the resistance arm, the greater will be the "moment of force" and the greater will be the speed of rotation. This means that in twisting or somersaulting

movements, it is advantageous to extend the arms and legs at the initiation of the movement in order to generate greater momentum. After the movement has been initiated, the arms and legs should bend in order to shorten the radius, thereby accelerating the speed of rotation. Once initiated, rotation, either in a somersault around the horizontal axis or in a twist around the vertical axis, cannot be stopped. It can, however, be appreciably decelerated by lengthening the radius through extending the body in somersaults or the arms in twists. This fact suggests the importance of throwing for a somersault or twist just hard enough relative to the height secured, the number of somersaults or twists desired, and the tightness of the tuck in a somersault or the wind-up in a twist.

12. *A number of forces may be added to one another to propel an object in a certain direction.* If these forces are applied simultaneously, the force generated will be limited by the weakest of the several forces. For greatest effectiveness, succeeding forces should be added at the point of greatest speed but least acceleration of the preceding forces. That is, the addition of the succeeding force should not be added while the preceding force is still accelerating, but should be delayed until the speed of the preceding force is at its maximum. If this is done, the resulting forces will be added to one another. This principle points up the importance of good timing and explains why fluidity is an important criterion in judging competitive gymnastics. Application of the principle is illustrated in leaping for height in the backward somersault. First, the arms drive upward; then the hips extend; next the knees extend; and, finally, the toes extend against the mat. Each succeeding movement is begun before the preceding one has been completed in order that the forces will be added to one another. While learning new skills, students sometimes need to be told when to initiate a movement.

13. *When several forces are applied simultaneously, the resulting direction and force is determined by the relative directions and amounts of the several forces according to a parallelogram of forces.* If two equal forces push at a 45° angle to the long axis of a body, that body will move directly forward. If the right-hand force is greater than the left-hand force, or if it pushes

at more than a 45° angle, the body will move to the left. This is why the faster the tumbler runs preparatory to executing the front salto, the greater must be the angle of his legs relative to the floor (blocking action) if he is to secure maximum height.

14. *There are three ways in which twisting movements are accomplished:*

a. *The simplest and most frequently seen method we will call the "direct" method.* In this method the twist is initiated from the mat or bed of the trampoline. As the feet leave the mat or bed, the head and shoulders turn to the left, and the extended right arm pulls across the face. After the twist has been initiated, the arms are held as close to the body as possible, or are moved parallel to the body's long axis. Since the twisting action is initiated while the feet are still in contact with the bed, the reaction is against the bed and the lower body cannot move in a direction opposite to that of the arms, head and trunk. The momentum generated by the head, shoulders, and arms is transferred to the body to bring it around for the twist.

b. *A second method of twisting LaDue and Norman call the "action-reaction twist."*[3] This method makes use of the law of physics that for every action there is an equal and opposite reaction. It is recommended that the tumbler or trampolinist first try the method while jumping vertically. After he is convinced that it will work, he should attempt the method with a somersault. In straight or vertical jumping, the method is executed in this manner: The feet leave the bed or mat with the arms extended directly in front at shoulder height and with the body straight. When the arms are next swung vigorously to the right at shoulder height, the body reacts by turning to the left. When the left arm runs into the chest, no more force or torque can be applied. In order that a twist of the body will not occur in the opposite direction when the arms are brought back, they are either dropped to the side or brought overhead in line with the body. This action shortens the radius of rotation, thereby increasing the speed of rotation. To do the back somersault with a twist utilizing this method, the

arms are lifted slightly above the horizontal before pulling them sideward, and the head and trunk are thrown backward. While this action produces a slight side somersaulting motion, it is negligible because the weight of the body is so much greater than that of the arms.

If more torque is desired, the shoulders and head can be squared, the arms then extended in front again, and the action repeated. While reverse twisting action will be present during the repositioning of the arms, it will be negligible owing to the small radius of rotation.

c. *A third method of twisting LaDue and Norman call "twisting from a pike."* This twisting procedure, like the one preceding, is initiated after the feet have left the bed, mat, or board. If this procedure is utilized during a front somersault, the twist is initiated when the body is in a sharply piked position by throwing the arm in the direction of the twist. The body is then extended and the twist follows.

This twisting action is made possible by the successive use of several laws of motion. With the body piked, when the arm is thrown across the chest in a plane which is at about a 45° angle to that of the chest, there can be little reaction to this movement, because the arm movement is parallel to the vertical axis, which in the piked position is forward of the hips. Sometimes there will be a slight side somersaulting movement, but this would be small because of the great mass of the body as compared to that of the arm. This makes it possible to build up considerable momentum without producing a reactive twist in the opposite direction. When the hips are extended, the momentum of the arm acts upon the body to twist it around its vertical axis, which at that time passes through the center of the extended body.

Twisting from an arch This move can also be done after the feet have left the supporting surface by applying the same principles. When the arms have reached a position in line with the vertical axis in their upward swing, they are swung sideward parallel to this axis. Since this movement is parallel to the vertical axis, no twisting reaction occurs. There is only a slight sideward somersaulting reaction produced. Momentum is thereby generated in the arms. This momentum, or force, acts to produce torque upon the vertical axis when

[3] Frank Ladue and Jim Norman, *This Is Trampolining* (Cedar Rapids, Iowa: Nissen Trampoline Co., 1954), p. 86.

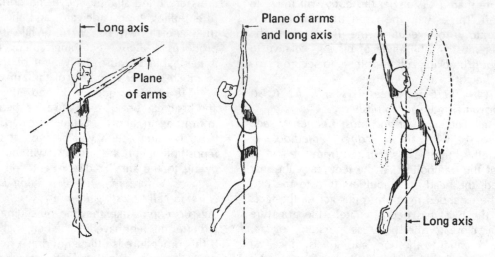

Twisting from an arch

the body moves from its hyperextended position into a straight position, at which time the arms are wrapped around the body.

15. *In planning a routine or exercise, let the position at the end of one move determine what the next move should be.* Following this principle not only will enable the gymnast to conserve energy by using the momentum of the preceding move, but also will make for an aesthetically more pleasing routine. With proper planning, the body position at the end of one move will be favorable to the execution of the succeeding move. Following are examples of routines in which this principle is applied:

a. Tumbling: Round-off—back handspring —back somersault with a half twist—walk-out—front handspring—front somersault—front roll—front somersault.

b. Parallel Bars: Front vault mount—peach basket to an upper arm hang—front uprise— "stutse" to a support—cast to an upper arm hang —back uprise cut and catch—handstand—back somersault dismount.

c. Horizontal Bar: Kip with a reverse grip—forward giant swing—half turn—three-quarter backward giant swing—hip circle—under-swing—back uprise into a rear vault catch—kip— front vault dismount.

16. *Good form should be based on good mechanics, not on super-rigidity.* Rigidity hin-

ders movement, which ought to be fluid, free, and graceful.

17. *The greater the distance, and therefore time, over which momentum is developed, the greater the momentum possible.* To state it another way: Velocity = acceleration × time of acceleration. In conformity with this principle, the tumbler initiating the back handspring swings his arms backward in an extended position before swinging them forward, upward, and backward. By swinging his arms backward, he increases the distance and consequently the time over which he can accelerate the speed of the forward arm swing. This increases momentum, which facilitates his getting around. For this reason, also, a high and long forward swing is advised in a back uprise to a handstand on the parallel bars or in the back uprise into a giant swing on the horizontal bar. Many other examples could be offered. These positioning or preparatory movements (which are in moves incorporated into the routine but are not eliminated) not only serve to build up the momentum necessary to execute the skill, but also place the muscles on a stretch. It is well known that muscles on a stretch can generate a greater pull than they can when they are already shortened. This is the reason for the "stretch" in baseball pitching. This physiological law applies to gymnasts as well as to pitchers. The preparatory

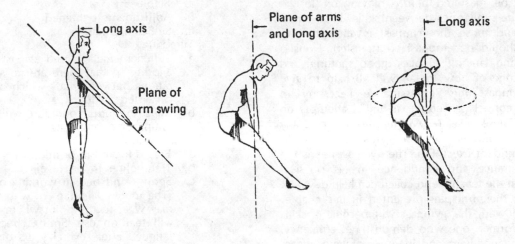

Twisting from a pike

stretch is also useful in directing the application of force. In doing a side somersault, the gymnast first brings his arms to the side opposite the direction he will somersault.

18. *After a swinging move has been completed, there is always a follow through during which the remaining momentum is absorbed.* Only awkward beginners attempt to stop immediately after completing a move involving momentum. When planning a routine, this follow through should be the preparatory movement for the succeeding skill. That is, it should be used to generate momentum, to place the muscles on a stretch, and to establish the direction of application of force for the next movement in the routine. The follow through also facilitates relaxation and conservation of energy.

19. *To produce linear motion, push or lift through the center of gravity or equally along the entire line of gravity.* In spotting somersaults, for example, if the gymnast lacks sufficient height, the spotter should lift at the center of gravity. To produce rotation, push at a right angle to the radius of rotation a distance from the center of gravity. If the gymnast is rotating too slowly in the back somersault, the spotter should push behind the thigh. If the gymnast is rotating too slowly in the front somersault, the spotter should push behind the neck with one hand. These suggestions indicate why it is stand-

ard spotting procedure to place one hand at the hips and the other varying distances away. One hand can then be used to impart lift while the other can be used to assist with rotation.

20. *All body parts possible should contribute to the desired movements.* In the cartwheel, for example, the gymnast bends his trunk sideward, swings his left arm downward, swings his right arm around, springs off his left foot, and swings his right leg up and around to establish the momentum necessary for the sideward rotation. The summation of all these forces facilitates execution of a smooth, effortless cartwheel. Application of all the principles arising from kinesiology will help bring the gymnast beyond the great rigidity, inefficiency, and unnecessarily great effort of the early learning stages.

21. *It needs to be emphasized that while practice does make for consistency, it does not make for perfection.* Faulty performance may become a habit as a result of practice. Thus sound teaching, coaching, and learning practices are needed. The principles presented in this chapter should be followed. Films, especially loop films, in which proper execution is depicted, should be used. Skilled gymnasts should be observed. Good spotting techniques and devices should be employed in order to give students the assurance necessary to execute the move correctly. Proper progressions should be fol-

lowed, and each step in the progression should be mastered before moving on to the next. The similarities between skills already mastered and those the gymnast is attempting to learn should be emphasized (transfer). Nonslip shoes and landing surfaces, good spotting, and knowledge of how to fall will all help to give the gymnast the self-assurance necessary to follow correct procedures in initial attempts on a skill. These measures will help to minimize any fear that inhibits and prevents concentration and confident execution. The gymnast needs the self-assurance and confidence in his physical skill that the teacher and coach can help develop.

If the principles presented in this chapter are followed, the gymnast will become a skillful performer, one who demonstrates efficiency, accuracy, judgment, and adequate strength, speed, and power.

SAFETY CONSIDERATIONS

In describing the procedure for developing a student's courage while at the same time keeping him safe, a safety procedure was described. The following additional procedures should be observed.

The instructor should attempt to develop in students the habit of checking equipment before using it. The instructor himself should also make daily checks on the equipment. The safety checks include:

1. Parallel Bars
   a. Wheels removed while bars are in use
   b. Width adjustment locked in place
   c. Height adjustment locked in place
   d. Mats positioned around and between bars.
2. Horizontal Bar
   a. Turnbuckle shafts securely threaded into adjusting position
   b. Guy wires sufficiently taut
   c. Sufficient mats butted up against one another
   d. Floor plates checked
3. Side Horse
   a. Wheels removed while it is in use
   b. Pommels tight
   c. Sufficient mats

4. Balance Beam
   a. Stable
   b. Adjustments tightened
   c. Sufficient mats
5. Tumbling
   a. Sufficient mats butted against one another so that there are no separations between mats which cause a twisted ankle
   b. Mats in good condition with no lumps or depressions
6. Trampoline
   a. Braces locked in position
   b. Trampoline frame level
   c. Springs and bed in working order (The individual straps of web beds may wear to the point where they will tear on use. Springs become fatigued after several years of use and sometimes snap at the hooked end and fly off. Beds and springs should be replaced when they are worn.)
   d. Frame pads all around
7. Rings
   a. Upper end attachments checked for wear.
   b. Straps checked for wear
   c. Chain properly hooked with hoisting types of rings.
   d. Sufficient mats butted up against one another.
8. Long Horse
   a. Wheels retracted while in use
   b. Holes (of pommel shafts) plugged
   c. Sufficient mats butted against one another.

The instructor has responsibilities when purchasing equipment to be sure that the equipment is safe. Savings on parallel bars that might crack, turnbuckles that might snap, and trampoline beds that wear out quickly are not very satisfying if a student is injured and a law suit results. It is far better to purchase standard equipment which can be depended upon to provide long service. Quality gymnastic equipment will last from 10 to 50 years when properly maintained.

Trampolines, springboards, and flying rings should be locked when not under supervised use.

The instructor should spend some class time in teaching students the various breakfalls.

The instructor should insist on a minimum of four spotters at all times on the trampoline. These spotters should position themselves on each side and each end of the trampoline. Their primary responsibility is to push the performer back onto the bed in the event he loses control. They should give the performer their undivided attention.

In addition to checking on equipment before using it, students have the following responsibilities with regard to their own safety:

1. Develop an amount of strength, power, flexibility, and endurance necessary to the successful achievement of the move or combinations of moves they are attempting to learn. (A student needs a minimum of arm and shoulder girdle strength to be able to swing in a cross arm support on the parallel bars.)
2. Observe all safety rules.
3. Learn skills in their progressive order of difficulty.
4. Master fundamentals.
5. Warm up properly.
6. Be willing to spot and to coach others.
7. Be willing to ask others to spot.
8. Avoid "horse play."
9. Use the necessary amount of carbonate of magnesium or rosin.
10. Possess the courage to follow a skill through to its completion once it has been initiated.
11. Possess knowledge of and sufficient skill to apply the principles of breakfalling in the event of an error. There are two principal methods by means of which the probability of an injury can be lessened as a result of a fall. These are:
    a. Distributing the impact over a greater area
    b. Distributing the impact over a greater period of time

Examples of application of the first method are provided in the fall forward and chest roll, the backward roll with legs straight, the headspring to the seat position, and the arm slap in backward falls (as demonstrated by professional wrestlers). In all of these skills, a relatively large body area contacts the mat at almost the same moment. Examples of application of the second method are provided in the arm bend in the diving forward roll, the bending of the knees and hips during the landing after a flyaway from the horizontal bar, and by the professional boxer when he "gives" with the punch.

Gymnasts should remember the following points with regard to breakfalls:

1. When catching the weight on the hands during a backward fall, the fingers should be pointed forward in order that the elbows can bend on impact.
2. The face should be turned in the direction of the fall if possible.
3. The chin should be tucked in or the face turned sideward just prior to impact in a forward fall.
4. The body should be tucked immediately after the landing to go into a forward, backward, or sideward roll if at all possible. This distributes the impact over a greater period of time.
5. Well-padded body parts such as the buttocks should contact the surface if possible.

LIABILITY

Liability and the possibility of lawsuits are unpleasant subjects, but teachers and coaches of gymnastics have been sued by parents of children who suffered an injury in gymnastics. Fear of suit has, unfortunately, caused some athletic directors, chairmen, physical education teachers, school principals and/or school boards to reach the decision that gymnastics should not be included in the curriculum. This decision is motivated by a desire for self-preservation, even though statistics gathered by the National Safety Council have shown that gymnastics is a relatively safe activity. The incidence of injuries is considerably higher in football, lacrosse, skiing, and several other sports where injuries have been accepted. Many skiers and football players, in fact, describe their injuries with pride. The remote possibility of legal action is not sufficient reason to deny students the benefits of gymnastics.

In some states, the school board, board of education, and the school trustees are immune to law suit; only the teacher is responsible.

Fortunately, in many states, the laws are being changed so that the burden does not fall entirely upon the teacher. In an increasing number of states, school boards and boards of trustees can be sued; hence teachers are less frequently sued.

A teacher cannot be held liable unless negligence is proven. Generally, a person is negligent when he has failed to act as a reasonably prudent person would act under the circumstances. A negligent act may be one of commission or one of omission. An example of an act of commission would be asking a student to do a front salto before he has learned to do cartwheels and the springs. An act of omission would be failure to put mats under equipment or failure to check on the condition of equipment. The primary guideline for the teacher or coach of gymnastics is: *Resist the temptation to be sloppy or lazy.* The teacher must be meticulous about checking equipment daily, teach his students the safety rules and spotting procedures, and resist the impulse to move students along too quickly. He must ground the students thoroughly in the fundamentals.

When equipment is defective or unsafe, the teacher or coach should write a letter notifying the authorities of this situation. He should retain a copy of this letter; meanwhile, he should refuse to use the defective equipment.

All interscholastic and intercollegiate athletes should be given a thorough medical examination just prior to the beginning of the time when practice for the competitive season is to begin. Various kinds of conditions (cardiac abnormalities, infectious diseases, kidney malfunctions, and the like) can develop between the opening of school and the beginning of the sports season. For this reason, it is inadequate to have an athlete undergo a medical examination in September when he begins practice in December. During the intervening three months, the student could suffer some debilitating injury or infection.

An equipment safety check list should be used at regular intervals. This will serve as a reminder to check all aspects of equipment safety and will also provide a record of the condition of the equipment.

All accidents should be reported in a standard accident report form, and a copy should be filed by the teacher. Litigation may take many months or years. Memories fade. An accident report form with all relevant details recorded and signed by witnesses (with their addresses) can prove invaluable in the event of litigation.

Following are examples of defenses to liability; however, it should be remembered that no defense is iron-clad, but ultimately subject to the interpretation of a court:

1. *Contributory negligence:* The plaintiff was himself negligent in some manner that contributed to the accident. However, it must be remembered that most of these cases come before a jury of laymen who are likely to feel great compassion for an incapacitated child.

2. *Voluntary assumption of risk:* People know there is a possibility of injury when they ski or play football. Members of a gymnastic team or club and their parents should be made aware of this risk in gymnastics. A letter explaining both the benefits and the risks sent to parents and accompanied by a permission slip to be signed by parents and the participant may be helpful in decreasing the probability of suit in the event of an accident. However, such a letter may deter some parents from allowing their child to participate in gymnastics.

3. *Act of God:* The accident was unforeseeable, unpredictable, and nothing could have been done to prevent it. No one has been negligent. If a bolt of lightning strikes the generator, causing the lights to go out just as the gymnast releases the horizontal bar for a double flyaway, no one could likely be held blameable for the gymnast's injuries.

4. *An act of negligence must have substantial connection with the injury:* Parents of a boy injured on the mini-tramp would not be likely to sue successfully if they contended that the coach had not provided enough magnesium, since magnesium is not used on this apparatus.

With respect to the possibility of a law suit, one of the best actions a physical educator or coach can take is to purchase liability insurance. Needless to say, he should study the policy carefully to make certain the policy will cover him for the kinds of things he needs coverage for.

Many schools are members of athletic benefit funds with membership limited to members of school athletic teams. Although these organizations do not pay damages, they do provide reasonable financial payment for medical expenses. Membership is usually voluntary.

METHODS OF CLASS ORGANIZATION

The first step in class organization is, as in any venture, to determine objectives. Since physical education is a part of general education, the objectives of a physical education class must be consistent with the objectives of general education in a democratic society.

The Educational Policies Commission in 1938 cited the following as objectives of education:

1. The objectives of self-realization: the inquiring mind; speech, reading, writing, and numbers; sight and hearing; health knowledge; health habits; public health; recreation; intellectual and aesthetic interests; and character.

2. The objectives of human relationships: respect for humanity; friendships, cooperation, and courtesy; appreciation and conservation of the home, homemaking, and democracy in the home.

3. The objectives of economic efficiency: work; occupational information and choice; occupational efficiency; occupational adjustment and appreciation; personal economics; and consumer judgment, efficiency in buying, and consumer protection.

4. The objectives of civic responsibility: social justice and activity; social understanding; critical judgment; tolerance; conservation; social application of science; world citizenship; law observance; economic literacy; political citizenship; and devotion to democracy.

The Educational Policies Commission statement on the objectives of education has probably been the most widely accepted of many such statements, but all others list essentially the same goals. School boards, administrators, curriculum builders, accreditation groups, facilities planners, and physical education teachers, when making plans for a unit on gymnastics, should consider this statement as one of their guides.

Physical education, and gymnastics as an important part of physical education, can contribute to the inquiring mind by developing a zest for living and broadening the variety of activities in which the student participates. Gymnastics contributes to health knowledge by serving as the means to teach the effects of exercise on the body and the factors governing physical performance.

Gymnastics can contribute to command of the fundamental processes by helping the student learn to judge distance, speed, and spatial relationships accurately; to estimate weight, force, and shock; to time movements of his body; and to select and read intelligently articles and books on health, recreation, and sports.

A student's knowledge of his body and its functions and his understanding of his physical achievements, capacities, and limitations will be improved by gymnastics. Gymnastics should be taught so as to develop attitudes conducive to the establishment of good health habits. It will aid in developing organic vigor, physical skills, and emotional control.

A unit on gymnastics adds another recreational skill to the student's repertory of recreational activities, as a participant and as a spectator.

The study of and participation in gymnastics develops an appreciation of pleasing, expressive, graceful, and efficient movement. The ability to appreciate skilled physical movement is akin to the ability to appreciate the classical fine arts. All are works of people with great and unique skill which add to the enjoyment of the audience. Gymnastics fosters an appreciation of pleasing proportions and contours. Ancient Greek art, poetry, and literature, which stressed the beauties of the human body, still is appreciated after thousands of years.

Gymnastics should be so taught as to aid students in developing a high level of self-discipline and self-direction. It should help them to develop skill in social relations and good emotional control. Students should learn to have regard for the well-being of others and to evaluate actions on the basis of the greatest good for the greatest number rather than on the basis of personal gain. Hopefully, friendships will develop in gymnastics classes and on gymnastics teams. They should identify with their group and establish satisfying relationships with people of both sexes and of all ages.

Opportunities should be provided to develop skill in democratic leadership and followership. Students should be encouraged to practice courtesy, sportsmanship, and fair play and to respect the personalities of others.

Gymnastics can help people to keep themselves physically fit to meet the demands of school work or jobs.

Gymnasts should be taught in such a manner as to develop tolerance for people of different social, racial, religious, and economic backgrounds and for individuals who hold opinions different from their own.

The instructor should take advantage of opportunities to develop world understanding by discovering the achievements of the people of other nations. He can accomplish this through movies of gymnasts of other nations or of the Olympic Games, or through promoting the sponsorship of touring gymnastic teams from foreign countries.

Finally, sudents should be aided in developing positive attitudes toward conforming to rules, regulations, and laws.

These, then, are the ways in which gymnastics, as a part of a physical education curriculum, can contribute to the objectives of education as stated by the Educational Policies Commission. Certain courses contribute more fully to certain objectives than do other courses. Teachers of the same subject may emphasize certain objectives more than will other teachers of that subject. Students' age, sex, and ability; facilities and funding available; knowledge, skills, and abilities of the teacher; class size; and other factors will determine the relative emphasis placed on different objectives. This diversity is desirable and is needed in a democracy.

The teacher should first describe the general objectives of all his units on gymnastics. These would be long-range goals such as those centering around improved social behaviors and improved physical fitness. Secondly, the teacher should list the specific, measurable objectives of each unit on gymnastics. These are the objectives which could be achieved within the limitations of the particular unit. These might be the ability to do the forward roll, handspring, or handstand in reasonable good form; knowledge of safety procedures; or appreciation of gymnastics.

Next, the teacher should decide on the principles which will guide him in his progress toward his goals. These could be drawn from the principles of anatomy, physiology, sociology, psychology, kinesiology, and physics already presented.

Now, the teacher must determine the methods that he will apply in progressing toward his goals. These would include selection of the specific knowledges, skills, attitudes, and behaviors which will be taught or developed during the class periods and by homework assignments, films, field trips, and class projects. The following can serve as a guide in the selection of skills:

1. Start where the students are and thereafter present skills in their progressive order of difficulty.

2. Present as great a variety of skills as possible in order that progressions are as gradual as possible and in order that students experience success as frequently as possible.

3. Select different kinds of skills so that the slender and the heavy, the flexible and the stiff, those with a good sense of balance and those with a poor sense of balance, the fearless and the fearful, and the strong and the weak can all find some skills in which they will experience success.

4. The range in difficulty of the skills should be great enough that the most inept can experience success and the most skillful will be challenged.

5. Select "theme" skills for each day. These theme skills should be related to one another or be similar in some respect. Forward and backward rolls and their varieties could be the theme for one day. The springs could be a theme for another day, the somersaults for another, the circles for another, the balances for another, the kips for another.

6. Select skills so that the one learned yesterday will contribute to the one presented today and the one learned today will contribute to the one to be presented tomorrow.

7. Prepare more than enough skills for a day's lesson so that the class is kept moving and makes maximum use of the available time with a resulting greater productivity.

Evaluating Evaluative devices selected should measure the extent to which the general and specific objectives have been met, because the evaluative devices become the objectives of the students. The teacher wants the students' objectives to be similar to his own. The evaluative devices should be easily administered and should not consume more than 10 percent of the total class time. They should lend themselves to as much objectivity as possible, although subjectivity in evaluating should not be completely condemned.

BIBLIOGRAPHY

Baley, James A., and Field, David A. *Physical Education and the Physical Educator*. Boston: Allyn and Bacon, Inc., 1970.

Bowen, Wilbur Pardon. *Applied Anatomy and Kinesiology*. Philadelphia: Lea and Febiger, 1934.

Broer, Marion R. *Efficiency of Human Movement*. Philadelphia: W. B. Saunders Company, 1960.

Campbell, Oscar J., Van Gundy, Justine, and Shrodes, Caroline. *Patterns for Living*. New York: The Macmillan Company, 1940.

Cooper, John M., and Glassow, Ruth B. *Kinesiology*. 3rd ed. St. Louis: C. V. Mosby Co., 1972.

Davis, Elwood C. *Philosophies Fashion Physical Education*. Dubuque, Iowa: William C. Brown Company, 1963.

Duvall, Ellen N. *Kinesiology: The Anatomy of Motion*. Englewood Cliffs, N.J.: Prentice-Hall, Inc., 1959.

Finch, Stuart M. *Fundamentals of Child Psychiatry*. New York: W. W. Norton and Co., 1960.

Frohse, Franz, Brodel, Max, and Schlossberg, Leon. *Atlas of Human Anatomy*. New York: Barnes & Noble, Inc., 1959.

General Education in a Free Society. Harvard Report. Cambridge: Harvard University Press, 1945.

Gray, Henry. *Anatomy of the Human Body*. Philadelphia: Lea and Febiger, 1948.

Griffith, Coleman R. *Psychology Applied to Teaching and Learning*. New York: Farrar and Rinehart, Inc., 1939.

Hart, M. Marie, ed. *Sport in the Socio-Cultural Process*. Dubuque, Ia.: William C. Brown Co., 1972.

Henry, Nelson B. *The Forty-First Yearbook of the National Society for the Study of Education*. Washington, D.C.: The National Society for the Study of Education, 1942.

Johnson, Warren R. *Science and Medicine of Exercise and Sports*. New York: Harper & Row, 1960.

Karpovich, Peter V., and Sinning, Wayne E. *Physiology of Muscular Activity*. 7th ed. Philadelphia: W. B. Saunders Co., 1971.

Kluckhohn, Clyde, and Murray, Henry A. *Personality in Nature, Society, and Culture*. New York: Alfred A. Knopf, 1949.

Mathews, Donald K., and Fox, Edward L. *The Physiological Basis of Physical Education and Athletics*. Philadelphia: W. B. Saunders Co., 1971.

Metzger, Paul A., Jr. *Elementary School Physical Education Readings*. Dubuque, Ia.: William C. Brown Co., 1972.

Morehouse, Laurence E., and Miller, Augustus T. *Physiology of Exercise*. 3rd ed. St. Louis: The C. V. Mosby Co., 1959.

Nash, Jay B. *Philosophy of Recreation and Leisure*. Dubuque, Ia.: William C. Brown Co., 1953.

Rasch, Philip J., and Burke, Roger K. *Kinesiology and Applied Anatomy*. 2nd ed. Philadelphia: Lea and Febiger, 1963.

Ricci, Benjamin. *Physiological Basis of Human Performance*. Philadelphia: Lea and Febiger, 1967.

————. *Physical and Physiological Conditioning for Men*. Dubuque, Ia.: William C. Brown Co., 1966.

Schur, Evelyn. *Movement Experiences for Children*. New York: Appleton-Century-Crofts, 1967.

Seidentop, Daryl. *Physical Education—Introductory Analysis*. Dubuque, Ia.: William C. Brown Co., 1972.

Sweeney, Robert T. *Selected Readings in Movement Education*. Reading, Mass.: Addison-Wesley Publishing Co., 1970.

Wells, Katherine F. *Kinesiology*. 5th ed. Philadelphia: W. B. Saunders Co., 1971.

4

COACHING GYMNASTICS

A coach of gymnastics has a difficult and unique role because of the diverse responsibilities which he must assume. He must be guide, counselor, and sometimes a surrogate parent to the young people on his team. He must be a worthy representative of the school and the community, whose integrity, social conscience, and morality cannot be questioned. He must be skilled in public relations. He must be an effective organizer and administrator. And he must be an effective teacher of gymnastics who can make practical application of the theories of educational psychology, teaching methods, kinesiology, and physiology of exercise; who possesses skill adequate to demonstrate, at the minimum, beginning and intermediate level skills; and who has a personality attractive enough that people will enjoy his company. All of these qualities, knowledge, and skills combine into one package that is seen by members of the gymnastic team, colleagues, administrators, and townspeople as an effective coach of gymnastics. Weakness in one area may be overcome by strength in another area. It is extremely difficult to make great improvements in some areas, such as personality, but in most areas (those requiring knowledge and skill), the coach can make great improvements if he is sufficiently motivated to devote the necessary time and energy to advancement.

THE ROLE OF THE COACH

If the coach has inspired the confidence of his team members through his knowledge and through manifestations of concern for them as individuals rather than members of a team, the team will come to him for counseling in all areas. Members will ask him not only how to do a certain routine or how to increase strength but also to seek his counsel on academic, financial, and psychological problems. They will ask such questions as "How can I become better liked by the other members of the team?" or "Should I marry now or wait?"

A few coaches during their individual counseling are guided by only one criterion: "What will be the influence of this course of action upon my reputation as a winning coach?" But most see the varsity team experience as a modality for helping students to become better people and will be guided in their counseling by another question: "What is best for the student?" Some coaches have even advised outstanding performers to enroll in other schools that could better meet their professional goals or better match their native abilities. These coaches are much more than outstanding coaches—they are outstanding individuals! Their personalities are so secure that they will not be crushed by a losing season. Observation indicates that such coaches actually have few losing seasons because students with the qualities necessary to become champions are attracted to them. The word gets around surprisingly fast that one coach uses the competitors to enhance his own self-esteem while another coach is truly interested in the welfare of the competitors as individuals and not only as members of a team.

The coach of any sport must know the personality of each of his team members. In the individual sports, such as gymnastics, it is essential that the coach know and understand the psychologic make-up of each team member. Some need more ego bolstering than others. Some need to be driven and want to be "scolded." Others are psychologically more fragile and need to be treated with tact and diplomacy. They all respond to criticism, frustration, and failure in different ways. Some will sulk, others will become depressed, and some will lose their temper. The good coach knows that he cannot give a stock answer to various questions and problems but must approach each one on an individual basis after considering the personality structure of each of his charges.

Some gymnasts work best under a highly structured and rigid schedule. Others require a greater degree of self-direction. It will be advisable for the coach to set up a day-by-day practice schedule for some members, to do this *with* the team members for others, and to allow still others to work according to the dictates of their mood and feelings. Some gymnasts experience a fear of new skills which is detrimental to coordination and judgment. A coach can help these students by moving them up slowly through the progressions, spotting them effectively, and instilling them with self-confidence. Other gymnasts have little or no fear. These students may have to be restrained.

Some gymnasts want a thorough explanation of the procedures for doing a skill or combination of skills and listen attentively while these explanations are made. Others become bored with lengthy explanations and prefer to see the skill done. The coach needs to understand and be guided by these individual preferences.

The coach cannot and should not be a "buddy" to his team members. His relationship to the gymnasts should be that of the understanding and helpful father—but a father to whom one can talk frankly, openly, and without fear of reprimand. If the coach is to be maximally effective, he must command the respect of his team members. He must maintain a measure of dignity. He cannot do this if he "horses around" with team members. Age has less to do with this than does the position of coach.

THE APPEARANCE, BEHAVIOR, AND DRESS OF GYMNASTS

The coach and team members are representatives of the school and community wherever they perform or compete. Since, in most cases, their expenses are paid for by the community or the state, team members must behave and dress within the bounds of propriety. It needs to be pointed out that behavior and attire which is acceptable on today's liberal and unrestricted college or university campus is not acceptable in some communities. A major educational outcome of membership on an interscholastic or intercollegiate team is a heightened regard for discipline, teamwork, and individual sacrifice. These objectives are undermined if there are no regulations regarding attire, length of hair, or facial hair. Outlandish costumes and hair styles not commonly accepted will undermine team discipline and *esprit de corps*.

Coaches can establish the necessary philosophical evidence for the necessity of these regulations by posting the regulations with a preamble which might read: "In order to inculcate good sportsmanship, respect for rules and authority; to establish leadership, team pride, teamwork, and team discipline, as well as to eliminate disruptive influences, disturbances in the locker room, gymnasium, on trips, and off school grounds, the following rules are established: ... Then the regulations concerning length of hair, beards, and clothing styles, as well as other regulations, should be stated. Where this has been done, when suits were pressed by the Civil Liberties Union and similar groups, the courts have usually ruled in favor of the coach and school.[1]

PERSONAL QUALITIES DESIRED IN COACHES

The coach must be a person of great integrity. He should make no promises he is not reasonably certain he can fulfill. Lest his actions belie his claim that participation in sports builds character, he must follow the spirit as well as the letter of the rules. He can not bend the rules for his own advantage. If he calls on the judges to correct an error in interpretation of the rules which is advantageous to his team, he must likewise point out errors which are disadvantageous to his team. If all coaches behaved in this manner, gymnastics would become a most beautiful sport—one that would attract many of today's highly idealistic youth.

The coach must have a social conscience. Since his salary is paid by society, he is obligated to give society a good return. Society's "money's worth" is not quality entertainment. Entertainment is the job of Warner Brothers, Walt Disney, and Joe Namath. The job of the coach in an educational institution is to shape an educational tool from the varsity experience. The coach should be guided in his decision making by a desire to improve society. He uses gymnastics to accomplish this goal by encouraging the boys' and girls' great desire to excel. In addition, there are many occasions when he can influence large groups of spectators or readers of the sports pages. He can also progress toward this goal via comments on sportsmanship or physical fitness on radio and television programs, in news releases, and while narrating gymnastic demon-

strations. Other manifestations of a social conscience include encouraging minority groups to come out for the team and lending time and energy to worthwhile social causes.

HOW TO BECOME A MORE EFFECTIVE COACH

Preparation for becoming an effective coach of gymnastics should begin during high school years or earlier by joining a competitive team. However, many coaches of gymnastics with national and international reputations, who have never competed in gymnastics, have achieved their preeminence through study and hard work. They have read articles, textbooks, and research reports. They have attended clinics and workshops. They have learned from others through discussions and questions.

There are currently a number of textbooks on gymnastics. The *Gymnast* is one magazine published in the United States devoted exclusively to gymnastics. Articles on gymnastics appear in the *Physical Educator*, the *Journal of Health, Physical Education, and Recreation*, the *Research Quarterly*, the *Scholastic Coach*, and the *Athletic Journal*. Dates and locations of clinics are announced in the *Journal of Health, Physical Education, and Recreation* and the *Gymnast*. The Eastern Gymnastic Clinic is held in Sarasota, Florida, and the Western Gymnastic Clinic is held in Tucson, Arizona. The coach who wishes to excel will continue to study kinesiology, physiology of exercise, psychology, and group dynamics and to draw from these disciplines ideas which he can use. He will observe the coaching techniques used in other sports and will adapt ideas and procedures for use in coaching gymnastics. He will constantly study, evaluate, modify, and revise his own teaching and coaching methods. He will eliminate unsuccessful techniques and retain those which are effective. He will observe and study his team members: he will identify their strengths and weaknesses; study their personality structure to determine the most effective ways to influence them; and evaluate their potential based on body type, motivation, coordination, strength, power, balance, agility, and flexibility. He will maintain his own fitness level at as high a level as possible in order to continue demonstrating skills as long as possible.

[1] "Coaches and the Courts," *Journal of Health, Physical Education, and Recreation*, June, 1970, p. 10; *Richards v. Thurston*, 304 F. Supp., 449, 454; *Akin v. Board of Education of Riverside, ... District*, 262 C.A., 2nd 161, 167; *Farrell v. Dallas Independent School District*, 392 F. 2nd 697, 702; *Ferrell* V. *Des Moines School District*, 393 U.S. 503, 507, 508.

DUTIES OF THE COACH

The coach has numerous responsibilities. He must promote gymnastics in his area; select candidates for the competitive team; plan practice sessions by day, week, and season; plan, organize, and administer gymnastic meets; select and purchase equipment and supervise its proper maintenance; arrange competitive schedules; and arrange for travel, meals, and housing for team members while traveling

There is no sharp line of demarcation between promotion and the other responsibilities of the coach. Effective work in all areas will help the coach in popularizing gymnastics. The more effectively he promotes gymnastics, the greater the number who will try out for the team, and the more selective he can become in choosing members.

UNIQUE QUALITIES NECESSARY FOR SUCCESS IN DIFFERENT EVENTS

For all gymnastic events, strength relative to body weight, power, flexibility, agility, coordination, perseverance, determination, and physical courage are needed. Yet, certain gymnastic events require a greater measure of certain qualities.

Long Horse and Side Horse Vaulting These two events require a good measure of power (the explosive force of muscles), particularly of the hip, knee, and ankle extensors, and the shoulder girdle. Achievement of excellence in these events does not require as much practice or gymnastic ability as do the other events if the performer possesses power. Boys and girls with power and little time to practice should be encouraged to specialize in these events.

Balance Beam A good sense of static and dynamic balance will be extremely helpful to the female gymnast in this event. Graceful movements and a sense of rhythm will also be helpful. Girls possessing these qualities should be encouraged to specialize on the balance beam.

Uneven Bars and Horizontal Bar Physical courage and long levers with strength adequate to cast out fully are the prime requisites for maximal learning in the shortest possible time for these two events. Great physical courage and self-confidence are required to "throw" for a giant swing or flyaway the first time. A tall gymnast can develop greater rotary momentum during the downward swing than can the short gymnast. Also, the same move looks more impressive when done by a tall gymnast. The taller gymnasts with physical courage should be encouraged to specialize in this event.

Parallel Bars and Still Rings These two events place a premium upon arm and shoulder girdle strength. Boys with a relatively wide shoulder girdle who enjoy stressing their muscles should be encouraged to specialize in these two events.

Side Horse Tall, slender individuals with relatively small hips and light legs, who possess great perseverance and determination, usually excel on the sidehorse. The long, slender types can generate the momentum necessary for execution of most moves and look more impressive when doing a move. Small hips and light legs require a smaller compensatory lean in the direction opposite the one toward which the legs are moving. Improvement in form and acquisition of new skills come slowly. For this reason, a gymnast who hopes to become an outstanding performer on the side horse must possess perseverance and determination.

Tumbling The shorter mesomorphic-endomorphs very often become outstanding tumblers. (However, individuals of other builds have also excelled.) Agility, power, kinesthetic sense (especially ability to orient oneself in space while revolving and spinning), and physical courage are the qualities essential for success in tumbling. Rather than counseling boys into tumbling on the basis of their physical characteristics (since tumbling is usually the first gymnastic event taught), the coach is advised to see first which boys or girls progress most rapidly and direct these to specialize in tumbling. These boys and girls will often become the better all-around performers.

Trampoline Outstanding kinesthetic sense, self-confidence, and physical courage are required to become an outstanding performer in rebound tumbling. Boys and girls with these qualities should be encouraged to work on the trampoline. But, because of the high risk factor, reckless students and those with poor judgment should be discouraged from concentrating on this event.

Floor Exercise This event permits the boy or girl to capitalize on his or her own strengths and to minimize weaknesses. The best performers in floor exercise are equally strong in all the physical and psychological qualities required for success in gymnastics—agility, strength, power, endurance, kinesthetic sense, determination, and perseverance. Probably the most important prerequisite for success in this event is the ability to appraise accurately one's strengths and weaknesses and to be creative enough to design an attractive routine with the materials at hand.

LONG-TERM PLANNING

In any undertaking, realistic goals must be established. In gymnastics, the coach must make a realistic appraisal of the potential of his team members and then select a long-term goal (winning the city, state, or national championships). Having done this, he should establish intermediate goals, each of which bring him closer to his ultimate goal. It would be well for the coach to write these down for periodic reference, with the realization that the time table may be too optimistic. He should not be too disappointed if the goal is more elusive than he had hoped.

Long-term planning should include all aspects of the program—equipment and facilities, public relations, selection of gymnasts, development of skills, and recruitment and development of skilled performers at lower grade levels who might later become team members.

Since there are great variations among different schools in all areas, no specific procedures can be presented for purchase of equipment. In some situations the coach may be able to purchase all the necessary equipment during the first year. In others, he may be able to purchase only one or two pieces of equipment each year, beginning with mats. Sometimes he may find it necessary to prove the worth of the activity before receiving an adequate budget.

In some situations, surrounding institutions may have on-going competitive programs in gymnastics. In others, the coach may have the problem of encouraging nearby schools to initiate

a competitive gymnastics program, and he may have to initiate a gymnastic league or association, hold clinics, establish rules, and generate interest and enthusiasm. In some institutions, the team may be made up of boys or girls with no previous gymnastics training. In others, the coach may be able to recruit gymnasts of international caliber. Whatever the total situation, the coach must start from where he is. If he is satisfied to stay at that point, life will be comfortable but dull, lusterless, and uninteresting. If he wishes to make improvements, to accept challenge, to lead a stressful but interesting and joyful life of competition, he should establish a master plan which is at once realistic and challenging.

A "dream" routine to be accomplished on each piece of equipment by each team member by the senior year should be written out. While such a routine represents an ideal, it should be within each student's reach. This routine will undoubtedly be modified and changed during the team member's school years. The coach should plan with each boy or girl the progressive steps (skills) which lead toward accomplishment of each move in this "dream" routine. Steps toward development of the endurance, strength, power, flexibility, and agility necessary to accomplish this "dream" routine should be thoroughly discussed with each team member.

After the "blueprint" has been drawn up, the beginning gymnast can start to lay the foundation for his "dream" routine. Each day he *should* strive to make a little progress toward that goal. Today he might learn a cast, next month a peach basket, the following month a peach basket into a glide kip, then a peach basket with a half twist, a peach basket to a support, the next year, or two years later, a peach basket into a handstand. Continuously, he should be improving his form, height, and elegance. He should also be mastering related skills on other equipment, such as the reverse kip on the rings and high bar, and the free hip circle and cast into a giant swing.

PLANNING FOR THE SCHOOL YEAR

Gymnastic team practice should begin at the start of the school year. Lack of adequate strength, power, agility, and flexibility are major deterrents to the acquisition of gymnastic skills, particularly among beginners. Gymnastics contributes to the improvement of these qualities of physical fitness perhaps more than does any other sport. However, there is a method even more effective than gymnastics for developing these qualities. We could call this the "direct" method. This consists of a number of exercises designed to develop flexibility in specific joints or strength and power in specific muscle groups. For example, flexibility of the hip joints can be worked on to facilitate accomplishment of the split. Flexibility of the shoulder joints can be developed to facilitate accomplishment of eagle giants. Strength of the deltoids and hip extensors can be increased to further learning of the straight arm, straight leg press into the handstand.

Strength, flexibility, and endurance are specific qualities. Different kinds of exercises are necessary to develop each quality. To increase strength, one must stress muscle fibers by endeavoring to overcome as great a resistance as possible. To increase flexibility, one must stress tendons and ligaments by stretching them to the point of some discomfort. To increase endurance one must stress the cardiovascular-respiratory system until the heart rate is over twice the normal rate, or about 150 beats per minute, and the amount of air breathed in and out per minute (minute volume of ventilation) is increased eight to ten times above the resting level.

Development of a high level of gymnastic skill requires expenditure of considerable time. The exertion necessary to improve strength and endurance through gymnastics could so fatigue the gymnast as to dangerously *increase* the chance of injury. For this reason, gymnasts should concentrate on physical fitness during the early months of the school year and, as the competitive season approaches, work less on fitness and more on moves, combinations, and finally routines.

The following schedule is based on the experience of the author. Study is needed of the most effective training methods. It is hoped that our gymnastic associations will soon undertake such experimental studies.

> September to November
> Strength work—30 to 40 minutes
> Stretching exercises—5 to 10 minutes
> Endurance work—15 to 40 minutes

> Work on individual skills—30 to 60 minutes
> November and December
> Strength work—30 to 40 minutes
> Stretching exercises—5 to 10 minutes
> Endurance work—15 to 30 minutes
> Work on skills and Combinations—40 to 70 minutes
> January and February
> Strength work—15 minutes
> Stretching exercises—5 minutes
> Work on combinations and routines—60 to 120 minutes
> March and April
> Work on combinations and routines—90 to 100 minutes
> May and June
> Taper off—fun and games ("add on," "follow the leader," exhibitions)

Note: The fitness work should be done after the gymnastics work.

IMPROVING STRENGTH

Of all the components of motor fitness—strength, power, flexibility, agility, endurance, and balance—the most important single component is strength. Moreover, it is most easily improved. Research has shown that an increase in strength does not cause a decrease in flexibility, endurance, or balance. Increases in muscular endurance, speed, agility, and power do result when strength is increased.

One of the most effective means for improving strength is exercise with barbells, sometimes called *progressive resistance exercises*. The gain in strength made possible through progressive resistance exercises is another manifestation of the marvelous adaptive powers of the human organism. The muscles are challenged to overcome a resistance which, with great effort, they just barely overcome. The muscles adapt by becoming stronger. Next time they can lift the same weight more easily.

In all the exercises described, a weight should be used with which the student can barely eke out six repetitions. When the gymnast's strength has increased to the point where he can do ten repetitions with this weight, he should increase the weight by 5 or 10 pounds. All exercises should be done slowly and in good form to ensure that the proper muscles are doing the major share of the work.

The Pull Over Lying supine with arms extended over the head and gripping the bar, the student pulls the barbell over his head, keeping arms extended throughout the pull. He then returns to the starting position.

The Supine Press The student lies supine, gripping the bar with the bar across the chest, elbows on the floor, and forearms perpendicular. He then presses the bar upward to arm's length and lowers the bar to the starting position.

The Dead Lift The student stoops over to grip the bar. Then, with legs and arms extended, he holds the bar while he comes to the erect position. He then lowers the bar to the floor in the same manner.

The Half Knee Bend A towel is placed around the knurled center of the bar or across the back of the shoulders. Two partners lift the barbell to the student's shoulders. The student, while supporting the barbell on his shoulders, flexes his knees to a 135° angle and then returns to the erect position.

   In executing the half knee bend, the gymnast places his feet shoulder width apart. The bar should be gripped near the plates. The back is held as nearly vertical as possible and the heels keep contact with the floor during the squat and during the return to the erect position.

Rise on Toes The bar should be held in front of the body, with the arms extended and hanging straight down. The student rises on his toes with the weight on the inside of his feet, and lowers his heels to the floor with the weight on the outside of his feet. He should keep his arms fully extended during the exercise.

Straddle Lift The student starts by straddling the bar. He bends his knees and grasps the bar with one hand in front of his body and the other behind it. The palms of both hands should face inward. He extends his legs and rises on his toes,

and then returns to the starting position. His back should be kept as nearly vertical as possible.

Straddle Hop The student holds the bar with a mixed grip in front of his body, with his arms extended, and springs up and down forcefully enough to leave the ground and to straddle his legs. On the next jump he brings his feet together again.

Front Curl The student stands in an erect position with the barbell held at arm's length, arms hanging downward. He grips the bar with palms facing to the front. Without hunching the shoulders or leaning backward, and with his elbows at his sides, he slowly flexes his arms to bring the bar to his shoulders. He then lowers the bar to the fully extended position of the arms.

Reverse Curl This exercise is executed in the same manner as the front curl, except that the knuckles rather than the palms face the front during the exercise.

Press Behind Neck With the bar across the shoulders, resting behind the neck, and being held with a wide grip with the palms facing forward, the student extends his arms to press the bar overhead. He then lowers the bar to the starting position.

Rowing Exercise The student starts in a stooped position, with his legs straight and with his trunk parallel to the floor. The bar is held at arm's length, arms hanging down. He pulls the bar toward the abdomen, along the chest, and pushes it forward away from the shoulders in as nearly a circular motion as possible.

Alternate Press: The student holds a dumbbell overhead in each hand, with one arm extended and the other flexed. His palms face inward. He alternately flexes the extended arm, while at the same time he extends the bent arm to press one dumbbell overhead as he lowers the other.

Abdominal Rise The student starts in a supine position. He holds a dumbbell, plate, or light barbell behind the neck; someone holds his feet or he hooks them under an object such as a couch. He sits up and then returns to the starting position.

Pull over

Supine press

Dead lift

Half knee bend

Rise on toes

Straddle lift

Straddle hop

Front curl

Reverse curl

 **Press behind neck**

 **Rowing exercise**

Alternate press

 **Lateral rise**

Press on Box The student begins by lying supine on a box or a bench narrow enough to enable him to lower both elbows to the side. With the bar across his chest and his elbows as low as possible, he presses the barbell to arm's length and then returns to the starting position.

Lateral Rise From a standing position with the arms at the sides, a dumbbell held in each hand, and palms facing inward, the student elevates the dumbbells directly sideward to shoulder height, keeping his arms fully extended, and then returns to the starting position.

ISOMETRIC EXERCISES

A simple, inexpensive, efficient, and time-saving procedure for doing isometric exercises has been developed by the author[2] which is especially appropriate for use by gymnastic teams. The method utilizes a canvas web belt 16 feet long and 3 inches wide, with two steel rings with a circumference of 4 inches on one end to facilitate quick adjustments in the length of the loop formed by the belt. The belt is stabilized against body parts or objects to make possible a large number of exercises. Over a 14-week test period, this method brought about an improvement in power, agility, speed, and muscular endurance three times as great as that effected through a sports program consisting of swimming, soccer, handball, and touch football. Another study showed, over an 8-week period, an average gain from 904.6 pounds to 1066.5 pounds in the leg lift; from 339.9 pounds to 396.9 pounds in the back lift; from 20.6 inches to 21.7 inches in the vertical jump; and from 19.17 seconds to 18.43 seconds in the agility run. All of these gains were statistically significant.[3]

Equal gains in improvement of measures of physical fitness are produced through isometric and progressive resistance exercises. However,

[2] James A. Baley, "A Comparison of the Effects Upon Selected Measures of Physical Fitness of Participation in Sports and in a Program of Mass Isometric Exercises Done with a Belt," *The Journal of Sports Medicine and Physical Fitness,* December, 1967.

[3] James A. Baley, "Effects of Isometric Exercises Done with a Belt Upon the Physical Fitness Status of College Students," *Research Quarterly,* October, 1966.

isometric exercises require considerably less expenditure of time. When using the barbells, after every exercise, the collar must be loosened and then removed, plates must be added or subtracted, and, finally, the collar must be replaced and tightened. More time is required to do six to ten repetitions of an exercise than is required to do a maximal contraction for six seconds. For these reasons, a half-hour workout with the Baley isometric belt will produce the same improvements in strength and power as will a two-hour workout with barbells.

A group of any number up to 100 or more students can do the exercises simultaneously at a cost of about $3 per belt compared to a cost of about $75 to $200 per barbell. Further, there is no danger of damaging the floor or toes by dropping barbells or plates. Storage is simply a matter of hanging the belts on a peg, and preparation time is minimal.

How Strength Is Developed

Muscle Physiology The exact nature of the physiological process accompanying an increase in strength is not, at this time, fully understood. Our understanding of the process is being continually enhanced as a result of research. It was suspected, when research on isometric exercises was first begun, that while isometric exercises increased strength, there was not a proportional increase in muscle size. This belief has since been proven false. Those body builders who exercise with barbells to improve their physical appearance can accomplish the objective of increasing muscle girth by doing isometric exercises. Morehouse and Miller[4] point out that when all factors are equal, the strength of a muscle is roughly proportionate to its circumference. Research also shows that increase in the size and strength of muscle is a result of the intensity of the work done by the muscle rather than the amount of foot-pounds of work done by it. Muscle strength and size are little affected when the muscle does a large number of repetitions of a movement against little resistance. Strength and size of a

[4] Laurence E. Morehouse and Augustus T. Miller, Jr., *Physiology of Exercise,* 6th ed. (St. Louis: The C. V. Mosby Co., 1971), p. 193.

muscle *are* affected when the muscle is overloaded by being required to overcome a substantial resistance or when the muscle attempts to overcome a resistance which it cannot overcome. Every muscle group is made up of many motor units, each of which is made up of a number of muscle fibers. Each motor unit has its own minimal nervous threshold stimulus which will cause all the muscle fibers in that motor unit to contract. Only the muscle fibers of motor units with low minimal threshold stimuli will contract when lifting light objects. The heavier the weight being lifted the greater the number of motor units called into play. Consequently, only during maximal contractions will all motor units be brought into play and developed. This is why, to develop strength, one must make maximal contractions as when doing isometric exercises.

Several changes have been noted to occur in a muscle when it increases in size. There is a great increase in the number of capillaries (45 percent in guinea pigs), an increase in the connective tissue, a small increase in the water content, a thickening of the sarcolema (covering of the muscle fibers), and increased phosphocreatine, glycogen, and non-nitrogenous substances. Regular exercise greatly increases the amount of buffers in the blood whose job it is to neutralize lactic acid, which is a fatigue product. This is one reason why training delays the onset of fatigue and increases muscular endurance. Still another result of training is that the electrical activity required for a muscle to produce a given degree of tension is reduced, indicating that the process of muscle stimulation by the central nervous system has become more economical.

From the standpoint of size and numbers, the voluntary muscular system is the most important system in the body. There are 434 voluntary muscles in the body. They account for 40 to 45 percent of the total body weight. Furthermore, when the muscles are used and developed, all the systems of the body improve in their functions. Alternately contracting and relaxing muscles aid in the venous return of blood to the heart as a result of their "milking" action upon the veins. Because activity creates a greater demand for oxygen and nutrients to be carried to the muscles and lactic acid and carbon dioxide to be carried away from them, stress is placed upon the heart muscle, and it adapts by becoming stronger so that with each beat it sends out a greater volume of blood. The result of regular physical activity is that the resting pulse rate becomes considerably slower, enabling the heart to rest for a greater proportion of time. The normal heart rate is 72 beats per minute. Well-conditioned athletes have resting pulse rates as low as 40 beats per minute. The muscular walls of athletes' hearts have become thicker, making possible a more complete contraction and therefore more complete emptying. This enables the heart to send out a greater volume of blood with each beat. From the standpoint of long-term health, a strong, muscular heart is even more to be desired than are well-muscled arms or legs.

The Valsalva Effect During a hard muscular contraction with the glottis closed, intrathoracic pressure is increased due to the contraction of the muscles of the abdomen and the thorax. The consequent pressure on the venae cavae slows down the return flow of blood to the heart with a resulting decrease in blood pressure. Then when the contraction has been completed and the pressure on the venae cavae is decreased, the dammed-up blood rushes into the heart and the blood pressure is increased. This phenomenon is known as the "valsalva effect." Senile and hospitalized people with weak vascular walls have been known to suffer ruptured blood vessels as a result of straining on the stool. However, no person in normal health has ruptured arterial walls while undergoing an isometric contraction of even maximal force. However, as insurance and for maximal safety, a simple procedure which easily circumvents this problem is recommended. This is exhaling in a controlled manner by making an s-s-s-s-s or f-f-f-f-f sound during the contraction. This procedure enables maintenance of nearly uniform intrathoracic pressure.

Human Levers Almost all levers in the human body are third-class levers with very short work or force arms and very long resistance arms. These kinds of levers favor speed at the cost of force. Because of the arrangements of these levers and because the muscle tendon usually inserts on the bone, which it is moving at a very small angle, great force must be generated to move the body. For example, 300 pounds of force must be developed by the deltoid muscle to enable it to raise the arm and hand holding a 10 pound weight to an elevation of 80°.[5] Tremendous force must be generated in doing a kip, uprise, or any gymnastic move. This points up why great strength is important for success. An athlete cannot increase the length of his anatomic levers to increase the speed of his hand during the act of throwing a ball or javelin, putting a shot, serving a tennis ball, or any other act. He cannot change the length of the work arm of his body levers. He cannot change the angle of insertion of the muscle tendon. He *can* increase the force generated by increasing his strength, with the result that he will be able to throw or hit the ball faster and farther.

Types of Muscular Contraction

Muscular contraction may be classified into three principal types: isometric or static; concentric, phasic, or isotonic; and eccentric. In an isometric contraction, the force of the muscle and the resistance applied to it are exactly equal and, consequently, there is neither shortening or lengthening of the muscle fibers. In a concentric (*con*—with; *centric*—center) contraction, the angle at the joint being moved becomes smaller, and the limb being moved approaches the one on which it is moving. In an eccentric (away from center) contraction, the resistance is greater than the force being generated by the muscle, and the muscle "gives" to the resistance. These three types of contraction could be illustrated in a wrist wrestling match. If A and B are equally matched and neither gives, they will both be undergoing an isometric contraction. If A wins the match, he will have undergone a concentric contraction while B will have undergone an eccentric contraction.

Following are general instructions and suggestions for use of the isometric belt:

1. It is of utmost importance that the person push or pull against the belt with maximum force. This maximal contraction is held for 6 seconds. Many people have never experienced a maximal contraction and consequently may believe they are contracting maximally when in actuality they are not. They must learn to make a maximal contraction. Some may be lazy. These the coach or physical educator must motivate with enthusiasm, and repeatedly. He must utilize every motivational device he can. This can include playing recorded march music, setting a good example, verbal urging, and rewards for improvement.

2. For maximal results, as many exercises as possible should be performed two or three times—each time at a different degree of flexion of the involved joint—in order to involve *all* the muscle fibers maximally. For example, the military press should be done with the forearms at a 45° angle to the upper arms, then at a 90° angle, and finally with the forearms at a 130° angle to the upper arms.

3. During the contraction, the person should maintain uniform intrathoracic pressure by means of a controlled exhalation making an f-f-f-f-f or s-s-s-s-s sound as he exhales air through closed teeth or lips. This procedure will prevent fluctuations in blood pressure.

4. Accurate adjustments in the length of the belt must be made before beginning each exercise in order to position the body segments properly. This will ensure that only those muscles which the particular exercise is intended to utilize will be involved in the exercise. For example, in the "shoulder shrug," the belt must be taut while standing on the lower loop with the upper held in the hands while the arms, hips, and knees are fully extended. (See pp. 55–56.) If the loop is too long, it will become necessary to bend the arms, which will cause the arm flexors as well as the trapezius and other shoulder elevators to become involved. If the loop is too short, it will become necessary to flex the hips, which will cause the back and hip extensors to become involved. As in body building with weights, each exercise is designed to develop specific muscle groups.

5. When time is limited (as it is in most situations), exercises should be carefully selected in order to accomplish the desired objectives. The typical physical education class is 30 minutes in length. Two to five minutes are required for roll call and other administrative procedures. In physical fitness classes, the instructor may wish to spend five minutes on stretching exercises to develop flexibility and ten minutes on running,

[5] Philip J. Rasch and Roger K. Burke, *Kinesiology and Applied Anatomy*, 2nd ed. (Philadephia: Lea and Febiger, 1963), p. 156.

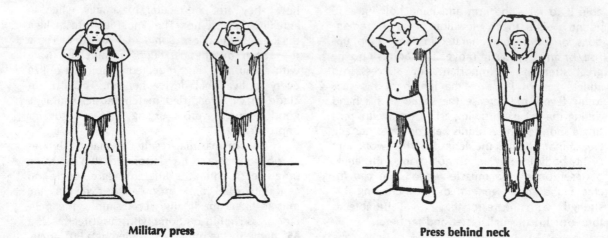

Military press   Press behind neck

wind sprints, or rope skipping to improve endurance. This leaves 10 to 13 minutes. All of the isometric exercises described in this book cannot be completed in that amount of time. For this reason, the instructor will find it necessary to select those isometric exercises which involve the largest muscle groups, such as the squat, bent-over rowing exercise, dead lift, suitcase lift, and rower's exercise. In other situations, the coach or physical educator might wish to develop the specific muscle groups which are principally involved in the activity being taught. Exercises should then be selected to accomplish the specific objectives.

6. Isometric exercises may be introduced to children when they are in the fifth or sixth grade. Children in the first grade have done them successfully; however, considerable class time is lost when working with primary school children because of the necessity of frequently adjusting the belt for individual children.

7. To expedite the exercise session it would be well to present the exercises in such an order that those exercises which require a long loop be presented first, and then exercises be presented which require progressively smaller loops. Further, all exercises done standing should be done first, then the sitting exercises, then those done in a lying position and finally those done with a partner or a group. However, exercises involving the same muscle group should not succeed one another.

Exercises for the Arm Extensors

Military Press The student stands on the lower loop of the belt. The straps should run up along the sides of his body and outside his arms. He grasps the upper loop above his head with his palms forward. His elbows should be flexed. He endeavors to extend his arms directly upward with a maximum force for 6 seconds at each of three different degrees of arm flexion. The first contraction should be done with the elbows flexed to a 45° angle, the second with them flexed to a 90° angle, and the third with the elbows flexed to a 135° angle. Adjustments of the belt are made unnecessary by moving the feet closer together or farther apart.

Press Behind Neck The student stands on the lower loop of belt. The straps should run up along the side of his body and behind his arms. He grasps the belt with his palms forward and pushes directly upward behind his head. His head should be forward. His elbows should be pointing sideward. His upper arms should be at an angle to his trunk. His forearms should be at an angle to the upper arms. He should do one maximal contraction for 6 seconds at each of three different degrees of flexion of the elbow joint as for the military press. To, in effect, shorten the belt, the feet are moved further apart.

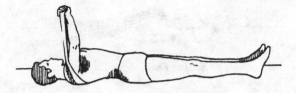

Supine press

Supine Press The student begins by lying on the floor in a supine position with the belt around the upper chest and shoulders. He grasps the belt at such a point that his forearms are perpendicular to the floor and at right angles to his upper arms. The belt will be outside the arms. He endeavors to extend the arms directly upward for a maximal contraction of 6 seconds at each of two different degrees of arm extension. The first contraction should be done with the elbows flexed to a 90° angle and the second contraction with the elbows almost fully extended.

Arm Depressor The student passes the belt behind his neck and over the front of his shoulders. He reaches between the belt and his body at waist height to grasp the belt at such a position that his elbows will be flexed. He pushes directly downward for a maximal contraction for 6 seconds at each of three different degrees of arm flexion. He should make one contraction with his elbows flexed to a 135° angle, another at a 90° angle, and a third at a 45° angle.

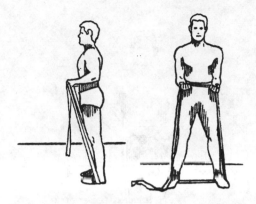

Front curl

Exercises for the Arm Flexors

Front Curl The student stands on the belt and grasps the belt with the palms up at such a position that his elbows are at the hips and his forearms are at an angle to his upper arms. He endeavors to flex his arms for a maximal contraction for 6 seconds at each of three different degrees of elbow flexion. The first contraction should be done with the elbows flexed to a 130° angle; the second with them flexed to a 90° angle; and the third with them flexed to a 45° angle. The feet are moved closer together to lengthen the belt for each succeeding contraction.

Reverse Curl The student stands with his heels on the belt. He reaches around the front of the upper loop of the belt, inserts his hands

Arm depressor

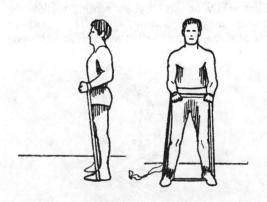

Reverse curl

53

Standing pull up

Supine finger flexor

Exercises for the Forearms and Wrists

Wrist and Forearm Exercise   The student starts in a squatting position with the belt under his feet. He grasps the belt with palms up and with his forearms resting along his thighs. He endeavors to flex his wrists for one maximal contraction of 6 seconds. He should avoid attempting to flex his elbows. He should do one contraction with the palms turned downward and one with the palms turned upward.

Supine Finger Flexor   The student begins in a supine position. He places his feet inside the lower loop and grasps the upper loop with both hands in such a manner that the fingertips are along the lower edge of the belt. His legs, body, and arms should be fully extended. He endeavors to flex his fingers for one maximal contraction for 6 seconds.

Sitting Finger Extensor   The student places the belt behind his neck in such a manner that two loops hang in front of the chest about chest height. He places the extended fingers of the right hand inside the loop on the right and those of the left hand inside the loop on the left with the palms up. The wrists should be slightly

between the straps and twists his hands counterclockwise to grasp the belt with the palms down. There will be a loop of belt over his hands and wrists. His elbows should be held alongside his hips throughout the exercise. He endeavors to flex his arms at each of three different degrees of elbow flexion. The first contraction should be done with the elbows flexed to a 130° angle, the second with them flexed to a 90° angle, and the third with them flexed to a 45° angle. The feet are moved closer together for each succeeding contraction.

Standing Pull Up   The student begins by standing on the belt with his knees and hips fully extended. He grasps the belt in front of his body with elbows flexed and pointed sideward. He pulls directly upward by attempting to flex the arms for maximal contractions of 6 seconds at each of three different degrees of elbow flexion; i.e., at 130°, 90°, and 45° of elbow flexion.

Wrist and forearm exercise

Sitting finger extensor

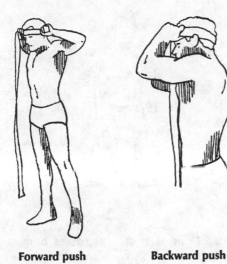

Head turn

Forward push   **Backward push**

flexed. He endeavors to hyperextend the fingers for a maximal contraction for 6 seconds. This exercise could also be done in a supine or in a standing position.

Exercises for the Neck

Forward Push The student places the belt against his forehead and endeavors to push his head forward against the resistance offered by the arms through the belt for a maximal contraction for 6 seconds.

Backward Push The student places the belt against the back of his head and endeavors to push his head backward against the resistance offered by the arms through the belt for a maximal contraction for 6 seconds.

Sideward Push The student places the belt against the side of his head and endeavors to tilt his head sideward against the resistance offered by the arms through the belt for a maximal contraction for 6 seconds. He should do one contraction to each side.

Head Turn The student places the belt almost completely around his head and across his forehead. He endeavors to turn his head as though trying to look sideward over the shoulder against the resistance offered by the arms through the belt. He should do one contraction for 6 seconds to each side.

Front Shoulder Shrug The student stands with his heels on the belt and with his hips, knees, and arms fully extended. He grasps the belt with his palms toward the body and pulls upward by elevating the shoulders. The arms should remain extended throughout the exercise. This exercise will develop principally the trapezius muscles which will give the neck the sloop that distin-

Sideward push

Front shoulder shrug

Back shoulder shrug

Sideward push

guishes the strong man from the weakling with padded shoulders. He should do one maximal contraction for 6 seconds.

Back Shoulder Shrug The student stands with his heels on the belt and the belt behind his body. His body is erect and his arms, hips, and knees are fully extended. He grasps the belt behind his hips with the palms facing rearward. He pulls upward by endeavoring to elevate his shoulders for one maximal contraction of 6 seconds. There should be no bending of the arms during the exercise. Only the shoulders should be elevated.

Exercises for the Chest

Chest Pull The student grasps the belt with both hands in front of his chin. His elbows are elevated. His hands should be about 6 inches apart. It will be helpful if he wraps the belt around his hands. He tries to pull outward for one maximal contraction of 6 seconds.

Sideward Push The student passes both straps of the belt behind his back and around the outside of his shoulders. He reaches under the two loops of the belt to grasp them with the palms turned downward and with the hands 2 to 6 inches apart. He endeavors to push his hands toward each other for one maximal contraction of 6 seconds.

Supine Extended Arm Elevator The student begins by lying on the floor in a supine position with the belt around his hips. He grasps the belt with his hands at shoulder width and with his arms at an angle to the floor. He endeavors to pull the extended arms upward for a maximal contraction for 6 seconds at each of two different degrees of shoulder elevation. The first contraction should be done with the extended arms at a 30° angle to the floor, the second with the arms at a 60° angle to the floor.

Bent Over Rowing Exercise The student stands with his heels on the lower loop of the belt. He keeps his legs fully extended and bends forward at the hips until his trunk is almost parallel to the floor. He places his hands inside the loop and then twists them around to loop the belt around his wrists. He pulls upward by trying to flex his

Chest pull

Supine extended arm elevator

Bent over rowing exercise

Suitcase lift

arms for three maximal contractions of 6 seconds each at three different degrees of elbow flexion. In each contraction the back should be parallel to the floor, but the elbows should be flexed to 130°, 90°, and 45° angles in the three contractions.

Exercises for the Back and Trunk

Dead Lift The student stands with his heels on the lower loop of the belt. He bends forward until his hips are flexed between a 170° and a 135° angle. His arms and legs should be held fully extended throughout the exercise. Because of the great amount of force generated, the belt should be wrapped around the wrists. The student endeavors to come to the erect position by pulling with the muscles of the back. He should do maximal contractions of 6 seconds duration at each of two different degrees of hip flexion. The

first contraction should be done with the trunk forming a 135° angle with the legs and the second with the trunk forming about a 170° angle with the legs.

Suitcase Lift The student stands on the lower loop of the belt with his right foot. He places his right hand into the upper loop and twists his hand halfway around to grasp both sides of the belt. His arm should be fully extended. He endeavors to pull directly sideward as though lifting a very heavy suitcase. He should do the exercise to each side for a maximal contraction of 6 seconds duration.

Exercises for the Thighs

Half Squat The student stands with his heels on the belt. He bends both knees to approximately a

Dead lift

Half squat

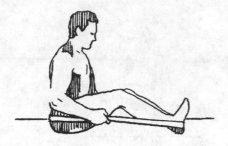

Sitting leg extensor

Supine hip flexor

130° angle. He passes the belt along the outside of his legs and up over the bony portion of his hips. He should keep his trunk as nearly vertical as possible. He endeavors to extend his legs for two maximal contractions of 6 seconds. The first contraction should be done with the knee joints at approximately a 130° angle and the second with the knees at approximately a 155° angle. The knees should not be flexed to less than a 120° angle.

Sitting Leg Extensor The student sits on the floor with the knees flexed so that the thighs are at a 135° angle to the lower legs. He passes the belt behind his hips and over the bony part, along the side of his legs and in front of his heels. He endeavors to extend his knees for one maximal contraction of 6 seconds.

Prone Leg Extensor The student lies on his abdomen with his knees bent. The belt should pass over his insteps along his back, over his shoulders, and be held in his hands in front of his neck. He should endeavor to extend his legs for one maximal contraction of 6 seconds.

Supine Hip Flexor The student assumes a supine position. He places his left foot in the lower loop with the belt against the bottom of the foot. He next places the right foot inside the upper loop with the belt against the instep. He maintains the left leg in a fully extended position as he endeavors to more fully flex the right hip. He reverses the positions of the legs to exercise the hip flexors of the left hip. He should do one maximal contraction of 6 seconds duration for each leg.

Sitting Leg Abductor The student assumes a sitting position. He places both feet inside the belt so that the belt runs outside his ankles. He endeavors to abduct (pull apart) the extended legs for one maximal contraction of 6 seconds duration.

Sitting Leg Adductor The student passes one loop of the belt around the inside of the right ankle. Someone may hold the other loop of the belt; it may be hooked around a stable object, or it may be held with the right hand against the floor to the right side of the body. The student

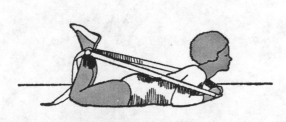

Prone leg extensor

Sitting leg abductor

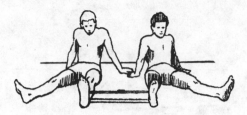

Sitting leg adductor

should endeavor to adduct (pull toward the midline of the body) the extended leg. The same exercise should be done for the left leg. One maximal contraction of 6 seconds duration for the adductor muscles of each leg should be done.

Side Leg Flevor   The student lies on his left side with his left leg extended forward and the right leg hyperextended backward with the right knee slightly bent. The belt should pass over the ankle of the left foot and over the heel of the right foot. He endeavors to flex the right knee for one maximal contraction of 6 seconds. Having done this, he reverses the procedure by turning onto his right side to do the exercise for the "hamstrings" (knee flexors) of the left leg.

Side Leg Extensor   The student begins by lying on his left side with his left leg forward and slightly flexed, his right leg backward and extended, his left arm along the floor overhead, and his right hand on the floor. The belt should

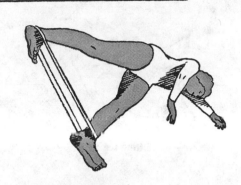

Side leg extensor

be passed around his left ankle and halfway over his right heel. He should endeavor to pull his extended right leg backward against the resistance of the belt for one maximal contraction for 6 seconds duration. One contraction should also be done while lying on the right side for the left leg.

Balance Kick   The student places the left leg into one loop of the belt and inserts his right foot into the other loop while in a standing position. He endeavors to kick the right leg as though kicking a ball, while maintaining balance standing on one foot. He does the same exercise for the left leg.

Side leg flexor

Balance kick

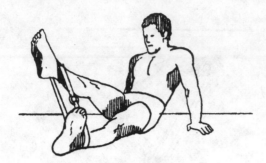

Sitting leg raiser

Sitting plantar flexor

Sitting Leg Raiser Starting in a sitting position on the floor, the student inserts both legs into the loop of the belt so that the belt is at ankle level of both legs. He endeavors to lift the extended right leg for one maximal contraction of 6 seconds as illustrated. He then does the same exercise for the hip flexors of the left leg.

Exercises for the Lower Legs

Rise on Toe The student stands on the lower loop with the balls of both feet. He brings the two straps up in front of his chest and places the upper loop behind the lower part of his neck. It is important that the belt be adjusted so that it will be taut and yet permit the student to stand erect and in good posture with the hips and knees fully extended, heels down. The student attempts to rise up on his toes against the resistance offered by the belt for one maximal contraction of 6 seconds duration. He should avoid hunching the shoulders.

Sitting Plantar Flexor The student starts in a sitting position with both legs extended. The belt should pass behind his hips alongside his legs and over the balls of the feet. The feet should be dorsi-flexed. The student attempts to plantar flex (point the toes) the feet against the resistance of the belt for one maximal contraction of 6 seconds.

Sitting Dorsal Flexor The student starts in a sitting position with his legs extended. He places both feet inside the upper loop. Another student may hold the lower loop, or it may be hooked over a stable object. He endeavors to dorsal flex the feet (pull the feet toward his face). If no partner or stable object is available, the student can achieve the same result by placing the left foot in the lower loop so that the belt passes across the bottom of the foot and the right foot in the upper loop so that the belt passes across his instep. With the right leg bent and the left extended, he then endeavors to dorsal flex the right foot. He should do one maximal contraction for 6 seconds for each foot.

Rise on toes

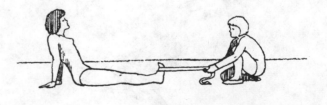

Sitting dorsal flexor

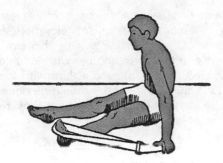

Sitting foot adductor

Sitting Foot Adductor The student starts in a sitting position on the floor with his legs straddled. He inserts the right foot into the lower loop so that the belt passes over the inside of the big toe. He holds the upper loop in his right hand with the right arm extended and at a 45° angle to the body. The belt may also be held by a partner or hooked to a stable object. He endeavors to bend the foot directly inward (adduction) using the heel as a fulcrum. He should do the same exercise for the left foot One maximal contraction for each foot, of 6 seconds duration, should be done.

Sitting Foot Abductor The student starts in a sitting position on the floor with his legs straddled. He inserts both feet into the loop so that

the belt passes over the outside of the little toes. He endeavors to bend the feet outward, using the heels as fulcrae. One maximal contraction of 6 seconds duration should be done.

Exercises for the Shoulders

Forward Extended Arm Depressor The upper loop of the belt is placed over a door or similar stable object. The student grasps the lower loop with both hands. He pushes downward with both hands while holding the arms in an extended position. He should do three maximal contractions of 6 seconds duration at each of three different levels of arm elevation. The first contraction should be done with the extended arms forming a 135° angle with the trunk; the second with arms forming a right angle with the trunk; and the third with them forming a 45° angle with the trunk.

Forward Extended Arm Elevator The student begins by standing on the loop of the belt. He grasps the upper loop with both hands and pulls upward with the arms in an extended position and elevated in front of the body. He does three maximal contractions for 6 seconds each at three different degrees of arm elevation. The first contraction should be done with the arms 45° from the vertical, the second 90° from the vertical, and the third with them 135° from the vertical.

Forward extended arm depressor

Forward extended arm elevator

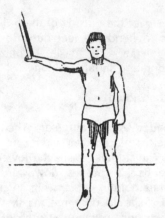

Sideward extended arm depressor

Sideward Extended Arm Depressor The upper loop of the belt is placed over a door or similar stable object at a similar height. The student grasps the lower loop with his right hand with his right arm extended sideward. He endeavors to push the extended arm downward. The same exercise should be done for the muscles of the left shoulder. Three maximal contractions for each arm at each of three different degrees (45°, 90°, and 130° from the vertical) of arm elevation should be done.

Sideward Extended Arm Elevator: The student stands on the lower loop of the belt with the heel of the right foot. He grasps the upper loop with the right hand with the right arm extended sideward. With the right arm extended, he endeavors to pull upward as hard as he is able. The same exercise for the muscles of the left shoulder should be done. Three maximal con-

tractions of 6 seconds for each arm at each of three different degrees of arm elevation should be done. One contraction with the arm at a 45° angle to the trunk, another with the arm at a 90° angle to the trunk, and a third with the arm at a 135° angle to the trunk should be done. The exercise may be done with the palms turned upward or downward.

INSTRUCTIONS FOR USE OF ISOMETRIC BELTS BY CLASSES OR TEAMS

It is as simple to lead a group of 10 to 100 students in doing isometric exercises with the isometric belt as it is for each person to do the exercise individually. The most effective class formation is with students in a circle or in two or more concentric circles. The students should face the center of the circle where the instructor will stand to explain and to demonstrate. In this formation, all students will be most easily able to see and to hear the instructor. By taking a few steps the instructor can reach any student to give manual and individual instruction and motivation. The interval between students should be approximately 5 feet. One or two of the students or team members can be assigned the task of distributing the belt to other students while the instructor or coach takes roll or makes necessary announcements.

For the initial demonstration, the instructor should demonstrate each exercise three times, facing a different direction each time to ensure that all students will see the procedures followed. The exercise should be named each time. At the second class meeting, one demonstration will very likely suffice. After a few meetings, it will become necessary that the instructor or coach merely name the exercise. During the initial demonstrations, hand, belt, and body positions should be described verbally as well as demonstrated. The degree of flexion should be indicated. In the military press, for example, the instructor could say: "Upper arms at a right angle to the trunk, forearms at a 45° angle to the upper arms, elbows pointed forward, palms forward, knees and hips fully extended."

To aid students in developing their sense of time, the instructor could count off the seconds during the contraction by counting:

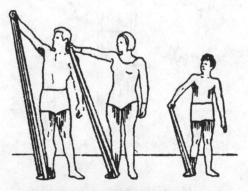

Sideward extended arm elevator

"One-two-three." This procedure makes it mandatory that students begin and end together. Since some students will require more time than others to adjust their belt, some time will be lost. After several class meetings, students will learn the sequence of the exercises (if the sequence followed is always the same). When this stage has been reached, each student can count for himself and proceed to the next exercise when he is ready. If each student begins the next exercise when he is ready, it will not be necessary for class members to wait for the slowest student, and time will be saved.

In most exercises, students will stabilize the belt against their own body segments. These exercises have been described. However, in a few exercises they should work in pairs or as a class. These exercises and class procedures follow.

Sitting Leg Adductor Students sit on the floor in the circle formation with their legs extended and apart. Each student loops one end of his belt around his own right ankle while he loops the other end around the left ankle of the neighbor to his right. Spacings can be adjusted so that all belts are taut by having students move forward or backward as necessary or by shortening or lengthening the belts. However, the necessary adjustments can be made more quickly if students slide themselves forward or backward as necessary. On a given signal, all students endeavor to adduct both legs while holding them extended with toes up. The instructor or coach should count off 6 seconds so that all students will stop together.

Feet Dorsal Flexor Students work in pairs sitting on the floor facing one another. One student holds one loop of the belt in his hands. The other loop is placed over the toes of both feet of his partner. The student who has the belt across his toes attempts to dorsi-flex his feet against the resistance of the belt for a maximal contraction of 6 seconds.

Pull-over The students are paired. One partner assumes a supine position with his arms on the floor extended over his head. He grasps the belt with his palms up. His partner stands on the end of the belt. The belt should be stretched out. The supine student endeavors to pull his exten-

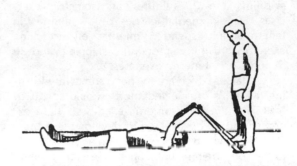

Pull-over

ded arms upward for three maximal contractions of 6 seconds each. The first contraction should be with the extended arms just above the floor, the second with the arms forming a 30° angle with the floor, and the third with the arms at a 50° angle to the floor.

Sit-up The students are paired. One partner assumes a supine position. His partner kneels to his side with one hand on his chest and the other on his thigh. The supine student endeavors to sit up against the resistance offered by his partner.

Students should be encouraged to do the isometric exercises in their rooms or elsewhere on those days that the class does not meet. Members of varsity teams could be required to do the exercises at home after being taught the correct procedures. This will save time at practice sessions, leaving more time to spend on teaching the individual skills of the game and for improving team play.

Low fitness or developmental classes of a half hour in length should spend 5 minutes on stretching exercises, 5 minutes on rope

Sit-up

skipping and 20 minutes on isometric exercises. Developmental classes of 45 minutes in length should spend 5 minutes on stretching exercises, 10 minutes on rope skipping, and 30 minutes on isometric exercises.

Classes which are to spend some time learning the skills of selected sports should spend 10 to 15 minutes on isometric exericses. These exercises should be selected to develop those muscles upon which the greatest demands are made in the sport being taught. Specific exercises which develop those muscles which contribute most to skilled performance in specific sports are listed in Chapter 3.

Procedure for Construction of the Isometric Belt

The isometric belt can be made quite easily if the necessary materials and equipment can be secured: a strong and heavy but soft and flexible web or cable belt 1¾ inches in width, 16 feet long, and strong enough to withstand a strain of 2,500 pounds, two steel rings 3½ inches in diameter, and heavy thread are needed for each belt. A shoemaker's sewing machine or one of the type used to repair athletic equipment is needed to sew the rings to the belt. The belting must be soft enough or flexible enough that it may be wrapped around the hands or wrists and not cut into the skin while pulling on the belt with several hundred pounds of force as will be done in the "dead lift."

The webbing is most difficult to locate. It may be found at local harness shops or surplus centers. The rings can be found in some hardware stores. A shoemaker or athletic equipment repair ship can sew the rings to the belt.

One end of the belt is passed through the center of the two rings, folded back about 4 inches of its length and sewn with heavy thread as illustrated below, left.

IMPROVING FLEXIBILITY

Anyone can improve his flexibility if he is willing to work at it. The rewards for these efforts will be improved mechanical efficiency in movement, increased gracefulness in movement, and a decreased likelihood of muscular, tendenous, or ligamentous strain or sprain.

Muscles work in antagonistic pairs. They can perform their functions with greater efficiency if they do not have to overcome the resistance of tight antagonists or of joint ligaments. If the muscles, tendons, and ligaments of a joint are elastic, that joint can be bent further before tissues are torn. Good flexibility is essential to development of skill in gymnastics since resistance from muscles, tendons, and ligaments will be minimal. Scales, handsprings, eagle giants,

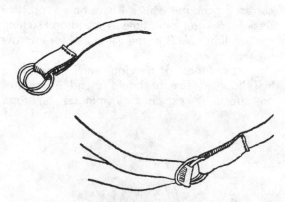

The belt is adjusted for length by passing the free end through the center of the two rings, doubling it back over the top of the uppermost ring, and passing it between the two rings.

The belt may be shortened by pulling on the outside strap. It may be lengthened by pulling on the inside strap while holding the rings apart with the fingers and thumb of one hand.

Hamstring stretcher

Side split

stoop vaults, splits, and many other moves require considerable flexibility. Every gymnast *needs* to spend some time each day throughout the year in improving and sustaining his flexibility. All of the exercises which are presented here should be done to the point of discomfort. However, determined people should not stretch so far that they injure themselves. All the exercises should be done with a strong, steady, slow pull, never in a jerky manner.

Hamstring Stretcher Sit on the floor with legs extended and straddled. Grasp the inner side of each foot with the hand on the same side of the body and pull the head as close to the floor as possible. Do 10 to 15 repetitions.

Fore and Aft Split Start from a standing position and slide one foot forward and the other backward to approach the split position until some pain is felt. Do only once.

Side Split Start from a standing position with the trunk parallel to the floor. Slide the extended legs sideward until some pain is felt. The body may be supported with the hands on the floor. Do only once.

Back Breaker Start from a sitting position with one leg extended forward and the other bent at the knee and turned sideward, as illustrated. With both hands, grasp the ankle of the forward leg and pull the head toward the knee. Endeavor to keep this leg fully extended. Then return to the starting position. Do 10 to 15 repetitions with the right leg extended forward, and then do the same number with the left leg extended forward.

Back breaker

Quadriceps Stretcher Start from a kneeling position with the toes pointed, the upper side of both feet and the shin bones along the floor, the trunk vertical, and sitting on the heels. Slowly bend backward until the head touches the floor or comes as close as possible. The hands may be placed on the floor to either side of the body during the lowering of the trunk. Return to the starting position. Repeat five or six times.

Fore and aft split

Quadriceps stretcher

Upper back stretcher

Bouncer

Upper Back Stretcher Sit on the floor with the legs extended and the hands clasped behind the neck. A partner stands behind with one knee placed between the shoulder blades. He will then grasp the elbows and rotate them forward, upward, backward, and downward as he presses forward with his knee between the shoulder blades with the assistance of the exerciser. Do not offer any resistance. Do 10 to 15 repetitions.

Trunk Twister Start from a standing position with the feet apart and the arms extended sideward at shoulder height. Swing the trunk downward with a twist to touch the right toe with the left hand, and return to the starting position. Repeat the exercise by touching the left toe with the right hand. Swing the top arm backward hard while touching the toe to stretch the muscles of the chest. Do 15 to 20 repetitions to each side.

Bouncer Start from a standing position with the feet apart and the arms extended above the head. Swing the arms downward between the legs as the hips are flexed and the knees bent, and return to the starting position. Do 20 repetitions.

Rotor Start from a standing position with the feet apart and the arms extended sideward at shoulder height. Swing the left arm backward and the right arm forward as the trunk rotates to the left. Repeat the exercise to the right side. Do 15 to 20 repetitions.

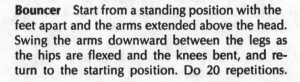

Trunk twister

Rotor

Back bend

Back Bend Begin in a supine position with the feet flat on the floor as near the buttocks as possible. Place the hands, palms down on the floor under the shoulders with the fingers pointing toward the feet. Extend the arms and legs to push up into the back bend position. Do only once.

Inch Worm Start in a front leaning rest position (push-up position), supported on the hands and feet with the front down. While keeping the legs extended, "walk" the feet up between your hands. Then "walk" the hands forward to return to the starting position. Do 5 to 10 repetitions across the room.

Inch worm

The preceding 11 stretching exercises will increase the range of motion in all the major joints of the body—ankles, knees, hips, spine, shoulders, and neck—in all directions of movement.

IMPROVING ENDURANCE

If a gymnast performed exercises and routines to the point of fatigue necessary to substantially improve cardiovascular-respiratory endurance, he would risk serious injury. The fine coordinations, delicate balances, and agile movements required in gymnastics are not possible when a performer is fatigued. Consequently, it is necessary for the gymnast to improve this quality by other means.

At basal or resting condition, the body uses between 200 and 250 milliliters of oxygen per minute. Under maximal physical exertion, oxygen consumption may rise to 4,000 milliliters per minute. This is 15 to 20 times the basal rate. This explains why athletes who participate in vigorous sports and people who do hard physical work are seldom fat.

The circulatory and respiratory adjustments which make possible a greater oxygen intake are made gradually; several minutes of heavy work may be necessary before the rate of oxygen intake balances the rate of oxygen consumption. For this reason, it is recommended that people begin their endurance work at a relatively slow pace and gradually increase the pace as circulatory and respiratory adjustments are made.

Endurance-type activities will benefit not only the heart and circulatory system, but other systems and organs as well. The respiratory system will be positively affected in several manners. The walls of the air sacs, the alveolar septa of the lungs, will become thicker, permitting a more effective exchange of oxygen and carbon dioxide. New alveoli will be produced. There will be an increase in the elastic fibers. The diaphragm, the broad, sheath-like muscle which lies at the base of the rib cage and which aids in breathing, will become stronger. These changes are adaptations made by the body to the stress placed upon it and permit the inhalation of a greater volume of air.

Physical activity may also affect the glandular system and increase tolerance for emotional as well as physical stress. Morehouse and Miller write: "Since exposure of the body to a given stress may result in the development of an adaptation that enables it to withstand that stress, it has been suggested that exercise may act to stabilize the homeostatic balance by providing a means of offsetting the physiological consequences of emotional stress. A possible mechanism for this is that exercise may increase the size and lower the threshold of stimulation of the adrenal glands, thereby resulting in a greater reserve of antistress steroids and a shorter time of response to stress."[6] Many coaches develop ulcers and die of heart attacks. Almost no players do—even though the game is, for them, equally stressful and exciting. A possible reason for this is not only that the coaches are older but also because they are less active physically.

Regular participation in vigorous physical activity increases the number of red blood cells, or erythrocytes, in the blood stream. The hemoglobin of the red blood cells carries oxygen from the lungs to the cells. The increase in red blood cells helps to delay the onset of fatigue in well-conditioned athletes. Another factor in this delayed onset of fatigue in well-conditioned athletes is the increase in the capillary bed of the exercised area, so that a greater volume of blood per minute can pass through the area. This makes possible more rapid removal of fatigue products and carbon dioxide from the muscle cells and more rapid transportation of oxygen and nutrients to the muscle cells.

Exercise not only results in the development of the muscular walls of the heart but also increases the vascular supply to the heart. In the event of a coronary occlusion, blood can be supplied to the heart muscle via the auxiliary blood vessels.

The average heart beats 70 times per minute; 4,200 times per hour; 100,800 times per day; 36,792,000 times in a year; and 2,575,440,000 times during the average life span of 70 years, without stopping. It deserves excellent care,

which involves stressing it regularly and progressively so that it can adapt to any unusual forthcoming stresses and so that it will beat fewer times per minute while at rest.

Distance runs of one to five miles, wind sprints, grass drills, or rope skipping can all serve to improve endurance with a small expenditure of time. In wind sprints, the students line up across the width of the gymnasium or playing field. They begin in a sprinter's crouch (starting position). On the first whistle, they take off and sprint as fast as they can. On the succeeding whistle, they stop quickly and drop into the crouch again. The length of the sprints can be varied from five to fifty yards. These are repeated until one or more lengths of the gymnasium or field have been traversed.

In grass drills, the students form a circle (or two or more concentric circles) and run in place, lifting their knees high. When the instructor calls "Front," they quickly drop to the prone position. When he calls "Back," they quickly move into the supine position. When he calls "Right," or "Left," they quickly move into the prone position, with their legs thrown either to their right or left side. On the signal "Up," they stand quickly and again run in place, lifting their knees high. *Commands should not be given in any definite pattern.*

Rope Skipping

Rope skipping is among the best activities for improving cardiovascular respiratory condition. Rope skipping will improve agility and sense of rhythm. It is an activity in which a person can participate throughout his lifetime. A minimum of space and equipment is required. People can skip rope in their bedroom, basement, garage, or most anywhere. Rope skipping can be made very interesting and challenging by attempting to skip in a variety of manners, by seeing how many skips can be done in a specified unit of time, and by seeing how many times the rope can be turned in one jump. It can be simple enough for a six-year-old child or difficult enough to challenge a professional athlete. It lends itself well to individual work when space and equipment are limited and can also be done by classes or teams with a hundred students skipping rope simultaneously.

[6] Laurence F. Morehouse and Augustus T. Miller, Jr., *Physiology of Exercise,* 6th ed. (St. Louis: The C. V. Mosby Co., 1971), p. 296.

Groups should form a circle around the instructor or coach with individuals spaced at approximately a single-arm interval. Large groups should form two or more concentric circles around the instructor. This formation facilitates individual instruction better than does the usual line or rectangular formation.

Ordinary sash cord 8 or 9 feet in length with a knot tied in each end or taped to prevent unraveling will serve well enough. However, heavier cord serves better and will last longer.

While hopping, the student should take his little jumps on the balls of feet just high enough to clear the rope. Beginners err in attempting to jump higher than is necessary and in bending the knees. The body should be kept erect and in good posture at all times. The hips should not be flexed, the head should be erect, and the back should not be rounded. The spring should come from the feet and ankles. The rope should be turned by rotating the wrists rather than by flexing the elbows. The hands should be held about 8 inches from the hips while turning the rope. Following are a number of rope skipping exercises that will add variety and interest to the conditioning work being done by a class, varsity team, individual, or family group. They may also be presented as an exhibition number by a group of several or a hundred people.

Hopping on two feet while turning the rope forward. (Rope moving upward behind the body and downward when it is in front of the body.)

Hopping on the right foot only or on the left foot only.

Hopping alternately on the left and then the right foot.

Hopping on two feet, on one foot, or alternately on one foot and then the other with the rope crossed. As the rope is moving forward above the head, bring the hands toward one another so that the wrists are crossed at waist height. Be certain to keep momentum on the end of the rope during crossing and while turning the rope in the crossed position by "flipping" the wrists.

Hopping and alternately crossing and uncrossing the rope. This may be done while hopping on two feet, on one foot, or alternately on one foot and then the other.

Skipping in place while turning the rope forward.

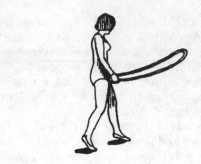

Skipping and traveling while turning the rope forward.

Running while turning the rope.

Skipping with the rope crossed.

Skipping and alternately crossing and uncrossing the rope.

Turning the rope backward and hopping on two feet. When turning the rope backward, the skipper should hold his hands slightly further forward of the hips than when turning forward.

Turning the rope backward and hopping on the right foot only or on the left foot only.

Turning the rope backward and hopping alternately on the right and the left foot.

Turning the rope backward while skipping and traveling.

Turning the rope backward while running backward.

Turning the rope forward and hopping on one foot while holding the other leg extended forward parallel to the ground. The rope must describe a flattened circle. This requires lifting the arms as the rope passes over the head in order that it will clear the extended and lifted leg.

Turning the rope forward and hopping on one foot while swinging the other leg forward on one hop and backward on the next.

Turning the rope forward and hopping with the feet spread sideward on one turn and brought together on the next turn.

Turning the rope forward and hopping with the feet spread forward and backward with the left foot forward on one turn and the right foot forward on the next turn. The body weight should be evenly distributed on both feet at all times.

Hopping while swinging the rope alternately forward and sideward so that it describes a figure 8.

Turning the rope forward and jumping and landing with the feet crossed on alternate jumps, placing first the right foot in front of the left foot, and then on the next jump, the left foot in front of the right.

Turning the rope forward and hopping and clicking the heels together on each hop.

Turning the rope forward twice on each jump. The hips and knees may be flexed (pulled upward) to give more time for the second turn of the rope.

Hopping twice for each forward turn of the rope.

Turning the rope forward and hopping while in a full squat position. The rope must be shortened while assuming the squatting position by moving both hands up the rope while turning it. The back should be vertical while hopping in the squat position.

PARTNER JUMPING
No. 1 turning the rope forward (rope moving downward when it is in front of the jumper and upward when it is behind the jumper) and No. 2 running in to face his partner and jumping with him.

Same as before but turning the rope backward.

No. 1 turning the rope forward; No. 2 running in and turning his back to No. 1.

No. 2 running behind his partner to jump with him.

Partners standing side by side holding hands while turning the rope forward or backward with their outside hands.

Partners clasping hands, facing opposite directions, and turning the rope in either direction with their outside hand.

Partners standing back to back and hopping while turning the rope in either direction with their outside hands.

As before, with partners holding one knee raised.

Three partners—one rope: No. 1 turning the rope. No. 2 running in front while No. 3 runs in behind and all three skip together.

Two partners, each turning a rope. No. 1 turning his rope forward while No. 2 is turning his rope backward. They may turn their ropes so that they jump both ropes simultaneously or so that they jump over one rope and then the other.

REVOLVING DOORS
(Long rope turned by two people)

Running in the front door (when the rope at the top of its arc is moving toward the jumper) and jumping while the partners turn the rope.

Running in the back door (when the rope at the top of its arc is moving away from the jumper), jump once and run out.

Touching the floor with the hands on every second jump.

Hopping while in a full squat position. (Keep the back vertical.)

On each jump lifting the legs forward (jackknifing) to touch the toes with the fingers.

"BUCKING BRONCO"

The hands clear the rope first and then the feet in "bucking bronco" style. The head stays low with the hips flexed, and the feet go above the head toward a headstand. Then the hips are flexed to bring the feet back to the floor. During the maneuver, as the hips move upward, the head and shoulders move downward to land on the hands over the moving rope. The feet then move upward to allow the rope to pass under them.

Partners facing one another with their hands on one another's shoulders and hopping while kicking one leg forward on one jump and the other forward on the succeeding jump.

Two jumpers facing each other, grasping one another's right ankle in their right hand and hopping on the left foot.

TRENDS IN GIRLS' AND WOMEN'S GYMNASTICS

The number of girl and women gymnasts in the United States is certain to continue to increase, which should result in improvement in the quality of women's gymnastics at the championship levels. The rise in popularity of women's gymnastics began when the rules were changed to adapt the activity to the unique physical and psychological characteristics of women. Because of their lower center of gravity and weaker muscular development, particularly of the shoulder girdle, girls cannot learn giant swings, the crucifix, planche, back somersault to a catch, and similar skills, with the same facility that boys can. However, they can present a routine on the balance beam, uneven parallel bars, or floor exercise which has considerably more aesthetic appeal than an exercise presented by a male. These rules changes, in addition to the televising of gymnastic meets and more vigorous promotional efforts by coaches of women's gymnastics teams, have contributed to the phenomenal growth of women's gymnastics.

Further growth will result from changing concepts regarding the nature and role of women. Today, few, if any, women believe that they become less feminine as a result of participation in sport. An increasing number of girls and women find in gymnastics a path to an interesting and challenging life.

Self-expression Girls and young women find in gymnastics an opportunity to use the body as a medium of expression, a means for communicating with others. The gymnast's vocabulary consists of the skills and body movements which she has mastered. The greater the range of skills, the more effectively she can communicate. The impressiveness, elegance, and effectiveness of the communication is enhanced by good form, kinesthetic sense, change in tempo, direction, movement and level, rhythm, balance, gestures, and sincerity. Sincerity means that movements, compositions, and expressions are in harmony with the gymnast's personality and physical appearance. The gymnast can become sensitive to this harmony by watching herself on video tape, performing before audiences, and listening to the comments of her coach and teammates.

Physical Fitness Like male gymnasts, female gymnasts can accelerate their learning rate, increase their endurance (necessary when doing routines and particularly when competing in the all-around event), and improve the quality and beauty of their performance by improving their physical fitness. Vannie Edwards, former U.S. women's Olympic coach, has pointed out that a prime reason for the improved performance of United States women gymnasts in the 1968 Olympic games was their improved physical fitness. They were stronger, more flexible, more enduring, and had greater agility. To improve their physical fitness women should follow the procedures that were presented earlier in this chapter.

Floor Exercise Optimum time for the floor exercise routine seems to be between 1:05 minutes to 1:15 minutes. The tumbling portion of the routine should include forward and backward tumbling with alternates and twists. Ballet, folk dance, jazz, and modern dance movements can be incorporated. Female gymnasts should receive dance instruction and become thoroughly grounded in several dance forms. Efforts should be made to maximize expression through gestures of the hands, arms, head, and shoulders. Principles of force, tempo, and rhythm, and utilization of space (direction, level, and design) need to be learned and applied in the design and presentation of the routine. Dance movements can be of tremendous value in the design of a floor pattern, moving the competitor over the entire floor exercise area while avoiding sudden, jerky changes in direction.

Balance Beam The gymnast should demonstrate complete control and assurance the moment she arrives on the beam. Five to ten passes should be made down the beam incorporating at least one strength move, two to five acrobatic moves, leaps and turns, dance movements, and a dramatic dismount such as a cartwheel, somersault, or vault from a handstand. Variation in tempo, high leaps, good form, and elegance will all contribute to a higher score.

Uneven Parallel Bars The trend is toward a greater number of release moves (seven or eight) and more twisting moves. Substantial strength and endurance is required. Originality and creativity is often rewarded by judges. Swinging movements should predominate.

Vaulting Girls are advised to strive for a high on-flight and off-flight by approaching the horse at a fast run and by utilizing a more direct take-off. The habit of running fast should be established early in the training program. Good spotting is essential to establish confidence and to minimize fear. To compete in the top echelons, girls will need to be able to do such moves as the full twisting cartwheel and handspring, the yamonshita, and the one and only quarter twisting cartwheel.

TRENDS IN BOYS' AND MEN'S GYMNASTICS

Just as football has evolved from the use of the flying wedge to its present form and continues to be modified, so changes are made in gymnastics. Spectators, participants, coaches, and officials have valued and regarded different qualities at different periods in the development of the sport. For instance, in the 1930s there were more holds and presses in Olympic parallel bar competition than there are today. Coaches and competitors must keep up with trends in moves combinations, and routines. The latest edition of the F.I.G. *Code of Points* should be studied thoroughly, analyzed, and accurately interpreted by every coach and gymnast. The *Code* provides a model for gymnasts at all levels, and can serve as a guide for routine building.

Parallel Bars When planning a routine on the parallel bars, the gymnast should include one C move, four B moves, and six A moves in order to satisfy the requirements for difficulty. The C part should be a swinging move. Classification of moves can be found in the F.I.G. *Code of Points*.

The routine should include moves of swing, flight, holding, and strength. It should contain one strength part, one B part above or below the bars with a simultaneous release of the hands, and no more than three held positions. Swinging movements should predominate. A straight arm bent body or straight body bent arm press into a handstand or a planche are examples of

strength moves. A gymnast should use whichever strength move he does best. The requirement calling for simultaneous release of the hands means just that—the hands must be released at the same moment. The stutzkehre will not satisfy this requirement, but the cast to a straight arm support, peach basket from above the bars or into a handstand, forward or backward salto to a regrasp, hop pirouette, rear uprise straddle cut and catch, or strueli will.

The limitation to three held positions mandates that the gymnast swing *through* a handstand by incorporating such moves as forward or backward swinging pirouettes or hop pirouettes, stutzkehre handstand, streuli handstand, and peach basket handstand (without holding the handstand) in order to continue moving and yet initiate moves from a handstand position. Holds should be for 2 seconds.

The gymnast should avoid excessive repetitions of the same move. The rules require a .1 to .2 deduction when a move is repeated more than once, even though the moves preceding and following are different. Gymnasts must strive for variety with moves above and below the bars and with alterations in pace and tempo.

Side Horse Work on the side horse should consist entirely of swinging movements with no stops or hesitations. Some moves must be done on each part of the horse—saddle, croup, and neck, both in a clockwise and in a counter-clockwise direction. It is not enough to merely pass over the part. Double leg circles should predominate; however, front and back scissors must be done, and either the front or back scissors must be done twice in sequence.

Horizontal Bar The exercise must consist exclusively of swinging without stops. The mount should be an explosive move at the B level of difficulty. Circles both backward and forward, with the back toward the bar, vaults (rear vault catch), moves in which there is simultaneous release and regrasp by both hands (back-uprise full pirouette and catch), full turns around the body's vertical axis (full twisting flyaway, full pirouette), and moves in which a dorsal or cubital grip is used (eagle giant) must all be included. Some moves satisfy more than one requirement. The dismount should be high and explosive. Multiple somersaults and twists and hechts are all desirable dismounts.

Floor Exercise   The floor exercise should consist of a harmonious, rhythmic pattern of movement alternating from movements of strength, balance, rhythm, and agility. The entire area (20 meters square) should be used. Somersaults (saltos) should be done at shoulder height. Handstands should be held for at least 2 seconds. A free support scale (planche) may be used instead of a press into a handstand.

Still Rings   Work on the still rings must contain movements alternating between swing, strength, and hold parts, without excessive swinging of the rings. The exercise must contain at least two handstands, one executed with strength and the other arrived at with a swing from a long hang, inverted hang, half-inverted hang or support. Holds must be for 3 seconds. The exercise should contain one strength move of at least B level of difficulty, such as a front lever or cross.

Movements of swing, strength, and holding must be presented in relatively equal proportions. The swinging movements should be done with dynamic rhythm or minimal use of strength. Strength moves must be executed slowly with no swing. It is advisable to do giant swings in both directions and with great speed, to strive for straight arm swing work, and to change pace (from hold to swing to sudden stop and hold). The gymnast should execute the routine with no obvious signs of strain or effort. He should present an impression of confidence, assurance, and ease. The exercise should be climaxed with an impressive dismount, such as a somersault with multiple rotations around the vertical or transverse horizontal axis of the body.

Long Horse   The competitor should demonstrate a forceful, accelerating run, high pre- and post-flight (feet above the head), and well-controlled landing with no steps or hops after initial contact with the mat.

Trampoline   The routine should begin with a move of superior difficulty. This can be followed with two moves of lesser difficulty. One or more moves of great difficulty should be presented in the middle of the routine followed by two or more moves of lesser difficulty. The routine should close with several moves of great difficulty. The routine consists of 10 to 12 contacts with the bed, beginning with the one preceding the first move. Skills should be executed in a mechanically sound manner, in complete control, and with good form.

MOTIVATION

Ego strength and level of motivation are as important in selecting students for the gymnastic team as are such physical considerations as body type, strength, balance, and neuro-muscular coordination. The coach cannot assume that his gymnasts will always be highly motivated. He must plan for and work toward maintaining a high level of motivation in his gym team members.

Gymnastics require a high level of personal motivation because the gymnast performs alone most of the time. It is easier to drive oneself when one belongs to a group which performs tasks together. This phenomenon explains the success of "Weight Watchers," "Alcoholics Anonymous" and similar groups. The gymnast is not subjected to as much group pressure as is the member of a football, basketball, or soccer team. The gymnast's drive must come almost entirely from within.

Gymnastics requires great amounts of self-discipline. The gymnast suffers torn hands, bumps, bruises, frustration, and humiliating falls. Only those who are highly motivated and can delay gratification will continue participation until they succeed. The greater the motivation toward the goal, the greater the willingness to accept the disciplines imposed by the sport. Consequently, the coach should select as team members boys and girls or young men and women who have a strong need to prove themselves and to meet and conquer challenges. This quality cannot be measured statistically. Some manifestations of a high level of motivation are: regular attendance, perseverance and persistence in pursuing achievement of a skill or combination, and determination in the execution of skills.

All people in our culture have certain common psychological needs. Some people have more intense needs than others. Such psychological requirements are ego satisfaction, self-acceptance, achievement and recognition, belonging, new experiences, and mastery. Membership on a gymnastic team can lead to satisfaction of all these needs. The coach who ensures satisfaction is likely to have a successful and happy team.

Self-acceptance, ego satisfaction, achievement, and recognition are similar though not identical needs. A person with a very low level of ego needs may accept himself even though his achievements are normal. Our society uses activities such as gymnastics to provide moments of euphoria through achievement, which some, unfortunately, seek through chemicals, at great expense to their health and well-being.

Undoubtedly, the greater the motivation, the greater the willingness to accept discipline of both the externally and internally imposed kinds. This is as true in gymnastics as it is in any other endeavor. Motivation will be increased if there is frequent evidence of self-improvement and success. Periodic evaluation is helpful. This can be accomplished through video tapes with instant playback, movies, critiques by the coach and teammates, and, of course, the more stressful gymnastic meet.

BIBLIOGRAPHY

Baley, James A. *An Illustrated Guide to the Development of Physical Fitness.* Danielson, Conn.: Racine Printing of Connecticut, 1968.

Beisser, Arnold R. *The Madness in Sports.* New York: Appleton-Century-Crofts, 1967.

Bund, John W. *Scientific Principles of Coaching.* Englewood Cliffs, N.J.: Prentice-Hall, Inc., 1955.

Cooper, Kenneth H. *Aerobics.* New York: Bantam Books, Inc., 1968.

Cureton, Thomas Kirk, Jr. *Physical Fitness Appraisal and Guidance.* St. Louis: The C. V. Mosby Co., 1947.

Davis, Elwood C. *Philosophies Fashion Physical Education.* Dubuque, Ia.: William C. Brown Co., 1963.

Editors of *Esquire* magazine. The Art of Keeping Fit. New York: Avon Book Division, 1940.

Exercise and Fitness. Papers presented at the Colloquium on Exercise and Fitness at The University of Illinois College of Physical Education and the Athletic Institute, 1959.

Fait, Hollis F. *Health and Fitness for Modern Living.* Boston: Allyn and Bacon, Inc., 1965.

Frohse, Franz, Borodel, Max, and Schlossberg, Leon. *Atlas of Human Anatomy.* 5th ed. New York: Barnes & Noble, Inc., 1959.

Grombach, John V. *The 1968 Olympic Guide.* New York: Pyramid Publishing, Inc., 1968.

Hein, Fred V., Farnsworth, Dana L., and Richardson, Charles E. *Perspectives on Living.* Glenview, Ill.: Scott, Foresman and Co., 1962.

Hoffman, Bob. *Weight Lifting.* York, Pa.: Strength and Health Publishing Co., 1939.

Johnson, Perry, and Stolberg, Donald. *Conditioning.* Englewood Cliffs, N.J.: Prentice-Hall, Inc., 1971.

Johnson, Warren R. *Science and Medicine of Exercise and Sports.* New York: Harper & Row, Publishers, 1960.

Morehouse, Laurence E., and Miller, Augustus T., Jr. *Physiology of Exercise.* 6th ed. St. Louis: The C. V. Mosby Co., 1971.

Murray, Jim, and Karpovich, Peter V. *Weight Training in Athletics.* Englewood Cliffs, N. J.: Prentice-Hall, Inc., 1956.

Nash, Jay B. *Physical Education: Interpretations and Objectives.* New York: A. S. Barnes & Co., 1948.

Olson, Edward C. *Conditioning Fundamentals.* Columbus, O.: Charles E. Merrill Publishing Co., 1968.

O'Shea, John Patrick. *Scientific Principles and Methods of Strength Fitness.* Reading, Mass.: Addison-Wesley Publishing Co., 1969.

Prentup, Frank B. *Skipping the Rope.* Boulder, Colo.: Pruett Press, Inc., 1963.

The President's Council on Youth Fitness and the President's Citizens Advisory Committee. *Fitness of American Youth.* Colorado Springs, Colo.: United States Air Force Academy, 1959.

Sanborn, Marion A., and Hartman, Betty G. *Issues in Physical Education.* Philadelphia: Lea and Febiger, 1964.

Steen, Edwin B., and Montagu, Ashley. *Anatomy and Physiology,* vol. 1. New York: Barnes & Noble, Inc., 1959.

————. *Anatomy and Physiology*, vol. 2. New York: Barnes & Noble, 1959.

Tutko, Thomas, and Richards, Jack. *Psychology of Coaching*. Boston: Allyn and Bacon, Inc., 1971.

Wallis, Earl L., and Logan, Gene A. *Figure Improvement and Body Conditioning Through Exercise*. Englewood Cliffs, N.J.: Prentice-Hall, Inc., 1964.

Webster, Randolph W. *Philosophy of Physical Education*. Dubuque, Ia.: William C. Brown Co., 1965.

Wessel, Janet A., and MacIntyre, Christine M. *Body Contouring and Conditioning Through Movement*. Boston: Allyn and Bacon, Inc., 1970.

Wittenberg, Henry. *Isometrics*. New York: Universal Publishing and Distributing Corp., 1964.

Zoethout, William D., and Tuttle, W. W. *Textbook of Physiology*. 10th ed. St. Louis: The C. V. Mosby Co., 1949.

5

LEAD-UP ACTIVITIES

Self-Testing Skills, Contests, and Relays

Relays and self-testing activities can serve as an extension of conditioning exercises while at the same time serving as an introduction to gymnastics and tumbling.

SELF-TESTING ACTIVITIES

A circle is the best formation for the conduct of self-testing activities for the following reasons:

1. All the students will have an unobstructed view of the instructor's demonstrations.

2. The instructor is near enough to every student in the class so that with only two or three steps he can give any student individualized spotting or coaching.

Following are a number of self-testing activities which will supplement the gymnastic program.

Foot and Toe Balance   The students lift one foot off the floor and maintain balance while standing on one foot. Arms may be extended forward-sideward. Variations: Balance on the ball of one foot, or balance with the bottom of one foot against the inside of the knee of the supporting leg. (Kindergarten–6th grade.)

Truck Extension Flexibility   The children begin in a prone position with their hands clasped behind their necks. A partner is needed to hold the one being tested. This partner should stand between the feet of the first child, kneel down with his knees outside those of his partner and place his hands on his partner's buttocks. The child being tested attempts to lift his head and chest as high off the floor as he is able. The vertical distance from his chin to the floor may be measured. (Kindergarten–9th grade.)

Extension Press-Up   The children lie prone with their arms extended above their heads and

Extension press-up

Trunk flexion flexibility

One-arm push-up

their elbows off the floor. Their toes should be curled under. They press down and forward with their hands to lift the entire body 3 to 5 inches off the floor. The shoulders must not be retracted, the head must not be lifted, and the back must not be arched. Variation: With both forearms along the floor. (3rd–12th grade.) (Boys only.)

Trunk Flexion Flexibility The children begin in a supine position with their feet 18 inches apart and with their hands clasped behind their neck. Their partners should kneel between their feet and hold their legs just above the knees. The backs of the knees can be held in contact with the floor more easily if the child being tested points his feet upward (dorsal flexed). The child being tested attempts to bring his head as close to his knees as possible. This distance can be measured. (Kindergarten–6th grade.)

Backward Leg Raise The children begin in a prone position with their hands clasped behind their necks. A second child places himself in a

kneeling position facing his partner's feet with one knee at each side of his head. His hands are placed on his partner's shoulder blades. While the second child helps him to hold his chest in contact with the floor, the child in the prone position lifts his extended legs as high as he is able. He should hold his feet together. The perpendicular distance from his ankle bone (external maleolus) to the floor can be measured with a yardstick. (Kindergarten–6th grade.)

One-Arm Push-Up The children support themselves on three points—one hand and the two feet. Their feet should be 3 to 6 inches apart. Their bodies should be turned sideward. If they will bend slightly at the hips as they lower themselves and will extend their hips again as they push up, the move will be made slightly easier. (Kindergarten–12th grade.) (Boys only.)

V-Sit The children assume a supine position with their arms extended beyond their heads. They simultaneously lift both legs and the trunk as they swing their arms upward-forward to while in the V-sit. (Kindergarten–9th grade.)

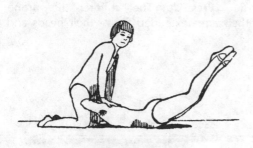

Backward leg raise

V-sit

Bridge

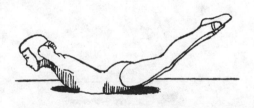

Jump and tuck

Push-Up and Chest Slap The children assume a front leaning rest position. They then do a push-up vigorously enough that they can slap their chest with both hands before catching themselves again in push-up position. (Kindergarten–12th grade.)

Bridge The children lie on their back with knees bent and both feet flat on the floor near their buttocks. Their hands are flat on the floor under their shoulders with their fingers pointing toward their feet. They then extend their knees, hips, and arms to finish in the arched position. (Kindergarten–12th grade.)

Arching The children are in a prone position with their hands clasped behind their neck. They pull their head, shoulders, chest, legs, and feet as high off the floor as they are able by contracting all the posterior muscles. Only their abdomens maintain contact with the floor. Variations: Elements of competition can be interjected by counting the length of time the position is held or by measuring the distance of the feet and the head from the floor. (Kindergarten–9th grade.)

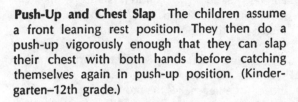

Arching

Jump and Tuck The children leap into the air drawing their knees to their chest with their legs bent and grasp their shins. They then release their grasp, extend their bodies, and land in a standing position. The back should remain vertical throughout the move, with head erect. A forward lean to bring the chest to the knees should be avoided; the knees are brought to the chest. The arms should be "driven" upward at the initiation of the jump. (Kindergarten–12th grade.)

Jump and Straddle Toe Touch The children leap into the air lifting their extended legs forward-upward with feet apart so that they can touch their toes. The legs should be fully extended when the toes are touched. The back should be vertical throughout the move with the head held erect. (Kindergarten 12th grade.)

Jump and Jackknife The children leap into the air lifting their extended legs forward-upward with feet together to touch their toes. The back should be vertical throughout the move and the head should be held erect. (Kindergarten–12th grade.)

Jump and Half Turn The children leap into the air throwing their left arm behind their hips and their right arm across the front of their hips as they look over the left shoulder to execute a half turn before landing on their feet. The body is held fully extended and the arms should be held close to the body in order to rotate around the vertical axis of the body. (Kindergarten–12th grade.)

Jump and half turn

Jump and Full Turn The children leap into the air and execute a full turn before landing on their feet. (Kindergarten–12th grade.)

Jump and Full and a Half Turn The movements are the same as those for the jump and full turn except that they must be executed with greater vigor. (Kindergarten–12th grade.)

Jump and Double Full Turn (Kindergarten–12th grade.)

Jump and Swan The children leap into the air "driving" their arms high over their heads as they pull their bodies into an arched position.

Jump and swan

The hips should be forward, the head and feet should be pulled backward hard, and the legs should be extended to the rear. The hips are flexed slightly before landing. (Kindergarten–9th grade.)

Note: All of the preceding jump skills can be done from a run, from a stand facing forward, from a run and hurdle off a springboard, or from a stand facing rearward off a springboard. They can also be done from platforms of varying heights, a diving board, or a mini-tramp or trampolette.

Forward Bend The children stand with their feet apart and bend forward to touch their fingers to the floor. The teaching principles of progression and of providing a reachable but challenging goal apply even to simple moves such as this one. Moving the feet closer and closer together makes the move increasingly difficult. When the child can touch his fingers to the floor with his feet together, ask him to place his palms on the floor, then to bring his head to (or between) his knees, and finally to bring his elbows close to (or down to) the floor. (Kindergarten–6th grade.)

Russian Dance The children begin in a full squatting position with one leg extended in front. They then reverse the position of the legs and repeat this procedure as many times as they are able. The back should be held vertical. The weight should be to the side of the supporting leg. (Kindergarten–12th grade.)

Double Kazotski The children start in a full squat position. They leap upward, simultaneously extending both legs forward at right angles to their body and bend them again to drop into the

Russian dance

Double kazotski

Single leg circles

full squat position. The move may be done repeatedly and in rhythm. The back should be held vertical. The legs should be kicked out and bent again quickly. (Kindergarten–12th grade.)

Rocker The children assume a prone position. They grasp their ankles and rock forward and backward.

Single leg Circles The children assume a squatting position with both hands on the floor. Their left knee is between their arms. Their right leg is then extended sideward. They next swing their right leg forward and when it meets the right arm, they lift their right hand and place it to the right of the right leg. They next shift their weight to their right arm as the right leg continues to circle under the left leg and the left hand and back to the starting position. Several leg circles should be done in series. A forward lean should be avoided. The back should be held nearly vertical. The left leg should remain bent. (Kindergarten–12th grade.)

Blind Balance The children stand with their right foot placed against their left knee. Their hands are on their hips and their eyes are closed. They should maintain balance for as long as they are able. (Kindergarten–6th grade.)

Stick Jump The children hold a wand in both hands in front of their bodies. They then attempt to jump over the stick without releasing their grip. Variation: The wand may be held behind the body and the students then jump backward over it. The wand should be held lightly in the fingertips so that it will be knocked out of the hands in the event of a failure. The wand should be swung under the legs as they are drawn upward. The trajectory of the jump should be straight up and down. (Kindergarten–9th grade.)

Pick-Up The children stand with their backs to the wall and attempt to pick up a clean handkerchief or a piece of paper placed on the floor in front of them. (Kindergarten–6th grade.)

Front Scale The children start in a standing position. They bend forward at the hips lifting their extended right leg up behind themselves until their right leg and trunk are parallel to the floor and nicely arched. The arms should be extended diagonally forward-sideward with palms down to help maintain balance. The head should

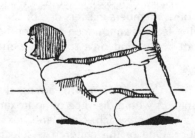

Rocker

Front scale

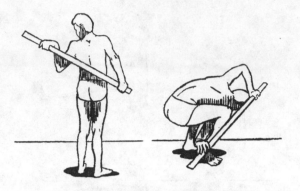

Through the stick

be pulled backward in order to enable the student to look at a point on the wall directly in front of himself. For good form, both legs and both arms should be fully extended. It may be necessary to angle the supporting leg slightly backward of the vertical. (Kindergarten–12th grade.)

Side Scale The children assume a standing position with their left foot and leg pointing diagonally to the left. They then lower their trunk to the left, sliding their left hand down along their left thigh until it comes to rest on their lower leg. Meanwhile, they have elevated their right leg until in the final position, their trunk, right leg, and extended right arm form one continuous line parallel to the floor. The supporting leg can be angled forward or backward of the vertical depending upon the distribution of the child's body weight to help in maintaining balance. For good form, both legs should be extended and the right leg, trunk, and right arm should form a straight line which is parallel to the floor. (Kindergarten–12th grade.)

Smell the Toe The children stand on one foot, grasp the other foot with both hands and by bending forward and pulling bring the foot to their nose. (Kindergarten–6th grade.)

Through the Stick The children stand holding a wand behind their back with their palms facing forward. They bring the wand up over their head and in front of their body without releasing the stick. Next, they bring their right leg around their right arm, between their hands and over the stick. Finally they crawl through head first and back over with their left foot. (Kindergarten–6th grade.)

GAMES

Following are several games in which many of the self-testing activities described above could be utilized:

Follow the Leader A leader is selected and the class follows the movements made by him.

Team Competition The class is divided into two or more teams. A point is awarded to a team each time one of its members masters one of the skills. The winning team is announced at the end of the semester or at the end of a specified period of time.

Simon Says The children are arranged in a circle formation with a distance of approximately two yards between each child and his nearest neighbor. One of the children is selected as the leader and goes to the center of the circle.

Side scale

The leader gives commands and executes the particular skill called for. Some of his commands are prefaced by the words "Simon says," and some are not. The children respond only to those commands prefaced by the words "Simon says." Any player who responds to a command not preceded by the words "Simon says" is eliminated. Those not responding when the command is appropiately preceded are eliminated. Those failing to perform a skill properly are eliminated. If the leader calls for a skill which he is unable to execute, he is eliminated, and the teacher selects a new leader. Variation: Instead of using the words "Simon says," use "Miss (name of teacher) says."

I Say Stoop The children are in the same formation as they are for "Simon says." The leader, who is in the center of the circle, gives the command, "I say stoop," or "I say do the front swan." He may do the action he has called for or he may do another action. Students follow the leader's commands, not his actions. Those not executing the action called for sit down. If the leader attempts a skill and is unsuccessful, he sits down and the teacher selects a new leader. Begin with simple actions and gradually increase their complexity and difficulty.

RELAY RACES

Selected relay races can supplement the conditioning exercises and self-testing activities in helping students to develop the strength necessary for success in gymnastic activities. Furthermore, relay races provide the added fun of identification with a team.

Animal Relays

In order to organize the class quickly for relays the following procedures are suggested:

1. The instructor should ask the children to line up abreast and facing forward.

2. He then has the children count off by the number of relay teams to be organized. For example, if four relay teams of ten on each team were desired in a class of forty students, the class would be asked to count off by fours. If eight relay teams of five students on each team were desired, the class would be asked to count off by eights.

3. The instructor should ask all number "ones" to form a single file at a point he indicates. He does the same for the remaining numbers.

4. The line behind which the single files are formed can serve as the starting line.

5. The finish or touch line should be placed at a distance from the starting line appropriate to the difficulty of the particular skill the children are being asked to do.

6. On the starting signal, the first child in each line progresses toward the touch or finish line. He could do the skill called for during the entire round trip from starting to touch line and return; he could run to the touch line and do the skill on the return trip; or he could do the skill from starting to touch line and then run back to the starting line. There might also be several lines drawn parallel to one another and the contestants could then be required to execute a different skill each time they cross over a line. For example, they might do the crab walk to the first line, the lame duck to the second line, and the ape walk to the third line, and then run back. The other students could repeat the procedure in like manner in their successive turns. Still another variation is to have each child imitate a different animal. For example, the first child on each team could imitate a bear, the second a rabbit, the third a seal, and so on.

7. While the children are lined up and before they count off to determine the membership of the several teams, the instructor should demonstrate and have the students try each of the several skills they will be asked to do during the relays.

8. To make it more easy to determine the winning team, all members of a team should line up single file and at attention with their right arms raised immediately after the last child has completed his turn.

Following are descriptions of a number of animal skills which could be used in animal relays.

Chicken Walk The contestant assumes the squatting position and reaches around behind and between his ankles to grasp the front of each ankle. He can move forward or backward while

Chicken walk

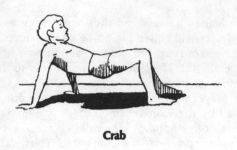

Crab

maintaining this position. (Kindergarten–6th grade.)

Elephant The contestant bends forward at the waist until his trunk is parallel to the floor. He then clasps his hands in front of his body and swings his arms from side to side as he takes long lumbering steps. (Kindergarten–6th grade.)

Donkey Kick The contestant makes forward progress by repeatedly diving forward-upward into a semi-handstand and snapping down to his feet. The student should start from a stooping position, driving his elbows up and backward and at the same time springing from both feet to upend near the handstand position. After he is in the up-ended position, he should bend his knees, and as his body falls off balance he should forcefully extend his knees and flex his hips to land on his feet. He should bend his knees upon landing on his feet. He should keep his shoulders low and his head pulled backward throughout the move. Some practice will be required before incorporating this skill into a relay. (6th–12th grade.)

Bunny Hop The student assumes a squatting position with his hands on the floor between his feet. The student hops forward. Variations of increasing difficulty would be to land on the feet first, on the hands and feet simultaneously, or on the hands first. (Kindergarten–6th grade.)

Crab The student squats down. He then places his hands on the floor behind his hips. With his back toward the floor and his abdomen up, he walks on his hands and feet. He should keep his body straight from knees to head. (Kindergarten–6th grade.)

Seal The student assumes a "front leaning rest" position. He "walks" on his hands, dragging his legs with his back extended, his head up and his toes pointed. (Kindergarten–6th grade.)

Ostrich Walk The student bends at the hips to grasp his ankles. He walks forward keeping his legs fully extended. (Kindergarten–6th grade.)

Bear Walk The child walks on "all fours" with his legs and arms fully extended and his head up. The arm and leg on the same side of his body should move together. (Kindergarten–9th grade.)

Stunt Relays

Stunt relays, like animal relays and self-testing activities, are useful in the elementary grades for helping students to improve their physical fitness status. The procedures are the same as those recommended for use in animal relays. Children from kindergarten through 9th grade would find these challenging and interesting. Following are a number of stunts which could be presented as relays:

Seal

1. Backward walk or run
2. Forward hop on two feet
3. Forward hop on right or left foot
4. Backward hop on two feet
5. Backward hop on right or left foot.
6. Skip
7. Walk on toes only
8. Walk on heels only
9. Hitler strut: The students walk without bending their knees swinging their forward extended leg to waist height with each step. They swing their opposite arm in extended position to shoulder height with each step.
10. Toe hold: The children raise their right knee to their chest. They grasp their right toe in their right hand. They then hop on their left leg. On reaching the half-way point, the child could change legs.

Partner and Group Relays

In partner relays each team should form two adjacent parallel files. When all contestants of a team have taken their turns, they should signify that they are finished by standing in their files at attention with partners holding inside hands raised over their heads. Following are a number of partner stunts which could be presented as relays:

Wheelbarrow The first child on each team assumes a "front leaning rest" position. The second child grasps the first child's ankles and holds them as though they were the handles of a wheelbarrow. They make forward progress in this manner with the first child walking on his hands. (Kindergarten–9th grade.)

Monkey Walk The first child stands with his feet apart. The second child lies on his back between the first child's legs with his legs in front of his partner's feet and his head behind them. The first child bends forward to place his hands on the floor to either side of his partner's legs. The second child wraps his legs around his partner's trunk, reaches upward to place his hands on his partner's back with his arms outside his hips and pulls himself off the floor. The first child walks forward on all fours. (Kindergarten–6th grade.)

Monkey walk

Fireman's Carry The first child stands with his feet apart. The second child stands facing his partner and squats to place his right arm between his partner's legs. The first child lies across the back of the second child's shoulders. The second child's right arm passes around his partner's right leg to enable him to grasp his partner's right wrist with his right hand. He then extends his legs to come to the erect position, meanwhile keeping his back perpendicular to the floor. Partners should be paired in such a manner that their weight and height are reasonably equal. Obese or very weak boys should be given other skills to perform. The lift should be performed with the back vertical and the legs doing the major share of the work. (Kindergarten–9th grade.) (Boys only.)

Saddle Back Carry The first child stands erect. The second child stands facing to the side with his right shoulder against his partner's chest. He then squats and stoops to place his right arm around and behind his partner's knees. The first

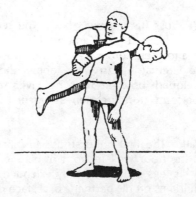

Fireman's carry

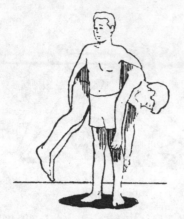

Saddle back carry
(Front view)

Saddle back carry
(Rear view)

child lies across his partner's back. The second child places his left arm around his partner's shoulders and then comes to the erect position. As in the Fireman's Carry, the obese and the underdeveloped boys should be given other skills to perform. (Kindergarten–9th grade.) (Boys only.)

Horse Walk   The first child stoops to place his hands on the floor well in front of his feet. His arms and his legs should be fully extended. The second child lies on his partner's back, face down and facing the opposite direction. He wraps his

Horse walk

legs around his partner's chest, places his hands on his partner's heels, and extends his arms. The first child then walks forward on all fours. (Kindergarten–6th grade.)

Tandem Walk   The first child stoops to place his hands on the floor about 24 inches in front of his feet. The second child stands in front of his partner facing the same direction. He bends forward to place his hands on the floor and then places his lower legs on his partner's back. Partners walk forward. (3rd–9th grade.)

Double Wheelbarrow   Child A stands facing the finish line. Child B stands facing the same direction directly in front of A. He then stoops down to place his hands on the floor and lifts his legs so that child A can grasp his lower legs directly behind the knees. Child C stands directly behind child A and facing the opposite direction. He stoops down to place his hands on the floor and lifts his legs to place them between child A's arms and body. Child A walks forward holding the legs of B with his hands and of C by pressing his arms against his body. B walks forward on his hands and C walks backwards on his hands. (4th–9th grade.)

Tandem walk

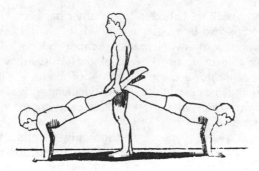

Double wheelbarrow

Tandem wheelbarrow

Partner Handstand Walk The first child stands with his feet apart. The second child, facing his partner, stoops to place his hands on his partner's feet and then upends into a handstand. The first child grasps his partner's legs and walks forward. (3rd–9th grade.)

Tandem Wheelbarrow Children A, B, and C stand directly behind one another facing the same direction. Child B assumes the "front leaning rest" position while C holds his ankles. Child A also assumes the front leaning rest position and places his lower legs along B's back. C walks his "tandem wheelbarrow" forward as A and B walk forward on their hands. (4th–9th grade.)

Forearm Carry Three children line up abreast of one another and facing the same direction.

The two on the outside bend their inside arm so that the forearm is horizontal. They may reach across their own body with their outside arm to grasp the wrist of their inside arm to lend it

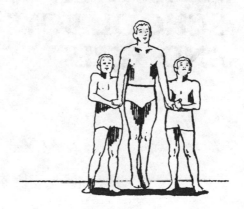

Forearm carry

greater stability. The child in the center grasps the wrists of the outside children and extends his arms to lift himself several inches off the floor. The two children on the outside walk forward carrying their partner who is in a cross arm support position. (4th–12th grade.)

BIBLIOGRAPHY

Daver, Victor P. *Dynamic Physical Education for Elementary School Children*. 4th ed. Minneapolis: Burgess Publishing Co., 1971.
Fait, Hollis F. *Physical Education for the Elementary School Child*. Philadelphia: W. B. Saunders Co., 1964.

Partner handstand walk

6

SKILLS FOR ELEMENTARY SCHOOL BOYS AND GIRLS

Every skill described in this chapter has been accomplished by an elementary school child. However, few, if any, elementary school children will be able to accomplish all of the skills. All will be able to accomplish some of them. Goals should be established and challenges issued which cause the most skilled child to extend himself.

Many elementary school physical education programs include little, if any, instruction in gymnastics and tumbling. And in many schools, where such instruction is offered, it is inadequate in quality or quantity, or in both.

While, ideally, the skills presented in this chapter should be introduced to children when they are in elementary school, they can be equally challenging to college students who have not been exposed to gymnastics. It is the striving for difficult goals which makes life interesting. Physical educators teaching at the high school or college level can, and should, draw heavily from this chapter.

It is the author's hope that this arrangement of material will serve as a challenge to physical educators to strive for a higher level of proficiency in their own teaching as well as in the performance of their students.

DOUBLES BALANCING

Double Crab The understander assumes a position on all fours with his front up, and the topmounter assumes a position on all fours with his feet on his partner's thighs and his hands on his shoulders. Both understander's and topmounter's arms and lower legs should be as nearly vertical as possible. Both partners' hips should be fully extended. (Boys and girls.)

Stand on Thighs The topmounter stands with his feet apart. The understander stands directly behind him as close as possible and facing in the same direction. He squats to place his head between the topmounter's legs, grasps his partner's thighs just above the knees and stands up with his partner sitting on his shoulders. While he is coming up to the erect position, he should keep his back as nearly vertical as possible in order to do the major portion of the lifting with the powerful knee extensors. After the understander has come to the erect position, he bends his knees and hips to about a 130° angle while the topmounter places his feet on his partner's thighs in such a manner that his toes are on the knee caps and his feet are along the thighs. The understander holds his partner's thighs just above the knees as the topmounter stands straight up with no forward bending at his hips. At the same time, the understander moves his head from between his partner's legs to complete the move. The understander's arms should be fully extended in the final position. (Boys and girls.)

Hand-Knee Shoulder Balance The understander assumes a supine position with his feet flat on the mat as close to his buttocks as possible and with his arms extended upward. The topmounter places his hands on his partner's knees and his shoulders in his hands. He springs from both feet simultaneously to elevate his hips over his head with his knees and hips bent. As he upends, he extends his arms horizontally in order that the understander will be enabled to support all his weight on his hands. The topmounter should not support any of his own weight. He uses his hands on the understander's knees only to aid in maintaining balance. He should pull his head backward to look into the face of his understander. After upending, the topmounter extends his hips and knees to assume an arched position with his heels directly over his head. The understander's arms, in the final position, should be as nearly perpendicular to the floor as possible. The spotter stands alongside the topmounter and grasps his ankle. (Boys and girls.)

Sit on Feet The understander assumes a supine position with his hands on the mat, palms up, next to his ears. The topmounter stands on the understander's hands facing away from him. The understander lifts his legs to place his heels on the topmounter's buttocks and his feet along the back of his thighs. The topmounter sits on his partner's feet. The understander extends his legs and brings his legs to a position perpendicular to the floor with his partner sitting on his feet. (Boys and girls.)

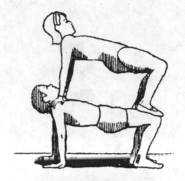

Double crab

Stand on thighs

Hand-knee shoulder balance

Sit on feet

Front lever between knees

Chest Balance on Back The understander assumes a position on his hands and knees. The topmounter places his chest across the understander's back and wraps his arms around his partner's chest and abdomen. He then upends into the chest balance. (Boys and girls.)

Front Lever Between Knees The understander assumes a supine position with his extended legs elevated perpendicular to the floor. The topmounter stands with his heels next to the understander's buttocks. He grasps the toes of the understander and lies back between his legs. In the final position, the topmounter's hips are just above his partner's knees. He should pull the

understander's legs together and keep his own arms and legs extended. The understander must keep his legs perpendicular to the floor and squeeze his legs together. (Boys and girls.)

Front Swan on Feet The understander assumes the supine position. The topmounter stands with his toes next to his partner's buttocks. The understander places his feet on his partner's abdomen with his heels on his partner's hip bones and his toes over his lower ribs. The topmounter leans forward in order that he be enabled to grasp the hands of his partner. The topmounter shifts his weight to his partner's feet and pulls his legs up to assume an arched position with his head, shoulders, and feet pulled upward. The understander should keep his feet parallel to one another and his lower legs perpendicular to the floor at all times. After balance has been secured, the partners may release hands. The instructor can assist by pushing up on the topmounter's chest and legs to place him in an arched position and horizontal. (Boys and girls.)

Chest balance on back

Front swan on feet

Back swan on feet

Giant wheel

Back Swan on Feet The understander assumes the supine position. The topmounter stands with his heels next to his partner's buttocks. The understander places his heels on his partner's buttocks and his toes on the small of his back. His feet should be parallel to one another. The understander grasps the topmounter's upper arms as he lies backward to assume the arched position with legs extended and head down. The understander should keep his lower legs perpendicular to the floor at all times. After balance has been secured, the understander may release his partner's arms. (Boys and girls.)

Stand on Hands The understander assumes a supine position with his legs elevated and his hands on the floor, palms up, next to his ears. The topmounter stands in his partner's hands facing him and grasps his feet. The topmounter jumps straight up. As he moves upward, he pushes down on his understander's feet while the understander extends his arms under his part-

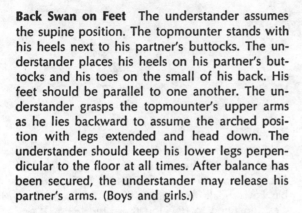

Stand on hands

ner's upward moving feet. The understander's arms should be perpendicular to the floor. The topmounter should keep his legs vertical and his weight centered over his partner's shoulders. Spot by standing behind the topmounter ready to catch him under his arms if he loses balance. (Boys, or a boy understander and a girl topmounter.)

Giant Wheel This move should be attempted only after both topmounter and understander are able to do a diving forward roll. The understander assumes a supine position with his legs elevated. The topmounter stands facing his partner's feet with one foot at each side of his head. Each partner grasps the other's ankles. The topmounter does a diving forward roll, lifting his hips high while retaining his grip on his partner's ankles. This action will pull the understander around to his feet. The partners have now reversed positions. The understander now does a diving forward roll while holding his partner's ankles. The procedure is repeated down the length of the mats. (Boys and girls.)

Hand-Knee Shoulder Spring The understander is in a supine position with his feet flat on the floor near his buttocks and his arms elevated. The topmounter jogs toward his partner and places his hands on his partner's knees and his shoulders in his hands. He springs off one leg and swings his other leg over his head to swing his body up and back around to his feet. The topmounter should extend his arms horizontally forward to bring his center of gravity over his partner's shoulders. His center of rotation should be over his partner's shoulders—not over his

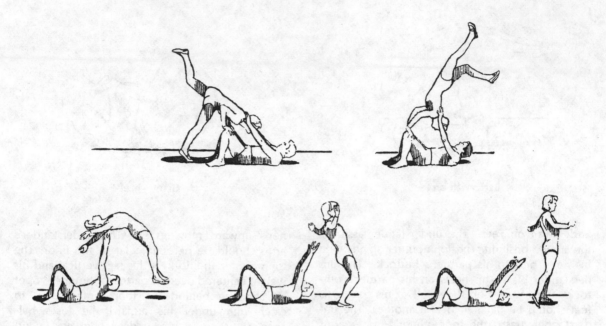

Hand-knee shoulder spring

knees. Spot by kneeling alongside the under-stander's head ready to lift the topmounter and also to check overspin. (Boys and girls.)

HORIZONTAL BAR AT CHEST HEIGHT

Skin the Cat The student grasps the bar with a front grip. He flexes his knees and hips and pulls his legs up between his arms and under the bar. He slowly continues to rotate until his hips are

lower than his head. He extends his hips and knees. Students unable to lift their legs to the bar have weak abdominal, iliac, and psoas muscles and need to develop these by doing sit-ups and leg raises. Note: In all skills on the horizontal bar, the thumbs should always be on the side of the bar opposite the fingers. Spot by holding the gymnast's wrist with one hand while slowing the descent of her legs with the other. (Boys and girls.)

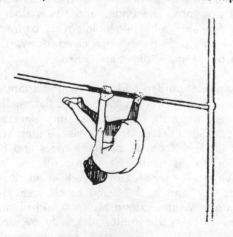

Skin the cat

Single-knee hang

Double-knee hang

Single-knee circle mount

Single-Knee Hang The student grasps the bar in a front grip with the hands set shoulder width apart and his body hanging below the bar in an "L" position. He pulls his hips up and hooks one knee over the bar between his hands. (Boys and girls.)

Double-Knee Hang The student grasps the bar in a front grip with hands set shoulder width apart and hangs in an "L" position (legs elevated) below the bar. He pulls his hips up and bends his knees to place the back of both knees over the bar and between his hands. He then releases his grip to hang by both knees. (Boys and girls.)

Pull-Over The student stands facing the bar and grasping it in a front grip with his hands set shoulder width apart. He swings his right leg forward, up, around, and over the bar while pulling himself toward the bar to finish in a front support on the bar. As he circles up and over the bar, the student must pull his head backward and attempt to get his center of gravity to the other side of the bar by pulling hard with his arms. His left leg, of course, joins his right leg as he circles up over the bar. Assist by pushing upward against the hip with one hand and push his leg up over the bar with the other hand. (Boys and girls.)

Single-Knee Circle Mount The student gets into the single-knee hang position, swings his extended leg downward and backward, pulls the bar toward his hips with extended arms, and rotates to a straddle support position on the bar.

It is very important that neither the arms nor the swinging leg be bent in order to utilize a longer lever to gain greater momentum. The swinging leg should be swung all the way back to a hyperextended position of the hip joint. Assist by pushing downward on the performer's extended leg with one hand and upward on his back with the other hand. (Boys and girls.)

Single-Knee Circle The student mounts to a straddle support position on the bar by means of the single-knee circle mount. He swings his extended leg forward and then backward. As this leg swings backward, he slides backward along the bar to catch it in the crook of his bent leg. He then immediately swings his extended leg forward as he throws his head and shoulders backward to completely circle the bar while being supported by one knee and two hands. A spotter should stand alongside the performer.

Single-knee circle

Penny drop

He can assist by pushing downward on the performer's extended leg or by pushing upward on his chest as he is about to complete the move. (Boys and girls.)

Penny Drop The student starts from the double-knee hang position and causes his body to swing back and forth. At the end of the backward swing, he releases his hands and swings his arms forward to gain impetus. At the very end of the forward swing when his body is parallel to the floor, he extends his knees to come free of the bar and lands on his feet. The move should be spotted until it has been mastered. The spotter should stand alongside the performer and to the front of the bar. He should be ready to extend one arm across the performer's chest in the event that he does not spin enough. At the same time, he should be ready to extend the other arm across the performer's back in the event he spins too far. (Boys and girls.)

Front Vault Dismount The student starts this move from a front support on the bar. He bends his arms slightly and sags at the shoulders in order to lower himself so that the bar is across his waist. He brings his legs forward by bending at the hips and then swings them backward vigorously. He carries his shoulders slightly forward of the bar as his legs rise upward behind him. He releases his right hand and pivots on his left hand to pass his extended body over the bar face down, and lands on his feet facing sidewards. A spotter should stand directly in front of the performer to catch him under the chest in the event of a miss. (Boys.)

Flank Vault Dismount The starting position and the technique of execution are the same as for the front vault dismount. The only differences are that the performer's side passes over the bar; he must carry the shoulder of his supporting arm sideward so that his center of gravity (his hips) will be over his point of support (his hand); and he will land with his back toward the bar. The spotter should stand to the side of the supporting arm and should hold the upper arm and wrist. (Boys.)

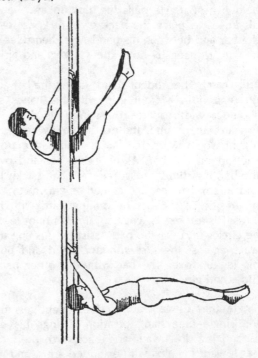

Flank vault dismount

Bar snap

Bar Snap The student stands facing the bar and grasps it with a front grip. His feet are about 18 inches behind a point directly under the bar and his arms are extended. He lifts both feet off the floor simultaneously and brings his toes to the bar. This will cause his body to rotate forward under the bar if he keeps his arms straight. At the proper point during his forward swing, he extends at his hips and shoulders, releases his grip, and shoots forward to land on his feet some distance from the bar. Caution: Students may strike their face against the bar if they bend their arms. Note: Contests can be held to see who can cover the greatest distance. (Boys and girls.)

PARALLEL BARS AT CHEST HEIGHT[1]

Hand Walk The student jumps to a cross arm support position on the bars. Keeping his arms fully extended, he "walks" the length of the bars on his hands by shifting his body weight from one hand to the other. Students should follow one another across the bars at 3-foot intervals. A spotter should stand at the end of the bars to aid children who require help in dismounting.

Hop Across The student jumps to a cross arm support. By shrugging his shoulders and flexing his arms slightly (15–20°) and then extending his arms, he hops the length of the bars. Students should follow one another at 3-foot intervals. A spotter should stand at the end of the bars prepared to aid children in the dismount.

Grasshopper walk

Grasshopper Walk The student jumps to a cross arm support with arms bent at a 90° angle. He "walks" the length of the bars with his arms bent by shifting his weight from one arm to the other. Students should follow one another across the bars at 3-foot intervals. This is an excellent exercise for developing the pectoral and deltoid muscles, as the students will testify when they complain of the ache in these muscles. A spotter should stand at the end of the bars.

Inverted Walk The student stands between the bars, just inside the uprights, with an outside grip on the bars. He flexes his hips to lift his extended legs over his head to assume a piked position while hanging from his hands. In the hang, his arms should be fully extended. His body weight should be evenly distributed to either side of his arms. Balance is maintained by positioning the hips and by the amount of hip flexion. His legs should be at right angles to his hips. He shifts his weight from one arm to the other as he "walks" to the far uprights. A spotter should stand alongside the performer with one hand under his neck and the other grasping his near wrist.

Hop across

[1] Only boys perform on the parallel bars.

Inverted walk

Inverted hop

Inverted Hop The starting position is the same as in the inverted walk. The student extends slightly but sharply at the hips and pulls with his arms to "hop" upward and forward. He repeats this procedure to travel to the opposite uprights. A spotter should follow the performer with one hand under his back and the other under his head.

Back Foot Leaning Rest The student jumps to a cross arm support at the center of the bars and places his feet on the bars in front of his body. He extends his body fully to complete the move.

Back foot leaning rest

Front Foot Leaning Rest The student jumps to a cross arm support at the center of the bars and places his feet on the bars behind his body. He extends his body fully to complete the move.

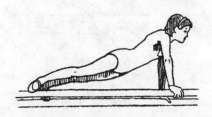

Front foot leaning rest

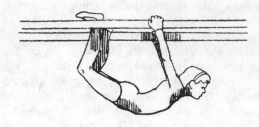

Bird's nest

Bird's Nest The student stands between the bars at their center and grasps them with an outside grip. He lifts his legs to pass through the inverted hang position and backward to hook his feet on the bars. He extends his legs, body, and arms fully to complete the move.

Inside Cross Riding Seat The student starts in a cross arm support. He sits on the right bar with his legs between the bars. He extends his left leg and hip and bends his right leg and hip to complete the move.

Outside Cross Riding Seat The procedures for this move are identical to those for the preceding, except that the legs are outside the bars.

Cross Foot Hang Facing Upward The student stands between the bars at their center and grasps them with an outside grip. He lifts his legs to hook his heels on the bars in front of his body and extends his body fully to complete the move.

Swinging in an Upper Arm Hang Two laws of physics are applicable to the learning of this move. The first states that the speed of move-

Inside cross riding seat

Outside cross riding seat

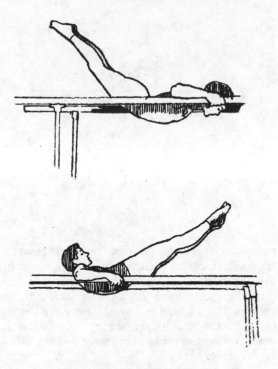

Swinging in an upper arm hang

ment at the end of a long lever will be greater than that of a short lever if they are making the same number of revolutions per unit of time. Therefore, to generate the momentum necessary to accomplish most moves, the student should extend his hips at the beginning of the backward swing. This gives his body greater speed (from hips to toes) and consequently greater momentum (momentum = mass × velocity). His body should remain extended as he swings backward and through the first part of the forward swing. During the forward swing, when his feet are approximately under his head, he flexes at the hips. In so doing, he makes application of another law of physics which states that shortening the radius will accelerate the speed of rotation. This flexion will enable the student to get his feet up over his head with little effort. Now, he is back where he started and he simply repeats the movements in sequence. These principles and these movements are fundamental to many of the more advanced skills.

Swinging in a Cross Arm Support   In this move, as in the preceding one, the body is extended at the beginning of the backward swing and flexed slightly in the center of the forward swing. However, we have an added problem—that of maintaining balance. If the arms were held vertical throughout the swing, the student would fall backward during the backward swing and forward during the forward swing due to centrifugal force and to the unbalanced distribution of his body weight. Therefore, as his legs and body

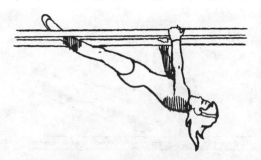

Cross foot hang facing upward

Swinging in a cross arm support

Still dips

Swinging dips on the backward swing

swing backward, the student must compensate for these forces by inclining his arms forward of the vertical; and as his legs and body swing forward, he must incline his arms backward of the vertical. During the learning stages, the coach or instructor should support the student with one hand on the performer's wrist and the other on his upper arm.

Still Dips The student begins in a cross arm support position with his arms fully extended and his body motionless. He lowers his body by flexing his arms until his upper arms are at right angles to his forearms. He then returns to a fully extended position of the arms using care to avoid swinging his body. This is an excellent exercise for developing the muscles most used on the parallel bars—triceps, pectoralis major and minor, and the deltoids.

Swinging Dips on the Forward Swing After the student has learned to swing properly in the cross arm support, he is ready to try swinging dips. Between the end of the backward swing and the beginning of the forward swing, when his body is practically weightless, the student bends his arms to drop into the position illustrated. Then at the end of the forward swing, while

momentum is carrying his body upward, he extends his arms. Contests can be held to see who can do the most consecutive swinging dips. Spot by holding the performer's wrist and upper arm.

Swinging Dips on the Backward Swing This time at the beginning of the backward swing, the student bends his arms; and at the end of the backward swing, he extends them again. Spot by holding the performer's wrist and upper arm. A double dip can be done by dipping on both forward and backward swings.

Rear Vault Dismount The student swings in a cross arm support at the center of the bars. As his feet rise above the bars on the forward swing, he leans to the right and brings both legs over the right bar, flexing at the hips as the legs pass over the bar. At the same time, he grasps the right bar with his left hand and releases his right hand. He lands alongside the bar facing his original direction. A spotter should hold his right wrist. He should land on the balls of his feet and

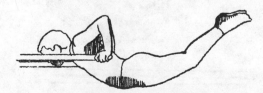

Swinging dips on the forward swing

Rear vault dismount

Front vault dismount

Corkscrew mount

bend his knees to take up the shock of landing. A few students may need to practice jumping from a height of 1 to 3 feet to learn how to land in balance and how to absorb the shock of landing by bending their knees and hips.

Front Vault Dismount The student swings in a cross arm support at the center of the bars. As his feet rise above the bars on the backward swing, he leans to the left shifting his weight to his left arm and brings both legs over the left bar. At the same time, he grasps the left bar with his right hand and releases his left hand. He lands alongside the bar facing his original direction. A spotter should grasp his left wrist.

Corkscrew Mount The student stands at the outside center of the bars and facing them. He grasps the near bar with his left palm facing away and his right palm facing him. He lifts both legs simultaneously to "shoot" his feet between the bars and over the far bar, landing to rest on his left hip or thigh. He pulls with his arms to get his head, shoulders, and chest above the bars, rotates on his thigh to face the bars, and then brings his right leg to rest across the opposite bar to finish the move in a straddle lying position.

STILL RINGS AT SHOULDER HEIGHT

Hang and Lift Legs The student hangs with his arms extended and lifts his extended legs to the point where they form a right angle with his trunk. (Boys and girls.)

Hang with Bent Arms The student hangs with his arms fully flexed. (Boys and girls.)

Leg Circling The student hangs and swings his legs around in circles. (Boys and girls.)

Inverted Hang with Body Extended The student starts in a hanging position and by flexing his hips and knees pulls them over his head. He

103

Skin the cat

Hang by the knees

then fully extends his body in the inverted position. For his first attempts, he can aid in maintaining balance by placing his feet against the ring straps, cables, or ropes. Later he should learn to do the move with his feet together. (Boys and girls.)

Piked Hang The student upends as in the previous move, but instead of extending his body he assumes a piked position with his legs at right angles to his trunk. His weight should be evenly distributed to either side of his arms. (Boys and girls.)

Skin the Cat The student starts in a hanging position. He bends his hips and knees and pulls with his arms to bring his hips over his head. He continues rotating until his hips and feet are below his head. He then extends as fully as possible, pushing his toes toward the mat. He returns to the hanging position by assuming a tucked position and rotating in the opposite direction. A spotter is advisable. (Boys and girls.)

Monkey Hang The student executes a skin the cat and, while in the extended position, releases his grasp with one hand to complete a full turn on the hanging arm. He regrasps the ring upon completing the move. Centrifugal force during the turn will be diminished if the student fully extends his body. Spot by standing alongside the gymnast ready to catch him around the waist. (Boys.)

Chin-Ups with Legs in "L" Position The student raises his extended legs until they form a right angle with his trunk. He performs as many chin-ups in this position as he can. (Boys and girls.)

Chin-Ups and Extend One Arm The student forms a regular chin-up and while the arms are flexed extends one arm sideward and then flexes it again. He then extends the other arm to the side and flexes it again to return to the starting position. (Boys.)

Hang by the Knees The student assumes the piked hang position and then inserts his lower legs into the rings up to his knees. He releases his hand grip and hangs by his knees to complete the move. (Boys and girls.)

Bird's Nest The student assumes a piked hang position and puts his insteps into the rings. He arches his back and pulls his head backward to complete the move. (Boys and girls.)

Bird's Nest with One Foot The student does a bird's nest and then removes one foot from the ring and extends that leg. (Boys and girls.)

Bird's Nest with One Hand The student does a bird's nest and then releases his grip with one hand extending that arm forward. (Boys and girls.)

104

Bird's nest

Bird's nest, one foot and one hand

Bird's Nest with One Foot and One Hand The student does a bird's nest, removes one foot from the ring, releases the grip of the hand on the opposite side of his body and extends the free leg and arm. A spotter should stand alongside the performer ready to catch him around his waist in the event an error is made. (Boys and girls.)

Dislocate The student first assumes the piked hang position. He then extends his hips vigorously to shoot his feet upward and backward at about a 30° angle from the vertical (or 150° to the floor). At the same time, he pulls his head backward, rotates his hands in such a manner that his thumbs move outward away from his body, and pushes his arms sideward. The student extends into an arched position, and then as he completes the rotation he pikes slightly and flexes his arms to absorb the jar. When he has mastered the move, he should execute it with his arms fully extended throughout and should continue rotating to return to the piked hang

position. The spotter should place one hand on the performer's shoulder to lift him and the other hand on his near hip to guide the movement (Boys.)

Single-Leg Cut-Off—Forward The student starts in the piked hang. With his arms slightly flexed he swings both legs forward, bringing one leg between the rings and the other outside the rings When his outside leg is about to strike his arm he releases his grasp, allowing the leg to pass under the ring. He then regrasps the ring. During the leg cut, he should pull his head and shoulders forward to facilitate the regrasp. A spotter should stand directly behind the performer with

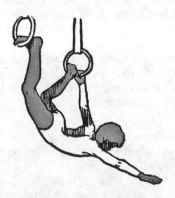

Bird's nest with one hand

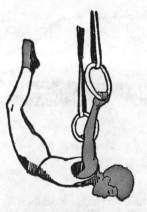

Dislocate

105

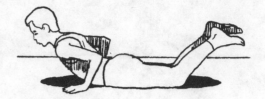

Chest roll from the knees

Single-leg cut-off—forward

both hands under his armpits. The rings may be lowered to facilitate spotting. (Boys.)

TUMBLING[2]

Front Break Fall   The student starts in a standing position and then, keeping his knees and hips fully extended, falls forward to catch himself on his hands. His arms should be almost fully extended at the moment of the catch and should flex on contact with the mat to distribute the impact over ⌐ greater period of time.

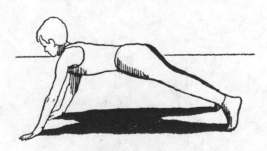

Front break fall

[2] All of the tumbling skills described in this section can be done with equal facility by both boys and girls

Chest Roll from the Knees   The student starts in a kneeling position with his hips extended and his hands at his waist; his wrists are flexed and his elbows bent. He arches as far backward as he is able and rolls forward contacting the mat first with his thighs, then with his hands and abdomen, and finally with his chest.

Chest Roll from a Standing Position   The student arches backward as far as he is able while standing and drops to his knees. From this point, he follows the same procedure as in the chest roll from the knees. After he has mastered both the chest roll and the handstand, the student can learn to execute the chest roll into a handstand.

Front Roll from a Squatting Position with the Arms Between the Legs   The student starts in a squatting position with his hands on the mat, his fingers pointing forward, and his arms between his legs. He elevates his hips by extending his legs slightly, tucks his chin into his chest, rotates to his shoulder blades, tucks tightly by grasping his shins, and continues to roll around until his feet contact the mat. As he rolls around, successive points on his back should contact the mat. It is considered poor form to place the hands on the mat before completing the roll back to the feet after the tucked position has been assumed. When a student finds it necessary to place his hands alongside his hips in order to come around to his feet, it is likely that the roll has not been executed in proper form.

Front Roll from a Squatting Position with the Arms Outside the Legs   The starting position and the execution of this move are identical to those of the preceding one except that it is begun with the arms outside of instead of between the legs.

Skills for Elementary School Boys and Girls

Front roll from a squatting position with the arms between the legs

Front roll from a squatting position with the arms outside the legs

107

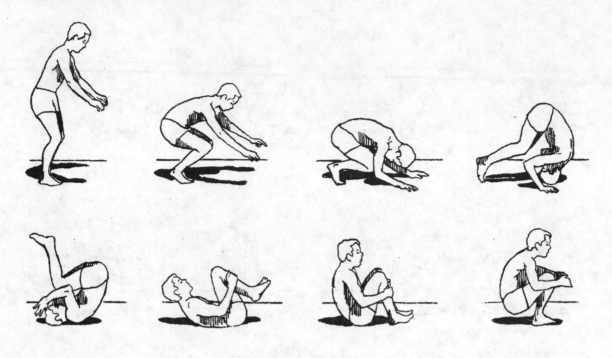

Forward roll from a stand

Forward roll from a walk

Forward Roll from a Stand The student starts from a standing position, squats to place his hands on the mat with his arms outside his legs, and executes the forward roll as previously described.

Forward Roll from a Walk When one leg is forward during the walk, the student stoops to place his hands on the mat in front of his body, tucks his chin into his chest, permits momentum to carry his hips over his head, "balls up," grasps his shins, and completes the roll.

Forward Roll with a Half Twist The student begins the move in the same manner as a regular forward roll, but when he is in an inverted position he crosses his legs. Then when he comes around to his feet, he spins on his toes to finish the move facing in the opposite direction.

Forward Rolls in Series The student executes the first forward roll from a standing position. As he completes the roll in coming to his feet and while still in the tucked position, he reaches forward with extended arms to place his hands on the mat well in front of his feet. He then moves into the next forward roll without coming to the standing position.

Dive and Forward Roll The student takes a short run, takes off from both feet into a flat horizontal dive, lands on his hands, tucks, and executes a forward roll. The student should keep his body horizontal and extended as it floats through the air. He should reach out well in front of his body with his hands in order to be able to cushion the shock of landing by bending his arms. The obese or frail should not be permitted to attempt this move. Long dives should

Forward roll with a half twist

Dive and forward roll

be discouraged except for those children who are well muscled relative to their body weight and who also have demonstrated a high level of skill in this move.

Side Roll The student starts in a supine position on the mat and rolls around his long or vertical axis.

Side roll

Backward roll from a squatting position

Backward Roll from a Squatting Position The student starts in a squatting position with his back toward the mat. He drops back to his buttocks and rolls around on his back until his shoulder blades contact the mat. At this time, he places his hands on the mat, palms down with fingers pointing toward his body. As he pushes against the mat with his hands to give his head room to come through, he pulls his knees toward his chest and comes around to his feet. The student should keep his head forward throughout the roll. During the push with his hands, he should pull his knees toward his chest to shorten the radius of rotation and thereby ac-

celerate the speed of rotation. Children can assist one another by placing one hand under their partner's shoulder to lift him and one on his back to help him to rotate.

Shoulder Roll The student starts standing, facing to the side. He throws his right arm across his waist, turns his head to the left, drops to his right knee, breaking the fall with his left hand, and rolls around the vertical (long) axis of his body. As he completes the roll, he comes to his left knee and right foot and then stands up facing sideward.

Shoulder roll

Backward roll from a stand

Backward Roll from a Stand The student starts from a standing position with his back toward the mat. He squats and goes immediately into the backward roll as described above.

Backward Roll in a Straddle Position The student starts in a standing position with his back toward the mat and with his feet straddled. He bends his hips to bring his hands to the floor. He then falls backward keeping his legs fully extended and his hands in contact with the mat until his buttocks contact the mat. He rolls around his rounded back with his head well forward. When his shoulder blades come in contact with the mat, he places his hands on the mat, pushes with his arms, tightens his pike (pulls the extended legs closer to his body), and comes around to his feet. The student should lean well forward during the backward drop to the buttocks. He should also tighten the pike during the final stages of the roll.

Backward roll in a straddle position

Backward roll in a jackknife position

Backward roll with an extension

Backward Roll in a Jackknife Position The student starts in a standing position with his back toward the mat and his feet together. He stoops to touch his toes and falls backward to his buttocks, keeping his legs fully extended during the fall. When his shoulder blades contact the mat, he places his hands on the mat under his shoulders, pushes with his arms, and comes around to his feet. The student should lean as far forward during the drop backward as his flexibility will allow. He should tighten the pike after his hands come in contact with the mat.

Backward Roll with an Extension The student begins the backward roll with an extension in the same manner as he does the backward roll in jackknife position; however, after he places his hands on the mat under his shoulders, he extends vigorously at the hips to "shoot" his feet vertically upward, pushes hard with his arms, pulls his head backward, "shoots" into the handstand position, and then flexes at the hips to snap his feet to the mat. A spotter can grasp the ankles of the student as he "shoots" into the handstand to pull him upward toward the handstand. This will help the student to learn when and at what angle to initiate the "shoot" or vigorous extension at the hips. Obese or frail children will find this move difficult.

Backward Rolls in Series All the varieties of backward rolls (tucked, straddle, jackknifed, and with an extension) can be done in series. As he comes around to his feet when completing one backward roll, the student immediately leans backward to initiate the next backward roll.

Cartwheel The student starts by standing oblique to his proposed direction of travel. He bends forward-sideward to place his left hand on the mat, meanwhile swinging his right arm across his body and to the mat. He then swings his extended right leg directly upward over his head, at the same time springing off his left foot. These actions will cause him to upend into a handstand position. He then flexes forward-sideward at the hips and pushes off his hands to bring first the right foot and then the left foot to

Cartwheel

the mat to finish in a standing position facing the side of the mat. While upended, the student's head should be pulled backward and he should look at a point on the mat between and slightly in front of his hands. The rhythm in contacting the mat is hand, hand, foot, foot—or 1, 2, 3, 4. Both hands and both feet do *not* contact the mat at the same moment. All four points of support —the two hands and the two feet—should contact the mat along a straight line. The instructor can help those students having difficulty by kneeling at such a point that their back will pass directly in front of him. He should grasp their waist as they pass him to help them to rotate.

Neckspring The student starts in a supine position with his hands under his shoulders, his palms on the mat, and his fingers pointing toward his feet. He lifts his extended legs up over his head until his toes touch the mat beyond his head. He then rolls forward on his shoulder blades keeping his feet low, until his back is at about a 55° to 60° angle to the floor. At this

point, he "whips" his legs around by extending his hips, pushes with his arms, and brings his head forward so that he lands on his feet. The vigorous extension at the hips must be made at precisely the correct moment during the forward roll of the body in order to: (1) utilize the momentum of the body, (2) get the feet under the hips (if the extension occurs too late, the student will be unable to get his feet under his hips), and (3) avoid shooting straight up. The student's legs must remain extended until his feet contact the mat so that he will have the long lever arm necessary to generate the needed momentum. The instructor must insist upon good assistance or spotting procedures. The spotter should kneel on both knees to the left side of the student and facing him. He should place his left hand on the student's lower back and his right hand under his left shoulder. The spotter's right forearm should rest on his own thigh for better leverage. The spotter's left hand will prevent the child from striking his back, and his right hand will ease him down in the event he should shoot straight up.

Neckspring

Neckspring to a straight leg landing

Neckspring with Hands on Knees The student begins in a position on his back with his hips flexed, his legs behind his head, and his hands on his knees. He pushes his hands against his knees instead of against the floor. In all respects, the technique is identical to that of the regular neckspring.

Neckspring to a Straight Leg Landing This move is executed in the same manner as is the regular neckspring, except that the extension of the hips is begun slightly earlier and the extension of the hips and the push of the arms must be more vigorous.

Neckspring with hands on knees

Headspring

Headspring The student squats to place his hands on the mat a shoulder width apart. He then places his head on the mat in front of his hands at such a position that if a line were drawn connecting the three points of support (head and hands), an equilateral triangle would be formed. Next, he brings his hips up over his head, keeping his toes on the mat with his legs extended. He then tilts forward until his back is at a 55° to 60° angle to the floor with his toes still near the floor. When he is about to lose balance, he vigorously extends his hips and pushes with his arms to come about to his feet. Every student must be spotted while learning this move. The skill is spotted in the same manner as the neckspring. Following are common errors in execution of the headspring:

1. Extending the hips as they are brought over the head so as to lift the legs over the head. The student thereby shortens the arc of rotation during the "whip" of the legs.

2. Bending the knees during the whip of the legs. This shortens the radius of rotation, limiting the amount of momentum that can be generated.

3. Whipping the legs around too soon. The student should wait until his back is at a 55° to 60° angle to the floor.

Headsprings in Series After completing the first headspring, the student immediately places his hands and then his head down on the mat and executes another headspring. These can be continued for the full length of the mats.

Headspring to a Straight Leg Landing The student should execute the extension of his hips more forcefully and should push harder with his arms than he did in the regular headspring so that he lands with his legs fully extended.

Headspring to a straight leg landing

Headspring from a Walk The student walks toward the mat. He stoops to place his hands on the mat, flexes his arms to place his head on the mat in front of his hands, and executes the headspring as previously described. Due to the momentum resulting from the walk, the extension of the hips should occur slightly earlier (when the back is at a 60° to 65° angle to the floor) than it does in the regular headspring.

Headspring from a walk

Headspring to a seat (side view)

Headspring to a Seat   In this move, instead of landing on his feet, the student lands in a sitting position. To do this he avoids hyperextending his hips during the snap. The push with his arms is in a horizontal direction, and his feet do not come under his body. The landing is made with the entire underside of both legs contacting the mat at almost the same instant. The heels, however, contact the mat slightly before the other parts of the leg.

Headspring to a seat (front view)

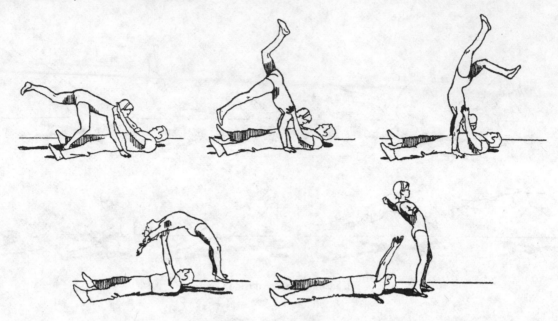

Assisted straight arm handspring

Handspring on a rolled-up mat

Assisted Straight Arm Handspring This is a partner move leading to the front handspring. The understander lies supine on the mat with his arms extended vertically and his legs apart. The topmounter runs toward his partner taking his last step between his partner's legs. He flexes quickly at the hips to place one hand on either side of the understander's chest and whips his legs over and around his head to land on his feet. The understander assists the topmounter by placing his hands on his partner's shoulders and pushing as he comes around.

Handspring over a Rolled-Up Mat A mat is rolled up tightly and placed in the center of two mats that are end to end. The student takes a short run toward the mat, skips after the final step to make it possible to place his hands closer to his feet and directly in front of the rolled mat. This will establish greater rotary momentum. He whips his legs over and around his head to land on his feet. The student should keep his arms fully extended and his head pulled backward throughout the move. As his body passes through the handstand position, he should push upward

from the shoulders (not the elbows). He should also push his hips upward by hyperextending his back after the handstand position has been passed. His arms should be perpendicular to the floor throughout the move. Two spotters should be seated straddling the mat so that the handspring will be done between them. They should place one hand under the performer's shoulder and the other on his upper back to assist him throughout the move.

Handspring on a Rolled-Up Mat The student executes a handspring placing his hands on top of the mat. The techniques of execution are identical to those described above for the handspring over the rolled-up mat. Two spotters should position themselves astraddle the rolled-up mat. As before, they place one hand on the tumbler's upper back. The other hand is used to grasp the tumbler's wrist or arm.

Handspring Having mastered the preceding moves, the student is ready to attempt a regular front handspring. The techniques of execution

Front handspring

Walk-out handspring

One-arm handspring

are as previously described, as are the spotting procedures.

Walk-Out Handspring In the walk-out handspring, the student takes off from one foot, his legs are apart throughout the move, and he lands first on one foot and then the other. In all other respects, the techniques of execution are identical to those previously described except that a more vigorous whip and shoulder push must be utilized. This style of front handspring is useful in advanced tumbling since the gymnast can run out of the move into a round-off.

One-Arm Handspring The techniques of execution are identical to those previously described for the handspring with the exception that only one arm is used.

Round-Off The student takes a short run to the mat, skips on his right foot, steps to his left foot, whips his arms downward, and quickly flexes his hips to place his hands on the mat directly in front of his feet with his fingers pointing sideward. His legs whip up over his head, his body turns 180°, and he flexes his hips and extends his knees to snap his feet down to the

mat. Both feet should contact the mat simultaneously on landing. The 180° turn cannot be easily made unless the student places his hands on the mat in the proper position. His hands should be relatively close together with his fingers pointing to the side of the mat, his forward hand a few inches closer to the side of the mat than the other hand. His head should be pulled backward and his arms should be extended throughout the move.

One-Arm Round-Off The techniques of execution for the one-arm round-off are identical to those described for the round-off, the obvious difference being that only one hand touches the mat.

Bucking Bronco The student starts in a standing position. He flexes his hips, drives his elbows backward and upward and springs from both feet simultaneously to upend in the handstand position. He then flexes his hips, pushes with his arms, and pulls his head backward to snap to his feet. He does this several times. Throughout the several repetitions his head and shoulders are below his hips.

Round-off

One-arm round-off

Bucking bronco

BALANCE BEAM[3]

All of the following skills can be done on a line painted on the floor, on the low balance beam, or on a regulation balance beam. Some of them could be done on a slack wire or on a tight wire.

[3] The balance beam is a competitive event for girls only. However, boys of elementary school age do enjoy executing the moves described and will be challenged by them

Forward Walk The student walks forward taking small steps with arms extended sideward for easier balancing.

Backward Walk The student walks backward placing the toe of one foot behind the heel of the other. Arms are extended sideward for better balance.

124

Walk on heels

Walk on toes

Cat walk forward   Sidestep

Heel-Toe Forward The student moves forward by placing the heel of one foot in front of the toe of the other.

Hop Forward The student makes forward (or backward) progress by a series of short hops. These may be done with arms sideward, forward, overhead, behind the back, or folded across the chest.

Walk Forward (or Backward) on Heels The student walks forward with toes elevated and only the heels contacting the beam. Variations: arms forward, sideward, overhead, or held behind the back.

Walk Forward (or Backward) on Toes The student walks forward (or backward) with only the toes contacting the beam.

Squat on One Leg The student stands on one leg and squats. The shoulders should be kept forward and the arms extended sideward. The nonsupporting leg should be held horizontally forward.

Cat Walk Forward The student walks forward on both hands and feet. Short steps should be taken.

Sidestep The student faces sideward and moves the left foot to the left and then brings the right foot next to the left foot. This procedure is repeated for the length of the beam.

Side Cross Step The student faces the side and then crosses her right foot in front of and to the left of the left foot. Then she moves her left foot, crossing it behind and to the left of the right foot. This procedure is repeated the length of the beam.

Turn The student does a 180° turn on the balls of her feet. She should extend her arms sideward to help maintain balance.

Jump Turn The student starts standing sideward across the beam. She leaps into the air, does a 180° turn, and lands in balance facing the opposite direction. The student should take a low jump, look over her left shoulder, bring her left arm slightly behind her body, and swing her right arm across the front of and close to her body to aid in execution of the turn.

Full Turn on One Leg The student executes a

Full turn on one leg

180° turn on the ball of one foot. She should extend her arms sideward for better balance.

Full Turn in a Cat Walk Position The student starts in a cat walk position; that is, with both hands and both feet in contact with the beam. She releases her hand grip and turns on the balls of her feet while maintaining the squatting position throughout the turn. On facing the new direction, she regrasps the beam with both hands.

Sit on Beam The student begins the move standing on the beam on one foot. She leans well forward as she squats as low as she can on her supporting leg. She holds her arms extended sideward. She completes the move by sitting on the beam. To return to the standing position, she places one foot on the beam as close to her buttocks as she can, rocks forward over her supporting foot and extends her supporting leg.

Skip Across The student starts by standing on one end of the beam facing inward with one foot forward. She then skips across the beam.

Cat Walk Sideward The student starts standing across the beam facing the side. She stoops down to grasp the beam with her hands. She walks sideward in this position by moving her left foot, left hand, right hand, and finally her right foot, in that order, to the left. This procedure is repeated until she has walked the length of the beam.

Pelican Stand The student stands on her right foot with her left foot placed against the side of her right knee. Her hands are on her hips.

Knee Scale The student starts in a kneeling position on the beam with one knee behind the other. She leans forward to grasp the beam with both hands and hyperextends her rear leg. In the final position, her arms are extended; she is supported on her two hands and one knee; her head is pulled backward and her back is arched.

Side Scale The student starts in a standing position facing sideward with her right foot along (rather than across) the beam. She bends her trunk sideward and at the same time lifts her

Full turn in a cat walk position

left leg until her trunk and her left leg form a straight line that is parallel to the beam. Her left arm should be extended backward along her body, and her right arm should be extended forward in line with her body.

Backward Roll The student starts in a supine position on the beam. She reaches over her head to grasp the underside of the beam with both hands, places her head to one side of the beam, and by pulling with her arms and bending her hips, rolls over backward. As she completes the roll, she places one knee on top of the beam. During a portion of the roll, her weight is supported on her shoulder. After coming around to her knee, she may go into a knee scale, or come up to her feet. The spotter should assist by grasping both hips of the gymnast and lifting upward.

V-Sit The student sits on the beam with her extended legs elevated to form a right angle with her trunk. Her trunk is at a 45° angle to the beam. She may hold the beam behind her hips with her thumbs on top and fingers on the side of the beam, or she may extend her arms sideward.

Backward roll

V-sit

Straddle stand

Front Scale The student stands on one foot, leans forward to bring her trunk to a position parallel to the beam and at the same time elevates her other leg until her back is nicely arched. Her toe should be pointed, her legs fully extended, her head pulled backward, and her back arched.

Straddle Stand The student stands across the beam facing sideward with her legs straddled, her trunk parallel to the floor, and her arms extended directly sideward.

Split The student starts in a standing position on the beam facing one end and slides one foot backward and the other forward until the entire undersides of both legs are in contact with the beam. Her arms may be extended horizontally sideward or she may hold the beam. Spot by standing alongside the gymnast, ready to catch her around the waist.

FLOOR EXERCISE

A number of skills have been described in Chapter 5 under self-testing activities that could be incorporated into floor exercise routines. These include:

V-Sit
Bridge
Jump and Tuck
Jump and Straddle Toe Touch
Jump and Jackknife
Jump and Half Turn
Side Scale
Jump and Full Turn
Jump and Full and a Half Turn
Jump and Double Turn
Jump and Swan
Single-Leg Circles
Front Scale

Several skills described in the section on tumbling can also be done as floor exercises. These include:

Front Break Fall
Half Turn into a Front Break Fall
Chest Roll from the Knees
Chest Roll from a Standing Position

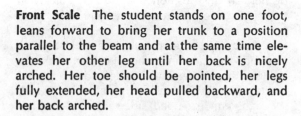

Front scale

Split

Dive and Forward Roll
Backward Rolls (all varieties)
Cartwheel
Necksprings (all varieties)
Headsprings (all varieties)
Front Handspring
Walk-Out Front Handspring
One-Arm Handspring
Round-Off

Several skills described in the section on the balance beam can be used as floor exercises. These include:

Knee Scale
Straddle Stand
Split

The skills just listed will not be described again. Additional floor exercise skills suitable for elementary school boys and girls will be described. Some of these are suitable for girls only, some for boys only, and some for both.

Toe Stand The students begin in a standing position and rise up on their toes extending their arms sideward with palms down. (Girls.)

Ballet Touch The students begin in a standing position with one foot forward. They flex their hips to touch the forward foot lightly with one hand and return to the standing position. (Girls.)

Body Sweep The students assume a position with their weight distributed on three points of support—the left hand, the left shin, and the inside of the right foot. They are sitting on their left heel. They swing their right arm across their body and raise their hips. (Boys and girls.)

Pirouette The students start in a standing position. They execute one or more full turns on the ball of the left foot by lifting their right foot off the floor and throwing their left arm across and around their body and throwing their right arm behind their body. The student should look straight ahead toward the starting direction as long as possible. When the head can no longer be held in this position, it is turned quickly in the direction of the turn. (Boys and girls.)

Stag Leap The student takes several steps to leap upward into an arched position with the right leg hyperextended. The left foot is placed inside the right knee with the left knee flexed, the right arm extended sideward, and the left arm extended overhead. She lands with feet apart and in balance. (Girls.)

Straddle Lean The students do a side split and then flex at the hips to bring their chest to the floor. (Boys and girls.)

Body Weave The students start in a standing position with their hands at their sides. They swing their arms forward-upward as they flex their knees and hips slightly. They then swing their arms backward-upward as they extend into an arched position and rise on their toes. (Girls.)

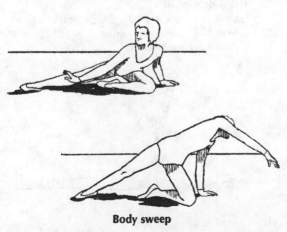

Body sweep

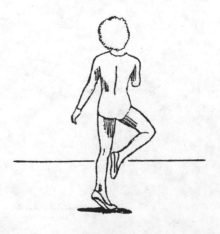

Pirouette

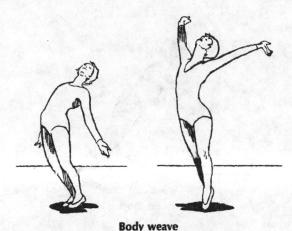

Body weave

Needle scale

One-leg balance

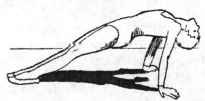

Arch-up

Back walk-over

Needle Scale The students start in the front scale position and then slowly flex their hips to grasp the shin of the supporting leg, or they may bring their hands to the floor with their head against the shin bone of their supporting leg. The other leg is elevated overhead until it is in line with the back. (Boys and girls.)

One-Leg Balance The students start in a standing position. They raise the left leg sideward as high as they can, grasp the instep with their left hand, and raise their left arm and leg sideward while maintaining balance. (Boys and girls.)

Arch-Up The students sit with their legs extended and their hands on the floor next to their hips, fingers pointing to the rear. They then push their hips upward to assume an arched position of the back. (Boys and girls.)

Back Walk-over The students start in a standing position. They bend backward until they can place their hands on the floor. They then kick one leg over their head and spring from the other to pass through the handstand position (with legs straddled forward and backward) and around to their feet. During the backward bend, they should carry their hips forward of their feet. They should pull their head backward throughout the move. Students should be spotted until they have learned the move. The spotter should kneel alongside the performer and assist with one hand in the middle of her back and the other under her shoulder. (Boys and girls.)

129

Forward drop

Front walk-over

Arabesque The students start in a standing position. They raise both arms forward-upward and lift one leg backward to assume a nicely arched position of the back. (Girls.)

Forward Drop This move is similar to the front break fall described in the section on tumbling except that one leg is raised backward during the fall. (Boys and girls.)

Shoulder Balance The students start in a supine position. They elevate their hips and legs over their head and then extend their legs and hips fully to balance on the back of their head, neck, and shoulders. Their arms may be placed along the floor or extended upward along the sides, or may be placed on the back. (Boys and girls.)

Squat Balance The students start in a squatting position with their arms between their legs; the hands are on the floor set shoulder width

Front Walk-over The students start in a standing position. They place their hands on the floor in front of their feet and kick up toward the handstand, continue on past the handstand (with legs straddled forward and backward), land on one foot, lift their hands off the floor, and whip the other leg over to return to the standing position. Their head should be pulled backward throughout the move. They should endeavor to push the hips forward of the foot after landing on it. The instructor should spot students on their initial attempts. Later, students can spot one another. The move should be mastered before being attempted without a spotter. The spotter should kneel alongside the performer and assist with one hand under the performer's shoulder and the other in the middle of the back. (Boys and girls.)

Shoulder balance

Squat balance

Forearm balance

apart. They place the inside of their knees on their upper arms just above their elbows, flex their arms to about a 130° angle, lean forward, lift one foot off the floor, lift the other foot off the floor, and hold the balanced position. Their head should be pulled backward throughout the move and their thighs should remain in contact with their upper arms. (Boys and girls.)

Head Balance The students start in a kneeling position with their hands on the floor a few inches in front of their knees. They place their head on the floor in front of their hands at such a point that the three points of support (head and two hands) form an equilateral triangle. They elevate their hips to a point directly overhead with their feet still on the floor. They then tuck their legs into their chest and extend them slowly overhead into an arched position. The students should resist the temptation to move their hands forward (in line with or beyond their head) because doing so may make them overbalance. If they overbalance, they should bend at the hips and knees and

roll over. The move should be learned on a mat before being attempted on the floor. (Boys and girls.)

Squat Balance into a Head Balance The students assume the squat balance position and then lower their heads to the floor in front of their hands. They next elevate their hips over their head with their legs tucked in. They then slowly extend their legs into the arched position. (Boys and girls.)

Forearm Balance The student begins in a kneeling position with his forearms on the floor; the palms are down and the index fingers and thumbs of the two hands are touching in such a manner as to form a hole into which the head is placed. He extends his right leg and swings it up overhead, at the same time springing off the left foot to upend into the balanced position. (Boys and girls.)

Elbow (Tiger) Balance The students start in a kneeling position with their forearms on the floor, parallel to one another with the palms down. They extend their right leg to swing it up overhead and spring off their left foot to upend into the balanced position. The head should be pulled backward and should not touch the floor. (Boys.)

Two-Arm Half Lever The students assume a kneeling position with their hands on the floor just outside their knees, fingers pointing to the

Head balance

Elbow (tiger) balance

Hand balance

rear. They extend their right leg and place their right elbow just inside the pelvic bone. They next extend the left leg and place their left elbow inside the pelvic bone. To complete the move, they lift their feet and pull the head and shoulders up to assume an arched position with the back parallel to the floor. The upper arms should be at no less than a right angle to the forearms throughout the move, and the forearms should be held perpendicular to the floor. (Boys.)

Hand Balance The students flex their knees slightly, stoop to place their hands on the floor set shoulder width apart, extend the right leg to swing it up overhead while springing off the left foot, and upend into the hand balance position. The arms should remain fully extended throughout the move. As the trunk and legs move overhead, the arms should be angled slightly forward of the vertical. After the feet are over the head, the arms should return to the vertical position. The head should be pulled backward throughout the move. An underbalance is checked by carrying the shoulders forward and bending the arms. An overbalance is checked by pulling the

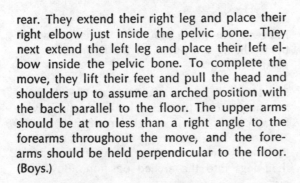

Two-arm half lever

head backward hard and pressing with the finger tips. The move is best learned with a partner who stands facing the back of the performer with one foot between the performer's hands. When the performer upends, the partner catches his ankles. He can prevent a cave-in of the arms by bending one knee so that the performer's shoulder rests on his thigh. He places the performer into position with his heels directly over his head, thereby helping him to gain the kinesthetic feel of the balanced position. As the performer gains skill, the spotter assists less and less.

The handstand can also be practiced against a wall. The hands should be placed 12 to 18 inches away from the wall. The feet rest against the wall. When the student feels he has secured balance, he can gently push first one foot away from the wall and then the other to hold the balance. When doing the hand balance without the assistance of the wall or a partner and an uncontrollable overbalance occurs, the student should pivot on one hand and flex at the hips to land on his feet facing sideward. (Boys and girls.)

Bent Arm–Straight Leg Press into a Head Balance The students begin in a kneeling position with the hands on the floor in front of the knees and their head on the floor in front of their hands. Keeping their legs fully extended, they move the hips over the head. After the hips are over the head, they extend their hips to move their feet over their head to complete the skill. (Boys and girls.)

Flying Leap The students take off from the left foot and leap into the air swinging the other leg forward to execute a half turn landing on the right foot in a front scale position. (Boys and girls.)

REBOUND TUMBLING (TRAMPOLINING)[4]

Jumping Techniques In rebound tumbling, a good jumping technique is basic to all the skills to be learned later.

During the initial lesson, after having explained the safety and maintenance procedures, the instructor should teach his class correct jumping procedures. He can do this most effectively by demonstrating on the trampoline. The students should be dispersed around the trampoline with sufficient interval between students to allow them freedom in swinging their arms. The instructor should explain and demonstrate the procedures and then ask the students to execute them with him while they are on the floor and he is on the trampoline. The students begin with their arms overhead and are asked to imagine that they are at the height of their jump and are in the act of dropping down. They bring their arms downward to their sides with their elbows slightly flexed. Their arms should be at about shoulder height at the time they simulate contacting the bed with their feet. Their arms continue the downward swing as the knees flex slightly and they imagine the bed being depressed under themselves. Then as the bed begins to move them upward in its rebound, they begin to extend their legs, bend their elbows, and begin to swing their arms and shoulders upward. During the upward swing of the arms, the hands should move vertically upward directly in front of and close to the body. At the height of the simulated jump, the arms should be fully extended overhead and the legs should also be fully extended.

At all times the body should be in good alignment with no inclination of the trunk either forward or backward. The head should be held erect. The eyes should be focused on the end

[4] All of the rebound tumbling events described in this section can be done by both boys and girls.

Kill spring

of the frame. The student should not look down at his feet or at the bed under his feet since this will bring his head out of alignment, which will impart a forward rotary force to his body. The student's arms should never be carried behind the frontal or lateral plane of his body. The height of the spring should be only gradually increased as control is developed. All skills, including plain jumping, should first be mastered with a low bounce. Precise *control* is more difficult to achieve than is the simple *accomplishment* of most skills.

Kill Spring This is a safety skill useful in the event that a student lands on his feet near the edge of the bed. On contact with the bed, the student absorbs the rebound of the bed by bending his knees and hips.

Jump and Tuck During his leap, the student draws his knees up toward his chest to grasp his shins momentarily in a tucked position. He then extends again to land on his feet. His back should be held vertical throughout the move. He should not bring his chest to his knees but instead should bring his knees to his chest.

Jump and tuck

Jump and straddle toe touch

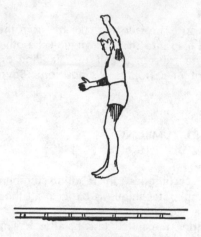

Jump and half turn

Jump and Straddle Toe Touch The student leaps into the air lifting his extended legs in a straddled position until they are at a right angle to his trunk, touches his toes, and extends his hips again to land on his feet. He should not incline his trunk forward to touch his toes. His back should be held vertical throughout the move.

Jump and Jackknife The student leaps into the air lifting his extended legs, feet together, to touch his toes with his hands, then drops his legs again to land on his feet. His back should remain vertical throughout the move.

Jump and Half Turn As the student leaves the bed, he throws this right arm across the front of his hips as if swatting a fly on his backside and pulls his other arm above his head. This action will cause him to pirouette.

Jump and Full Turn This move is executed in the same manner as the preceding one except

that a slightly harder initial throw is required. To stop the turning action, the student simply extends his arms sideward.

Jump and Full and a Half Turn The techniques of execution for this move are the same as those for the two preceding ones.

Knee Drop The student leaps straight up and bends his knees to land on his insteps, shins, and knees, then rebounds to his feet. His instep, shins, and knees should all contact the bed simultaneously. He should land with his hips extended (not hyperextended), and he should avoid "caving in" at the hips on landing. An arched position on landing may produce a strained back muscle. "Caving in" absorbs the bed's rebound with resulting insufficient lift.

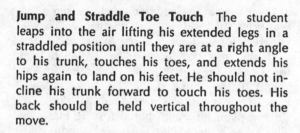

Jump and jackknife

Knee drop

Knee drop with half turn

Seat drop

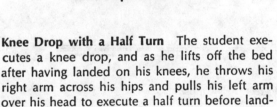

Knee Drop with a Half Turn The student executes a knee drop, and as he lifts off the bed after having landed on his knees, he throws his right arm across his hips and pulls his left arm over his head to execute a half turn before landing on his feet.

Knee Drop with a Full Turn The student executes a knee drop and as he lifts off his knees, executes a full pirouette following the same procedures as those described in executing a knee drop with a half turn.

Seat Drop As the student drops toward the bed, he flexes his hips to lift his legs so that he lands on his buttocks and the underside of his legs. He then rebounds to his feet. The student's feet should never be high above the bed. He should not suddenly flex the hips to bring the legs parallel to the bed. The hips are flexed, or the legs lifted, as he drops to the bed so that at the moment of landing his legs are parallel to the bed (but not before). His buttocks and the entire underside of both legs should contact the bed simultaneously. On contact, his hands should be alongside his buttocks with his fingers pointing forward. He should lean slightly forward as he rebounds from his seat.

Knee Drop into a Seat Drop The student does a knee drop, and as he rebounds from his knees, he flexes his hips and extends his knees to land in a seat drop position. In lifting off after the seat drop, if he will extend his hips and bend his knees, he will go back to the knee drop po-

sition. A good arm lift makes this combination easier. All action other than the arm lift should occur below the hips. The trunk should remain vertical throughout the execution of both moves. The students should first learn to do a knee drop to the feet followed by a seat drop to the feet to a knee drop. After having mastered this combination, they can learn to move directly from the seat drop to the knee drop to the seat drop without an intermediate spring onto the feet. Contests can be held to see which student can execute the greatest number of seat and knee drops in swing.

Seat Drop with a Half Twist to the Feet The student executes a seat drop, and as he rebounds from his seat he swings his arms over his head with his left arm pulling backward and his right arm pulling across his face. At the same time, he should turn his face to the left. These actions will cause him to twist. He should then pull his feet under his body. As he lifts off from his seat, the angle between his legs and hips should increase so that his feet are at no time high above the bed. Twists are more easily executed when the body is extended than when it is piked. The twist should be executed when the body is near a fully extended position.

Seat Drop with a Half Twist to the Seat (Swivel Hips) This move is initiated in the same manner as is the previous one except that instead of landing on his feet, the student lifts his leg in front of his body after having completed the half twist so that he lands on his seat again.

Seat drop with half twist to feet (swivel hips)

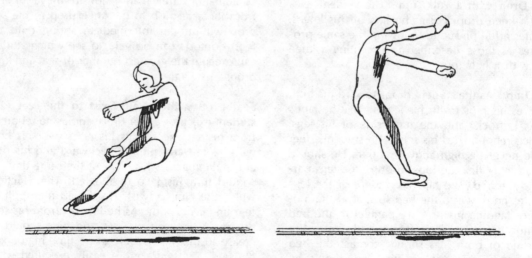

Seat drop with half twist to seat

Seat Drop with a Full Twist to the Seat When rebounding from the seat, the student leans slightly backward from his hips and allows his feet to stay low. These actions will cause his hips to move to the extended position. Twists are very difficult to perform in a piked position due to the centrifugal force generated at the end of the lever arm. The student follows the same procedures in executing the full twist that he did in doing the half twist except that the twist is executed with the body in a nearly horizontal position. As he completes the twist, he flexes his hips to bring his trunk to the vertical position again so that he lands on his seat.

Seat drop with full twist to seat

Hands and Knee Drop As the student leaps upward, he elevates his hips until they are at the same height as his head. He then drops to the bed landing simultaneously on his hands, knees, and shins. He rebounds to his feet by lifting his head, pushing off his hands, and pushing his hips forward.

Front Drop While teaching this move, the instructor should remove two springs (or shock cord) from the center of one side. This will enable him to stand between the bed and frame of the trampoline and place him in a more favorable spotting position. In the event the student lands on the bed in the front drop with either his chest or his legs leading, the instructor can extend his arms over the legs and back of the student to prevent him from hyperextending his back.

The student should first "get the feel" of the landing by lying prone on the bed with his arms overhead and his forearms in contact with the bed. Next, the student should go into the front drop from a standing position with no preliminary bounces. It should be emphasized that there should be no travel, i.e., that the trajectory should be straight up and down. The abdomen should land on the spot where the feet last left the mat. The landing should be made with the abdomen striking the bed first and with the arms overhead at a 45° angle to the body and the elbows flexed at about a 135° angle. The student's body will pivot on its horizontal axis from the vertical to the horizontal position while in the air, when the student lifts his hips, drops his head, and moves into a loosely tucked position. After his body has pivoted 90°, the student extends his body for the front drop landing. He rebounds from his abdomen to his feet by flexing his hips to bring his feet under his body.

Hands and knee drop

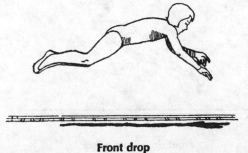

Front drop

137

Front drop from a jackknife

Half turntable

Front Drop from a Jackknifed Position During his leap, the student lifts his hips, drops his trunk to touch the toes of his extended legs, and then extends his hips to lift his legs and his trunk. These actions place his body into a horizontal position for the front drop landing.

Front Drop from a Swan Position The student pulls directly into a swan position out of his leap by pulling his head, shoulders, and arms upward and backward and by hyperextending his hips. At the height of his leap, while in the swan position, the student's body should be at a 45° angle to the bed. As he drops toward the bed, his body will pivot about its horizontal axis so that he will land on his abdomen with his body horizontal.

Half Turntable The student executes a front drop, and as he rebounds from his front, he

pushes sideward against the bed with his hands, tucks, and pulls his head and trunk sidewards. He pivots around his transverse axis with his front toward the bed throughout the move until he has completed a 180° turn. At this time, he extends his body again to land on his front. The student's feet should not move under his body. They should move around to the side in a circular pattern. He should resist the temptation to open up before he has completed the turn.

Full Turntable The full turntable is executed in the same manner as is the half turntable except that the movements must be initiated with greater vigor and it may be necessary to delay the extension of the body slightly longer in order to complete the turn.

Back Drop In teaching the back drop, as in teaching the front drop, the instructor should

Front drop from a swan

Full turntable

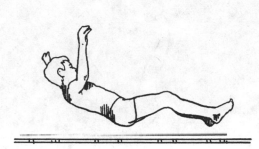 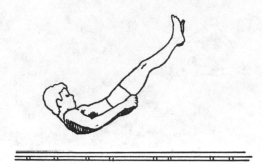

Back drop

stand between the bed and the frame. He should hold the performer's near wrist with one hand and his near ankle with the other.

The performer should first "get the feel" of the landing position by lying on his back with his hips off the bed and his legs elevated at a 130° angle to his trunk. Next, the student should learn to do the back drop from a standing position with no bounce. To do this, the student, on take-off, should lift his legs forward-upward to land on his upper back in a piked position. After landing on his back, he should extend at the hips (kip) to come back up to his feet. His head should remain in alignment with his trunk throughout the move. The instructor can help the student to learn the kinesthetic feel of the movements by assisting him in moving through the positions while holding his ankle and wrist.

Having progressed this far, the student is ready to learn the back drop from a bounce. His first attempts should be with a low bounce. As he gains skill, he can increase the height of his bounce.

Back Drops in Swing Time The student rebounds from his back to his feet and immediately moves into another back drop. In rebounding from his back to his feet, he should not come completely to the upright position. His back should remain slightly behind a line drawn from his feet that is perpendicular to the bed. This will make it easier to move into the succeeding back drop. With the development of skill, he will be able to do successively lower back drops and then build them up successively higher.

Back Drop from a Layout Position The student takes a high bounce pushing his chest and hips

upward and allowing his legs to drag with his head forward. Then just before he strikes the bed, he lifts his legs by flexing his hips to land on his upper back. With the exception of the forward head, the move, at its outset, looks like a back somersault in layout position.

Back Drop to a Back Drop The student lands on his upper back, extends his hips to "kick" his legs almost directly upward and lands on his upper back again. He does this repeatedly. He should avoid pulling his head forward or hyperextending his hips. His hips and feet should at times be over his head.

Back Drop with a Half Twist The student executes a back drop and as he rebounds from his back, pulls his left arm across his chest as though slapping a fly on his right shoulder. At the same time, he turns his head to the right.

Back drop to a back drop

Back drop with a half twist

Turnover to back from knee drop

These actions cause him to turn about and he then lands on his feet facing the opposite direction.

Cradle The student executes a back drop with a half twist, but instead of landing on his feet, he pulls his legs under his body and over his head to land on his back.

Before learning this move, the student should master the back drop with a half twist and the back drop with a half twist to a seat drop.

Cat Twist The student executes a back drop of the type he would do if he intended to drop back onto his back. In other words, he does not hyperextend his hips or bring his head forward.

Cat twist

His feet and hips remain above his head throughout the move. As he rebounds off his back, he throws his left arm across his chest and turns his head and shoulders to his right. This will cause him to twist around completely with his body in an extended and nearly vertical position and to land on his upper back.

Front Drop into a Back Drop After rebounding from the front drop, the student flexes his hips to pull his extended legs under his body and over his head to land on his upper back. He then executes a back drop.

Back Drop into a Front Drop The student executes a back drop, but instead of landing on his feet, he pulls his legs under his body and backward to land on his front. He should lift his hips in moving into the front drop position.

Front Turnover to the Back from the Knee Drop The student lands in the knee drop with his hips slightly bent and his thighs angled slightly backward. This take-off position will cause his hips to move upward at a faster rate than his head, thus initiating the flip. The student lifts his arms upward and then moves into the tucked position grasping his shins and bringing his head and trunk forward and downward. He should use very little bounce in order to land on his back.

Turnover to seat from knee drop

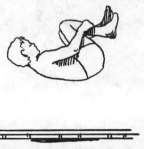

Front somersault from the feet

Front Turnover to the Back from the Feet This move is done in exactly the same manner as the preceding one except that the student begins from his feet.

Front Turnover to the Seat from a Knee Drop This move is done in exactly the same manner as the front turnover to the back from a knee drop except that the student turns over slightly farther to land on his seat.

Front Turnover to the Seat from the Feet This is the next step in the progressions toward a front somersault. It is executed in exactly the same manner as is the preceding move except that it is begun from the feet.

Front Somersault from the Knees This move is done in the same manner as a front turnover to the seat from a knee drop except that the student continues the somersault around to his feet. The student must tuck tightly on this move. Spotters, particularly at the ends of the trampoline, are mandatory.

Front Somersault from the Feet The procedures in executing a front somersault from the feet are the same as those for executing the move from the knees except that the problem of control becomes greater, particularly with respect to overspin. The move should be learned with a very low spring. Height can be increased as control and self-assurance are gained.

Front turnover to back from feet

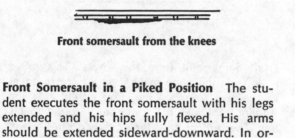

Front somersault from the knees

Front somersault in a piked position

Front Somersault in a Piked Position The student executes the front somersault with his legs extended and his hips fully flexed. His arms should be extended sideward-downward. In order that he not travel and so that his trajectory will be straight up and down, his hips should be slightly behind his feet at the moment of take-off and his hips should be slightly bent.

Front One and One-Quarter Somersault into the Front Drop The student overspins his front somersault until he can see the bed, at which time he extends his hips and knees to land in a front drop position. After mastering the move in a tucked position, the student may wish to attempt it in a piked position. The instructor should position himself between the bed and frame and follow the spotting procedures previously described for a front drop.

Backover to Hands and Knees The student lands on his upper back, but instead of extending his hips and pulling his head forward as he would do in executing a back drop to his feet, he flexes his hips and pulls his head backward after rebounding from his back. This action enables him to do a partial back somersault to his hands and knees.

Backover to the Feet The student follows the same procedures that he did to do a backover to the hands and knees except that by pulling slightly more vigorously, he will come around to his feet.

Back Somersault with Hand Spotting At the moment of take-off, the back is hyperextended, and the student's arms are lifting upward and backward. He then brings his knees to his chest

Front 1¼ somersault to front drop

Backover to the feet

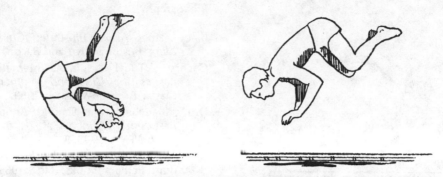

Backover to hands and knees

and grasps his shins in a tightly tucked position, pulling his head backward to somersault around. When he has completed the somersault, he should extend his hips and legs sharply and fully and pull his head forward into alignment with his spinal column. He should extend his knees and his hips at the same time.

To spot, the instructor should stand on the trampoline with the student. He should stand to the student's right holding his trousers or twisted shirt with his left hand and use his right hand to assist him in the somersaulting action by tapping him behind the hips. With a little practice,

the instructor will learn to coordinate his own knee bends with the bounces of the student. As the student gains proficiency, the instructor can use only his right hand to tap the student around. An overhead belt, of course, can also be used.

Back Somersault Unassisted Having mastered the previous move, the student is ready to attempt the somersault unassisted. Spotters should be stationed on all four sides of the trampoline, and the instructor should position himself between the bed and the frame.

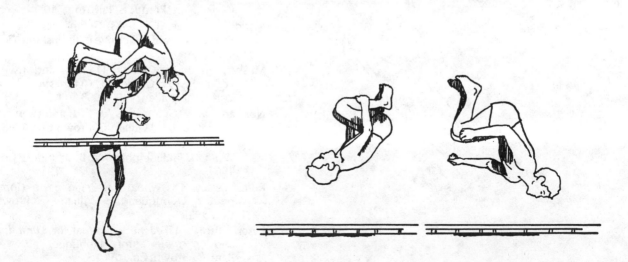

Back somersault with hand spotting

Back somersault unassisted

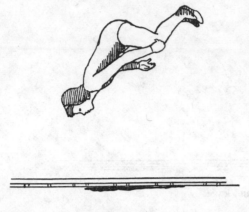

Swingback

Swingback This is a somersault with the body in a piked rather than a tucked position. The student initiates the move in the same manner as he would a tucked back somersault except that he flexes only his hips, keeping his legs extended.

Back Somersault in Layout Position The student initiates the move from a high bounce. At the height of his leap, he pulls his arms, head, and upper back backward hard, and lifts his chest. He somersaults around with his body arched and his legs fully extended. Just before landing, he flexes his hips slightly.

Back somersault in layout position

Bibliography

Baley, James A. *An Illustrated Guide to Tumbling.* Boston: Allyn and Bacon, Inc., 1968.

Cochrane, Tuovi Sappinen. *International Gymnastics for Girls and Women.* Reading, Mass.: Addison-Wesley, 1969.

Drury, Blanche J., and Schmid, Andrea B. *Gymnastics for Women.* Palo Alto, Calif.: The National Press, 1965.

Dunn, Walter G. *Gymnastics for Schools.* London: Pelham Books, Ltd., 1965.

Edwards, Vannie M. *Tumbling.* Philadelphia: W. B. Saunders Co., 1969.

Griswold, Larry. *Trampoline Tumbling.* Fred Medart Manufacturing Co., 1948.

Holzaepfel, Norman R. *Gymnastics, How to Do It.* Schillar Park, Ill.: Porter Athletics Equipment Co., 1964.

Horne, Virginia Lee. *Stunts and Tumbling for Girls.* New York: Ronald Press Co., 1943.

Kenny, Charles J. *Fundamental Tumbling Skills Illustrated.* New York: Ronald Press Co., 1966.

Ladue, Frank, and Norman, James. *This Is Trampolining.* Nissen Trampoline Co., 1954.

Laporte, William R., and Rennar, A. G. *The Tumbler's Manual.* Englewood Cliffs, N.J.: Prentice-Hall, Inc., 1938.

Loken, Newton C., and Willoughby, Robert J. *Complete Book of Gymnastics.* Englewood Cliffs, N.J.: Prentice-Hall, Inc., 1959.

Maddax, Gordon T. *Men's Gymnastics.* Pacific Palisades, Calif.: Goodyear Publishing Co., 1970.

Musker, Frank F., Casady, Donald, and Irwin, Leslie W. *A Guide to Gymnastics.* New York: Macmillan Co., 1968.

Norman, Randi. *Gymnastics for Girls and Women.* Dubuque, Ia.: William C. Brown Co., 1965.

Roys, Betty Maycock. *Gymnastics for Girls and Women.* Philadelphia: W. B. Saunders Co., 1969.

Ruff, Wesley K. *Gymnastics, Beginner to Competitor.* Dubuque, Ia.: William C. Brown Co., 1959.

Ryser, Otto E. *A Teacher's Manual for Tumbling and Apparatus Stunts.* Dubuque, Ia.: William C. Brown Co., 1961.

Szypula, George. *Tumbling and Balancing for All.* Dubuque, Ia.: William C. Brown Co., 1957.

United States Gymnastic Federation. *Age Group Gymnastics Workbook*. United States Gymnastic Federation, 1964.

United States Naval Institute, Aviation Training Division Office of the Chief of Naval Operations. *Gymnastics and Tumbling*. United States Naval Institute, 1943.

West, Wilbur. *The Gymnast's Manual*. Englewood Cliffs, N.J.: Prentice-Hall, Inc., 1955.

Yeager, Patrick A. *A Teacher's Guide for Tumbling and Pyramids*. Statesboro, Ga.: Wide World Publications, 1963.

7

SKILLS FOR JUNIOR HIGH SCHOOL BOYS AND GIRLS

All of the skills presented in this chapter have been done by boys and girls of junior high school age. However, no child of junior high school age has done all of the skills, nor is it likely that any will; "but a man's reach should exceed his grasp,/or what's a heaven for?"

Junior high school children who have had no previous instruction in the activities described in this chapter should first receive instruction in the skills described in Chapter 6. Gymnastics, like swimming, diving, mathematics, foreign languages, or, for that matter, most any subject, must be taught in such a manner that skills and knowledge become progressively more difficult. Fundamentals must be mastered in order to provide a foundation for more advanced work. If this procedure is followed, participants will experience less frustration and a greater measure of success.

Junior high school children, it is believed, possess the strength, neuromuscular development, and capacity to comprehend that are necessary to learn the skills described in this chapter—provided they have mastered the fundamental skills described in Chapter 6.

DOUBLES BALANCING

Stand on Shoulders. The partners begin by facing one another. They grasp one another's right hand as though shaking hands. The topmounter steps close to the right side of the understander and facing him so that the frontal or lateral plane of his body is at right angles to that of the understander. They grasp left hands. The understander squats with his back perpendicular to the floor. His left upper arm is horizontal, with his elbow forward, and his left forearm is held vertically. His right forearm is held vertically. The topmounter steps with his right toe onto the understander's right thigh as close to the trunk as possible. As he does this, he pushes directly downward on his partner's hands. He then steps with his left toe onto his partner's left shoulder and then with his right toe onto his partner's right shoulder. Only his toes should be on his partner's shoulders. His heels should be drawn downward and be pulled together. During the process of mounting, he should avoid introducing a lateral component of

Mounting to a stand on shoulders

force upon his partner. He should endeavor to keep his weight centered directly over his partner.

The understander should next release the right hand hold to grasp the belly of his partner's right calf or gastrocnemius muscle. He then grasps the left gastrocnemius muscle in the same manner. He should pull his head backward and pull forward and downward with his hands (with his elbows pointing sideward) to wedge his partner's legs between his head and hands, thereby making one unit of the two bodies.

The topmounter must avoid bending at the hips or neck and must avoid "flapping" his arms. His hands should be placed on his hips and he should look directly forward.

Stand on shoulders

The understander should stand with his feet spread laterally, one forward and one backward. His knees should be slightly bent and his back should be perpendicular to the floor.

To dismount, the partners regrasp one hand at a time, and the topmounter jumps forward and "rides" his partner's hands down. Or he can dismount by moving to a sitting position on his partner's shoulders. The understander then squats and stoops to bring his partner's feet to the mat. A more spectacular dismount is when the partners fall forward as a unit and then, when they are at about a 45° angle to the floor, the topmounter jumps off his partner's shoulders to his own feet. Both then immediately execute a forward roll.

The topmounter can also mount into the stand on shoulders from a sitting position on his partner's shoulders. In this method, the partners grasp hands and the topmounter pushes downward on his partner's hands while he pulls one foot under himself and onto his partner's shoulder. He repeats this procedure with the other foot. He then stands up and the understander grasps the topmounter's calves. While standing on the shoulders, the topmounter must keep his knees slightly bent and his back vertical. (Two boys or a boy as the understander and a girl as the topmounter.)

Two or three spotters should be used until the skill has been mastered.

Low Hands to Feet In the starting position, the understander is lying on his back with his

Low hands to feet

Low front swan on hands

extended legs elevated and his hands on the mat next to his ears with the palms facing upward. The topmounter is standing with his heels in his partner's hands and is holding his feet. On a signal, the topmounter leaps directly upward and pushes downward on his partner's feet. As he does this, the understander extends his arms. The understander should lock his elbows and hold his arms perpendicular to the floor. After balance has been secured, the topmounter releases his grip on his partner's feet, places his hands on his hips or along his sides and comes to the erect position. He should allow the understander to do all the balancing and should avoid movement of any kind including flexing his ankles or hips or waving his arms. A spotter should stand directly behind the topmounter until the skill has been mastered. (Two boys or a boy and a girl.)

Low Back Swan on Hands In the starting position, the understander is lying on his back with his arms extended upward and his hands

Low back swan on hands

on his partner's hips. The topmounter is standing astraddle of his partner's hips and facing his feet; he arches and lies backward onto his partner's hands. In the final position, the understander's arms will be perpendicular to the floor and the topmounter will be in an arched position with his legs extended, toes pointed, head pulled backward, and his arms extended in a direction between sideward and overhead, depending upon the location of his center of gravity. (Two boys or a boy and a girl.)

Low Front Swan on Hands The starting positions for both the understander and the topmounter are the same as for the low back swan on hands, except that the topmounter faces his partner's head in the starting position and his front is down in the final position. The understander places his hands on his partner's hip bones. The topmounter places his hands on his partner's shoulders, shifts his weight from his feet to his partner's hands, and pulls his head, trunk, and legs upward to assume an arched position as illustrated. He then extends his arms sideward or forward to strike the balanced position. The understander's arms must be perpendicular to the floor. (Two boys or a boy and a girl.)

Low Arm to Arm Balance In the starting position, the understander is in a supine position with his arms extended upward, his knees bent, and his feet flat on the floor near his buttocks. The topmounter's hands are on his partner's knees and his shoulders are in his partner's hands. The topmounter swings his right leg over his head and springs off his left foot to upend in the hand-knee shoulder balance. As he upends, he should extend his arms horizontally in order that his understander be enabled to re-

Low arm to arm balance

Jump and turn

ceive all his weight on his vertically extended arms. After the balance has been secured, the topmounter shifts his weight to his right shoulder and transfers his left hand from his partner's knee to his right upper arm. After shifting the major portion of his weight to his left side, the topmounter releases the understander's knee to grasp his left upper arm with his own right hand to complete the moves. In the final position, the topmounter's head should be pulled backward, his back should be arched, and his feet should be directly over his head, while the understander's arms should be perpendicular to the floor. (Two boys, two girls, or a boy as understander and a girl as topmounter.)

Pull-up to stand on thighs facing

Pull-Up to Stand on Thighs Facing   In the starting position, the understander is lying on his back with his feet flat on the floor as close to his buttocks as he can place them; his hips are up so as to present a horizontal thigh surface for his partner to stand on, his knees are forward of his feet, and his right hand is grasping the right hand of his partner. The topmounter is standing facing his partner with his toes on the understander's knees and grasping his right hand with his own right hand. The topmounter moves his hips backward to angle his extended legs backward, meanwhile keeping his right arm extended. At the same time, the understander allows his knees to move still further forward of his feet. These actions will cause the understander's back to be lifted off the mat. As he comes up, the topmounter should extend his hips. The move is completed when the partners have assumed the position illustrated. (Two boys or a boy and a girl.)

Jump and Turn   In the starting position, the understander is in a crab position, that is, on his hands and feet facing upward. His arms and lower legs should be perpendicular to the floor, and his hips should be extended. The topmounter is standing with his toes on his partner's knees. His heels should be in the air and he should be in good posture. On a signal, the topmounter leaps directly upward, drawing his knees up toward his chest. The moment his partner leaves his knees, the understander spins around

149

to land on his hands and knees facing downward. He should keep his hips low as he spins. The topmounter extends his knees to land on his partner's hip bones in good balance. While students are learning this move, the topmounter should be spotted by two or three students.

Partners may move into the starting position for this skill from the final position of the pull-up to stand on thighs facing. To do this, the understander will place his left hand on the mat behind his hips. His fingers should point to the rear. He will then release his grasp with his right hand and place this hand behind his hips. The partners will now be in the starting position for the jump and turn. (Two boys or a boy and a girl.)

Lever Around the Chest The topmounter kicks up into the handstand, and the understander steps up to him from the front, grasps his ankles to place his partner's legs under his own arms, and then grasps his partner's hip bones. The understander arches backward while the topmounter also arches backward to lift himself to the mat; when the topmounter is high enough off the mat, he places his hands on his partner's knees. This is made possible because the topmounter's body serves as a third-class lever; the fulcrum is the back of his knees, which are prevented from moving by the underarms of his partner, and the force is the understander's pull on his hips; the weight is the topmounter's trunk. The move can also be done with the topmounter's arms extended sideward. (Two boys.)

HORIZONTAL BAR AT CHEST HEIGHT

Back Pull-Over The student faces the bar to grasp it with both hands in a front grip. He then lifts both feet off the floor to pull his legs under the bar and between his arms. Next, he extends his knees and hips to push his feet above and as far to the opposite side of the bar as he can. His head is forward. He pulls as hard as he can with his arms to place his center of gravity over the bar. His body then rotates to place him in the final position sitting on the bar. (Boys or girls.)

Lever around the chest

Backward Double-Knee Circle The student starts in a sitting position on the bar with a front grip with his hands as close to his hips as possible. He raises his body slightly, moves his hips backward to catch the bar behind his knees, extends his arms, and throws his head backward to initiate the rotary movement. When his body is in an inverted position, he pulls with his arms and pushes his hips over the top of the bar to finish in a sitting position on top of the bar. As he completes the move, he should shift his wrists behind his hands in order to be enabled to check his rotary movement and to better support his body. A spotter should stand in front of the bar facing the student to be in position to assist during the last half of the rotation. (Boys or girls.)

Back Hip Circle (Muscle Grinder) The student starts in a sitting position on the bar, grasping it with a front grip. He lowers his body as far as possible by flexing his arms. He then releases his right hand to pass the right arm behind the bar.

Back pull-over

He does the same with his left arm. The bar is now between his back and his upper arms. He interlaces his fingers in front of his abdomen or grasps his pants, shirt, or belt. He next lifts his extended legs by flexing his hips and whips them backward to cause his body to rotate around the bar. To dismount from this position, it would be advisable that another student assist the performer by lifting him until he can disengage his arms.

While this skill cannot be used in competitive gymnastics, students enjoy doing it and in competing with one another to see who can do the most consecutive "muscle grinders." The skill lends itself well to exhibition work since the audience can count and a drum can beat for each "muscle grinder." Some students will be able to do a hundred or more consecutive "muscle grinders." (Boys.)

Backward Hip Circle The student starts in a front support position on the bar with a front grip. To initiate the move, he flexes his arms slightly to position his body so that he can flex his hips. He swings his legs forward slightly and then swings them backward as he extends his arms. He then swings his legs forward and pulls his head backward, arching his back while holding himself against the bar with his arms extended. These actions will cause his body to rotate around the bar. As he passes through the inverted position, he flexes slightly at the hips to shorten his radius and thereby accelerate his speed of rotation. As he completes the hip circle, he checks his rotation by arching his body. A spotter should stand in front of the bar and facing the performer's plane of motion in order to give him aid in circling the bar if necessary. (Boys and girls.)

Backward Free Hip Circle The starting position and the techniques of execution for the backward free hip circle are the same as those for the backward hip circle. The only difference is that the movements are more vigorous and the hips are a few inches away from the bar during the circling. (Boys.)

Frontward Hip Circle The student starts in a front support position with a front grip on the bar. He elevates his hips to place the upper part

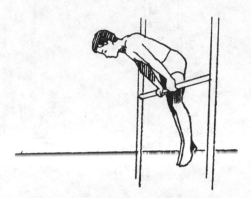

Frontward hip circle

of his thighs against the bar. He extends his arms, elevates his chest, and stretches his head forward to bring a greater portion of his weight in front of the bar. These actions will initiate his rotation. As he passes through the inverted position under the bar, he pulls the bar toward his thighs with his extended arms, pulls his head forward, and extends his hips to whip his legs around and to return to the starting position. A spotter should stand alongside the performer to push on his back to aid him in coming around. (Boys and girls.)

Rear Vault Dismount The student starts in a front support position with a front grip on the bar. He flexes his arms slightly to place his hip joints against the bar. He flexes his hips to swing his legs first forward and then backward. As his legs swing backward, he extends his arms and carries his shoulders forward of the bar. He then lets go with his left arm as he brings his legs to

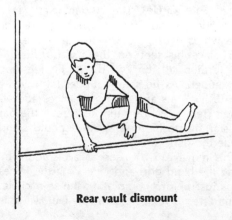

Rear vault dismount

151

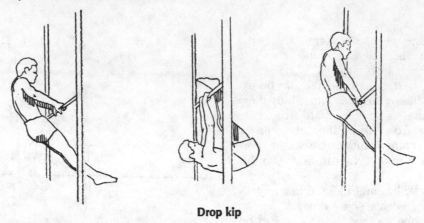

Drop kip

his left over the bar and under his left arm; he shifts his weight to his right arm, turns so that his rear passes over the bar, regrasps the bar with his left hand, and lands facing the side. A spotter should stand in front of the bar and behind the performer ready to catch him under the arms in the event he misses the move. (Boys.)

Drop Kip The student starts in a front support position with a front grip on the bar. He drops backward, at the same time bringing his toes to the bar with his legs and arms held in an extended position. His piked body swings forward in a pendular movement. When it begins to swing backward, he extends his hips to kick his legs upward, forward, then downward. This will cause his body to rotate under, around, and above the bar to enable the gymnast to complete the move in a support position above the bar. A spotter standing alongside the performer can help him to move above the bar. (Boys.)

Backward Sole Circle The student starts in a front support position with a front grip on the bar. He whips his legs backward and flexes his hips to place his feet on the bar outside his hands. He then falls backward with his legs and arms extended. As he swings under the bar, he pulls with his arms and flexes his knees and elbows sufficiently to bring himself above the bar to the starting position. A spotter should stand alongside the performer.

This move can be used as a dismount by releasing the hand grip and extending the knees and hips just before completing the sole circle. The gymnast will then land on his feet with his

back toward the bar. A spotter should stand alongside the anticipated landing point of the gymnast to guard against over- or underspin. These can be checked by the spotter by extending his arm across the gymnast's chest in the event of an underspin and across his back in the event of an overspin. (Boys and girls.)

Forward Sole Circle The starting position for this move is the same as for the backward sole circle except that the reverse grip is used. The move is initiated when the student whips his legs backward and flexes his hips to place his feet on the bar outside his hands. He extends his head forward and holds his arms and legs extended as he initiates the forward rotation. As he passes through the inverted position under the bar, he flexes his arms and legs to shorten his radius. This will accelerate his speed of rotation and cause him to ride up above the bar. A spotter should stand alongside the performer. (Boys and girls.)

HIGH HORIZONTAL BAR (7–8 FEET)

Kip The student starts in a standing position slightly behind the bar. He leaps upward to grasp the bar with a front grip. His body swings forward and then backward. During the backward swing, the gymnast flexes his arms and hips to bring his toes to the bar with his legs maintained in an extended position. He completes his backward swing with his body in a jackknifed position. Near the end of the forward swing he extends his arms and hips to push away from the bar. These actions initiate the swing necessary

Back uprise

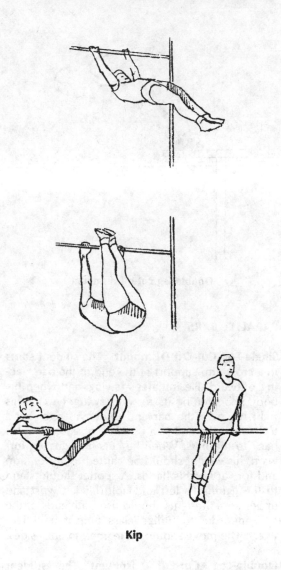

Kip

for the kip. The same procedure is also utilized to secure the swing necessary to do the back uprise. In the kip a small swing is used while in the back uprise a big swing is necessary.

The gymnast's body swings backward with his arms extended. His body then swings forward under the bar. As it does, the performer arches his back to lead with his abdomen. Near the end of this forward swing, the gymnast flexes his hips to bring his toes to the bar. As his body begins to swing backward in a jackknifed position, he extends his hips and pulls downward with his extended arms to complete the move in a front support position above the bar. (Boys.)

Back Uprise This move is initiated in the same manner as is the kip. The procedure used is described in the first paragraph of the procedures describing the kip. However, the big swing must be secured.

As his body swings backward, the gymnast flexes his hips slightly and pulls downward

hard with his extended arms to complete the move in a front support position. (Boys.)

Back (Reverse) Kip The student initiates a swing as previously described. Just before the end of the forward swing is reached, the gymnast flexes his hips to bring his feet between his hands and under the bar. He swings backward in the jackknifed position. In his forward swing, just after he passes the center of the swing, he extends his hips, arches his back, and pulls his head backward to complete the move in a sitting position on the bar. A spotter should stand directly under the bar. (Boys.)

Back (reverse) Kip

153

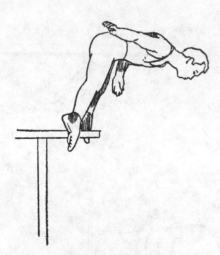

Double-leg cut-off dismount

Double-leg cut-off over one bar

PARALLEL BARS[1]

Single-Leg Cut-Off Dismount The student starts in a cross arm support at the end of the bars, facing outward. He initiates a swing, and when his body is beginning its forward swing, he cuts his right leg over the bar and under his right hand to land on the mat in a standing position with his back to the bars. When he cuts his right leg forward, his weight should be shifted to his left arm and forward of his hands. A spotter should stand to the gymnast's left and hold his left wrist and upper arm. Students should use both ends of the bars in order to utilize class time more effectively. The move should be learned to both sides.

Double-Leg Cut-Off Dismount The student starts in a cross arm support at the end of the bars facing outward. He initiates a swing and when his body is in a horizontal position at the end of its backward swing and it is beginning to swing forward, he flexes at the hips to cut both legs over both bars and under both hands to land in an erect position with his back to the end of the bars. He should angle his arms forward during the cut and avoid hyperextending his back after the cut before landing. A spotter should stand directly in front of the performer ready to catch him under the arms in the event of a miss.

[1] All skills on the parallel bars are to be performed by boys only.

The spotter should not stand so close to the gymnast that he hampers his movements. The class should use both ends of the bars simultaneously in order to utilize class time more effectively. Students should first learn to do the move with the bars at their lowest level and after each successful attempt move them up one notch until they have succeeded at the regulation height.

Double-Leg Cut-Off over One Bar The student starts in a cross arm support at the end of the bars facing outward. He initiates a swing, and at the end of the backward swing, when he is beginning to swing forward and his body is in a horizontal position, flexes his hips to cut both legs over the right bar and under his right hand to land in an erect position with his back to the end of the bars. As he initiates the cut-off, he shifts his weight to his left arm. Students should learn to do the move to both sides. Both ends of the bars should be used simultaneously in order to utilize class time most effectively. A spotter should hold the wrist and upper arm of the gymnast's supporting arm until the student has mastered the move.

Rear Vault Dismount with a Half Twist The rear vault dismount has been described in the section on parallel bars for elementary school children. To do the rear vault dismount with a

Single-leg cut-on mount

Double-leg cut-on over one bar

half twist, the gymnast extends his hips during the vault and turns his head toward the bar after he has regrasped the bar with his right hand. This will cause his body to turn in a clockwise direction toward the bar. As he completes the turn, the performer will grasp the bar with his left hand. A spotter should stand alongside the performer ready to catch him in the event of a miss.

The move may also be done with a half-twist in a counterclockwise direction away from the bar. To do this, the gymnast extends vigorously at the hips, turns his head toward his left, and pushes off his right hand as his hips clear the bar. He will land in an erect position alongside the bars facing in the opposite direction from his starting position.

Single-Leg Cut-On Mount The student starts in a standing position on the mat facing the end of the bars, grasping them with an outside grip. The gymnast leaps upward, pulling and then pushing (after his shoulders are above his hands) with his arms. His hips are behind his hands. As he comes into the cross arm support position, he shifts his weight to his right arm and cuts his left leg over the bar and under his left arm. He regrasps the bar to complete the move in a cross arm support position. Students should first learn the move with the bars at their lowest level and after each successful attempt move the bars up one notch for the next attempt. Both ends of the bars should be used. A spotter should stand directly behind the performer ready to catch him under the arms if he should miss.

Double-Leg Cut-On over One Bar This move is done in the same manner as the single-leg cut-on mount except that both legs pass simultaneously over the left bar and under the left hand. The lean to the right must be slightly greater, however. As in the other mounts, both ends of the bar should be used simultaneously by class members. Spotters should stand behind the performers, ready to catch them under the arms. Students should start at the lowest level of the bars, moving them up one notch after each successful attempt.

Double-Leg Cut-On Mount The initial movements and procedures for the double-leg cut-on mount are identical to those for the preceding two moves. However, the right leg passes over the right bar while the left leg passes over the left bar. The move is completed when the gymnast catches in a cross arm support position. The gymnast should start from a position standing with his toes just behind an imaginary perpendicular line dropped from the ends of the bars. Beginning students often fail because they start from a stand so far from the bars that their trajectory leads directly into the bars. The trajectory described by the body should be almost directly upward. Another error that students frequently commit is that of attempting to elevate the hips too high. This increases the difficulty of elevating the feet. The hips need to be only slightly higher than the bars, with the legs being lifted to a right angle to the trunk on

Double-leg cut-on mount

Single-leg cut and catch in the center of the bars

clearing the bars. The trunk should be nearly vertical throughout the stunt.

Following are recommended progressions for learning this skill:

1. Start with the bars at their lowest level and move up a notch at a time after each successful attempt.
2. At each height, first jump to a straddle seat position with the legs behind the hands.
3. After succeeding in doing the above, jump to a straddle seat position with the legs in front of the hands after having cut them under the hands. The student can then see that to complete the move, it will be necessary only that he bring his legs together before they land on the bar.
4. Having progressed this far, the student should attempt the complete move.

The spotter standing directly behind the gymnast can push up on his buttocks to lift him over the bar and to give him confidence.

Single-Leg Cut and Catch in the Center of the Bars The student starts in a cross arm support position at the center of the bars. He initiates a swing, and when his body is horizontal and beginning its forward swing, he shifts his weight to his right arm and flexes his left hip to cut the left leg over the bar and under his left hand. This movement must be made very quickly. He catches the bar to finish in a cross arm support between the bars. A very small swing is needed.

After learning to do the move with the left leg, the student should learn it with the right leg.

Double-Leg Cut and Catch over One Bar The techniques of execution for this move are identical to those for the single-leg cut and catch with the exception that both legs are cut simultaneously over the bar. A slightly greater lean in the direction of the supporting arm is necessary. The move should be learned to both sides.

Front Uprise to a Straddle Seat The student starts in an upper arm hang position at the center of the bars. He initiates a swing and executes the move during the forward swing of his body. On this forward swing, as his feet come under his body, the gymnast arches his back to lead with his hips while dragging his feet. He maintains this arched position until his body is about 45° beyond the vertical. At this time, he quickly flexes his hips and pulls with his arms to cause his body to rise upward. When his feet are above the bar, he straddles his legs to complete the move in the straddle seat position.

Double-leg cut and catch over one bar

Back uprise

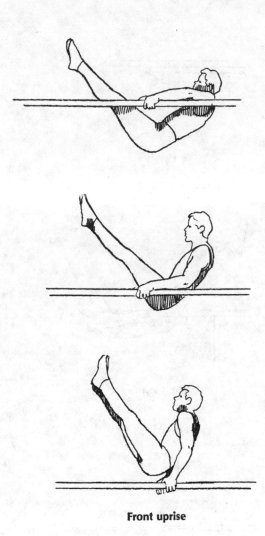

Front uprise

Front Uprise The starting position and the techniques of execution for this move are the same as those for the preceding with the exception that this move is completed in a cross arm support position instead of in a straddle seat. This requires a slightly more forceful whip of the legs and pull with the arms. Correct initial arm position also becomes more important. The forearms should be at right angles to the upper arms, and there should be no sagging at the shoulders during the swing in the upper arm hang. A spotter can stand alongside the bars to push on the performer's pelvis with one hand to help him to rise up above the bars. The spotter must always spot from below the bars. Spotting above the bars places the arm between the performer and the bars at the risk of a broken arm.

Back Uprise The student starts in an upper arm hang at the center of the bars. His forearms should be at right angles to his upper arms and there should be no sagging at the shoulders. He initiates a big swing and on the backward swing, as his legs begin moving upward, he pulls vigorously with his arms to bring his body over his hands and completes the move in a cross arm support position. It is considered poor form to slide the hands backward on the bars or to complete the move with the arms bent. The spotter can reach under the bar to push upward on the gymnast's thigh.

"Monkey" Kip The student starts in a standing position facing the end of the bars with an inside grip on the bars. He jumps upward, flexes his hips, and places his feet against the uprights. He then flexes his legs and extends them again to bring himself to the cross arm support position. The gymnast's arms should remain extended throughout the move. Two students can practice simultaneously by using opposite ends of the bars.

The "monkey" kip may also be done at the side of the bars. The student starts from a stand

157

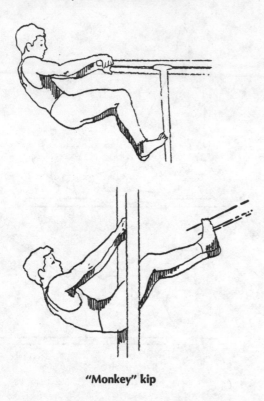

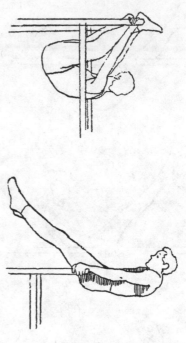

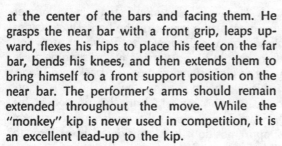

"Monkey" kip

Short kip

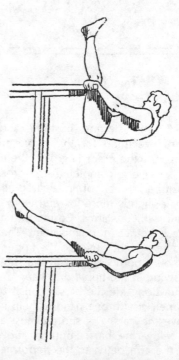

at the center of the bars and facing them. He grasps the near bar with a front grip, leaps upward, flexes his hips to place his feet on the far bar, bends his knees, and then extends them to bring himself to a front support position on the near bar. The performer's arms should remain extended throughout the move. While the "monkey" kip is never used in competition, it is an excellent lead-up to the kip.

Short Kip The student starts in a standing position on the mat facing the end of the bars. He has an inside grip. He should stand with his toes about 18 inches behind an imaginary perpendicular line dropped from the ends of the bars. He initiates the move by flexing his hips to bring his extended legs and his toes up between his hands. As a result of these actions, his jackknifed body will swing forward and then backward. During the backward swing, the gymnast extends his hips and pulls hard with his extended arms to finish in a cross arm support. The performer may be aided during the learning stages by the spotter, who pushes upward on his buttocks as he rises toward the cross arm support. This move may also be done at the center of the bars.

Drop kip

Glide kip

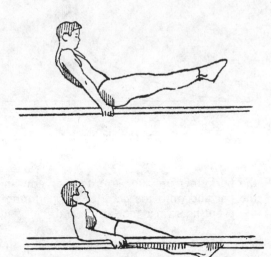

Top kip to straddle seat

Drop Kip The student starts in a cross arm support at the end of the bars facing inward. He falls backward with his arms extended, flexing his hips as he drops backward. His shoulders and hips should move in a circular pathway. He swings forward under the bars, and then as he swings backward, he pulls hard with his extended arms and extends his hips to finish in a cross arm support. This move may also be done at the center of the bars.

Glide Kip The student starts in a standing position facing the end of the bars with an inside grip and his feet directly under the end of the

bars. He bends his knees and springs directly backward. As his body swings forward, he keeps his toes just an inch or so above the mat until the end of the swing is reached. At this time, his body is arched and his arms are extended. He then flexes his hips to bring his extended legs up with his toes between his hands. His jackknifed body will swing backward. Near the end of the backward swing, he pulls hard with his extended arms and extends his hips to complete the move in a cross arm support. This move may also be done at the center of the bars.

Top Kip to a Straddle Seat The student starts in an upper arm hang at the center of the bars. His upper arms are at right angles to his forearms. He flexes his hips to bring them above the bar and to bring his feet directly over his head. He extends his hips to swing his extended legs upward and forward and pulls hard with his arms to move his center of gravity upward and forward. He straddles his legs as he rises off the bars to complete the move in a straddle seat position.

Top Kip The starting position and the techniques of execution for this move are identical to those for the preceding except that it is finished in a cross arm support rather than a straddle seat position. A spotter should stand alongside

Top kip

Pirouette in a cross arm support

the performer prepared to extend an arm under the bar and onto the chest of the performer in the event he swings too far forward.

Shoulder Balance The student starts in a straddle seat position at the center of the bars. He grasps the bars in front of and as close to his thighs as possible. He bends forward to place his shoulders on the bar keeping his elbows abducted in order that he will not slip down between the bars. He moves his hips upward over his head, keeping his feet low. After his hips are over his head, he extends them to bring his legs over his head. In the final position, his back is arched, his head is pulled back, and his feet are directly over his head. To achieve aesthetically pleasing lines, his legs should be extended, his back arched, and his toes pointed. The gymnast can move into the shoulder balance from a swing, kip, front or back uprise, or lower into

it from a handstand. A spotter should stand alongside the beginner and bring one hand under the bar and to the performer's back if he goes over.

Chest Balance The student starts in a lying position across the bars with one bar across his chest. He grasps the other bar with palms down and flexes his hips to bring them over his head while keeping his feet low. After his hips are over his head, he extends them to bring his legs up over his head. Throughout the move, the gymnast should pull the far bar toward himself. The spotter, standing outside the bars at their

Shoulder balance

Chest balance

Pirouette in the "L" position

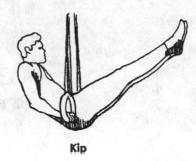

Kip

center, should place one hand on the performer's back and the other under his shoulder.

Pirouette in a Cross Arm Support The student starts in a cross arm support at the center of the bars. He shifts his weight to his left arm, looks to his left, pushes off his right hand, and makes the turn to a front support on the left bar. He then shifts his weight to his right arm, looks to his left, pushes off his left arm, and completes the move in a cross arm support position facing in a direction opposite to his starting position.

Pirouette in the "L" Position The student starts in a cross arm support at the center of the bars with his legs elevated at right angles to his trunk. He shifts his weight to his left hand, turns his head to his left, pushes off his right hand, and moves into an "L" position on the left bar. He then shifts his weight to his right arm, turns his head to his left, pushes off his left hand, and completes the turn to finish in the cross arm support in "L" position facing a direction opposite to that from which he started.

STILL RINGS²

Inlocate The student starts in an inverted hang in the jackknifed position. He extends his hips to swing his legs forward and around. As his legs are rising in the backward swing, he simultane- and tucks his head to complete the move in an ously turns his thumbs downward, jackknifes, inverted hang in the jackknifed position. After he masters this, he can learn to do the move with

² All moves on the still rings are to be done by boys only.

his body extended. A spotter should assist the performer during the learning stages by lifting upward with one hand on his near shoulder and the other on his thigh.

Kip The student starts in an inverted hang in jackknifed position. He increases the degree of flexion of his hips in order to secure a rebound and on the rebound extends his hips and pulls with his arms extended to complete the move in a support position.

Front Uprise The student starts in a hanging position. He swings his feet backward and forward several times and at the end of one of the backward swings flexes his hips slightly, pointing his toes at a spot directly below the point of suspension of the rings. As his body swings forward, he continues to point his feet toward this spot. This brings him into an arched position. When his body reaches the fully arched position, he flexes his hips to swing his feet upward and

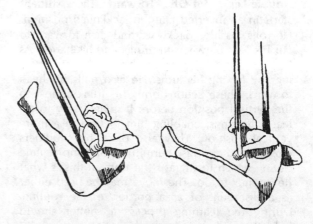

Front uprise

Double-leg cut-off backward

Double-leg cut-off forward

pulls hard with his arms. He next thrusts his chest toward the rings and swings his legs downward. As he rises above the rings, he shifts his wrists from a hanging to a support position.

Back Uprise The student starts in an inverted hang in jackknifed position. He extends his hips vigorously to swing his legs forward and downward. A forceful downward swing will cause the gymnast to rebound from the bottom of the swing. As his legs rise during the backward portion of their swing, the student pulls with his arms, flexing his elbows, to come to the support position.

Double-Leg Cut-Off Forward The student starts in an inverted hang in jackknifed position. He rolls his hips backward and then forward to cut his legs between the rings and his hands. As he rolls forward, he pulls his trunk toward his legs by flexing his arms. He also pulls his head forward. These actions bring his trunk almost to the vertical position before it is necessary to release the rings, enabling him to land in a more vertical position. They also place his shoulders closer to the rings, permitting him more time during which to regrasp the rings, if this is what he intends to do. The move may be used either as a dismount or as a portion of the routine. During the learning process a spotter should hold the performer under his arms.

Double-Leg Cut-Off Backward The student starts in a hanging position. He initiates a swing and on the forward swing flexes his hips slightly to bring his legs over his head. When his legs strike his arms, or slightly before, he releases his grasp, pulls his head backward, and extends into an arched position to somersault around to his feet. As his legs circle upward over his head, he should pull hard with his arms. During the learning process spotters should stand on both sides of the performer. They should grasp him by the upper arms to assist in the move.

Forward Roll The student starts in a support position. He elevates his hips, pulls his head forward, and rolls around slowly in a jackknifed position, holding his body high by flexing his elbows. After completing the roll, he extends his elbows slowly to lower himself into a hanging position. Having mastered this move, the student may wish to try a forward roll into the support position. The techniques of execution in the two moves are essentially similar. To return to the support position, the gymnast must keep his center of rotation between the rings. As his legs come around, he kips slightly to aid his return to the support position.

TUMBLING

Tinsica The student takes a short run, skips on his right foot, lands on his left foot, flexes his hips to place his left hand on the mat directly in front of his left foot with fingers pointing to the rear, places his right hand directly in front of his

Tinsica

left hand with fingers pointing to the front, and swings his legs over his head to land on his feet facing in his original direction. The performer secures the necessary rotary force by flexing at the hips and swinging his extended right leg over his head as he springs off his left leg. Throughout the move, his head should be pulled backward. The tumbler lands first on his right foot and then on his left foot. A spotter should assist during the learning process by kneeling alongside the anticipated point of landing. He should place one hand on the performer's upper back and the other on his lower back to lift him around. (Boys and girls.)

Back to Back Pull-Over To start this move, partners stand back to back with their arms locked. The understander's elbow should be above the topmounter's elbows. The understander squats slightly to get under his partner. He then bends forward and extends his legs to lift the topmounter over his back and around to the mat. The topmounter should permit the understander to do the lifting. He should not spring. The topmounter flexes his knees and hips and rolls over his partner. As the topmounter rolls over him, the understander should extend his arms sideward to prevent his partner from sliding off his back. A spotter should stand alongside to assist the topmounter if necessary. This move orients the tumbler for the back handspring. (Boys and girls.)

Foot-Push Back Handspring This skill is started with the understander lying on his back with his feet on the buttocks of the topmounter, who is standing astride the understander's buttocks and facing his feet. The topmounter arches backward, dropping his arms and head backward until the understander catches his shoulders with his hands. After upending, the topmounter flexes his hips and snaps down to his feet. The topmounter is assisted in this movement by the understander, who pushes with his feet against the topmounter's buttocks. The topmounter should not lift for

Back to back pull-over

Foot-push back handspring

height but should throw his arms directly backward. He should keep his elbows straight throughout the move. The understander should delay his leg push until all of the topmounter's weight is on his feet. This move is another lead-up to the back handspring. (Boys and girls.)

The Sit-Back and Arm Swing for the Back Handspring The next step, after having learned the foot-push back handspring to become accustomed to turning over backward, is to learn to sit properly. During all the years of their lives, whenever people sit down, they angle their lower legs and back forward so that their shoulders and knees are in front of their feet during the sit back. In the back handspring, the lower legs and back must be kept perpendicular to the floor during the sit-back in order to initiate momentum in a horizontal direction backward. It is difficult to overcome this habit of long stand-

ing. The sitback will require practice. If it is done properly, the tumbler will drop down hard on his partner's thigh. He should not, therefore, endeavor to sit down gently. The tumbler should stand his own thigh's length from his partner's thigh. If he stands closer than this, he will be forced to carry his knees and shoulders forward. The tumbler can also learn to move into a backbend position from the sit-back as an additional lead-up to the back handspring. After doing the sit-back, he bends backward over his partner's knee to place his hands on the mat and to assume the backbend position. (Boys and girls.)

Belt Spotting for the Back Handspring Having progressed this far, the tumbler is ready to try the back handspring in a safety belt with two spotters. The spotters should wrap the rope around the hand nearest the performer and use the other hand to help him around by pushing

Sit-back and arm swing

with it against the back of his knees. The spotters should stand behind the starting point of the performer since he will move backward. (Boys and girls.)

Back Handspring The performer sits back and swings his arms backward-downward. When he is about to lose balance, he swings his trunk backward and simultaneously swings his arms upward-backward. His take-off should be from his heels. As his arms swing beyond his head,

his head is thrown backward, he arches his back, and he lifts his hips toward the ceiling. His arms should be carried backward as far as his flexibility will permit and should remain fully extended throughout the move in order to generate greater momentum. His hands contact the mat just as his feet are leaving the mat. The momentum generated will carry the performer into the handstand. From the handstand, the performer simply "snaps" down to his feet to complete the move. (Boys and girls.)

Hand Spotting the Back Handspring After the performer is able to do the back handspring correctly in the belt, he can attempt it without a belt. He should master the move first with two and then with one hand spotter. The one spotter should kneel to the left side of the performer and use his right arm to support him at the small of his back and his left arm to help him upend by pushing against the back of the performer's thighs. In order to lift effectively, he must be near enough to the performer so that he can hold his forearm in a vertical position. (Boys and girls.)

Back handspring

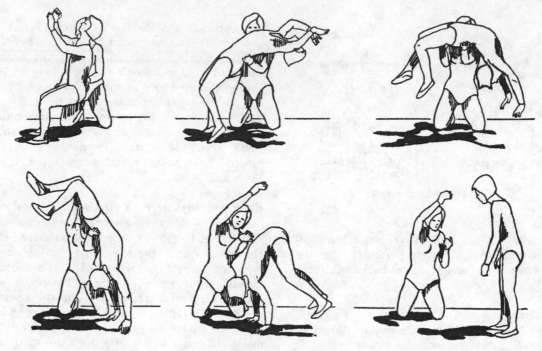

Hand spotting the back handspring

Snap-down back handspring

Round-off back handspring

Snap-Down Back Handspring The student starts from a handstand on the mat, flexes his hips and bends, and then extends his knees to snap down to his feet. He then executes a back handspring. In this procedure, the tumbler's arms need not swing downward-backward. Backward momentum generated in the snap-down takes the place of that generated in the arm swing. This move is lead-up to the round-off back handspring and to back handsprings in series. (Boys and girls.)

Round-Off Back Handspring After the snap-down back handspring and the round-off have been mastered, it will be easy to combine the round-off with the back handspring. This combination should be learned in a belt first, then with two hand spotters, next with one hand spotter, and finally alone. When using the safety belt, the rope from the performer's right side should cross in front to the spotter on his left while the rope from the performer's left should cross behind his body to the spotter on his right. This applies if the performer turns counterclockwise in the round-off. The procedures are reversed if he turns clockwise. (Boys and girls.)

Back Handsprings in Series After having mastered the previously described skills, back hand-

springs in series can be attempted by the student. The tumbler should avoid "diving" into his back handsprings. The handsprings should be done in a snappy, rhythmic manner, the tumbler moving without hesitation out of one back handspring immediately into the succeeding handspring. (Boys and girls.)

Side Leg Pitch The understander stands alongside the topmounter and places his left hand on his buttocks or lower back and his right hand under the calf of the topmounter's uplifted leg. As the topmounter flexes the knee of his supporting leg, the understander bends his knees. The topmounter springs straight up, lifting with his arms at the same time that the understander lifts with his arms and extends his legs. During the lift, the topmounter should keep his supported leg fully extended. At the end of the lift, he should pull his head backward and flex his hips to somersault around to his feet. During the learning stages, a spotter should assist the performer by placing his right hand on the tumbler's shoulder and his left hand under the tumbler's buttocks. He should be alert to protect for overspin. This move is relatively easy to execute since the understander assists the tumbler in both the lift and the spin. (Boys and girls.)

Back handspring in series

Side leg pitch

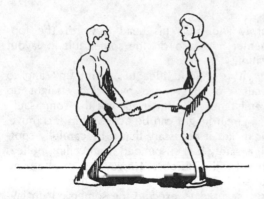

Front leg pitch

High foot pitch

Front Leg Pitch To start the front leg pitch, the understander and topmounter face one another. The understander grasps the topmounter's ankle with his right hand and his calf with his left hand. As the topmounter dips on his supporting leg, the understander bends his knees. As the topmounter springs off his supporting leg and lifts upward with his arms, the understander extends his legs and lifts with his arms. The topmounter swings his head, arms, and trunk backward to secure the necessary rotation. Following are suggestions for accomplishing this move:

1. The topmounter should keep his supported leg fully extended throughout the move.
2. Movements of the topmounter and of the understander should be fully co-ordinated.
3. Spotters should watch for overspin.

During the learning stages, this move should be spotted by two men in the same manner as described for the side-leg pitch. This move is of slightly greater difficulty than the side leg pitch since the understander assists only in the spin but not in the lift. (Boys and girls.)

Pitch from a Sitting Position In the starting position, the understander is sitting on the mat with his legs extended and straddled and his hands on the mat, palms up, between his thighs. The topmounter is standing with the balls of his feet in his partner's hands and is facing him. As the topmounter leaps upward and throws his head, arms, and trunk backward, the under-

stander lifts with his arms. To provide a greater lift, the understander rolls backward to his back. The topmounter should be spotted until he has mastered the move. (Boys and girls.)

High Foot Pitch The understander grasps his own left thumb with his right hand. His left hand lies across his right hand and wrist with the palm turned upward. This grip permits the understander to continue the support and lift well over his head. When the fingers are intertwined, as is often done, the understander can lift only to his chest, at which point the fingers prevent further lift. The understander stands with his feet spread, squats low, and places one foot slightly ahead of

Partner lift drill

the other. His back should be vertical with his chest out and his head erect. The topmounter places one foot in the understander's hands and his hands on his partner's shoulders. As he springs upward off his supporting leg, the topmounter pushes downward with his other leg into his partner's hands to extend his leg fully and at the same time pushes down on his partner's shoulders with his arms. As he does this, the understander extends his legs and lifts with his arms. His hands move upward close to his body. The partners' movements must be carefully coordinated. At the height of the lift, the topmounter pulls his head backward and tucks to rotate. At the completion of the rotation, he opens up

sharply and pulls his head forward. The top-mounter may also do the somersault in layout position.

It is a good idea to "warm up" and to practice for this move by lifting straight up several times without executing the somersault.

Great height can be achieved in this move. This makes it necessary that it be carefully spotted. A safety belt suspended from ceiling pulleys is best for this purpose. However, it can be hand spotted by two men. Sufficient height can be easily secured to execute the somersault in layout position. (Two boys or a boy as understander and a girl as topmounter.)

Partner Lift Drill This drill is practiced to enable the tumbler to learn the tucking procedures for the back somersault. The understander is standing directly behind the topmounter, holding him under the arms. The topmounter leaps upward, "driving" his arms over his head, pulls his head backward, and draws his knees up into a tightly tucked position, grasping his shins and pulling with his arms. These actions would cause him to somersault around. However, he is prevented from doing so by the understander who checks his rotation by pushing on his back. In order to support the tumbler, the understander must stay under his partner so that his forearms may be held in a vertical position. If the top-mounter is too far away from the understander, he will have to angle his arms forward, which will prevent him from giving necessary support. (Boys and girls.)

Standing back somersault

Snap-down back somersault

Standing Back Somersault The tumbler starts in a standing position. He drives his arms downward as he bends his knees and then drives his arms upward as he extends his knees. Before leaving the mat, he pushes his hips slightly forward and arches his back slightly. He lifts his knees up to his chest with knees bent and grasps his shins, pulling into a tightly tucked position. At the same time, he pulls his head backward. These actions will cause him to somersault around to his feet. He should avoid throwing his arms or trunk forward during his efforts to move into the tucked position.

This move should first be learned in a safety belt. After reasonable success has been achieved in the safety belt, the performer can attempt the move first with two people hand spotting him, then with one person hand spotting, and finally (after he can do the back somersault successfully in ten out of ten trials), he can try it unassisted.

One successful hand spotting procedure is the following:

The spotter stands to the performer's left side and uses his right hand to help in the lift and the left hand to "slap-lift" the performer around. The right hand lifts on the performer's lower back and the left hand slaps him behind the thigh to assist in the rotation. Spotting for overspin is accomplished by sliding the right hand along the performer's back to his neck as he revolves. After the gymnast has developed adequate skill, he can be spotted with only one hand by "slap-lifting" against his buttocks. (Boys and girls.)

Snap-Down Back Somersault The tumbler begins in a handstand position. He underbalances his handstand and vigorously flexes his hips to snap his feet down to the mat just behind his hands. He rebounds off his feet to leap vertically upward by extending his knees and hips and driving his arms upward. He pulls his head and trunk backward and then tucks to spin around to land on his feet again. (Boys and girls.)

171

Back somersault from a round-off

Back somersault from a back handspring

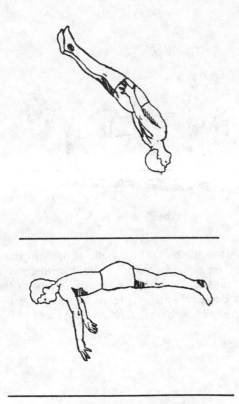

Back somersault in layout position

Back Somersault from a Round-Off After the back somersault and the round-off have been mastered, it is quite simple to combine the two. The gymnast should execute his round-off vigorously and should snap his feet down close to his hands. Safety progressions should be followed. That is, the move should first be attempted in a safety belt, then with two hand spotters, next with one hand spotter, and finally unassisted. When using the safety belt in the round-off into the back somersault, it is necessary to turn the belt so that the rope from the spotter to the performer's left leads to his right hip in front of his body, and the other rope leads from his left hip behind his body and to the spotter to his right. If he twists to his right (clockwise) in his round-off, the belt is turned in the opposite direction. (Boys and girls.)

Back Somersault from a Back Handspring After the tumbler has mastered the back handspring, the back somersault, the snap-down back somersault and the back somersault from a round-

off, he can easily learn the back somersault from a back handspring. Progressions should be followed with regard to safety procedures. His first attempts should be made with two spotters and a safety belt. After succeeding in this step, he should have only one spotter holding the belt (the free rope can be wrapped around his waist). Next, he can try the move with two hand spotters who should position themselves just behind the point of the anticipated landing of his feet as he comes out of his handspring. Then he can try the move with one hand spotter. After he has mastered the skill to the point where he can perform it successfully in ten out of ten trials, he will be ready to try it alone. (Boys and girls.)

Swing Back This is a variation of the back somersault. While the movements are less complex, they are more vigorous. The tumbler swings his arms downward and flexes his knees, then drives his arms upward and backward as he extends his knees. As his arms swing backward, he throws his head and trunk backward and lifts his hips. When he is halfway around in a layout position, he flexes his hips to land on his feet. While the tumbler cannot secure the height that he can in the regular back somersault, he can get around very quickly. The same progressions in spotting should be followed in learning the swing back as have been described for the back somersault. (Boys and girls.)

Swing Backs in Series Tumblers have done twenty or more consecutive swing backs. As soon as the tumbler lands on his feet in coming out of one swing back and bends his knees to absorb the impact, he extends his knees and swings his arms to move into the succeeding swing back. (Boys and girls.)

Round-Off into a Back Somersault in Layout Position Having mastered the round-off, round-off into a back somersault, and swing backs, the student is ready to attempt the round-off into a back somersault in layout position. He must execute a very vigorous round-off. When snapping down out of the round-off, the gymnast's body should be about 30° forward of vertical when his feet hit the mat (blocking action). He leaps directly upward and pulls his head backward

Straddle lift front somersault

Wheelbarrow pitch

hard, pulls his shoulders and extended arms backward, and lifts his chest by arching his upper back. As he somersaults around, his back is arched and his legs are extended. Just before landing, he flexes his hips slightly, and on landing he bends his knees to absorb the impact.

During the tumbler's initial efforts, he will most likely do a swing back, but as he gains increased height and self confidence, he will approach the layout position and will learn to delay the hip flexion until just before landing. (Boys and girls.)

Front somersault from a run in tucked position

Straddle Lift Front Somersault In the starting position the topmounter is standing with his feet apart, his hips flexed, his arms extended backward between his legs, and his palms facing one another. The understander is standing facing the opposite direction, straddling his partner's head and holding his wrists. The topmounter springs upward and tucks his head as the understander pulls on his wrists to flip him around and to the standing position. The topmounter must hold his legs in a straddled position until just before his feet contact the mat. The purpose of this move is to have the topmounter become accustomed to somersaulting forward. The move may also be performed with both partners facing in the same direction and the understander standing behind his partner. No spotters are necessary. (Boys and girls.)

Wheelbarrow Pitch In the starting position the topmounter is in a front leaning rest position. His feet are being held by the understander, who is standing facing his partner. The understander flexes his knees and then extends them, tossing his partner's feet upward and forward. The topmounter tucks and somersaults around to his feet. This move should first be mastered in a safety belt. Caution should be exercised to prevent overspin. (Boys and girls.)

Front Somersault from a Run in Tucked Position The tumbler takes a short run, leaps upward to land on both feet with his legs angled backward, springs upward, and throws his arms and trunk downward to move into a tucked position, and opens up again to land on his feet after having completed the somersault. To translate horizontal momentum to vertical momentum, the tumbler must lift off for the somersault with his legs angled backward so that his hips are behind his feet. The tighter the tumbler's tuck, the more rapidly he will spin. Efforts should be made to make the trajectory as nearly vertical as possible. A vertical trajectory not only adds to the aesthetic appeal of the move but will also give the tumbler more time in which to complete the somersault. The move should first be learned in a safety belt with two spotters holding the ropes and another spotter standing in front of the point of anticipated landing. This third spotter will protect for overspin. After having mastered

this first step, the tumbler should attempt the move in the belt with one spotter; then with two hand spotters over a rolled-up mat; then with one hand spotter over a rolled-up mat; then with two hand spotters and no rolled mat; then with one hand spotter; and finally unassisted. Following these safety progressions will give the tumbler the feeling of having made progress, while at the same time they will keep him safe from injury. (Boys and girls.)

Front Somersault in Piked position This move is executed in the same manner as is a front somersault in tucked position except that the tumbler keeps his legs extended and his arms extended and his arms extended sideward-downward. An unusually high leap and a tightly piked position are required. (Boys.)

Walk-out Front Somersault This move is executed in the same manner as is a front somersault in tucked position except that in opening up for the landing the tumbler's legs are straddled forward and backward so that he lands on one foot a split second before his other foot strikes the mat. This enables the tumbler to move immediately into a round-off out of the somersault to initiate backward tumbling moves. (Boys.)

Front Somersault from a Standing Position This move requires a very tight tuck since a fast spin is necessary. Good leg power is necessary to secure height. A good arm lift is also necessary. Because the tumbler is spinning very fast, overspin must be guarded against by the spotter. It is wise to use a double thickness of mats. (Boys.)

Front Roll into a Front Somersault The tumbler executes a forward roll, and as soon as his feet are on the mat, he leans forward slightly and leaps upward, lifting hard with his arms to execute a front somersault. There should be no hesitation between the roll and the somersault. Overspin must be guarded against. (Boys and girls.)

Front Handspring into a Front Somersault The tumbler must have mastered the front somersault and must be able to do a front handspring with straight legs before attempting this move.

Needle scale

Forward shoulder roll

He executes a high front handspring with a vigorous push-off from his hands. On landing, he bends his knees slightly and immediately springs upward for the front somersault. (Boys.)

Back Somersault into a Front Somersault The tumbler executes a tucked back somersault, coming out of it slightly early so that on landing his body is angled forward. On landing, he bends his knees slightly in order to be enabled to spring upward. His arms remain over his head in order to move them quickly downward into the tucked position. He immediately rebounds from the mat into a front somersault. (Boys and girls.)

BALANCE BEAM[3]

Cartwheel This move may be used as a dismount off the end of the balance beam or done in the middle of the beam into a handstand or completely around to the feet on the beam. In any case, the gymnast should master the move on the floor first, being certain that she can start and finish on the line. When used as a dismount, the gymnast should increase the distance covered by pushing sideward during the last half of the move. When it is done into the handstand, the gymnast should lift her right leg as she bends her trunk to the left to place her left hand on the

beam. She next springs off her supporting leg and swings her right leg upward as she places her right hand on the beam. A spotter should stand alongside to hold the gymnast's left upper arm with her right hand and her right hip with her left hand. To continue around to her feet, the gymnast will flex her hips to her right, land on her right foot, push off her left hand, bring her left foot onto the beam, lift her right hand off the beam, and come to the erect position.

Needle Scale This move is also used in free exercise routines. The student starts in a front scale position and lowers her trunk as she elevates her left leg. She continues to lower her trunk and to elevate her leg until her trunk meets her supporting leg and her left leg is in line with her trunk. She may grasp the balance beam or her right ankle with her hands.

Forward Shoulder Roll The student starts balanced on her lower legs with her left knee behind her right toe. She bends forward to place her right shoulder on the beam and her head to the left of the beam. She grasps the underside of the beam with both hands, moves her hips over her head by extending her knees and continues to roll over until she is in a supine position on the beam. A spotter should hold her hips as she rolls over.

Straddle Leap The student takes several steps and leaps upward and forward to land in balance on one foot.

[3] While boys often enjoy performing on the balance beam, this is a competitive event for girls only.

Jump to forward roll mount

Backward walk-over

Shoulder Balance The student starts in a kneeling position as described for the forward shoulder roll. She places her shoulder on the beam, with her head to one side of it. She places her hands on the beam and extends her legs to bring her hips over her head. She then slowly extends her hips to bring her feet over her head and arches her back to assume the shoulder balance position. A spotter should stand alongside to hold her waist as she upends.

Jump into a Forward Roll Mount The student starts from a standing position on the floor at one end of the beam facing the opposite end. She places her hands on top of the beam and leaps upward to bring her hips over her head as she lowers her right shoulder to the top of the beam with her head to the left of the beam. At this point, her hips are flexed, her legs are extended, and her feet are low. She lowers her hips over her head to the beam, shifting her hands to grasp the underside of the beam, and then lowers her extended legs to finish in a supine position on the beam. A spotter should assist in lowering her to the bar gently by placing one hand under her shoulder and the other behind her hips.

Backward Walk-Over The student must master this move on the mat before attempting it on the beam. She starts in a standing position with her right foot in front of her left foot. She arches over backward maintaining balance by pushing her hips forward of her feet. She places her right hand on the beam and then her left hand on it directly behind the other hand. She springs

off her feet to pass through the handstand position and over to her feet. A spotter should assist the gymnast as she turns over by placing one hand on her shoulder and one in the middle of her back.

Forward Walk-Over Because the gymnast cannot see the beam during the last half of this move, she must master the move on the mat so thoroughly that she can land on a line in balance ten out of ten trials before attempting it on the balance beam. She starts in a standing position with her left foot in front. She flexes her hips to place her hands on the beam with her left hand farthest forward, pushes off her feet to upend, passes through the handstand position and arches over to land on her left foot first and then on her right foot. She then pushes her hips forward and pulls herself up to a standing position. Two spotters standing on the mat to either side of the gymnast during the learning stages are mandatory. They should grasp the gymnast's upper arm with one hand and help to ease her down with the other hand on the small of her back. Another method of spotting is with one

177

Forward walk-over

Handspring dismount

hand on the lower thigh and the other on the lower back.

English Handbalance The gymnast starts in a standing position on the beam. She bends forward to place her hands on the beam with her thumbs on top and her fingers along the sides. She then kicks up into a handstand facing the length of the beam.

English Handbalance Dismount The gymnast kicks up into a momentary English handbalance and then lowers her body to one side of the balance beam as though doing a high front vault dismount.

Handstand Arch-Over Dismount The gymnast starts in a handstand position facing sideward and allows her feet to overbalance beyond her head,

arching over to land on the mat on her feet. She should flex her hips and knees upon landing. During the learning stages, a spotter should stand alongside the performer between the anticipated point of her landing and the beam. She should hold the gymnast's upper arm with one hand and place the other on her lower back.

Handspring Dismount The gymnast starts in a standing position at the center of the beam and facing one end. She flexes her hips to place her hands on top of the beam and then executes a front handspring off the beam, her body passing to one side of the beam. A spotter should stand on the side of the beam opposite the dismount side ready to push the gymnast to the side if it appears she may land on the beam.

Squat Vault Dismount from a Handstand The gymnast starts from a handstand position at the center of the beam, facing sideward. She overbalances slightly until her feet are beyond her head. She then flexes her hips vigorously and

English handbalance

English handbalance dismount

Handstand arch over dismount

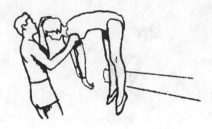

Straddle vault dismount from a handstand

Jump to a squat stand mount

bends her knees to bring her legs between her arms in order to land on her feet with her back toward the beam. A spotter should stand on the side of the beam toward which the performer will dismount and to the performer's right. He should grasp the gymnast's upper arms.

Straddle Vault Dismount from a Handstand The gymnast starts from a handstand position at the center of the beam, facing sideward. She overbalances slightly and then vigorously flexes her hips to bring her straddled and extended legs over the beam and outside her hands in order to land on the mat on her feet with her back toward the beam. A spotter should be utilized in the same manner as described in the previous move.

Leg Raise The gymnast begins in a standing position facing sideward with the left foot along the beam. She grasps the inner side of her right

foot with her right hand, with her fingers on the underside of her foot and her thumb on top. She extends her right leg upward while retaining her grip on her foot. She holds the position.

Stoop Vault Dismount from a Handstand This move is executed and spotted in the same manner as is the straddle vault dismount from a handstand except that the legs are held together throughout the move.

Squat vault dismount from a handstand

Leg raise

One-arm half lever

Arabesque

Arabesque The student raises one leg backward to assume an arched position while balanced on one foot.

Jump to a Straddle Stand Mount This move is identical in every respect to the jump to a squat stand mount except that the gymnast brings her feet onto the beam outside her hands to finish in a straddle stand.

Jump to a Squat Stand Mount The student runs toward the side of the beam, places both hands on top of the beam, springs simultaneously from both feet, and pushes upward with both arms. She draws her knees toward her chest to land on the beam on both feet in a squat position facing sideward with her hands on the beam. A spotter should stand on the side of the beam opposite the mounting side and grasp the gymnast's upper arms as she mounts.

FLOOR EXERCISE

One-Arm Half Lever The student starts in a kneeling position on his hands and knees. He places his right hand directly in front of his right knee with his fingers pointing to the rear. He extends his right leg and places his right elbow just inside his right pelvic bone. He extends his left leg and pulls his shoulders and legs upward to place his body in an arched position parallel to the floor. His body should be tilted sideward so that his left shoulder and hip are higher than his right shoulder and hip. When he has secured his balance, he extends his left arm in line with his body. In the final position, his right forearm should form a right angle with his lower arm; his body should be horizontal and arched; and his head should be pulled upward. (Boys.)

Planche (Free Lever) The student starts in a handstand. He slowly levers his arched body downward until it is parallel (or as nearly parallel as his strength will allow) to the floor by angling his arms forward. His arms should remain fully extended throughout the move. This move requires tremendous strength relative to body weight. (Boys.)

Jump to a straddle stand

Planche (free lever)

Valdez

Stoop through

Valdez The student starts in a sitting position with his left leg extended, his right knee flexed, his right foot flat on the mat next to his left knee, his left hand on the mat behind his buttocks with his fingers pointing to the rear, and his right arm extended forward. He extends his right leg, throws his right arm over his head and backward to the mat, swings his left leg over his head, pushes his hips upward, pulls his head backward and upends into the handstand or continues over to his feet. A spotter can facilitate the learning process by kneeling next to the gymnast and assisting him around with one hand on his shoulder and one in the middle of his back. (Boys and girls.)

Straddle Through The student starts in a front support position. He lifts his hips and springs off his toes to bring his body into an arched position parallel to the floor. He then flexes his hips quickly and pushes with his arms to bring his extended legs outside his arms and around in front to finish in a back leaning rest with his feet together. (Boys.)

Stoop Through This move is executed in the same manner as is the straddle through except that the gymnast keeps his legs together to bring his extended legs between his arms. As in the straddle through, he finishes in a back leaning rest position with his feet together. (Boys.)

Double-Leg Circles The student starts by doing two or three single-leg circles to generate the necessary momentum. This procedure was described in Chapter 5, the chapter on self-testing activities for students of all ages. As the gymnast's right leg circles under the left leg during single-leg circles, he extends the left leg and circles it with the right leg. As his legs swing to his right, he shifts his weight to his left hand. As his legs circle toward the front, he extends his hips; and as they circle toward the rear, he lifts and flexes his hips. In this manner, he cir-

Straddle through

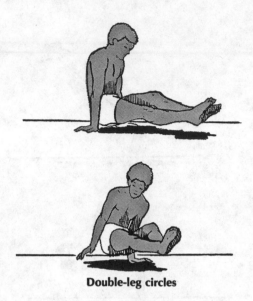

Double-leg circles

Japanese handstand

cles both legs around his body without touching the floor with his feet while being supported on his hands only. (Boys.)

Straight Arm–Straight Leg Press into a Handstand
The student starts in a standing position. He stoops to place his hands on the floor, shoulder width apart, directly in front of his feet, with his fingers pointing forward. Keeping his arms extended, he angles them forward and pulls his hips upward over his head. His feet remain close to the floor until his hips are directly over his head. When his hips are over his head, he extends them to bring his feet up over his head. As his feet move upward, he brings his shoulders back over his hands. Hamstring and shoul-

der girdle flexibility are as essential to success in this move as is strength. (Boys.)

Straight Body Press into a Handstand The student starts in a prone position on the floor with his hands on the floor next to his hips and with his fingers pointing toward his head. He pulls himself into an arched position with his back muscles and pushes with his arms. This will bring his feet a portion of the way over his head. He continues to press up in an arched position until he reaches the handstand position. (Boys.)

Reverse Lever The student starts in a handstand position. He allows his extended legs to move beyond his head while he maintains balance by angling his arms backward. He continues to arch over until his legs and lower back are parallel to the floor. He then pulls his head forward between his arms. He holds this position momentarily. Balance is difficult because it must be maintained by kinesthetic sense entirely. (Boys and girls.)

Japanese Handstand The student starts in a handstand position and slowly "inches" his hands sideward until his arms are almost horizontal and his face almost touches the floor. (Boys.)

Straight arm-straight leg press into a handstand

TRAMPOLINE[4]

Baroni The baroni is similar to the front somersault with a half twist. The difference is that in the baroni the twist is initiated immediately after the lift-off so that the gymnast can see the bed at all times; whereas in the front somersault with a half twist, the twist is not initiated until after the performer has completed half of the somersault. The baroni is very useful move in routines because it is relatively easy to do out of and into other moves.

The student initiates a front somersault looking at the center of the bed. As his hips move upward over his head, he initiates the twist by turning his head toward the left, pulling his right arm across his chest, and pulling his left arm behind his back. When he has upended, he extends his hips and continues the somersault. When the twist has been completed, he flexes his hips to bring his feet to the bed for the landing. The twist may, of course, be done in the opposite direction. The student should twist in whichever direction seems most natural to him.

We like a method of teaching the baroni recommended by LaDue and Norman.[5] They urge the student to learn the move by following the progressions outlined here:

1. Knee drop into a front three-quarter somersault. The spin during the first half of the somersault should be fast in order that the opening of the body in preparation for the landing on the back will occur as high above the bed as possible. The landing on the back must be made with the body fully extended and horizontal. The trajectory of the move should be straight up and down with no travel. Mastery of this step will require considerable practice.

2. Knee drop into a front three-quarter somersault with a half twist to the front drop. Before attempting this move, it would be well for the student to learn to leap upward lifting his legs forward (as though he were to land flat on his back for a back drop). After this, he should

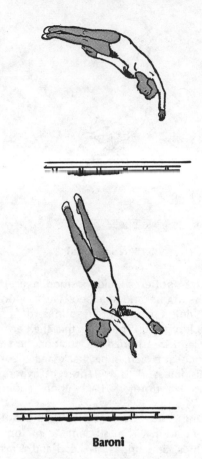

Baroni

leap upward as though to land on his back but look over his shoulder to execute a half twist before landing on his front. While working on this step, the student should wear sweat clothes to prevent mat burns.

3. Knee drop into a front three-quarter somersault with a half twist to the hands and knees.

4. Knee drop into a front three-quarter somersault with a half twist to the knee drop.

Steps 5, 6, 7, and 8 repeat steps 1, 2, 3, and 4 except that the move is initiated from the feet.

Back Three-Quarter Somersault The student leaps upward, pushes his hips forward and upward, pulls his head and arms backward, arches his body, somersaults three-quarters of the way around, and lands in a front drop landing. Before attempting this move, the student should have mastered the back somersault in layout po-

---

[4] All of the trampoline moves described in this section have been done by both boys and girls.
[5] Frank LaDue and Jim Norman, *This is Trampolining,* (Cedar Rapids, Ia.: Nissen Trampoline Co., 1954), p. 49.

Back ³/₄ somersault

Front 1¼ somersault in piked position

sition. The spotter should position himself between the frame and the bed. He can do this by removing two or three springs, depending upon his hip girth. If he notes that the performer will not land in a horizontal position, he should extend one arm across his back and the other across his knees. This will prevent hyperextension of the performer's back upon rebound.

Front One and One-Quarter Somersault in Tucked Position The student leaps upward, lifts his hips, and brings his head and arms forward to move into a tightly tucked position. He retains the tucked position until his feet pass the bed. He then opens up sharply to land in a front drop position. The spotter should position

himself between the bed and the frame to prevent hyperextension of the performer's back by extending his arms across his upper back and legs.

Front One and One-Quarter Somersault in Piked Position The move is executed in the same manner as is the preceding, the only difference being that the legs are extended throughout this move and the arms are also extended and are thrown in a downward-sideward direction. The head should be lifted to check the forward rotation before the front drop landing is made. The student's initial efforts should be spotted in the same manner described for the two preceding moves.

Back One and One-Quarter Somersault The student performs a back somersault in tucked position as described in the section on trampoline skills for elementary school children. He holds his tuck until his hips have passed under his body. At this time, he extends his legs (but not his hips) to land in the back drop position with his feet above and slightly in front of his head. He then continues over into a back-over or kips up to his feet. The student should first learn to do a back somersault to a seat drop position.

Back Somersault with Twist The student initiates the back somersault in an arched position. However, after the somersault has been initiated, he straightens his body. On take-off he lifts his arms straight up over his head with his hands

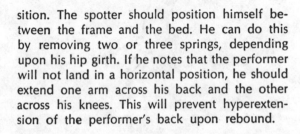

Front 1¼ somersault in tucked position

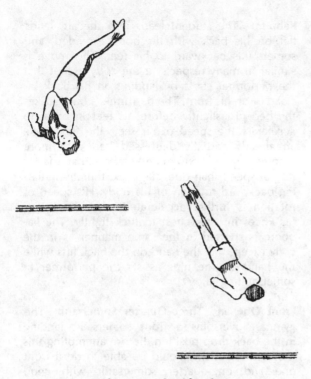

Back somersault with twist

slightly farther apart than shoulder width. His elbows are almost fully extended. At this point, to twist to his left, he extends his right elbow to push his right arm sideward. He then sweeps it across his abdomen and upwards toward his chest, flexing his elbow only after his arm has reached his abdomen. At the same time, his flexed left arm is driven backward and downward and then moves into a folded position across his chest. When the twist has been completed, he extends his arms sideward to check the spin.

LaDue and Norman[6] recommend that the following progressions be observed:

1. Back three-quarter somersault into the front drop.
2. Back three-quarter somersault with a half twist into the back drop.
3. Back three-quarter somersault with a full twist into the front drop.
4. Back three-quarter somersault with a full twist into the hands and knee drop.
5. Back somersault with a full twist.

[6] LaDue and Norman, p. 52.

Initial efforts should be made in a twisting belt or a spotter may stand on the bed to hand spot the performer. An excellent hand spotting procedure has been described by Rich Harris.[7] If the performer twists toward his left, the spotter should stand to his right and slightly behind him. He places his hands on the hips of the performer in such a position that he can pull with his left hand and push with his right hand. The spotter should not spring with the performer but should absorb the rebound of the bed by bending his knees. To develop the performer's confidence in his spotter and in order that both the performer and the spotter will learn to coordinate their movements, the performer should take three jumps and on the third jump the spotter should twist him around in a full pirouette (no somersault). This should be done several times. Next, the performer should do several back somersaults in layout position while the spotter assists. During this procedure it will be necessary that the spotter release his grasp momentarily and then regrasp the performer as he completes the somersault. When this step has been mastered, the performer should throw for the back somersault with a full twist, assisted by the spotter. As the performer's hips are lifted upward, the spotter initiates the twist by pulling with his left hand and pushing with his right hand. It will be necessary that he release his grasp momentarily and regrasp during the last half of the twist. With each successive attempt, the gymnast should assume an increasing share of the responsibility for executing the move until he can finally do it alone.

Cody The student does a three-quarter back somersault in layout position. When he lands on his front, his knees are bent and contact the bed just slightly in advance of his chest. This accelerates the speed of his chest (rotation is around the hips) and causes it to strike an already partially depressed bed with greater force so that it will rebound faster than his feet. This initiates backward rotation. He provides additional rotary force by pushing off the bed with his hands. He then pulls his head backward, pulls his knees forward into a tight tuck, and somer-

[7] Rich Harris, *Safety and Rebound Tumbling* (New York: Barnes Publishing Co., 1960), pp. 18–19.

185

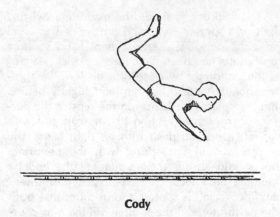

Cody

saults around to his feet. With a higher bounce and by pulling his head backward and arching hard, he can execute the cody in layout position. He can also land in the front drop position.

The cody may be spotted with an overhead belt or by two hand spotters. This procedure is described by Rich Harris.[8] A spotter stands on the frame on one side of the trampoline, and a second spotter stands on the frame on the other side of the trampoline. The spotters might also stand on two tables, the exact height of the trampoline, placed on either side of the frame. Both spotters should be prepared to step onto the bed the moment the performer has left it but not a moment before since this would "kill" his spring. Each spotter places one hand on the performer's near shoulder to lift him. They place their other hand behind his buttocks to help him to somersault. The performer should continue to utilize spotters until he has mastered the move.

Kaboom The student leaps into the air, lands flat on his back with his body extended, and somersaults backward to his feet. This move is similar in many respects to the cody except that the performer starts by landing on his back instead of on his front. The performer's back strikes the bed just slightly before his feet in order to accelerate the speed of his feet; the feet strike an already partially depressed bed with more momentum and consequently rebound at a faster rate of speed than does his back, thereby initiating backward rotation of his body. His speed of rotation is further accelerated when he brings his knees into his chest to tuck tightly. The kaboom is spotted in the same manner as in the cody except that the hand on the back lifts while the hand on the hips assists the performer in somersaulting. (Boys.)

Front One and Three-Quarter Somersault The gymnast overspins a front somersault landing in the back drop position. Before attempting this move, the student should be able to do a front one and one-quarter somersault with good height and control. It would also be well for him to learn a front one and one-half somersault from a diving board. The student secures an early fast spin, then lifts his head momentarily to look at the bed as he arrives at the one and one-quarter position; he then tucks it under again to land on his back in the back drop position.

Front Double Somersault Having mastered the front one and three-quarter somersault, the

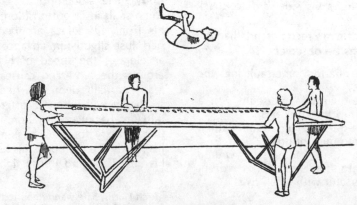

[8] Harris, p. 20.   **Front double somersault**

Shoot over the low bar from a hang on the high bar

gymnast is ready to learn the double front somersault. His first step should be to learn to do front somersaults in swingtime; that is, with no intermediate bounce between successive front somersaults. He should then learn a front one and three-quarter somersault to the seat drop. When he does the double front somersault, the gymnast should endeavor to (1) bounce straight up; (2) tuck as tightly as possible on the first somersault; (3) come out of his second somersault slightly early on his initial attempts since this is not as hazardous as is overspinning.

The move should not be attempted unless there are at least six spotters—two on each side and one at each end of the trampoline.

UNEVEN PARALLEL BARS[9]

Jump to a Front Support The gymnast starts by standing on the mat opposite the center of the low bar, facing it and grasping it with a front grip. She jumps upward to finish in a front support with her thighs against the bar, her arms extended, and her head and chest elevated.

Cross Seat Mount The student starts standing between the bars at their center facing the end of the bars. She jumps up to grasp the low bar with her right hand and the high bar with her left hand and then swings both legs up and over the low bar, doing a quarter turn to finish in a seat position across the low bar.

Shoot over the Lower Bar from a Hang on the High Bar The student starts by standing on

[9] While the uneven parallel bars are used as a competitive event for girls only, elementary school boys do enjoy doing and are challenged by these moves.

the mat opposite the center of the high bar and facing it. She leaps upward to grasp the high bar in a front grip and swings her legs over the low bar to finish in a seat position across the low bar with her body extended while continuing to hold the high bar.

Pull-Over The student starts by standing on the mat opposite the center of the low bar, facing it and grasping it with a front grip. She swings one leg under, around, and over the bar, pulls herself toward the bar, brings the other leg alongside the first, and circles the bar to finish in a front support position on the bar. This is the same move done by boys on the horizontal bar.

Squat Stand Mount The student starts from a standing position several feet away from and facing the center of the low bar. She takes the necessary steps, grasps the bar with a front grip, leaps from both feet simultaneously, pushes down with her arms, elevates her hips, and flexes her knees to place both feet on the bar between her hands. She completes the skill by moving into the erect position and grasping the high bar. A spotter should stand alongside the performer ready to grasp her by the waist in the event she loses her balance.

Flank Vault Dismount from a Straddle Seat The student starts from a sitting position astraddle the low bar with her outside knee flexed, and her inside leg extended, with a reverse grasp on the low bar and a front grip on the high bar. She swings her inside leg forward and over the low bar, supports herself principally on the hand grasping the low bar, pivots around on this arm to face the opposite direction, and lands on the mat still holding the low bar. She should lean well over her supporting arm.

Cast off the Low Bar with a Quarter Turn The student starts in a front support position at the center of the low bar facing inwards. She flexes her hips to bring her legs forward and then swings them backward, pushing away from the bar, releasing her right hand and turning her head to the right to land on the mat facing the end of the bars with her left shoulder toward the bars. She should retain her grasp with her left hand until she lands on her feet to aid in maintaining balance.

"L" Position Cast Dismount The student begins in a seat position across the center of the low bar facing outward and grasping the bar to either side of her hips with a front grip. She lifts her feet and pushes away from the bar to land on the mat a few feet from the bar with her back toward it. A spotter should stand alongside the performer and lift with one hand under her hips. The spotter's other hand should grip her wrist.

Underswing Dismount from the Low Bar The student starts in a front support position at the center of the low bar facing outward. She has a front grip on the bar. She swings her legs backward and then forward. As her legs swing forward, she flexes her hips and swings under the bar. She then pulls with her arms and extends her hips to shoot her foot upward and away from the bar to land on her feet several feet from the bar. During the shoot, her arms should extend and her back should be arched. A spotter should stand alongside the performer to place one hand on the performer's hips and the other on her upper back.

Underswing Dismount from the High Bar The student starts in a standing position on the center of the low bar and facing the high bar which she grasps in a front grip. She jumps upward, flexing her hips to bring her feet toward the high bar. At the same time she pulls with her arms, causing her body to swing forward under the bar. She then extends her hips and arms in order to shoot away from the bar and land several feet away from the high bar with her back toward it. A spotter should stand alongside the performer ready to grasp her waist if necessary.

Rear Vault with a Quarter Turn Dismount The student starts in a support position between the bars at their center. She swings her legs forward and upward by flexing her hips, then pushes away from the high bar to pivot on the hand on the low bar and to bring her feet over the low bar. She moves her other hand from the high bar to the low bar and passes over the low bar with her body in an "L" position. She then

Underswing dismount from the low bar

pushes away from the bar to land with her back toward the bar, several feet from it. During the learning stages, a spotter should hold the wrist and upper arm of the supporting arm of the performer.

Seat Balance The student starts in a crotch seat position on the low bar. She releases her grip on the low bar and regrasps the bar behind her hips. She places her right foot on the bar with her knee flexed and elevates her extended left leg until it is at a 45° angle to the bar.

One-Leg Squat into a Scale The student starts from a squatting position on her right foot on the low bar, with her left leg extended forward. She is holding the high bar with her right hand and the low bar in front of her supporting foot with her left hand. She extends her right leg, extends her left arm forward in line with her body after releasing her grip, and moves her left leg backward to finish in a front scale position while continuing to hold the high bar with her right hand.

One-leg squat into a scale

Swan support

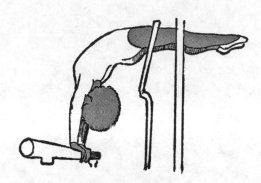

Arch back

Swan Support The student starts in a front support position on the high bar. She extends her arm sideward, lifts her head, and arches her back to balance on her hips in a swan position.

Thigh Rest The student starts in a front support position on the high bar facing inward. She releases her grasp, pivots slowly about her hips to grasp the low bar, and lifts her legs to finish supported on her extended arms with her body arched and her thighs resting against the high bar.

Kick Off the Low Bar and Single-Leg Kip to High Bar The student starts in a hanging position at the center of the high bar facing inward. She has a front grip. She takes a small swing forward to place her right foot on the low bar and to lift her extended left leg until her toes touch the high bar. As she swings backward, she extends her right leg and whips her left leg downward while pulling with her arms to finish in a front support position on the high bar.

Leg Bounce into a Pull-Over on the High Bar The student starts in a hanging position at the center of the high bar facing inward. She has a front grip. She flexes her hips to lift her legs over the right side of the low bar and allows them to drop forcefully against the bar, striking it with the upper back part of her thighs. As her legs rebound upward, she pulls with her arms to execute a pull-over, finishing in a front support on the high bar.

Arch Back The student begins hanging by her knees from the high bar and facing the low bar. She grasps the low bar with both hands and pulls her body over it. She then extends her arms and legs to finish in an arched position with the back of her legs resting against the high bar. A spotter should hold her wrist and upper arm during the move.

BIBLIOGRAPHY

Baley, James A. "Beginning Tumbling Stunts, Part I." *Athletic Journal*, December, 1963.

———. "Intermediate Tumbling Stunts, Part I." *Athletic Journal*, January, 1964.

———. "Intermediate Tumbling Stunts, Part II." *Athletic Journal*, February, 1964.

———. "Advanced Tumbling Stunts, Part II." *Athletic Journal*, April, 1964.

Goier, J. G. "Safety Procedures in Gymnastics." *Athletic Journal*, March, 1953.

Holzaepel, Dick. "Tumbling—A Comparison and Analysis." *Athletic Journal*, October, 1954.

———. "Handsprings and Headsprings." *Athletic Journal*, January, 1955.

———. "Somersaults, Gainers, and Routines." *Athletic Journal*, February, 1955.

———. "Stunts and Combinations." *Athletic Journal*, October, 1955.

———. "Safety First in the Gym." *Scholastic Coach*, January, 1956.

Loken, Newton. "Advanced Tumbling Hints." *Athletic Journal*, January, 1951.

8

SKILLS FOR
SENIOR HIGH
AND COLLEGE
MEN AND
WOMEN

While most of the moves described in this chapter have been done by a child of high school age, it is unlikely that any child has done all of them or that any ever will. Most of the moves are too difficult to be taught in the typical high school physical education class. However, all of the moves could serve members of interscholastic or intercollegiate gymnastic teams and exhibition troupes at the high school or college level.

The moves described in this chapter are a continuum, in the order of difficulty, of moves presented in Chapters 6 and 7. High school and college students should not attempt the moves described in this chapter until they have mastered the lead-up skills. In school systems where children have been given an excellent program of instruction in gymnastics throughout their elementary and junior high school years, many of the moves included in this chapter could be presented to them in high school physical education classes. While this is the situation in few school systems at the present time in the United States, it is hoped that this situation will improve. This text is organized as it is in the hope that the challenge will be accepted by physical educators and school administrators.

DOUBLES BALANCING

Hand to Feet Get-Up In the starting position, the partners are in a low hand to foot balance. The topmounter initiates the move by leaning forward to get himself off balance. If he merely flexes his hips to angle his legs backward and his trunk forward, he will not be off balance. He should lean forward from his head to his feet with his body straight. The understander angles his arms forward and lifts his trunk to come to a sitting position. As he sits up, he bends his elbows, placing them next to his trunk in order to keep his forearms vertical. However, he should not flex his elbows until after the sit-up has been initiated. He then flexes his left knee, leans forward from his hips, and rises to a kneeling position. He next places his left foot on the mat. Then he places his right foot on the mat to assume a squatting position and rises to a standing position. To complete the move, he presses his partner to arm's length overhead. Until the move has been mastered, at least three

Hand to feet get-up

spotters are needed. (Two boys or a boy understander and a girl topmounter.)

Hand to Feet Get-Down This skill is done in the same manner as the preceding except, of course, that the partners move from the high hand to feet to the low hand to feet position and all the movements are reversed. (Two boys or a boy understander and a girl topmounter.)

Hand to Feet Seal Roll The partners begin in a low hand to feet position. The topmounter shifts his weight to his left foot, and the understander flexes his right arm to place his right elbow on the mat alongside his head. The topmounter then shifts his weight to his right foot, and the understander flexes his left elbow to place it against his hips and rolls around into the supine position. As he does this, he brings

191

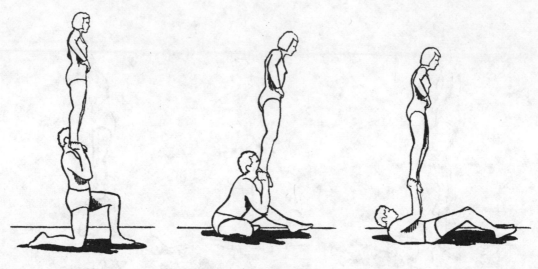

Hand to feet get-down

his left elbow to the mat about 12 inches to the left of his right elbow. At the same time, the top-mounter turns his head to the right to facilitate the turn. The topmounter next shifts his weight to his left foot while the understander rolls to his back and extends his arms to complete the move in a low hand to feet position. It is neces-sary that the understander keep his forearms as nearly vertical as possible at all times. (Two boys or a boy understander and a girl topmounter.)

Hand to Feet Pretzel The partners begin in a low hand to feet position. The topmounter shifts his weight to his left foot and the understander flexes his right elbow to bring it to the mat along-side his head. The understander then flexes his

knees and hips to bring his body between his arms and to place his knees on the mat behind his elbows. As his knees come to the mat, he bends his left elbow to place the backs of both hands against his hips. He then places his left elbow on the mat and rolls around with his head on the mat to a jackknifed position, resting on his shoulder blades and the back of his head. To finish the move, he brings his hips and legs between his arms, ending in a low hand to feet position. (Two boys or a boy understander and a girl topmounter.)

High Arm to Arm Balance The partners begin standing facing one another and gripping one another's upper arms. The topmounter leaps up-

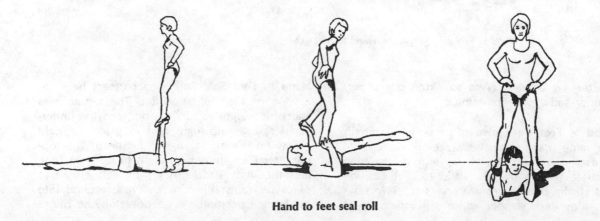

Hand to feet seal roll

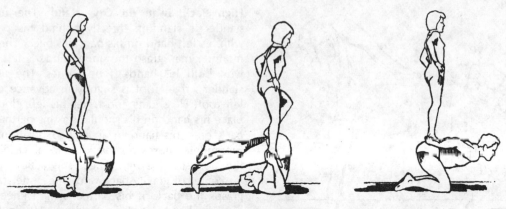

Hand to feet pretzel

ward and flexes his hips to place his legs under his partner's arms. The understander bends forward and then whips up to the erect position to bring the topmounter over his head. At the same time, the topmounter lifts his hips over his head. He then extends his hips to complete the skill with his body in an arched position. Until the balanced position has been secured, the understander should have one foot slightly in advance of the other for greater stability. Partners should look into one another's face throughout the skill. (Two boys or a boy understander and a girl topmounter.)

High Front Swan on Hands The partners begin by standing facing one another. The understand-

er's hands are on the topmounter's hips while the topmounter is grasping his partner's wrists. The topmounter leaps upward to elevate his hips as his partner squats and bends his arms to get under him. The understander then extends his legs and arms in one continuous motion as the topmounter pulls into an arched position with his arms extended sideward to complete the skill. Some experimentation in positioning of the understander's hands may be necessary in order to find the center of balance. The topmounter can move her center of balance forward or backward slightly by positioning her arms. (Two boys or a boy understander and a girl topmounter.)

High arm to arm balance

High front swan on hands

High back swan on hands

High Back Swan on Hands The skill is begun with the understander standing directly behind his partner with his hands on his partner's hips. The topmounter is grasping the understander's wrists. The topmounter leaps upward and lies back into an arched position as the understander squats and bends his elbows to get under him. After his partner is over his head, the understander extends his arms and legs to complete the move while the topmounter is in an arched position with his arms extended sideward. (Two boys or a boy as understander and a girl as topmounter.)

High Back Swan on One Hand The understander is standing directly behind his partner with his left hand on his partner's back. The topmounter may grasp the understander's left wrist with both his hands if he wishes. The understander's right foot is slightly in advance of his left foot. He squats and flexes his left elbow to place his hand on his shoulder as his partner lies back onto his hand in an arched position. The topmounter flexes his left knee to place his left toe alongside his right knee. This action moves his center of gravity backward. The understander grasps the back of his partner's right knee with his right hand. He then stands up. He flexes his knees slightly and extends them quickly and vigorously as he extends his left arm under the rising body of his partner. When balance has been secured, the topmounter extends his arms sideward and the understander places his right hand on his hip to complete the move. The spotter should stand behind the understander. (Two boys or a boy as understander and a girl as topmounter.)

Stand on Head In the starting position, the topmounter is standing on his partner's shoulders. The topmounter squats and the understander releases his grip with his right hand on his partner's lower leg and grasps his hand. He does the same with his left hand. The topmounter pushes directly downward on his partner's hands

High back swan on one hand

Stand on head

194

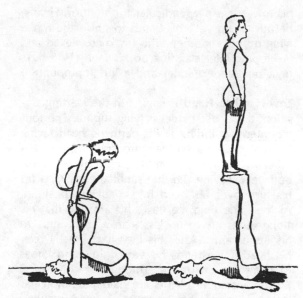

Feet to feet balance

Jump into feet to feet balance

and places his left foot on his partner's head, leaving room for his right foot. He then places his right foot on his partner's head. The arches of his feet should cup the understander's head. The understander shifts his right hand to his partner's right ankle and then shifts his left hand to his left ankle. His fingers are behind the ankles while his thumbs are in front. The understander does all the balancing. The topmounter must resist the temptation to balance himself (by flexing his hips, waving his arms, or pushing with his toes). During their initial attempts, the performers should be guarded by at least three spotters. (Two boys or a boy as understander and a girl as topmounter.)

Feet to Feet Balance In the starting position, the understander is lying on his back with his extended arms elevated perpendicular to the floor. His knees are on his chest with his lower legs perpendicular to the floor. The topmounter is standing at his partner's head, facing his feet and holding his hands. The topmounter supports himself on his hands as he flexes his hips and knees to place his feet on his partner's feet. He hunches his shoulders forward to shift his center of gravity over the understander's feet. The partners release one another's hands as the topmounter moves into a squatting position on the

understander's feet. The understander extends his legs as the topmounter moves into an erect position to complete the move. Throughout the move, the understander's lower legs have been perpendicular to the floor. Until the move has been mastered, the topmounter should be guarded by at least two spotters. (Two boys or a boy understander and a girl topmounter.)

Jump into a Feet to Feet Balance In the starting position, the understander is lying on his back with his head elevated and his hips and knees flexed. His lower legs are angled slightly forward of the vertical. The topmounter is standing several feet away from his partner (on his feet side) and facing him. He takes several steps, leaps from both feet simultaneously, draws his knees up, and lands on both feet on his partner's feet in a semi-squatting position. Both partners then extend their legs to complete the move. Until the move has been mastered, the topmounter should be guarded by a spotter at each side. (Two boys.)

Body Breaker: In the starting position, the partners are in a feet to feet balance. The topmounter shifts his center of gravity slightly to the rear and the understander elevates his hips and flexes his knees to roll backward around his shoulders and to place his left knee on the mat as far over his head as he can. As his knee moves backward, he reinforces his leg by placing his left hand against his left lower leg. He next places his right knee on the mat as far beyond his head as he is able. At all times, he endeavors to keep

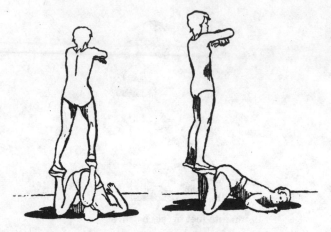

Body breaker

Low hand to hand balance

his lower legs perpendicular to the floor. Finally, he pushes up with his hands to finish the move lying on his abdomen with his knees flexed and the topmounter standing on his feet. (Two boys or a boy understander and a girl topmounter.)

Low Hand to Hand Balance In the starting position, the understander is lying supine. The topmounter is standing at his partner's head facing his feet, and the partners are grasping one another's hands. The topmounter springs upward, both feet leaving the mat simultaneously, to lift his hips over his head into a tucked position. At the same time, he flexes his arms so that his upper arms are at no less than a 135° angle to his upper arms. After his hips are directly over his head, he extends his arms, hips, and knees to complete the move. Throughout the move, the understander's arms are held perpendicular to the floor and the topmounter's head is pulled backward. In the final position, the topmounter's feet are directly over his head. (Two boys.)

High Hand to Hand Balance In the starting position, the topmounter is standing directly in front of the understander, facing the same direction and gripping his hands. The topmounter jumps upward lifting his hips backward between his arms and pushing with his arms as the understander flexes his knees and steps forward to get under him. Both boys continue to extend their arms as the topmounter moves upward. When the topmounter's hips are over his head, he extends his hips, knees, and arms to finish with his body arched and his feet directly over his head in the handstand position. Throughout the move both performers' heads should be pulled backward. (Two boys.)

Hand to Hand Get-Up Before attempting this move, the partners should learn to do a hand to feet get-up. This will speed up the learning process since the procedures followed by the understander are identical in both moves. The topmounter also follows the same procedures except that he is balanced on his hands instead of his feet. As the understander sits up from the supine position, the topmounter must overbalance his handstand to fall forward under his partner's forward-moving hands. When the understander reaches the sitting position, the top

High hand to hand balance

mounter must check his overbalanced position by moving his hands forward slightly and by pulling his head backward. As the understander flexes his left knee to place his left foot on the mat, the topmounter must shift his weight forward and to his left hand when the understander places his right foot on the mat. He must shift it forward again slightly when the understander stands up. The move is finished when the understander has pressed his partner into the high hand to hand balance. To dismount, the topmounter underbalances. (Two boys.)

Hand to Hand Seal Roll Before attempting this move, the partners should learn to do a hand to feet seal roll since the procedures followed by the understander are identical, as are those followed by the topmounter except that he is standing on his hands instead of his feet. As the understander lowers his right elbow to the mat beyond his head, the topmounter flexes his left elbow slightly and shifts his weight to his left arm. He initiates the turn by turning his head to the right. He shifts his weight to his right arm

after the understander's right elbow is on the mat. He shifts his weight to his left arm as the understander rolls from his front to his back. (Two boys.)

Jackknife Hand to Hand In the starting position, the understander is standing with his hips flexed and his arms elevated behind himself and perpendicular to the floor. The topmounter is standing on his partner's hips, facing in the same direction and grasping his hands. He moves into an "L" support position on his hands and presses up into a hand to hand balance. As the topmounter's weight moves from his hips to his hands, the understander must angle his legs backward in order to keep the center of support under the center of weight. The topmounter must squeeze his hands toward one another. Only understanders with good shoulder girdle strength should attempt this skill. (Two boys.)

Handstand on the Feet In the starting position, the understander is lying on his back with his extended legs elevated and perpendicular to

Hand to hand get-up

Hand to hand get-down

Hand to hand seal roll

the floor. His elbows are on the mat and his hands are against his thighs to brace them. The topmounter is straddling the understander's waist, facing his feet, and holding his insteps. He takes a little jump to bring himself to a support position on his hands on his partner's feet. His hips are flexed and his legs are extended. He flexes his arms and his knees to make it easier to bring his hips over his head. If he flexes his elbows so that his upper arms are at less than a 135° angle to his forearms, he will experience difficulty in pressing up. After his hips are over his head, he extends his arms, hips, and knees to finish in a handstand

position. Throughout the move the understander's legs should be held perpendicular to the floor. (Two boys.)

Jackknife Roll Through The partners start this move in a jackknife hand to hand balance. The understander bends his knees and tucks his head to place his shoulders on the mat. He shifts his weight to his shoulders and pushes off his feet to roll his body and legs between his arms to finish in a low hand to hand balance. He must flex his knees as his legs swing between his arms in order to avoid striking his partner with his heels. (Two boys.)

Jackknife hand to hand

Handstand on the feet

Jackknife roll through

Foot flag

Cannonball into a High Hand to Hand Balance
In the starting position, the topmounter is lying supine and the understander is gripping his hands and standing several feet away facing the topmounter's feet. He steps forward quickly to straddle his hips in a stooped position, pulls very hard with his arms, extends his hips to come to the erect position, and flexes his knees to get under his partner's rising body. As his partner steps forward to straddle his hips, the topmounter moves into a tucked position. He maintains this tucked position and pulls very hard with his arms until he has been moved opposite his partner's face. At this time, he extends his arms, hips, and knees to shoot up into a high hand to hand balance. As the topmounter shoots into the handstand position, the understander extends his arms. (Two boys.)

Foot Flag This move is started from a stand on thighs. The topmounter turns to hook his left foot behind the neck of the understander. The understander wedges his partner's left leg between his neck and right shoulder by grasping his left thigh with his right hand. The understander leans sideward as the topmounter moves into the final position. (Two boys or a boy understander and a girl topmounter.)

Shoulder Balance on Feet The understander starts in a supine position with his legs elevated. The topmounter stands at the understander's head facing his feet and grasping his hands. He places his shoulders on his partner's feet and upends into a shoulder balance on his partner's feet. The understander's feet should be positioned along the topmounter's upper arms so that the topmounter can lever against them to aid in maintaining balance. The topmounter should be in a slightly underbalanced position. When balance has been secured, the partners should release hands. (Two boys.)

Front Lever on Knees This move is usually begun from a high hand to hand position. The

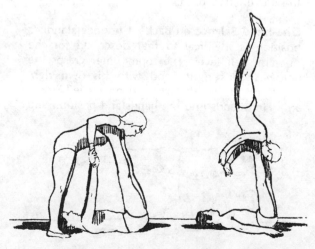

Free shoulder balance on feet

Front lever on knees

understander flexes his arms to lower the top-mounter. The topmounter flexes his arms and slides down along the chest and abdomen of his partner bringing his shoulders to rest on his thighs. He rolls around his shoulders with his hips flexed as the understander moves toward the final position. The topmounter extends his hips to complete the move. Note that the top-mounter's upper arms are at right angles to his trunk and his forearms are at right angles to his upper arms.

One-Arm Half Lever In the starting position the understander is lying on his right side with his right arm behind his back and his right hand resting on his left hip. His left hand is on the mat and his left arm is flexed to brace himself against sideward movement. He further braces himself by flexing his left leg and placing his left knee on the mat. The topmounter grasps the understander's right hand in his own right hand and does a one-arm half lever with his left hand on his partner's shoulder. After he has secured a steady balance, the topmounter lifts his left arm and extends it in line with his body to complete the move. (Two boys.)

One-Hand Balance on Back The understander's position is identical to that described for the one-arm half lever. The topmounter grasps the understander's right hand with his own right hand and places his left hand on his left upper arm. He upends into the handstand position and

One-hand balance on back

then moves into the one-hand balance to complete the move. The topmounter's back (frontal or lateral plane) should be as nearly vertical as possible. (Two boys.)

One-Hand to Hand Balance The partners begin in a high hand to hand balance. The understander flexes his left (or right) arm while the top mounter flexes his right (or left) arm. The understander's left (or right) forearm is perpendicular to the floor. The topmounter shifts all his weight to his left (or right) arm by angling his body sideward. His supporting arm should at all times remain perpendicular to the floor. He "locks" his shoulder joint. When balance has been secured, the partners release one another's

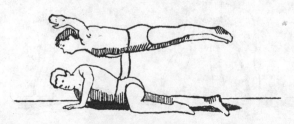

One-arm half lever

One-hand to hand balance

Front swan, kick, and half twist to back swan

right (or left) hands. The understander should do all the balancing by shifting his weight from one foot to the other or by bending his trunk to one side or the other as necessary. (Two boys.)

Front Swan, Kick, and Half Twist to Back Swan
The partners begin in a front swan on the feet. The understander flexes his knees and then extends them sharply to kick the topmounter upward. The topmounter must not permit his body

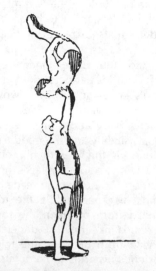

High one-arm to arm balance

to fold under the force of the kick. As he leaves his partner's feet, the topmounter turns his head to the left and swings his right arm across his chest. These actions will cause him to execute a half turn. The understander catches him on his feet in a back swan on feet. (Two boys or a boy understander and a girl topmounter.)

One-Arm to Arm This move is begun from a high arm to arm balance. The topmounter shifts his weight to his right arm by angling his body sideward. When balance has been secured, the partners release left arms to complete the move. (Two boys.)

TRIPLES BALANCING

Triple Crab In the starting position, the understander is in a crab position. His hips are extended in order that his thighs will be in a horizontal position. His lower legs and arms are vertical. The middle man is standing to the understander's left and is facing his feet. He places his left foot on the understander's left knee and then his right foot on his right knee. He next places his left hand on the understander's left shoulder and his right hand on his right shoulder and extends his hips. The topmounter places his right foot on the understander's left thigh and then his left foot on the middle man's left knee. As he climbs up, he keeps his weight centered over his partners. He then places his right foot on the middle man's right knee and places his hands on his shoulders to complete the move. (Three boys or two boys and a girl.)

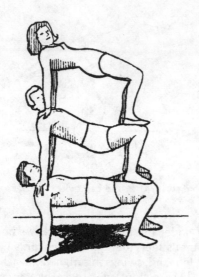

Triple crab

Triple thigh stand (three airplanes)

Tepee In the starting position, the understander is supine with his extended arms elevated. The middle man is standing a few feet from the understander's head with his back toward him. He arches back and then drops onto the hands of the understander. The topmounter stands next to the understander's chest and facing his head. He grasps the middle man and leaps upward into an "L" sit supported on the middle man's hands. He then presses up into a hand to hand balance to complete the move. (Three boys.)

Triple Thigh Stand (Three Airplanes) The three partners are standing behind one another about a foot apart and facing in the same direction. The middle man squats to place his head between the legs of the topmounter who then sits on his shoulders. He grasps the topmounter's knees to steady him as he extends his own knees to lift him. He keeps his back as nearly vertical as possible as he lifts. After he is up, the topmounter clamps his feet behind the middle man's back and squeezes. The middle man grasps the topmounter's knees and pulls downward. These actions make one unit of the two men, making it easier for the understander to balance them. The understander squats to place his head between the middle man's legs. The middle man sits on his shoulders and the understander extends his knees to lift both his partners. He then grasps the middle man's knees and pulls downward while the middle man clamps his feet behind the understander's back and squeezes. The understander squats slightly and the middle man places his feet along his thighs with his toes over the kneecaps. The topmounter places his feet in a similar position on the middle man's thighs, and then extends his knees while the middle man pulls his head from between the topmounter's legs and extends his arms. The understander next pulls his head from between the middle man's legs and extends his arms to complete the move. It is helpful if the understander places his index

Tepee

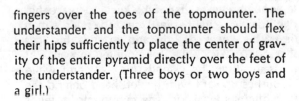

Two and a half high

High front swan on thighs

fingers over the toes of the topmounter. The understander and the topmounter should flex their hips sufficiently to place the center of gravity of the entire pyramid directly over the feet of the understander. (Three boys or two boys and a girl.)

Two and a Half High The two and a half high is started from the triple thigh stand. The middle man places his head between the legs of the topmounter and then extends his knees to stand straight up. At this time, the middle man's body should be perpendicular to the floor. The topmounter and the middle man then grasp hands. The middle man keeps his forearms vertical as the topmounter pushes down on his hands to place one foot on the middle man's shoulder and then the other foot on his other shoulder. He next extends his legs to come to the erect position. The middle man releases the topmounter's hands one at a time, and grasps his calves in the same manner as in the two high to complete the move. (Three boys or two boys and a girl.)

Thigh Stand and Arch Back This move is also started from a triple thigh stand. The topmounter twists around to grasp the shoulders of the middle man. He moves his left foot to the right thigh of the midde man and then moves his right foot to the left thigh to complete the turn. The middle man grasps the topmounter behind the knees and the topmounter arches backward to complete the move. (Three boys or two boys and a girl.)

High Front Swan on Thighs This move begins from the thigh stand and arch back. The top mounter comes to the erect position and the middle man places his hands on her hips. His arms are flexed. She bends forward to place her weight on his hands. He then extends his legs and arms to lift her to arm's length overhead as she pulls her legs, shoulders, and head backward into an arched position. (Two boys and a girl.)

High One-Hand Back Swan on Thighs This move is started from a triple thigh stand. The

High one-hand back swan on thighs

Thigh stand and handstand on back

High hand to hand on thighs

middle man places his right hand on the topmounter's lower back. The topmounter lies backward to assume an arched position on the middle man's hand. The middle man's arm is flexed and the back of his hand is on his shoulder. The topmounter flexes her right knee to place her right toe alongside her left knee. The middle man flexes his knees slightly and extends his legs sharply to "kick" the topmounter upward. At the same time, he extends his right arm while he pushes upward with his left hand behind the topmounter's left knee. The topmounter extends her arms sideward and the middle man places his left hand on his hip to complete the move. (Two boys and a girl.)

High Hand to Hand on Thighs This move is begun from a two and a half high. The topmounter squats and grasps the hands of the middle man. He then presses up into a hand to hand balance. (Three boys.)

Thigh Stand and Handstand on Back In the starting position, the middle man is standing on the thighs of the understander. She flexes her hips and places her hands on her knees. Her back is horizontal. The topmounter steps up on the thigh of the understander and places his right hand between the middle man's shoulder blades

Father time

and his left hand on her sacrum. He then presses up into the handstand, keeping most of his weight on his left hand. If the balance is secure, the middle man may extend her arms sideward. (Three boys, or a girl as middle man and boys as understander and topmounter.)

Father Time In the starting position, the understander is supine with his legs extended and elevated at right angles to his trunk. The middle man is standing with his heels directly in front

of the understander's buttocks and his back toward him. He sits back to place his pelvic bones between the understander's legs just above his knees. At the same time, he grasps his partner's feet just behind the toes with his fingers on top and his thumbs underneath. As he lies back into an arched position, he extends his arms and pulls the understander's legs inward. The topmounter, who has been standing alongside the understander's head and facing his feet, now grasps the understander's heels, jumps to an "L" support position, and presses up into a handstand to complete the move. If he wishes, the understander may place his hands on his own thighs to help stabilize his legs. (Three boys, or a girl as middle man and boys as topmounter and understander.)

Mongolians In the starting position, the understander is supine with his hands on the mat next to his head, palms up. The middle man is standing on the understander's hands with his back toward him. The understander lifts his legs to place his heels on the middle man's buttocks and his toes on the posterior upper portion of his thighs. The middle man sits back onto the understander's feet. The understander extends his legs and brings them to the vertical position as he stabilizes and lifts the middle man with his hands. The topmounter steps foward to face the middle man and to grasp his upper arms. The middle man grasps the topmounter's upper arms. The understander releases the middle man's feet

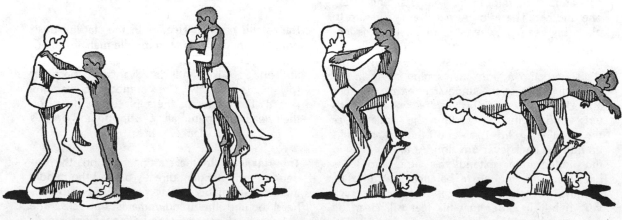

Mongolians

Jackson boys

Fulcrum on the feet

and places his hands on the mat, palms up, so that the topmounter may step onto them. The topmounter jumps upward on the mat, palms up, so that the topmounter may step onto them. The topmounter jumps upward to sit on the middle man's thighs. During the jump, the middle man assists by pulling with his arms while the understander assists by lifting with his arms. The topmounter now hooks his feet inside the understander's lower legs. The middle man and topmounter release one another's arms as they lie backward into a horizontal position to complete the move. The understander's legs must remain vertical throughout the move. (Three boys, or a boy as understander and two girls.)

Jackson Boys In the starting position, the understander and middle man are standing facing one another. The middle man bends forward to place his head between the understander's legs and his shoulders up against his knees. The understander grasps his wrists. The topmounter steps onto the middle man's hips facing in the same direction as the understander. He assumes an "L" support position on the understander's wrists and begins to press into the handstand as the middle man lifts his feet off the mat and pulls up into the back lever position. At the same time, the understander extends his arms and leans backward just enough to balance the entire assembly. In pressing up, the topmounter must tuck very tightly in order that his feet will clear the understander. (Three boys.)

Fulcrum on the Feet In the starting position, the understander is supine and the middle man is standing with his heels next to his partner's buttocks; the understander's feet are placed behind the middle man's knees in such a position that the middle of his feet overlap the knee joint. He supports the middle man with his hands against his back as he lies backward. As the middle man lies backward, the topmounter grasps the ankles of the middle man and presses up into the handstand. The understander very likely will find it necessary to experiment in positioning his feet as will the topmounter in placing his hands before the balanced position is found. (Three boys, or a girl as middle man and two boys.)

Handstand on Two Heads In the starting position, the understander and middle man are standing side by side. Their feet are spread sideward and one foot is slightly in advance of the other for greater stability. The topmounter, standing directly behind his partners, places his hands on their heads, jump into an "L" support and presses up into a handbalance. (Three boys.)

The Finafield In the starting position. the understander is standing directly behind the middle man. He flexes his hips to place the back of his head behind the middle man's buttocks. The partners hook arms and the understander extends

Handstand on two heads

Three high

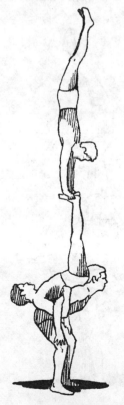

The Finafield

his hips to place his back at a 135° angle to the floor. The middle man lifts his legs to position them vertically while lying on the understander's back. The understander places his hands on his own thighs for greater stability. The topmounter is standing alongside his partners and facing in the same direction as the understander. He grasps the middle man's left leg with his left hand and steps on the understander's left thigh with his left foot. He pulls himself up and steps on the middle man's abdomen with his right foot. He brings his left foot up next to his right foot, grasps the insteps of the middle man, and presses up into a handstand. (Three boys.)

Three High The starting position is a three high sitting. Procedures for getting into this position have been described for the three airplanes skill. From this position, the understander and the middle man grasp hands. The understander's forearms should be vertical and his upper arms horizontal. The middle man pushes straight down with his arms so that he can place his right foot on the understander's right shoulder. He places

Roll around from a triple crab

his left foot on the understander's other shoulder. The understander then releases his grip on the middle man's hands and grasps his calves one hand at a time and reaches in as deeply as possible. He pulls his head backward and pulls forward and downward with his hands to press the middle man's lower legs against his head. Only the middle man's toes should be on the understander's shoulders. His heels should be unsupported and pulled downward. The topmounter moves into the standing position by following the same procedures followed by the middle man. All movements throughout the skill should be executed slowly and deliberately. The

Quadruple thigh stand

High father time

Pitch into a high hand to hand

The Springfield

weight should be centered over the understander's feet at all times. The topmounter must resist the temptation to balance herself, leaving this to her partners. Four spotters should guard the performers until the skill is mastered.

Another method for mounting into the three high is that illustrated. This is begun from a two high. The topmounter begins by standing directly in front of the understander, facing him. Beginners should be well spotted by two or three spotters. (Three boys or two boys and a girl.)

SINGLES BALANCING

"L" Handstand The gymnast starts in a handstand. He flexes his hips to lower his extended legs until they are at a right angle to his trunk. At the same time, he angles his trunk and his arms forward of the vertical to counterbalance the off-center weight of his legs. He tucks his head between his arms to complete the move. Maintaining balance is difficult in this position because the gymnast cannot see the floor. He must rely on his kinesthetic sense and pressure against his fingers. (Boys and girls.)

German Handstand The gymnast starts in a handstand. He removes all the arch from his body by stretching his feet toward the ceiling and tucking his head between his arms. (Boys.)

One-Hand Balance The gymnast starts in a handstand. He straddles his legs and, while keeping his right arm perpendicular to the floor, angles his body toward the right until all his weight rests on his right hand. He continues to

German handstand

211

One-hand balance

Handstand on the fingertips

touch the floor with the fingertips of his left hand until the balance is secured. In the final position, his left leg is in line with his right arm and his right leg is in line with his left arm. His shoulder joint is "locked" in extension. He checks an underbalance by flexing his right elbow an overbalance by pulling his head backward and pressing with his fingertips; he controls lateral balance by moving his left arm or right leg upward or downward. The one hand balance can also be done with the legs together. The same principles apply. However, a greater sideward lean of the body is necessary. (Boys.)

Handstand on the Fingertips The gymnast places his fingertips on the floor and kicks up into a handstand. The handstand may also be done on two fingers and the thumbs of each hand or on one finger and the thumb of each hand. The superb professional handbalancer Bob Jones did the handstand on his thumbs only. (Boys.)

Handwalk Down Steps The gymnast starts in a handstand at the top of a flight of stairs. He flexes his arms and shifts his center of gravity forward. He moves his right hand to the next step below and shifts his center of gravity over this hand as he moves his left hand alongside his right. This procedure is repeated down the flight of stairs. (Boys.)

Handwalk Up Steps The gymnast starts in a handstand at the bottom of a flight of stairs. He

shifts his center of gravity forward by overbalancing and places his left hand on the next step above. He shifts his center of gravity over this hand, does a one-arm press-up, and brings his right hand up alongside his left. He repeats this procedure up the flight of stairs. Another procedure is that of holding the left arm flexed until the right hand is brought up and then pressing up with both hands. (Boys.)

Bouncing on the Hands Down Stairs The gymnast starts in a handstand at the top of the stairs. He overbalances slightly by angling his arms forward while keeping his body and legs vertical. He flexes his knees slightly and then extends them sharply to lift himself off the step.

Handwalk up steps

Handstand on two chairs

He lands on his hands on the next step below, flexing his arms slightly to absorb the shock of landing. He repeats this procedure down the flight of stairs. (Boys.)

Bouncing on the Hands Up Stairs The gymnast starts in a handstand at the bottom of the stairs. The stairs must be low. He overbalances slightly by angling his arms forward, bends his knees, and then sharply kicks his legs directly upward to lift himself upward. He lands in a handstand position on the next step above with his arms bent. He then extends his arms. This procedure is repeated up the flight of stairs. (Boys.)

Clapping the Hands in a Handstand The gymnast starts in a handstand. He flexes his knees and then extends them sharply to lift himself off the floor. He claps his hands together before landing again in the handstand position. (Boys.)

Handstand on One Chair The gymnast begins in a side sitting position on a chair with his right hand grasping the seat and his left gripping the backrest. He pushes up into an "L" support, tucks his legs inward, and presses up into a handstand. About 70 percent of his weight is on his right hand. (Boys.)

Handstand on Two Chairs The gymnast stands on the middle of one chair facing sideward and gripping the back of the chair with his right hand. He places the back legs of another chair on the front portion of the seat of the first chair and grips the back of this chair with his left hand. He presses up into the handstand. (Boys.)

Handstand on Two Chairs and Four Bottles The gymnast places a soft drink bottle under each leg of a chair. He must exercise care to ensure that the bottles stand vertically. He then mounts the chair, taking care to keep his weight centered over the chair as he steps onto it. He

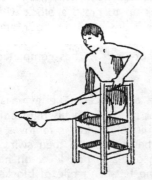

Handstand on one chair

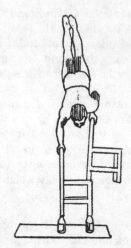

Handstand on two chairs and four bottles

Handstand on roller skates

places the second chair on the first in the manner described for the handstand on two chairs, then presses up into the handstand. (Boys.)

Handstand on Two Chairs and Three Bottles The gymnast starts as in the previous move but removes the left rear bottle before stepping up on the chair. From this point on, he follows the same procedures that he did in doing the handstand on two chairs and four bottles, the only difference being that he grasps the back of the chair on his left nearer the front and places a

Handstand on blocks

greater proportion of his weight on his right hand. An extremely steady press-up and handstand is mandatory for execution of this skill. (Boys.)

Handstand on Blocks The gymnast secures eight 2- by 4- by 8-inch wooden blocks. He places them in two stacks of four blocks in each stack, with the 4- by 8-inch surface on the floor. He upends into a handstand on the blocks. He shifts his weight to his right hand and removes the top block on the left-hand stack. He then shifts his weight to his left hand and removes the top block on the right-hand stack. He repeats this procedure until all the blocks have been removed.

He can also build up the blocks by starting his handstand on the floor with the two stacks of blocks between his hands or just outside his hands. He shifts his weight to his right hand, reaches up to grasp a block with his left hand, places it down on the floor, shifts his weight to his left hand, reaches up to grasp a block with his right hand, places it down on the floor, and repeats this procedure, placing successive blocks on top of one another until he has completed the move. (Boys.)

One-Arm Half Lever on Blocks The gymnast begins in a half lever position on his right arm on the blocks. With his left hand, he removes a block from the left-hand pile. He then swings his body over into a one-arm half lever on his left arm on top of the left-hand pile of blocks. With his right hand he removes a block from the right-hand pile. He repeats this procedure until

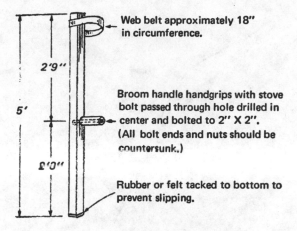

Web belt approximately 18"
in circumference.

2'9"

5'

Broom handle handgrips with stove
bolt passed through hole drilled in
center and bolted to 2" X 2".
(All bolt ends and nuts should be
countersunk.)

2'0"

Rubber or felt tacked to bottom to
prevent slipping.

Construction of handwalking stilts

all the blocks have been removed. The gymnast can also build up the blocks while balanced in a one-arm half lever by reversing the above procedures. (Boys.)

Handstand on Roller Skates The handbalancer upends into an underbalanced handstand, with his elbows flexed, while grasping a roller skate in each hand. He causes himself to roll forward on the skates by pushing first one hand forward and then the other in the same manner as when roller skating on the feet. (Boys.)

Handwalk on Stilts Stilts can be made of straight grained 2- by 2-inch hardwood with hand grips made of 6-inch pieces of broom handles. A hole is drilled through the length of each handle. A long bolt is passed through this hole to bolt the handle to the stilt. A belt is securely fastened to the upper end of the stilts; it will encircle the gymnast's upper arms. Felt or rubber pads are attached to the bottoms of the stilts to prevent sliding.

The gymnast starts by standing on a table. He slips his arms through the web belting and grasps the hand grips. He upends into the handstand in a slightly overbalanced position. He repeatedly moves the stilts forward under his forward moving center of gravity. In the event his center of gravity is behind the stilts, he moves them backward. If his center of gravity gets so far forward that he cannot move the stilts far enough forward to catch his balance, he should

flex his hips to bring his legs and body down between the stilts and land on his feet. (Boys.)

HORIZONTAL BAR[1]

Double-Knee Swing Up The gymnast secures a swing with a front grip. On the forward swing, he arches his back and then flexes his hips to bring his legs under the bar and between his arms; then he hooks the back of his knees over the bar. He pulls with his arms during the backward swing and swings forward again to complete the move in a sitting position on the bar, with the bar behind his knees. The spotter should stand under the bar prepared to slow the performer in the event he swings too far or not far enough. (Boys and girls.)

Seat Rise The gymnast secures a swing with a front grip. During the forward swing, he arches his back. At the end of the forward swing, he flexes his hips to bring his extended legs under the bar between his arms. He rides the backward swing in the jackknifed position. At the end of the backward swing, he depresses his extended arms and pushes his feet over the bar to finish the move in an "L" support position on the bar. Spot in the same manner as for the double-knee swing-up. (Boys.)

Cast-Off, Cross Hands, and Back Uprise The gymnast starts in a front support with a front grip. He casts his body backward away from the bar

Seat rise

[1] While competition on the horizontal bar is not held for girls, girls who plan to compete on the uneven parallel bars will find the horizontal bar a useful piece of equipment on which to learn moves that later can be done on the uneven parallel bars.

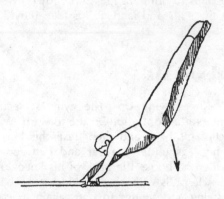

Cast-off, cross hands, back uprise

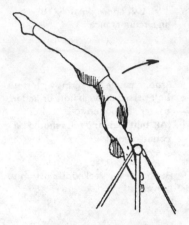

Three-quarter forward giant swing

and into an arched position. He releases his grip with his right hand and immediately regrasps the bar with his right arm crossed over his left. After he has passed under the bar, he twists to his right, pivoting around his right arm, releases his grip with his left hand and regrasps the bar with a reverse grip as he executes the back uprise to finish the move in a front support with a reverse grip. The spotter should stand under the bar ready to catch the gymnast around the waist on his downward swing if he fails to complete the back uprise. (Boys.)

Three-Quarter Forward Giant Swing The gymnast starts in a front support position with a reverse grip. He flexes his hips and then extends them vigorously to whip his legs and trunk over his head into a handstand position. As his legs and trunk move upward, he angles his arms forward to make it easier to get into the handstand position. As he is about to reach the handstand position, he brings his arms back to the vertical position. As he begins to circle the bar in the giant swing, he stretches his body to lengthen the lever and thereby generate greater momentum. During the circling, his body forms a straight line from his hands to his toes. As he is beginning to rise upward in the back portion of the swing, he flexes his hips slightly and pulls with his arms to execute a back uprise, finishing in a support position. Two spotters should stand under the bar and to either side of the performer ready to catch him around the waist in the event that his hands slip off the bar. (Boys.)

Forward Giant Swing The gymnast initiates this move just as he did the three-quarter forward giant swing. However, he delays flexing his hips on the backward swing until slightly later in the swing. Also he does not flex his shoulders or hips as much. He circles completely around the bar until he reaches the handstand position again. Use an overhead belt for spotting initial efforts. The ropes must be wrapped around the bar once in such a manner that it will unwind as the gymnast circles the bar. (Boys.)

Forward giant swing

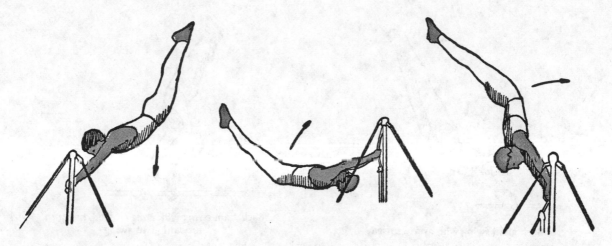

Back giant swing

Three-Quarter Back Giant Swing The gymnast starts in a front support position with a front grip. He flexes his hips and then extends them to whip his legs backward away from the bar. At the same time, he pushes away from the bar so that his body and arms are extended parallel to the floor. He initiates the rotation around the bar with his body and arms forming a straight line (no arch or pike). Just after his body has passed the uprights, he flexes his hips and shoulders and pulls with his extended arms to complete the move in a front support position. As his legs come up over the bar, he shifts his hands from a hang to a support position in order to check the momentum of his body as it approaches the bar. Two spotters should stand directly under the bar prepared to catch the gymnast around his waist in the event he misses the move. (Boys.

Back Giant Swing The gymnast starts in a front support position with a front grip. He flexes his hips and then extends them vigorously to lift his body up into a handstand position. He extends his arms, trunk, and legs so that they form a straight line. He rotates around the bar in an extended position until he has just passed the uprights. At this time, he flexes his hips and his shoulders slightly to shorten his radius of rotation and to thereby accelerate his speed of rotation. As his body rises above the bar, he shifts his hands from a hang to a support position. The move is completed as he passes through the handstand position. From this point, he may continue into another giant swing, lower his body into a free hip circle, or move into a number of other moves. Until the move has been mastered, two spotters should position themselves under the bar. They should be prepared to grasp the gymnast around the waist with both hands in the event of error. An overhead belt should be used if one is available. It will be necessary to wrap the ropes once around the bar in such a manner that it will unwind when the gymnast completes the giant swing. (Boys.)

Forward Giant Swing, Half Turn, Back Giant Swing The gymnast executes a forward giant swing. As he completes the giant swing in the handstand position, he shifts his weight to his left arm, turns his head to the left, releases his right hand, pivots around his left arm, regrasps

Forward gaint swing, half turn, back giant swing

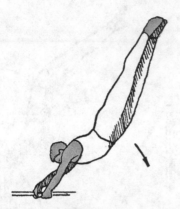

Back giant swing with arms crossed

Back giant swing with arms crossed, half turn,
forward giant swing

the bar with his right hand in a front grip on the other side of his left hand, and moves into the back giant swing.

This move should not be attempted until the gymnast has mastered both the backward and the forward giant swing. It would also be advisable that he master the half turn on a low horizontal bar. To do this, he should swing up into a handstand position on the low bar with the reverse grip and then execute the half turn. (Boys.)

Back Giant Swing, Half Turn, Forward Giant Swing The gymnast executes a back giant swing. When he has almost reached the handstand position, he shifts his weight to his left arm, turns his head to the left, twists his body, releases his right hand, and regrasps the bar with a reverse grip on the other side of his left hand. He continues to rotate around the bar in a forward giant swing. As he executes the twist, his hips flex slightly. This is a difficult move and should be attempted only by highly skilled gymnasts. Use an overhead twisting belt during initial efforts. Later use two spotters. (Boys.)

Back Giant Swing with Arms Crossed The gymnast executes a back giant swing with arms crossed. Just before his body reaches the vertical position above the bar, he releases his right hand, turns his head to the right, pivots around his left arm, regrasps the bar with a reverse grip to the right of his left hand, and continues to circle the bar in a forward giant swing. (Boys.)

Back Giant Swing with Arms Crossed, Half Turn, Forward Giant Swing The gymnast executes a back swing with arms crossed. Just before his body reaches the vertical position above the bar, he releases his right hand, turns his head to the right, pivots around his left arm, regrasps the bar with a reverse grip to the right of his left hand, and continues to circle the bar in a forward giant swing. (Boys.)

Back Giant Swing, Full Pirouette, Back Giant Swing The gymnast executes a back giant swing with arms crossed. Just before he reaches the vertical position above the bar, he turns his head to the right, releases his right hand, pivots around his left arm for a half turn, then regrasps the bar with a reverse grip with his right hand while still near the handstand position; then he releases his left hand, pivots a half turn around his right arm, regrasps the bar with his left hand in a front grip, and continues to circle around the bar in back giant swings. His body is stretched to form a straight line from his hands to his feet during the time he executes the full pirouette. This position minimizes the amount of unbalancing centrifugal force that will be generated. Use an overhead twisting belt during initial efforts. Later use two hand spotters. (Boys.)

Back Uprise and Rear Vault to a Catch The gymnast executes a back uprise with great vigor and height. As his shoulders begin to rise above the bar, he rotates his pelvis counterclockwise and flexes his hips to lift his legs upward to the

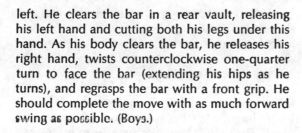

Back uprise and rear vault to catch

German giant swing

left. He clears the bar in a rear vault, releasing his left hand and cutting both his legs under this hand. As his body clears the bar, he releases his right hand, twists counterclockwise one-quarter turn to face the bar (extending his hips as he turns), and regrasps the bar with a front grip. He should complete the move with as much forward swing as possible. (Boys.)

German Giant Swing The gymnast begins in a rear support with a front grip. He hyperextends his hips and then flexes them to swing his feet, legs, and hips forward and upward over his head. As his feet move over his head, he angles his arms backward and then extends his hips to circle the bar in a "skin-the-cat" position. After he passes between the uprights under the bar, he flexes his hips slightly to shorten his radius of rotation. This action will increase his speed of rotation. His upward moving feet will also help to lift his body above the bar (as in a front uprise on the parallel bars). He completes the move in an "L" sitting position on the bar. The spotter should stand under the bar prepared to grasp the gymnast around his waist. He may assist

during early efforts by pushing up on the gymnast's hips as he comes up. (Boys.)

"Baby" Flyaway The gymnast jumps to a hang with a front grip and secures a swing. On the forward swing, just after his body passes the uprights, he flexes his hips to bring his legs under the bar and between his arms. He releases his grip to land on his feet after they have passed between his arms. He may or may not bend his knees, as is necessary. A hand belt should be

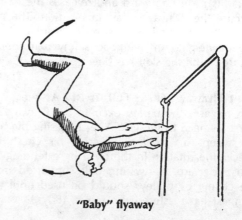

"Baby" flyaway

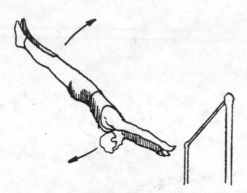

Front flyaway layout

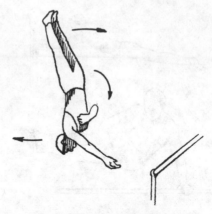

Front flyaway with a full twist

used as a safety measure for his first efforts. After several successful efforts in the hand belt, two spotters can be used instead of the safety belt. As the gymnast gains in skill and confidence, he should attempt the move with a greater swing to secure greater height and to release the bar earlier in the swing. (Boys.)

Front Flyaway Layout After the gymnast has learned the "baby" flyaway, he should learn the regular flyaway. He initiates this move from a front support with a front grip. He casts backward and away from the bar as though he were going to do a back giant swing. On his initial efforts, his cast should be low. However, as he gains in skill and confidence, he should secure a higher cast. Just after his body passes the uprights, he flexes his hips and his shoulders slightly. When his body is just a few degrees from the horizontal, he lifts his hips upward, pulls his head backward and releases the bar to execute the flyaway in layout position. The upward lift with his hips aids him considerably in gaining height. An overhead safety belt should be used until the skill has been mastered. (Boys.)

Front Flyaway with a Full Twist As the gymnast releases the bar to execute the flyaway, he turns his head to the left. After releasing the bar, he sweeps his right arm across his chest. He checks the rotation in the twist by extending his arms sideward. A twisting belt supported from the ceiling by pulleys should be used until the gymnast has mastered the move. (Boys.)

Double Front Flyaway The gymnast initiates the double front flyaway either from a back giant swing or from a cast into the handstand position. Just after his body has passed the uprights and is beginning its upward swing, he flexes his hips and shoulders. When his hips are at almost the same height as his head, he releases the bar, pulls his head backward and whips into a tightly tucked position to complete two somersaults before opening up to land on his feet. An overhead safety belt and a mat held by its handles by six gymnasts at a height of a foot or two above a double thickness of mats are the safety procedures that should be used until the gymnast has mastered the move. (Boys.)

Flyaway Backward The gymnast should first learn the flyaway backward from an underbar swing. To do this, he jumps upward to grasp the bar with a reverse grip and initiates a swing. On the backward swing, just as his body passes between the uprights, he flexes his hips and pulls with his arms. As his feet are swinging directly upward—that is, when his body is horizontal—the gymnast releases the bar, lifts his hips, tucks tightly grasping his shins, and pulls his head forward to somersault around to his feet. He extends his hips and knees as he completes the somersault. The gymnast should use an overhead safety belt until he has mastered the move. Since, even with an overhead safety belt, an overspin is difficult to spot, the gymnast should intentionally underspin his flyaways backward until he knows precisely where he is throughout the move and can control it well. Later he may learn the back flyaway in piked position. (Boys.)

Hecht The gymnast initiates this move from a series of forward giant swings. As his body passes between the uprights, he flexes his hips and pulls very hard with his arms. When his body is horizontal, he pulls his head backward and lifts his chest as he pushes forward-upward with his arms. These actions cause his body to move forward over the bar and to pivot around its central axis from the horizontal toward the vertical position. As he passes over the bar, his body is at a 45° angle to the floor. After he has released the bar, his body continues to move toward the vertical position and into an arched position. Before landing on his feet, he flexes his hips slightly in order to more effectively absorb the impact. The move should be mastered in an overhead safety belt before being attempted without the safety belt. (Boys.)

PARALLEL BARS[2]

Shoulder Roll Backward in Tucked Position The gymnast starts in an upper arm hang. He is gripping the bars with his forearms forming a right angle to his upper arms. He initiates a swing. On one of the forward swings, as his body passes through the vertical position, he flexes his hips and knees and pulls with his arms to bring his body over his head. He releases his grip and extends his arms sideward, pressing them downward against the bar while rolling around his upper arms. He regrasps the bars as soon as he can to finish the move in an upper arm hang. A spotter should stand alongside the bars. If the gymnast requires assistance in upending, the spotter should push on his hips. He should place his hand on the gymnast's chest as he completes the move. The spotter should never place his arm between the bar and the gymnast.

Shoulder Roll Backward The gymnast begins in a shoulder balance. He underbalances slightly, stretches his body, releases the bars, extends his

[2] All of the parallel bar skills described in this section are for boys only.

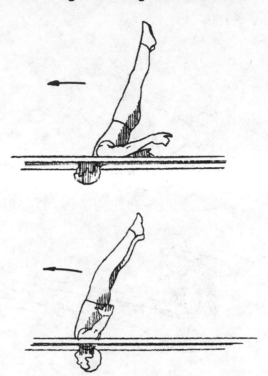

Shoulder roll backward

arms sideward momentarily, and begins to circle around his upper arms. As soon as he can, he regrasps the bars in front of his body. As his body passes through the vertical position when his feet are below his head, he flexes his hips and pushes with his arms to bring his hips and feet above his head. When they are above his head, he arches his body and extends his arms sideward to initiate another shoulder roll. The gymnast should at no time allow his shoulders to sag. This move should be spotted in the same manner as a shoulder roll backward in tucked position.

Shoulder Roll Forward The gymnast starts in a shoulder balance. He stretches his body so that it forms a straight line with no arch. He brings his head forward to sight upward along his body. He releases the bars and begins to circle around his extended upper arms holding his body extended and his head pulled forward. His arms are momentarily extended sideward and he then regrasps the bars forward of his shoulders. As his body passes through the vertical position

Hip swing-up

Glide kip, single-leg cut-off, and regrasp

when his feet are under his head, he flexes his hips slightly and pulls with his arms. These actions will bring him around and back into the shoulder balance position. A spotter can stand alongside the parallel bars to push against the gymnast's abdomen to help him around during the last half of the roll.

Glide Kip, Single-Leg Cut-Off, and Regrasp
The gymnast initiates a glide kip. As he executes the kip, he brings his left leg outside his right arm and releases the left bar to bring this leg between his hand and the bar. He regrasps the bar,

pushes his body backward with his hips flexed, and swings forward to execute a glide kip into a cross arm support. If he can secure enough lift as he kips and cuts his leg, he can regrasp the bar in a cross arm support position without executing the second glide kip.

Glide Kip, Double-Leg Cut-Off, and Regrasp
This move is executed in the same manner as is a glide kip, single-leg cut-off, and regrasp, except that both legs are cut over the bars and under the hands. After regrasping the bar, the gymnast can move into another glide kip; or he can do a short kip; or if he can secure the necessary height, he can catch in a cross arm support.

Hip Swing-Up The gymnast starts from a stand between the ends of the bars facing outward. He has an outside grip. He flexes his hips and pulls with his arms to raise his hips over an imaginary bar between his hands. He hooks his heels under the bars, pulls with his legs, and pushes with his arms to finish in a straddle seat position.

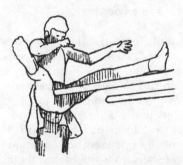

Glide kip, double-leg cut-off, and regrasp

Back uprise, cut, and catch

Having mastered this move, he can learn to do the move without hooking his heels.

Reverse Kip The gymnast starts from a stand between the ends of the bars facing outward. He has an outside grip with his thumbs next to his fingers. He lifts both feet off the mat simultaneously by flexing his hips and pulling with his arms. He shoots his feet upward by extending his hips, endeavoring to get his center of gravity above the bars. His hands rotate around the end of the bars as he completes the move in a cross arm support.

Back Uprise, Cut, and Catch The gymnast starts in an upper arm hang at the center of the bars. He flexes his hips to pull them above the bar and to bring his feet over his head. He extends his hips to press his feet forward-upward. The purpose of these movements is to give him a good backward swing. As his body passes through the vertical position with his feet under his head, he pulls with his arms. As his feet rise above the bars behind his body, he quickly flexes his hips to cut his legs forward over the bars and under his arms, releasing the bars to allow his legs to pass through. He regrasps the bars with his body in an "L" support position. Initiation of the leg cut when his hips are too high will cause the gymnast to drive his legs downward toward the bar. The movement of the legs during the cut should be a horizontal one that is directly forward.

Half Turn on the Backward Swing The gymnast starts from a cross arm support. He initiates a swing. On the backward swing he turns his head and trunk to the left, pushes off with his left hand, transfers his right hand to the opposite bar, grasps the other bar with his left hand, and finishes the move facing the opposite direction in a cross arm support. The turn should not be executed until the body is horizontal. Mats may be draped over the bars to prevent bruising of the legs.

Back Uprise, Half Turn into a Cross Arm Support The gymnast starts in an upper arm hang. He secures a swing in the same manner as he did in executing a back uprise, cut and catch. As his body rises upward during the backward swing,

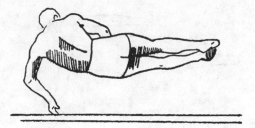

Back uprise, half turn into cross arm support

he executes a half turn as described in the previous move. A spotter should stand alongside the bars ready to catch the gymnast. A mat may be draped over the bar to prevent bruising of the legs.

Back Uprise into a Handstand The gymnast initiates a backward swing in the same manner as he did in doing the back uprise, cut, and catch. He delays his arm pull until his body is beginning to rise above the bars. At this time, he pulls vigorously to bring his center of gravity above his hands with his arms flexed and his feet moving over his head. Momentum will cause his body to continue to move upward as he extends his arms to complete the move in a handstand position.

Moore The gymnast starts in a cross arm support. He secures a small swing. On the backward swing he flexes his hips to lift them above his head so that his extended legs will clear the bar. He pushes off his left hand, pivoting a quarter turn on his right arm. He grasps the right bar with his left hand in a reverse grip and pivots a quarter turn on his left arm as he pushes off his right hand and grasps the opposite bar to finish in a cross arm support. As his feet circle outside the bar, the gymnast keeps them close to his hands and angles his arms forward in order to keep his center of weight over his hands. He can embellish the move by extending his hips and arching his body as he moves over the bar toward the final position. The move is best learned on the parallels by springing up from a stand between the bars.

Half Turn on the Forward Swing The gymnast starts in a cross arm support. He secures a small swing. On the forward swing, he turns his head

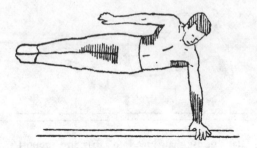

Half turn on the forward swing

Stutzkehre into a handstand

to the left, pushes off his right hand, transfers his left hand to the right bar, and grasps the left bar with his right hand to complete the move in a cross arm support facing opposite his starting direction. There is only a brief moment in the move when his body is not supported by one hand or the other. A mat should be draped over one bar during initial efforts.

Stutzkehre The gymnast starts in a handstand on both bars at their center. He stretches his body toward the ceiling and swings down freely between his arms by keeping his arms nearly vertical. When his extended body has passed the horizontal position in front, he turns his head to the left, pushes off his right hand to bring it around to the left bar, and then pushes off his left hand to grasp the opposite bar and to complete the turn with his body horizontal.

Stutzkehre into a Handstand The gymnast executes the stutzkehre as previously described but with a greater swing in order to catch in the handstand position.

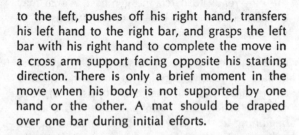

Stutzkehre

Peach Basket into an Upper Arm Hang The gymnast starts from a stand at the center of and between the bars. He may have either an inside or an outside grip. His arms are extended and his body is vertical. He takes a small jump directly upward, then flexes his hips; with his arms extended and his hips flexed, he rotates around his hands and his shoulders. When his shoulders are moving upward between the bars, he extends his hips vigorously, pulls his head backward, and pulls with his arms. He retains his grip until his hands are pulled off the bars. At this time, he swings his arms forward-upward between the bars to land in an upper arm hang with his body horizontal. Two spotters should be utilized. One should stand alongside the parallel bars ready to catch the gymnast under the bars. The other should assume a kneeling position between and outside the uprights at the end of the bars facing the gymnast. His arms should be extended ready to catch the gymnast under his chest in the event he misses. The peach basket may also be initiated from a cross arm support or a handstand by dropping between the bars and flexing the hips.

Peach Basket into a Cross Arm Support This move is executed in the same manner as is a peach basket into an upper arm hang. However, the gymnast must secure a greater swing, pull harder, and hang on longer.

Peach Basket with a Half Twist The gymnast initiates a peach basket. As he is completing the move, he turns his head to the left, pushes off his right hand, and then pushes off his left hand

Peach basket into an upper arm hang

to land in an upper arm hang facing the opposite direction.

Peach Basket into Glide Kip The gymnast initiates a peach basket, but instead of throwing his arms above the bars to catch in an upper arm hang, he reaches forward to grasp the bars with an inside grip with his arms extended. He then flexes his hips and continues into a glide kip between the bars.

Peach Basket into a Handstand The gymnast initiates a peach basket, but instead of moving his hips upward-backward, he moves them di-

rectly upward to catch on his hands with his arms and hips flexed and his hips over his head. With practice, the gymnast will be able to move into the handstand with no hesitation or press at any point in the move.

Flying Kip (Cast) into an Upper Arm Hang The gymnast starts from a stand between the bars at their center. He has an inside grip. His body is vertical and his arms are extended. He springs upward and flexes his hips to bring his feet over his head. His body swings forward in piked position around his hands. Just before his hips reach the highest point in their forward swing, he pulls with his arms, extends his hips slightly, and releases his grip. He "floats" upward for a moment and lands on his upper arms with his feet over his head and his hips above the bars. A spotter should stand alongside the bars to assist the gymnast on his initial efforts by lifting with one hand on his upper back and with the other on his lower back.

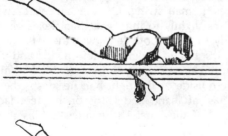

Peach basket into a cross arm support

Cast into an upper arm hang

Cast catch

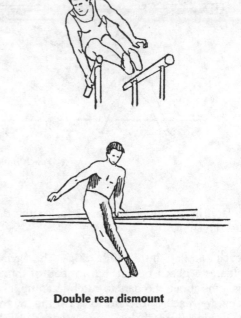

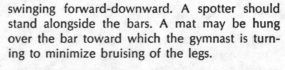

Double rear dismount

Flying Kip into a Cross Arm Support (Cast Catch) To do the flying kip into a cross arm support, the gymnast must execute the movements of the flying kip with greater vigor and height.

Flying Kip with a Half Twist The gymnast initiates a flying kip, but instead of releasing both hands to land in a piked position on his upper arms, he turns his head to the left, pushes off his right hand, extends his hips, then brings his right arm to the left bar and his left arm to the right bar to land on his upper arms facing opposite to his initial direction. For a split second, both his arms are on the left bar. As he completes the turn, his body is arched above the bars and

swinging forward-downward. A spotter should stand alongside the bars. A mat may be hung over the bar toward which the gymnast is turning to minimize bruising of the legs.

Double Rear Dismount The gymnast starts in a cross arm support at the center of the bars. He secures a small swing. On the backward swing, he leans slightly to the right, then flexes his hips quickly to bring both legs over the left bar behind his body, under his left hand, and then around in front over both bars. As his feet move to the outside of the right bar, he grasps the bar with his left hand and lands on his feet facing the end of the bars. The gymnast's hips should remain close to his right arm throughout the stunt. A spotter should stand alongside the bars to hold the gymnast's right wrist with his left hand and his right upper arm with his right hand.

Front Pirouette in a Handstand The gymnast starts in a handstand at the center of the bars. He shifts his weight to his left arm, looks at the left bar, pushes off his right hand, and turns to grasp the left bar with his right hand in a handstand on the left bar. During the turn, his left

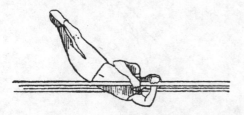

Cast with a half twist

Front pirouette in a handstand

Reverse pirouette in a handstand

arm remains vertical. He then shifts his weight to his right arm, looks to the left, and pushes off his left hand to complete the move in a handstand on both bars having executed at 180° turn. During the last half of the turn his right arm must remain vertical. The move should be learned on the parallets before being attempted on the parallel bars.

Swinging Front Pirouette in a Handstand The gymnast starts in a cross arm support. He secures

a big swing. He initiates the pirouette while his feet are moving over his head when his body is 15° to 30° from the vertical by looking at the left bar and pushing off his right hand. He then grasps the left bar with his right hand in a momentary handstand on one bar. He immediately pushes off his left hand and looks to his left to complete the pirouette in a handstand on both bars. This move should first be learned on the parallets by kicking up into the move.

Reverse Pirouette in a Handstand The gymnast starts in a handstand on both bars at their center. He looks to his left and pushes off his left hand to do a quarter turn on his right arm to a handstand on the right bar with a reverse grip. During the turn, his right arm remains vertical to serve as the axis of rotation. His feet remain above his head. He then releases the bar with his right hand, does a quarter turn around his left arm, and grasps the left bar with his right hand. He has completed the move in a handstand on both bars, having made a 180° turn. The move should first be learned on the parallets.

Swinging front pirouette in a handstand

Swinging Reverse Pirouette in a Handstand The gymnast starts in a cross arm support. He secures a big swing. On the backward swing, as his feet are moving over his head and when his body is about 15° from the vertical, he looks to the left, pushes off his left hand, pivots around

Swinging reverse pirouette in a handstand

his right arm through the handstand on one bar, and transfers his right hand to the opposite bar as he pivots around his left arm; he finishes in a handstand on both bars. The movements throughout the skill are continuous, with no hesitations. The move should first be learned on the parallets by kicking up into the move.

Flying Handstand Change The gymnast starts in a cross arm support. He secures a big swing. On the backward swing, when he is to do the move, he maintains his arms in a nearly vertical position. When his body is 15° to 30° from the vertical, he looks to the left, pushes off both hands (but harder off the right hand) and executes a half turn to catch the bars near the handstand position. He then swings downward to the cross arm support position.

Front somersault to an upper arm hang

Front Somersault to an Upper Arm Hang The gymnast starts in a cross arm support. He secures a big swing. On the backward swing he maintains his extended arms in a nearly vertical position. He flexes his hips to lift his center of gravity upward and forward, tucks his head to initiate rotation, and pushes off hard with both hands to gain added lift. He extends his arms sideward to land in an upper arm hang. Mats may be draped over both bars to ease the shock of landing on the upper arms.

Front Somersault into a Cross Arm Support This move is executed in the same manner as is a front somersault to an upper arm hang except that a greater lift is necessary. The gymnast should effect the hand change very quickly so that his body is unsupported for a very brief moment. He should regrasp with his hands slightly forward of his shoulders in order to more effectively absorb his body's forward momentum. The gymnast should master the move in an overhead safety belt before attempting it unsupported.

Front Somersault Dismount This move is done in the same manner as is a front somersault into a cross arm support except that the gymnast's body must move sideward to clear the bar. To accomplish this, he pushes sideward as well as upward off his hands. He also moves his head sideward. As he clears the left bar, he will grasp this bar with his right hand after he has cleared it in order to better control his landing. An overhead safety belt should be used until the move has been mastered. A mat may be draped over the bar as an added safety measure. Bruce Fredericks teaches this move to his gymnasts in a very short time by lowering the parallel bars, placing the trampoline next to the parallel bars and having the gymnasts do the front somersault dismount off the parallel bars to a seat drop on the trampoline.

Back Somersault to an Upper Arm Hang The gymnast starts in a handstand on both bars at their center. He stretches his body endeavoring to push his feet toward the ceiling by stretching his shoulders and hips. He swings his body downward between his arms, holding his arms nearly vertical throughout the swing. (Angling the arms forward will slow down the swing and decrease

Back somersault into a cross arm support

Back Somersault into a Handstand This move is executed in the same manner as is a back somersault into a cross arm support except that the gymnast's lift must be directly upward and he must regrasp very quickly in order to catch in the handstand position. Because even a very small amount of rotary momentum would carry the gymnast beyond the handstand position, he must regrasp the bars before the handstand position is reached. This will give him a little distance over which to apply braking forces. An overhead safety belt should be utilized until the move has been mastered in order that the gymnast will not become fearful of regrasping the bars too early.

Back Somersault Dismount The techniques of execution of this move are the same as those for the back somersault into a cross arm support except that the gymnast must move his head and trunk slightly to the left and push to the left as well as upward as he "goes for" the somersault. As he clears the left bar, he should place his right hand on this bar to steady his landing. The gymnast should master the move in an overhead safety belt before attempting it unsupported.

Squat Vault Dismount from a Handstand The gymnast starts in a handstand on one bar at its

the lift.) As his body passes between his arms, he flexes his hips slightly. He retains his grip until his body is horizontal in front. At this time, he lifts his hips upward to arch his body and pulls his head backward. His hands are pulled off the bar and he somersaults around to land on his upper arms with his arms extended sideward. The gymnast's initial efforts should be spotted with an overhead safety belt. A mat may be draped over each bar behind the gymnast's hands to cushion the impact against his upper arms. A hand safety belt may be used if the spotters stand on tables placed on either side of the bars. The move may also be hand spotted with a spotter on each side of the bars. These spotters grasp the gymnast's wrist with one hand (with the thumb down) and his upper arm with the other hand (with the thumb up). The bars must be lowered to their lowest point when this technique of spotting is utilized.

Back Somersault into a Cross Arm Support This move is executed in the same manner as is a back somersault to the upper arm hang except that the gymnast reaches back and down to regrasp the bars when his body is near the handstand position. He should not wait for his body to drop down toward the bars before regrasping but should begin reaching for the bars the moment his hands are pulled free of them. This means that he will be unsupported for only a very brief moment. The gymnast's initial efforts should be spotted with an overhead safety belt.

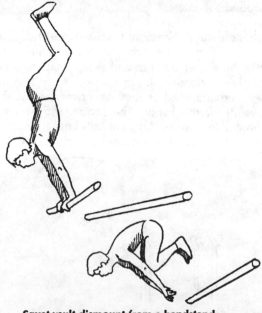

Squat vault dismount from a handstand

Straddle vault dismount from a handstand

Straddle vault dismount from a one-hand balance

center. He overbalances by angling his entire body forward in a straight line from his feet to his hands. (He should not, as some beginners do, angle his arms forward and his body backward.) When he has moved slightly forward off balance, he vigorously flexes his knees and his hips to bring his feet over the bar and between his arms. At the same time, he pushes off his hands. After his feet have cleared the bar, he extends his knees and hips to land in the erect position with his back toward the bar. A spotter should stand to either side of the gymnast ready to catch him around the chest.

Straddle Vault Dismount from a Handstand This move is done in the same manner as a squat vault dismount from a handstand except that the knees are held extended throughout the move and the legs are straddled as they pass over the bar and outside of the hands. The spotter should stand directly in front of the gymnast's anticipated spot of landing far enough away that he will not

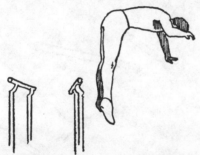

Stoop vault dismount from a handstand

hamper the gymnast's movements and near enough to assist him by extending his arms under his chest in the event of a miss.

Stoop Vault Dismount from a Handstand This move is identical to the straddle vault dismount from a handstand except that the extended legs are held together and pass over the bar between the arms instead of outside them. It is spotted in the same manner as is a squat vault dismount from a handstand. A vigorous hip flexion and push off the arms is mandatory.

Straddle Vault Dismount from a One-Hand Balance The gymnast starts in a handstand on one bar. He shifts into a one-hand balance and then straddles both legs over the bar to either side of his supporting arm. Ability to do a one-hand balance is, of course, prerequisite to this move. It is spotted in the same manner as is a straddle vault dismount from a handstand. The gymnast can also move into position by doing a swinging front pirouette and executing the straddle vault before grasping the left bar with his right hand. All the squat, straddle, and stoop vaults should be learned on the parallels before being attempted on the parallel bars.

Squat Vault Dismount from a Handstand over Two Bars The gymnast starts in a handstand on both bars at their center. He shifts his weight to his left hand momentarily in order to change his right grip to a reverse grip. He then shifts his weight to his right hand and pivots counterclockwise on his right arm into a handstand on one bar with his back toward the left bar. He angles his body well forward from his feet to his hands. He flexes vigorously at the hips and knees and pushes forward off his hands to execute a squat vault over both bars. The gymnast should first learn the move from the outside bar, vaulting over that bar and a pole held loosely by a partner at a distance from the bar equal to the distance between the bars. After having mastered the move over a pole, the gymnast may try it over both parallel bars with the bars adjusted to a narrow width. He should be spotted by two spotters standing to either side of his anticipated landing spot. As the gymnast gains in skill and confidence, the bars can be widened to the regulation width.

Straddle Vault Dismount from a Handstand over Two Bars This move is executed, practiced, and spotted in the same manner as is the squat vault dismount from a handstand over two bars except that the legs are held extended throughout the vault and are brought down outside the arms.

One-Arm Half Lever, Turn and Press into a Handstand on One Bar The gymnast may move into this position in any one of several manners. He might lever down from a handstand into the one-arm half lever. To do this, he angles his arms forward and his body backward until he can slowly place his right elbow just inside the crest of the ileum. He might move into the position from a back uprise. The easiest method for getting into position is by kneeling on one bar facing the opposite bar and gripping both bars. The gymnast tucks his right elbow inside his pelvic bone. His right forearm is perpendicular to the bar and his right upper arm forms a right angle with his right forearm. He pulls his head, shoulders and legs upward so that his body is in an arched position and horizontal. His body should be tilted with his left shoulder and hip slightly higher than his right shoulder and hip. When he has secured the balance, he should release his left hand and extend his left arm in line with his body. He then pulls his head to the right to cause his body to pivot on his right hand until he is in position to grasp the right bar with his left hand. He continues to pivot as he presses upward into a handstand on one bar. Before at-

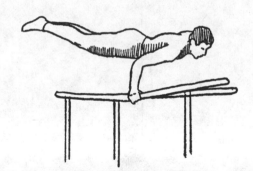

One-arm half lever, turn and press into handstand on one bar

tempting to press up into the handstand on one bar, the gymnast should learn to press up into a handstand on both bars.

STILL RINGS[3]

Muscle Up The gymnast starts from a hanging position. He has a false or over grip, in which the ring passes between his thumb and index finger, diagonally across his palm, behind the heel of his hand and across his wrist. He pulls up quickly keeping his elbows close together, leans forward, and flexes his hips slightly as he pulls up. He then extends his hips and raises his elbows to bring his shoulders above the rings and to place his arms in a pushing position. He extends his arms to complete the move.

Shoulder Balance The gymnast starts in a support position. He flexes his hips and his arms to bring his hips up over his head. He pulls his head backward throughout the move. His upper arms are pressed against the straps of the rings to aid in maintaining balance. If he bends his knees as he presses into the handstand, it will become easier to elevate his hips above his head and to lift his feet into the final position. However, if he keeps his legs extended, the move will look better and will gain more points in competition. In the final position, his head is pulled back, his back is arched, his legs are extended, and his toes are pointed.

[3] All the moves on still rings which are described in this section are to be done by boys only.

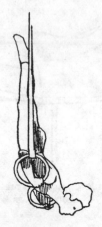

Shoulder balance

Hand balance

Hand Balance The gymnast starts from a support position. He flexes his hips, elbows, and knees to bring his hips up over his head. He bends his elbows until his upper arms are at a right angle to his forearms but no further. A greater degree of flexion will make it difficult to extend his arms again. He keeps his head pulled backward throughout the move. After his hips are above his head, he extends his arms, hips, and legs simultaneously to move into the handstand position. He should keep the rings pulled inward. He may press his upper arms against the straps to help stabilize the balance. After he has gained skill and control, he should learn to press up with his legs extended and to maintain the balance with his arms free of the straps. If he overbalances, the gymnast should flex his knees, hips, and arms to roll over into the hanging position. A spotter should be stationed directly under the rings ready to catch the gymnast around the waist if he overbalances.

Reverse Kip (Bird-Up) The gymnast starts from an inverted hang in piked position. He extends his hips to push his feet forward. His body then swings forward, downward, and backward—then forward again. When his body, during its forward swing, passes through the vertical position, he flexes his hips and pulls with his arms to bring his center of gravity above the rings. At the same time he pulls his head backward. As his body moves above the rings, he changes his hands from a hang to a support position. He then vigor-

ously extends his hips to complete the move in a support position with the rings held in front of his body. A spotter should stand alongside the gymnast. He can help the gymnast to gain the "feel" of the move by pushing upward on his chest.

Reverse Kip into a Handstand (Shoot) This move is executed in the same manner as is a reverse kip except that the gymnast shoots his feet directly upward between the ropes instead of up and back. He must, of course, also pull with his arms much more strongly and extend his hips with greater vigor to secure the lift necessary to finish in a handstand.

Back Uprise into a Handstand The gymnast may start from a piked inverted hang and gain the necessary swing by extending his hips as he chins up and then pushes away, or he may begin

Reverse kip (bird-up)

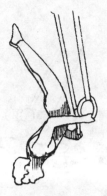

Reverse kip into a handstand (shoot)

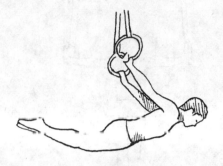

Back lever

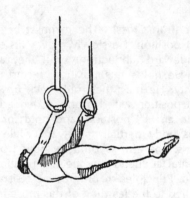

Front lever

from a handstand. If he begins from a handstand, he overbalances and keeps his shoulders and hips almost fully extended as he circles around his hands. When his body is beginning its upward swing, he flexes his hips slightly, whips into an arch, pulls with his arms, and then pushes upward to complete the move in a handstand position.

Back Lever The gymnast begins in an inverted hang in an arched position. He slowly lowers his body backward in the arched position until it is parallel to the floor. His palms face one another and he pulls the rings inward. His arms are angled forward and his head is pulled backward.

Front Lever The gymnast starts in an inverted hang with his body straight. His head is forward. He slowly lowers his body forward, keeping his arms, hips, and knees extended, until it is parallel to the floor.

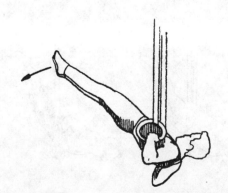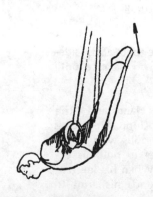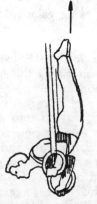

Back uprise into a handstand

Crucifix (iron cross)

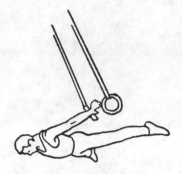

Double-leg cut-off backward

Crucifix (Iron Cross) The gymnast begins in a support position. He slowly moves his extended arms sideward (abduction) until they are horizontal. He holds this position against the pull of gravity. He may then pull back up into the support position with his arms extended; lift his legs into an "L" position, and hold; or he may turn his body partially sideward while holding the cross. The arms should be pulled backward (horizontal abduction) while the position is being held. Principles of progressive resistance can be applied to the learning of this move in several ways: (1) The lever arms can be shortened by having the rings at the elbows, forearms, or wrists, (2) a rope can be tied to the gymnast's belt which passes up through a pulley and down through another pulley with weights tied to it. (3) The gymnast can use wall pulleys in the same manner as when doing the crucifix, increasing the resistance as he gains in strength.

Inverted Crucifix The gymnast begins in a handstand. He lowers his extended arms sideward while maintaining the hand balance until his arms are horizontal.

Straight Body Press-Up into a Handstand The gymnast starts in a support position. He arches his body, flexes his arms, and pulls with all his back and hip extensor muscles to pull his extended legs up over his head. When his legs are almost over his head, he extends his arms to press up into the handstand.

Double-Leg Cut-Off Backward The gymnast initiates a swing in the hanging position. On the forward swing when his feet are under his head, he flexes his hips and pulls with his arms to bring his feet above his head. When his legs strike his arms, he extends his body into an arched position, pulls his head backward, and releases his grip to somersault around to a stand on the mat. Two spotters should be stationed under the rings during early efforts.

Front Flyaway The gymnast begins in a piked inverted hang. He secures a good swing. On the forward swing, as his body passes through the vertical position with his feet under his head, he flexes his hips and pulls with his arms. When his body is horizontal in front, he extends his hips to lift them upward, pulls his head backward, and releases his hands to somersault around to his feet in a layout position. He should learn the move in a safety belt.

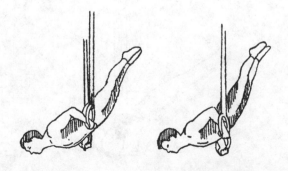

Straight body press-up into a handstand

Front Double Flyaway The gymnast initiates this move in the same manner as the front flyaway, but he tucks very tightly to complete two somersaults before landing on his feet. A safety belt and two thicknesses of mats should be used.

Front Flyaway with a Full Twist The gymnast initiates this move in the same manner as the front flyaway, but just before he releases the rings, he turns his head to the left. After he has released the rings, he pulls his right arm across his chest. These actions will cause him to execute a full twist as he somersaults. The gymnast should learn the move in a twisting belt.

SIDE HORSE VAULTING

The moves described in this section can be done by men as well as women either with the pommels on the horse or with them removed. This is one of the events included in competition for women. In competition, the vaults are done without the pommels. It also serves as an excellent physical education class activity for boys and men and is one which they enjoy.

Courage Vault The student starts from a kneeling position on the horse at its center. Her weight is on her shin bones; her knees are fully flexed and her trunk is vertical. She swings her arms upward and extends her hips and knees to lift herself off the side horse to land on her feet. A spotter should stand in front of the horse and

Squat vault

alongside the performer ready to extend her arm across the performer's waist in the event she misses.

Squat Vault The student runs toward the horse from a distance of approximately 20 feet. She takes off from one foot and brings her other foot up alongside the first to land on the beat or Reuther board with both feet striking the board simultaneously. This hurdle is executed in the same manner as is the hurdle in diving. She places her hands on the horse and immediately pushes off as she draws her knees and hips upward so that her feet can clear the horse. She keeps her head elevated throughout the move. Her hands should leave the horse as her feet clear the horse. In other words, she should push off her hands. A spotter should stand alongside the performer ready to extend an arm across her chest.

Courage vault

Straddle vault

Wolf vault

Stoop vault

Straddle Vault The gymnast initiates the straddle vault in the same manner that she does the squat vault. She lifts her extended legs sideward and pushes off vigorously to clear the horse and to land in balance with her feet together and her back toward the horse. The spotter should stand directly in front of the performer ready to lunge forward quickly and to catch her under the arms in the event she misses.

Stoop Vault The student initiates the stoop vault in the same manner that she did the squat vault except that as she springs upward off the beat board, she extends her legs and holds them extended until she lands on her feet. At this time, she bends her knees to absorb the impact of the landing. During the vault, she lifts her hips high and pushes hard off her hands. She also extends her hips the moment her feet have cleared the horse and pulls her head backward throughout the move if she wishes to land in good balance on her feet. A spotter should stand alongside the performer ready to extend an arm across her chest.

Wolf Vault The student runs toward the horse, takes off from the beat board from both feet simultaneously, places both hands on the horse, leans toward the left by angling her left arm sideward, lifts her legs and trunk up to the right,

bends her left leg to place the left foot at the right knee, releases her right hand, allows her body to move forward, and lands in good balance on both feet with her back toward the horse. The spotter should stand to the performer's left side and hold her left wrist and upper arm.

Flank Vault The student executes the flank vault in the same manner that she does the wolf vault except that both her legs are extended throughout the vault. Since there is more weight to the right of the point of support in the flank vault than there is in the wolf vault, the student must angle her left arm further to the left in order to move the center of gravity more nearly over the point of support. For excellent form, the student extends her hips as she clears the horse. This move is spotted in the same manner as is the wolf vault.

Front Vault The student initiates the front vault in the same manner as she does the flank vault except that as her body rises, she turns to

Flank vault

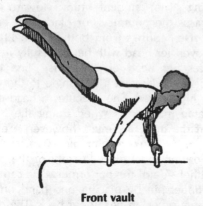

Front vault

Rear vault

face the horse. She leans well forward, holds her head up, arches her back, and extends her legs as she clears the horse. She lands on her feet in front of the horse with her left side toward it. The spotter should stand directly in front of the performer.

Rear Vault The student runs toward the horse, takes a small spring from both feet, grasps both pommels, lifts her legs to the left, turns so that her rear is toward the horse, leans backward on her extended right arm, cuts her legs under her left arm, regrasps the horse with her left hand, and lands on her feet facing the side with her left side toward the horse. The spotter should stand behind the performer ready to catch her under the arms if necessary.

Rear Vault with a Quarter Twist The student executes a rear vault and as her feet clear the horse she turns her head to the left and swings her left arm backward to land on her feet facing the horse. The spotter should stand behind the performer.

High Front Vault (Handstand with a Quarter Turn) The student runs toward the horse, takes a high hurdle, and springs vigorously from both feet to drive her hips upward over her head. She extends her arms as her hips move over her head. After her hips are over her head, she extends them to bring her body into the handstand position. She then pivots on her left arm to land on her feet facing the side with her left shoulder toward the horse. The spotter should stand in front of the horse and to the

side of the performer ready to grasp her under the arms.

Thief Vault The student runs toward the horse and takes off from her right foot from a point far enough away from the horse to permit her to swing her left leg in extended position forward over the horse. As she passes over the horse, she brings her right leg up in bent po-

High front vault

Thief vault

Headspring The student runs toward the horse, grasps the pommels (or places her hands on the horse), springs from both feet to lift her hips up over her head with her hips fully flexed, and places her head on the horse. She turns over until her back is at a 60° angle to the floor with her hips flexed. She executes a headspring in the same manner as when doing the headspring off the mat. She must, however, exercise caution to avoid overspinning. Two spotters should position themselves in front of the horse and to either side of the performer. One can protect for underspin by placing one hand on her hips and the other on her upper back. The other spotter should protect for overspin, being prepared to grasp the performer under the arms if it appears that she will overspin.

Handspring The gymnast initiates this vault in the same manner as she does the high front vault. After she reaches the handstand position, she brings her head forward and continues to rotate around her hands over to her feet with her body extended. She can embellish the move by pushing away from the horse to secure a short flight. This push-off is secured by means of a shoulder extension rather than an elbow extension. A spotter should stand alongside the performer with one hand on her upper arm and the other on the small of her back.

Handstand Squat Vault The gymnast moves into the handstand position in the same manner as when doing a high front vault. When her feet have moved beyond her head and her body is

sition alongside her left leg and extends it. At the same time, she places her hands on the horse momentarily and pushes off. The spotter should stand in front of the horse and alongside the performer. A second spotter could position herself behind the horse. Hurdling the horse without touching the hands is a helpful lead-up move.

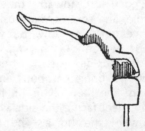

Headspring

Handspring

angled forward slightly, she flexes her hips and knees and pulls her head backward to bring her bent legs down between her arms. At the same time, she pushes off her hands. She lands on her feet with her back toward the horse. The spotter should stand in front of the performer holding her upper arms.

Handstand Straddle Vault The handstand straddle vault is executed in the same manner as is a handstand squat vault except that the legs are held extended and pass outside the arms rather than between them. The spotter should stand directly in front of the performer and facing her.

Handstand Stoop Vault The handstand stoop vault is done in the same manner as is a handstand squat vault except that the legs are held extended throughout the vault. A vigorous flexion of the hips and a vigorous push off the hands is required. This move is spotted in the same manner as is a handstand squat vault.

Handstand, Quarter Turn, Cartwheel The gymnast leaps into the handstand position, pivots on her left arm for a quarter turn, places her right hand on the horse, lifts her left arm, and pivots sideward on her right arm to land with her side toward the horse. The spotter should stand di-

rectly behind the performer to grasp her by the waist until the move has been mastered.

Giant Cartwheel The gymnast runs toward the horse, accelerating as she approaches. She leaps from both feet to dive up and forward, executing a quarter turn during the flight and before the hands land on the horse. Her left hand contacts the horse before she is in the handstand position. As she reaches the handstand position, her right hand contacts the horse. She then lifts her left arm to pivot sideward around her right hand to land with her right side toward the horse. The spotter should stand directly behind the performer prepared to grasp her waist.

Handstand straddle vault

239

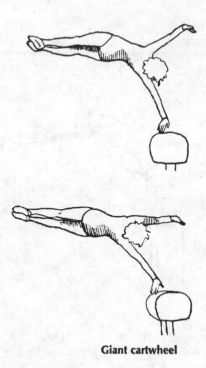

Giant cartwheel

The straight body ascent

The Straight Body Ascent The squat, the straddle, and the stoop vaults and the handstand with a quarter turn, the handspring, the quarter turn pivot cartwheel, and the giant cartwheel can all be done with a straight body ascent. In competition for women, all of these, with the exception of the squat vault, rate maximum in difficulty when done with a straight body ascent. The straight body ascent requires a very vigorous take-off and push with the arms as well as a strong pull by the back and hip extensor muscles. The feet should be driven directly upward so that the body rises in an extended position with no flexion at the hips or knees. In the squat, straddle, and stoop vaults, the hips are flexed vigorously when the body is about 30° above the horizontal in the extended position. From that point on, the vaults are executed in the same manner as when done without the straight body ascent. In the handstand with a quarter turn, handspring, quarter turn pivot cartwheel, and giant cartwheel, the body ascends in straight position to the handstand. From that point on, the moves are executed in the same manner as when done without the straight body ascent.

Swan Vault The gymnast runs toward the horse with good speed in order to execute a long dive with considerable forward momentum. She pushes up and forward off her arms very hard in order to clear the horse with her body arched and her legs extended. After she has cleared the horse, she continues to pull her head backward and to arch her upper back in order to cause her body to pivot on its horizontal axis to enable her to land on her feet. The spotter should grasp the performer's upper arms.

SIDE HORSE[4]

Single-Leg Half Circle The student starts in a front support. He shifts his weight to his left

Swan vault

[4] Side horse moves are done by boys only.

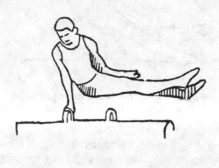

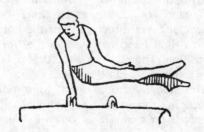

Single-leg half circle under opposite leg

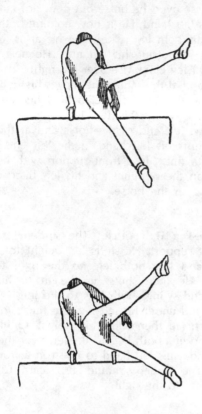

Single-leg half circle

arm and lifts his extended right leg upward directly to the right to cut it over the right pommel and under his right hand, finishing in a straddle seat position. The student returns to his starting position by shifting his weight to his left hand and lifting his extended right leg to the right to cut it over the horse and under his right hand. He regrasps to finish in the front support position. In all leg circling movements, the student's legs should move principally in the vertical plane. The student should also learn to do the single-leg half circle with his left leg.

Single-Leg Half Circle under Opposite Leg
The student starts in a front support. He shifts his weight to his right arm, turns his body slightly counterclockwise, and swings his extended right

leg upward to the left in front of his left leg, over the horse and under his left hand, and regrasps the left pommel, finishing in a straddle seat position with his right leg in front of the horse and his left leg behind it. The student should keep his chest and head elevated at all times in all work on the side horse. The student should also learn to do the move with his left leg.

Single-Leg Full Circle The student initiates this move in the same manner as he does a single-leg half circle. After his right leg has been cut forward under his right hand, he shifts his weight to his right hand and continues to swing his leg upward to the left, over the horse, and under his left hand. He regrasps the left pommel with his left hand and finishes in the front support. The student should also learn to do this move with his left leg.

Single-Leg Full Circle under Opposite Leg
The student initiates this move in the same man-

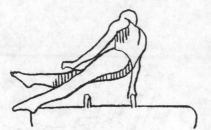

Single-leg full circle under opposite leg

ner as he does the single-leg half circle under the opposite leg. After his right leg has been cut forward under his left hand and he has re-grasped the left pommel, he shifts his weight to his left hand and continues to circle the right leg in a clockwise direction over the horse and under his right hand to finish in the front sup-port position. The student should also learn to do this move with his left leg.

The student should learn to combine all the preceding moves into a continuous routine. Following is an example of one of several pos-sible combinations of the preceding moves:

1. Right leg half circle counterclockwise to straddle seat (right leg in front).
2. Left leg half circle clockwise to rear support.
3. Right leg half circle clockwise to strad-dle seat (right leg in back).
4. Left leg half circle clockwise to front support.
5. Right leg full circle clockwise to front support.

Single-Leg Half Circle Travel The student does a right leg half circle counterclockwise to a straddle seat. He then swings his left leg clockwise over the horse but does not cut it un-der his left hand. He is now holding both pom-mels, his right leg is between his arms, and his left leg is outside his left arm. He next circles his right leg clockwise over the right side of the horse and at the same time moves his right hand to grasp the left pommel behind his left hand. He then swings his left leg counterclockwise over the left end of the horse and at the same time shifts his left hand to the left end of the horse to finish in a front support with his right hand on the pommel and his left hand on the left end of the horse.

Double-Leg Half Circle The student starts in a front support. He shifts his weight to his left hand and lifts both legs to the right to gain swing. He then shifts his weight to his right hand and swings both legs to the left, over the horse and under his left hand to finish in a rear support. He then shifts his weight to his right arm and lifts both legs to the left over the horse and under his left hand to finish in a front sup-port. The student should also learn to circle both legs to the right.

Double-Leg Full Circle The student initiates this move in the same manner as for a double-leg circle. However, he continues to circle his

Single-leg half circle travel

Feint

Scissors

legs in their original direction to finish in a front support. If he is circling his legs clockwise, when he reaches the rear support position, he shifts his weight to his left hand and lifts his legs to the right over the right side of the horse and under his right hand to finish in the front support position. The student should learn to circle his legs in both directions.

Feint The student starts in a front support. He swings his right leg over the right side of the horse until it meets his right arm. At the same time, he shifts his weight to his right arm. He lifts his right leg upward until it is at a right angle to his trunk. He then swings his right leg clockwise and pushes with his left knee against the horse. This move is used to gain the momentum necessary to accomplish the more difficult skills.

Scissors The student starts in a straddle position with his right leg forward. He shifts his weight to his right arm and swings his legs to the left. When they are above the horse, he moves the right leg backward and the left leg forward over the horse and under his left hand to finish in the straddle support with his legs having reversed their positions. The student should learn to move into the scissors from a right leg half circle. He should also learn to do scissors to both sides and in series.

Reverse Scissors The student starts from a straddle support with his right leg forward. He shifts his weight to his left arm and swings his

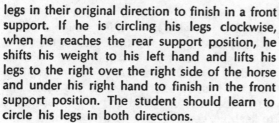

Reverse scissors

Single rear dismount

Triple rear dismount

legs to the right. When they are above the horse, he moves his right leg backward and his left leg forward cutting them under his right hand to finish in the straddle support with his left leg forward and his right leg to the rear of the horse. The student should learn to move into the scissors from a left leg half circle under the opposite leg. He should also learn to do the reverse scissors to both sides and in series.

Single Rear Dismount The student feints to the right. He swings his right leg around, and as it begins to rise over the center of the horse, he brings his left leg up to join it. As his legs cut under his left hand, the student turns so that his rear passes over the horse. As he circles around, his hips are held against his right forearm After his legs have cleared the horse, he grasps the right pommel with his left hand and extends his hips to land with his left side toward the horse.

Double rear dismount

Double Rear Dismount The student feints to the right. He swings his right leg around and then as it begins to move over the center of the horse, he brings his left leg up to join it. His hips are flexed so that his legs are at a right angle to his trunk; his head is turned to the right; and his right arm is extended and angled backward to keep his center of gravity over his right hand. After his legs have been swung over the left and the right sides of the horse, he extends his hips to land with his left side toward the horse. At the same time, he places his left hand on the horse to steady his landing.

Triple Rear Dismount The student initiates this move in the same manner as for a double rear dismount. However, instead of facing the end of the horse as he executes the second rear vault, he faces the side to pass through the rear support position with his legs at right angles to his trunk, with his right hand on the pommel, and his left hand on the end of the horse. From this point, he pushes with his left hand and his legs continue to circle around to pass over both pommels. After his legs have cleared the horse, he extends his hips to land alongside the end of the horse with his left shoulder toward it.

Double Rear Mount The gymnast stands facing the horse with his left hand on the left end and his right hand on the left pommel. He jumps upward and forward to bring both legs over the left side with his hips against his extended right arm and with his legs at right angles to his trunk. He turns his head to the

right and pushes off his left arm to circle around his right arm, finishing in a rear support between the pommels. As he circles, he should sit on his right hand and angle his right arm backward and sideward to maintain his center of gravity over his right hand.

Hip Circles The gymnast feints to the right. He circles his legs in a clockwise direction over the left side of the horse and under his left hand and continues to circle them over the right side and under his right hand to the front support position. As his feet move toward the front of the horse, he extends his hips, and as they move backward, he flexes and lifts his hips. When his legs are moving forward, he angles his arms backward. When they are moving backward, he angles his arms in the opposite direction. These actions keep his center of gravity between the pommels. The gymnast should develop ability to do several hip circles in series and in both directions. He should also learn to do them on either end of the horse.

Double rear mount

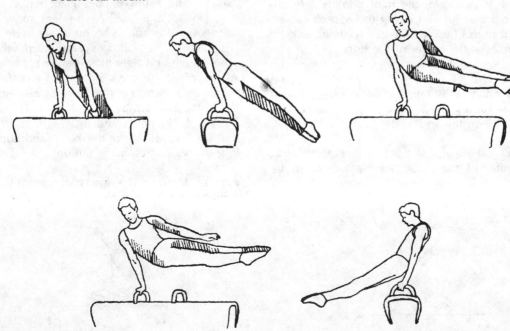

Hip circles

245

Double in

Moore

Double In The gymnast does giant hip circles on the left end of the horse. As his legs pass over the end of the horse, he leans toward the right and draws his hips in close to his right arm. He pivots around this arm executing a half turn as his legs pass over the right pommel. He finishes in a rear support facing the opposite direction. From this position, he can continue in giant hip circles at the center of the horse.

Double Out This move is executed in the same manner as is the double in except that it is begun from giant hip circles in the center and is finished on the end of the horse.

Tromlet The gymnast does giant hip circles at the center of the horse. As his legs clear the

right side of the horse, he angles his left arm well over to the left. As his legs swing toward the left behind the horse, he shifts his right hand to grasp the left pommel in front of his left hand. His legs begin to pass over the left side of the horse while he is holding the left pommel with both hands. He then shifts his left hand to the end of the horse and continues in giant hip circles on the end. The gymnast should also learn to do the tromlet from the end to the middle of the horse.

Moore The gymnast does giant hip circles in a clockwise direction. As his legs move backward over the horse, he turns his body clockwise on its vertical axis and grasps the left pommel with his right hand next to his left hand. At this point, his arms are angled well forward. He pivots around his right arm as his legs clear the horse and grasps the far pommel with his left hand. He flexes and lifts his hips in order that his feet will clear the horse and continues in giant hip circles facing the opposite direction.

Reverse Moore The gymnast starts by doing giant hip circles in a clockwise direction on the

Tromlet

Reverse moore

left end of the horse. As his legs begin to move over the right side, he turns his front upward and transfers his left hand from the end of the horse to the left pommel. As he completes the half turn facing in a direction opposite to his starting direction, he transfers his right hand to the end of the horse and continues in giant hip circles on the end of the horse in a clockwise direction.

Loops The gymnast does giant hip circles on the left end of the horse. As his legs swing to the left behind the horse, he pivots on his left arm to face the far end of the horse. At the same time he leans forward. He places his right hand on the end of the horse and swings his legs past the end of the horse. He lifts his left arm to allow his legs to swing forward and over the horse as he places his right hand on the horse again. His legs then move down along the side of the horse and he continues doing a series of loops.

TRAMPOLINE[5]

Front One and a Half Somersault with a Half Twist This move may be done in either of two ways. The easiest is to do a front one and a quarter somersault and then to execute the twist by turning the head to the left and pulling the right arm across the chest just before the horizontal position is reached to land on the upper back. The other method is to do a front somersault with a half twist or a baroni and to overturn the somersault to land on the upper back.

Back Somersault with a Double Twist This move is executed in basically the same manner as is a back somersault with a full twist described in the trampoline section of skills for junior high school children. The principal differences between the two moves are that in the double twist, the arms begin in a slightly wider position, the right arm whips across the chest with greater force, and both arms are pulled in closer to the body.

[5] All the trampoline moves described in this section, except those indicated, may be done by both boys and girls.

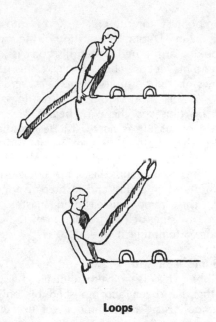

Loops

body. All of these actions give greater torque about the vertical axis. On take-off, the feet should push backward against the bed to lift the hips up and forward. There should be no sideward push from the feet or leaning of the body sideward since these actions will cause the trampolinist to travel sideward. The first twist is completed by the time the gymnast has upended. The second twist is executed during the next quarter of the somersault so that the trampolinist has completed the twist before he lands. The trampolinist's initial efforts should be made in a twisting belt suspended from the ceiling.

Back Somersault with a Triple Twist All the suggestions that have been made with reference to all the back somersaults with twists apply to the back somersault with a triple twist. Twisting back somersaults should be mastered in the progressive order of difficulty.

Front Somersault with a One and a Half Twist (Rudolph) As the trampolinist leaves the bed, he swings his arms upward and drives his hips upward and backward by pushing downward and forward against the bed with his feet. As his arms move upward, they are positioned farther apart than they are in the baroni or the front somersault. This wide position of the arms will enable the trampolinist to put greater force into the twisting action. During this portion of the move, he is looking at the bed. When his body is jack-knifed and his feet are about as high as his head, he throws his right arm across his chest and abdomen. As his arm swings past his legs, he extends his hips and the twist begins. He continues to somersault as he twists. He completes the twist when his body is approximately three-quarters of the way around in the somersault. At this time, he extends his arms sideward to check the twisting action and to prepare for the landing. The trampolinist should master this move in a twisting belt suspended from the ceiling before attempting it free.

Front Somersault with a Two and a Half Twist (Randolph) This is a very difficult twisting move that has been accomplished by only a few trampolinists. The techniques of execution are the same as they are for a front somersault with a one and a half twist except that greater twisting force must be applied. (Boys only.)

Fliffes The word *fliffes* refers to an entire group of moves in which a double somersault with a twist is executed. They might be double back or double front somersaults or the first somersault might be forward and the second backward or vice versa. The twist might be a half, full, full and a half, double, or even a triple twist. Students should attempt to learn fliffes only when being coached by a highly qualified coach. The gymnast or coach who would like to learn the most advanced moves should attend one of the many gymnastic clinics being conducted in the United States. (Boys only.)

UNEVEN PARALLEL BARS[6]

Flank Vault Mount to the Low Bar The student starts facing the low bar several feet from it. She takes a few running steps, places both hands on the bar, takes off from both feet, and executes a flank vault to the left, retaining her

[6] While the uneven parallel bars are used in competition by women and girls only, elementary school boys enjoy doing the moves, are challenged by them, and can profit from practice on them.

grip on the low bar with her left hand. She grasps the high bar with her right hand and finishes in a side seat position facing the high bar.

Flank Vault with a Half Twist The student starts several feet from the high bar and facing it. She runs toward the bar, takes off from both feet to grasp the high bar, and lifts both legs to the right over the low bar to finish with her hips on the low bar while retaining her grip on the high bar. As her legs pass over the low bar, she turns her entire body toward the floor.

Forward Roll off the High Bar The student starts from a stand on the low bar with a reverse grip on the high bar and her abdomen against it. She executes a forward roll around the high bar to a hanging position.

Squat Vault Dismount over the Low Bar The student starts in a front support position on the low bar facing outward. She flexes her arms slightly in order to lower her body so that the bar is across her hip joints. She flexes her hips to swing her legs forward. She then swings them backward, extends her arms, lifts and flexes her hips, flexes her knees, and brings her feet forward between her arms and over the bar so that she lands on her feet with her back toward the bars. The spotter should stand to the side of the performer and hold her wrist and upper arm.

Straddle Vault Dismount over the Low Bar This move is executed in the same manner as is the squat vault dismount over the low bar except that the legs are straddled and pass outside the arms. The spotter should stand directly in front of the performer. She should be prepared to catch the gymnast under the arms.

Front Vault Dismount from the High Bar over the Low Bar The gymnast starts in a swan support on the high bar. She flexes her hips to lower her trunk and to grasp the low bar with a reverse grip with her left hand and a front grip with her right hand. She vigorously extends her hips to whip her legs upward and sideward. She pivots a quarter turn on her left arm to execute a front vault with her body arched over the low bar landing with her left side toward the bar. She retains her grip on the bar with her left hand until after she has landed on her feet.

Single-Knee Circle Backward The gymnast starts in a front support on the low bar facing the high bar. She brings her left leg forward between her arms. She swings her right leg forward and then backward. As this leg swings backward, she slides her body backward to hook the back of her left knee on the bar. She immediately swings her right leg forward and pulls her head and shoulders backward to circle around the bar returning to her starting position. To check her rotation when the move is completed, she squeezes the bar with her hands and extends her left leg.

Single-Knee Circle Forward The starting position is the same as for the single knee circle backward except that a reverse grip is used. The gymnast initiates rotation by swinging her left leg backward and bringing her head and trunk forward. The bar is at her crotch as she circles. When she has completed the circle, she checks her rotation by squeezing the bar with her hands, bringing her head backward, and lifting her chest. The spotter should stand alongside the performer and push down on her extended leg to help her finish the move.

Back Hip Circle The student starts in a front support on the low bar. She flexes her arms to lower her body so that the bar will be across her hip joints. This position will allow her to flex her hips and to swing her legs forward. She swings her legs backward and then forward. As she swings her legs forward, she pulls her head backward. These actions cause her to rotate around the bar. As she circles the bar, she pulls herself against it. She checks her rotation by hyperextending her body. The spotter should stand alongside the performer and push on her legs or back as necessary to assist her in the rotation.

Half Turn Swing on the High Bar into a Back Hip Circle on the Low Bar The gymnast starts from a sitting position on the low bar facing inward and gripping the high bar with the left hand in a front grip and with the right hand in a reverse grip. She swings her legs backward and then forward to cast off the low bar into a hang on the high bar. At the end of her forward swing, she turns her body to the left to face the low bar and releases her left hand to regrasp the high bar in a front grip. When her abdomen strikes the low bar in her forward swing, she releases the high bar and grasps the low bar in a front grip to execute a backward hip circle on the low bar. A spotter should stand alongside the performer, ready to assist if necessary.

Half Turn Jump from the Low Bar to the High Bar The gymnast starts in a front support on the low bar facing outward. She flexes her arms to lower her body so that the bar will be across her hip joints. She flexes her hips to swing her legs forward and then swings them backward. As she swings her legs backward, she pushes off with her left hand and turns her head to the left. Immediately afterward, she pushes off her right hand and grasps the high bar with both hands in a front grip to finish in a hanging position. The spotter should stand between the bars and hold the gymnast by the hips to assist in the turn until the move has been mastered.

Double-Knee Hang to a Handstand on the Low Bar The gymnast starts in a double knee hang on the high bar facing the low bar. She grasps the low bar in a front grip and pulls her body over the low bar until her arms are fully extended and are supporting her weight. She places her left foot on the high bar and extends her right leg to bring her body into the handstand position. She then pushes gently off her left foot to move into the handstand on the low bar. The spotter should stand between the bars alongside the performer with one hand on her upper arm and the other on her lower back.

Pull Over on the High Bar The gymnast starts from a standing position on the low bar, facing the high bar, and gripping it with a front grip. She flexes her hips to lift her feet above the high bar and pulls with her arms to circle under it and to finish in a front support on the high bar. The spotter should stand between the bars and assist with one hand on the gymnast's upper back and the other on her lower back.

Stand on the croup

Basic position

Side Cross Hand Balance The gymnast starts from a front lying position on the high bar facing the low bar and gripping the high bar with a reverse grip with the left hand. She flexes her hips and lowers her body to grasp the low bar with a front grip with her right hand. She turns her body and presses up into a handstand between the bars with her right arm extended and her left arm flexed. The spotter should stand behind the performer.

Glide Kip The gymnast starts from a standing position under the high bar, facing the low bar and gripping it with a front grip. She springs backward flexing her hips to lift her feet an inch or two above the mat. She swings forward under the low bar until her body is arched and her arms are extended. At the end of this forward swing, she flexes her hips to bring her toes to the bar. She then pushes her feet upward and pulls with her extended arms to finish in a front support. The spotter should stand alongside the performer to push on her back or legs to assist her in coming to the support position.

LONG HORSE

While moves on the long horse appear very difficult to the uninitiated, many of them can be learned by typical high school students. Boys who have strength and power will find that they can progress to the more difficult moves in a relatively short time.

Combined long horse and side horse vaulting, with the boys vaulting across the length of the horse and the girls alternating with the boys and vaulting across the width of the horse, makes a very interesting exhibition number. Students should follow one another quickly to increase the number's effectiveness.

Students can gain self-confidence and an understanding of the techniques of execution of many of the moves by doing them from a stand on the croup before attempting them from a run.

Straddle Vault from a Stand on the Croup The student starts from a standing position on the croup. He flexes his knees and hips and takes a low dive to his hands, placing his hands on the neck of the horse. He pulls his body up into into an arched position so that it is angled about 30° above the horizontal. His legs are extended and his head is pulled backward. He has some forward momentum (henceforth called the basic position). He next flexes his hips and straddles his legs to land on his feet with his back to the horse. He lands on the balls of his feet, lowers to his heels, and bends his knees and hips on landing to absorb the impact of landing. The spotter should stand directly in front of the gymnast's anticipated point of landing ready to catch him under the arms if necessary.

Squat Vault from a Stand on the Croup The student starts from a stand on the croup. He dives forward into the basic position and then vigorously flexes his hips and pushes off his hands. After his hips have begun to flex, he

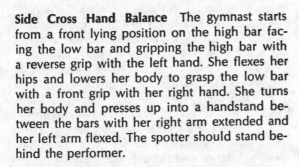

Straddle vault from a stand on the croup

draws his knees up toward his chest and flexes them. He lands with his back toward the horse. The spotter should stand alongside the performer's anticipated point of landing.

Squat vault from a stand on the croup

Stoop Vault from a Stand on the Croup This move is executed and spotted in the same manner as is the squat vault from the croup except that the legs are held extended throughout the vault. A vigorous hip flexion and push off the hands is mandatory.

Scissors Vault from a Stand on the Croup The gymnast starts from a stand on the croup. He dives forward to place his hands on the neck to strike the basic position. After he strikes the basic position, he turns his head to the left, pushes

Neckspring from a stand on the croup

off his left hand, and pulls his right leg to the left side of the horse. These actions cause his body to turn on its long axis so that his front faces upward. He straddles his legs and lands facing the horse. The spotter should stand directly in front of the gymnast's anticipated point of landing and be ready to catch him under the arms.

Neckspring from a Stand on the Croup The gymnast starts from a stand on the croup. He jumps forward-upward to lift his hips in a flexed

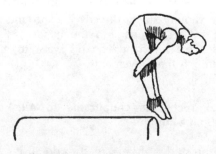

Stoop vault from a stand on the croup

251

Handspring from a stand on the croup

Cartwheel from a stand on the croup

position and places his hands on the horse at the location of the farthest pommel. He holds his legs extended and his feet low as his hips move forward beyond his head. When his back is at approximately a 57° angle to the top of the horse, he extends his hips and pushes with his arms to perform the neckspring. He lands with his back toward the horse. The spotter should stand to the performer's right and should hold his right upper arm with his right hand and place his left hand on his lower back.

Handspring from a Stand on the Croup The gymnast starts from a stand on the croup. He dives forward-upward to place his hands on the end of the horse with his arms and legs extended, his head pulled back, and his hips flexed and directly over his head. He extends his hips to bring his body to the handstand position. He rotates around his hands with his body and his arms in an extended position until he lands on his feet—at which time he bends his knees and his

hips to bring his center of gravity over his feet. The spotter should stand to the gymnast's right side. He should hold his right upper arm with his left hand and place his right hand on his shoulder blades.

Cartwheel from a Stand on the Croup The gymnast starts from a stand on the croup facing sideward. He flexes his trunk forward-sideward and bends his left knee to place his left hand on the site of the first pommel. He springs off the left foot, swings his right leg up over his head, and swings his right arm across his body to place his right hand on the site of the second pommel. These actions will bring him up into the handstand position. His head is pulled backward. He pushes off his left hand and flexes his trunk to the right to pivot around his right hand, cartwheeling off the horse to finish with his right side toward the horse. The gymnast directs his thrust so that it is in line with the horse. The spotter should stand directly behind the performer as he upends into the handstand and should place his hands on his waist to guide him through the movements.

General Techniques Applicable to All Vaults Done from a Run

When the student has learned to do all the preceding vaults from a stand on the croup, he is ready to learn them from a run. Execution of these vaults from a run will appear exceedingly difficult to the uninitiated because of the apparent difficulty in traversing the length of the horse. If the instructor will stand with his abdomen against the near end of the horse, bend forward, and stretch his arms forward to touch the far end of the horse, the student will easily see that the leap necessary to land in the basic position is not an impossible one. The instructor must emphasize that the body does not pass over the horse in a vertical position but dives horizontally into the basic position and then pivots about the shoulders, hips, and hands. Moves such as the squat, stoop, straddle, and scissors vaults require a modicum of forward momentum and therefore require a flatter trajectory than those which require that the feet be brought above and around the head such as the neckspring, handspring, and cartwheel; these moves require a higher trajectory during the flight. The swan (hecht) and all near tap moves require considerable forward momentum and therefore demand a flat trajectory. Moves requiring a high trajectory make it advisable that the beat (or Reuther) board be placed nearer the horse while moves requiring a flat trajectory make it advisable that the beat board be positioned farther away from the horse.

The student's run toward the horse should be forceful and should accelerate as he approaches. He should not "chop" his steps or skip in order to hit the board properly. He should hit the board with, and take off from, both feet. It is advisable for him to mark the spot for the start of his run much as track athletes do in the pole vault and the running broad jump.

Straddle Vault The gymnast runs toward the horse, dives into the basic position, flexes his hips, pushes off his hands, and pulls his head backward to clear the horse with his legs straddled, landing with his back toward the horse. The spotter should stand directly in front of the anticipated landing point of the gymnast ready to catch him under the arms.

Squat Vault The gymnast runs toward the horse, dives into the basic position, and flexes his hips and knees to draw his thighs toward his chest as he pushes off his hand to clear the horse

Squat vault

and to land with his back toward the horse. The spotter should stand alongside the anticipated landing spot of the gymnast, ready to catch him around the chest.

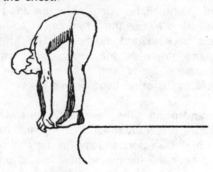

Stoop vault

Stoop Vault The gymnast runs toward the horse, dives into the basic position, pulls his head backward, flexes his hips, and pushes off his hands vigorously to cut his feet past the end of the horse with his legs extended and to land with his back toward the horse. The spotter should stand alongside the anticipated landing point of the gymnast and be ready to catch him around the chest in the event he loses control.

Scissors Vault The gymnast runs toward the horse, dives into the basic position, turns his head

Scissors vault

to the right, pushes upward off his right hand, cuts his left leg under his right leg, straddles his legs, and lands facing the horse. The spotter should stand directly behind the anticipated landing point of the gymnast ready to catch him under the arms in the event he misses.

Neckspring The gymnast runs toward the horse, dives forward-upward to place his hands on the site of the second pommel, and tucks his head between his arms to place the back of his neck against the horse while he flexes his hips to bring his hips over his head. His feet are low and close to the horse until he extends his hips. When his back is at approximately a 57° angle to the top of the horse, he extends his hips and pushes with his arms to execute a neckspring to his feet with his back toward the horse. The spotter should stand alongside the horse and grasp the performer's upper arm with one hand while he places his other hand on his lower back.

Handspring The gymnast runs toward the horse forcefully, then dives up and forward with a high trajectory to land on the end of the horse as near the handstand position as possible. The momentum should be sufficient to carry his feet above and beyond his head. If the momentum is inadequate to bring his feet over his head, he can flex his hips. When his body is 20° to 40° beyond the vertical, the gymnast pushes off with his arms to effect a flight before landing on his feet with his back toward the horse. The spotter should stand to the performer's right and grasp his right upper arm with his left hand and lift with his right hand against the performer's upper back.

Double tap cartwheel

Double Tap Cartwheel (Handspring with Quarter Pivoted Turn) The gymnast runs toward the horse, takes off from both feet simultaneously to dive into a momentary handstand on the site of the second pommel. He pivots a quarter turn around his left arm and places his right hand on the neck of the horse. He pushes off his left hand and flexes his trunk to the right to cartwheel off the horse with his right side toward the horse. The spotter should stand to the side center of the horse and place his hands on the performer's waist as he executes the move.

Single Tap (Giant) Cartwheel The gymnast runs forcefully toward the horse. He takes off from both feet to dive with a high trajectory so that he can place his left hand on the center of the horse. As he leaves the beat board, he drops his

Handspring

Single tap cartwheel

left shoulder, elevates his right shoulder, and pulls his head to the left in order to execute a quarter turn during the flight. He lands in a handstand position facing the side with his left hand in the center and his right hand on the end of the horse. He continues to cartwheel over the horse to land with his right side toward the horse. This move should be spotted in the same manner as the double tap cartwheel.

Hecht The gymnast runs forcefully toward the horse, dives forward with maximum forward momentum, strikes the basic position (with body extended rather than arched), and pushes off his hands very forcefully to clear the horse with his hips and legs extended. As he pushes off his hands, he lifts his chest, arches his back, and pulls his head backward. The spotter should stand alongside the anticipated point of landing ready to extend an arm across the gymnast's chest or abdomen.

Near Tap Straddle Vault The gymnast runs toward the horse forcefully. He hits the near end with his hands and pushes off to clear the length of the horse with his legs straddled.

Near Tap Squat Vault The board is placed 3 to 4 feet from the end of the horse. The gymnast secures a forceful, accelerating run. He hits the near end of the horse with both hands, pulls his hips upward, and brings his bent knees to his chest as he pushes off his hands. His forward momentum and the push off his hands should be adequate to enable him to clear the far end of the horse. To develop confidence and courage, the gymnast should, on his first attempts, land on his feet on the far end of the horse. With each succeeding attempt, he should try to land farther out on the end of the horse until he feels certain he can clear it by holding his feet up.

Near Tap Stoop Vault This move is executed in the same manner as is a near tap squat vault except that the legs are held extended throughout the vault. A more forceful run and push-off are required. During his initial attempts, the gymnast will, very likely, bend his knees as he draws his legs up between his arms and extend them as he passes over the horse. As he develops skill,

Near tap stoop vault

he should endeavor to keep his legs fully extended throughout the vault.

Near Tap Hecht The gymnast secures a forceful, accelerating run. He hits the near end of the horse with both hands and pushes off very forcefully to clear the horse with his body arched and his legs extended. Considerable forward momentum is required for execution of this move. The gymnast's body is horizontal as he passes over the horse. After his feet have cleared the horse, he pulls his head backward and lifts his chest to cause his body to pivot to the vertical position for the landing.

BIBLIOGRAPHY

Baley, James A. "Beginning Triples Balancing." *Athletic Journal*, February, 1952.
———. "Intermediate Triples Balancing." *Athletic Journal*, March, 1952.
———. "Advanced Triples Balancing." *Athletic Journal*, April, 1952.
———. "Beginning Singles Balancing." *Athletic Journal*, January, 1954.
———. "Intermediate Singles Balancing." *Athletic Journal*, February, 1954.
———. "Advanced Singles Balancing." *Athletic Journal*, March, 1954.
———. "Vaulting Stunts over the Side Horse." *Scholastic Coach*, February, 1958.
———. "Vaulting Stunts over the Swedish Box and Elephant." *Scholastic Coach*, September, 1959.
———. "Beginning Doubles Balancing Stunts." *Scholastic Coach*, October, 1959.
———. "Intermediate Doubles Balancing Stunts." *Scholastic Coach*, November, 1959.

————. "Advanced Doubles Balancing Stunts." *Scholastic Coach*, December, 1959.

————. "Beginning Parallel Bar Stunts, Part I," *Coach and Athlete*. February, 1962.

————. "Beginning Parallel Bar Stunts, Part II." *Coach and Athlete*. March, 1962.

————. Intermediate Parallel Bar Stunts." *Coach and Athlete*, September, 1962.

————. "Advanced Parallel Bar Stunts." *Coach and Athlete*, January, 1964.

————. "Vaulting Stunts over the Long Horse." *Coach and Athlete*, November, 1962.

9

INTERNATIONAL LEVEL SKILLS FOR MEN

RINGS

German Rise to "L" The gymnast begins from a straight body inverted hang. He allows his feet to drop forward in a free swing while looking at the floor. As he reaches the inlocated hang position, the gymnast flexes his hips to whip his legs forward into a tightly piked position. At this point, as he feels himself rising upward, he brings his head sharply upward, and pulls downward on the rings with his arms extended through the "L" cross to an "L" sit.

This move may also be initiated from a handstand or inverted cross. It may finish in a cross, "L" cross, or front lever. (When finishing in a front lever, the gymnast leans backward instead of throwing his head up after the vigorous hip flexion.)

Prerequisites: 1. Very flexible shoulders developed through static stretching in the inlocated hang position while stretching the toes toward the mat. 2. Ability to do the cross.

Spotting: The spotter should push upward with one hand on the gymnast's buttocks and one on his upper leg as he reaches the inlocate hang position.

Hollowback Press The gymnast begins from an "L" support, lowers his feet through the straight body support and continues pulling them over his head with his body arched until the handstand position is reached. The arms should be fully extended and forward of the vertical with the hands away from the body and turned outward (supinated), as in a reverse grip on the horizontal bar, while the head should be brought forward slightly. As his legs move over his head, the gymnast bends his elbows to no less than a right angle. When his feet have reached a point over his head, the gymnast extends his arms to finish in a handstand position.

Prerequisites: Sufficient strength to do a hollowback press on the floor from a lying position, is prerequisite. The gymnast may develop the necessary strength by pressing to the handstand from an "L" position in the rings, utilizing considerable whip of the legs and decreasing the amount of whip as he gains in strength.

Spotting: The danger of a fall is minimal in this move. The spotter can assist the performer in learning the kinesthetic feel of this skill by standing on a table to the performer's right side and placing his right hand on the performer's near shoulder and his left hand on the performer's thigh to push him upward into position.

Back Rise to Handstand The gymnast begins from an inverted hang with hips flexed and legs extended. He extends his hips forward and pulls upward with his arms and then extends his arms to lengthen the body lever and thereby gain greater momentum. As his body approaches the bottom of the descent, he increases his pike slightly. As his feet pass under the rings, he whips his legs backward forcefully, initiating the arm pull with the rings behind his head. As his legs, hips, and chest rise above the rings, he brings his extended arms to his sides with the palms turned outward. As soon as his body is above the rings, he presses upward to the handstand, aided by the momentum generated by his rising legs and hips. If he has generated enough momentum and enough rotary force, upon arriving above the rings he will find himself between an inverted cross and a planche. When he has reached this level of skill, he should endeavor to rise all the way to the handstand without bending his arms.

Common causes for failure are: (1) failure to press downward on the rings as the arms move toward the side during the rise, (2) inadequate extension of the shoulders at the bottom of the swing, (3) insufficient whip of the legs as the legs come under the rings, (4) failure to bring the rings next to the hips with hands supinated as the body rises above the rings, and (5) failure to continue pulling the legs upward throughout the drive.

Prerequisites: Ability to do a back uprise to a support and a hollowback press are prerequisite to this skill.

Spotting: The spotter stands on the floor to the performer's left side. As the performer descends in the downward swing, the spotter places his left hand on his thigh to assist the performer in whipping his legs backward.

Fall or Cast from a Handstand into a Reverse Giant Swing This move is initiated from a handstand. The gymnast stretches his body to eliminate the arch, pulls his shoulders about one inch

in front of the straps, pushes his hands backward while holding his arms extended and shoulder width apart, and allows his extended body to fall as one straight unit while keeping his head in position (neither ducking it nor pulling it backward). Because it is necessary to establish strong rotary force by having the feet circle faster than the hands and shoulders, he must avoid pushing the rings sideward; he must keep his body extended, and he must avoid bending his arms. As the gymnast approaches the hang position, the movements are the same as those described for the preceding skill, the back rise to handstand. That is, the legs whip backward, the arms pull to the sides in extended position, the hands are supinated, and the legs continue to pull upward into the handstand as the hollowback press is executed.

Prerequisites: The gymnast should master a back rise to a handstand before attempting this skill.

Spotting: Because of the danger of being pulled from the rings during the descent due to failure to establish rotation around the hands, the performer should be carefully spotted. If the gymnast flexes his arms, shoulders, or hips during the descent, the probability is great that he will be pulled from the rings on reaching bottom. For these reasons, spotters should stand to either side of the performer with one hand on the performer's upper back and the other on the front of his upper legs.

Cast into Regular Back Giant The gymnast begins from a handstand position and lowers toward a planche with arms either extended or bent. When his feet are level with his head, the gymnast pushes the rings forward rapidly keeping his arms straight and his head forward, and leading with his chest as his body drops below the rings. As he approaches the hanging position, he flexes his hips vigorously to whip his legs forward and upward, pulls his head backward, and as he rises above the rings, pushes downward against the rings to finish in the handstand.

Prerequisites: The gymnast must first learn the basic cast or layaway technique. The first step in learning this technique is to swing the legs forward and backward trying to get them as high as possible while in a bent arm support position. When the feet can be swung backward as high as the head, the gymnast can attempt the cast as previously described. However, he should be well spotted, for if he pushes the rings sideward instead of forward, if he bends his arms, if he raises his head, or if he moves his arms forward too slowly, he may be pulled from the rings because his feet will come down first. Pushing the rings forward rapidly, keeping the head down and the arms straight, and leading with the chest are all done to maximize rotary force.

After he has mastered the layaway with bent arms, the gymnast should learn the layaway (cast) with straight arms. Then he should learn the layaway from a planche. The planche may be done either with arms straight or bent; in either case, while the gymnast may utilize a slight swing to get into the planche position, he should get there principally through strength. Finally, the gymnast may attempt the cast and giant by lowering from the handstand into the planche and then casting into the giant. As his proficiency increases, the gymnast should endeavor to cast layaway earlier until finally he can layaway directly from the handstand position.

Spotting: Two spotters, one on either side of the performer should be used. These spotters should place one hand on the performer's chest and the other behind his upper legs as he drops below the rings. The hand on the chest can slow down a fall if the performer loses his grip, while the hand behind the legs can assist in the leg whip.

Double Dislocate Shoot into Handstand This move is initiated from a piked hang. The gymnast extends his hips and presses downward on the rings forcefully so that the first dislocate is done with the shoulders at ring level and with the arms fully extended. The second dislocate is lifted to the inverted cross position. In both dislocates, the body is arched during the downward swing to make possible a smooth swing. As he passes through the hanging position, after the second dislocate, the gymnast flexes his hips to whip his legs upward. As his feet rise above his head, the gymnast forcefully extends his hips, shooting his feet upward, and arches into the handstand position while his arms are extended sideward. At the same time, he pushes downward on the rings and continues to push until the handstand position is reached.

Prerequisites: The gymnast should master the dislocate and the shoot into a handstand before attempting this move.

Spotting: Spotters should stand alongside the performer with one hand on his shoulder to push him upward and the other behind his upper leg to assist in the whip.

Backward Somersault with Full Twist The gymnast obtains a big swing. On the forward swing, as he passes through the hanging position, he flexes his hips and pulls with his arms. As his body approaches the inverted vertical position, he first extends his hips and then he initiates the twist by turning his body slightly in the direction of the twist. On reaching the vertical position, he releases the hand opposite to the direction toward which he is twisting and swings this arm across his body as though swatting a fly on the opposite shoulder. He also turns his head in the direction of this shoulder. He endeavors to see the mat as soon as possible.

Prerequisites: The gymnast should master a back somersault with a half twist before learning this skill.

Spotting: A double thickness of mats should be used. The spotters should stand alongside the performer ready to catch him around the chest in the event the somersault is not completed.

Backward Straddle Dismount The gymnast secures a forceful swing. On the forward swing as his body is passing through the vertical hang, he flexes his hips to whip his legs upward. At the same time, he pulls the rings toward his waist and then up toward his chest. When his feet are over his head, he pulls his head backward to rotate his upper body above the rings. He next flexes his hips, straddles his legs outside the straps, and pushes the rings to the rear out of the way of his falling body. As he clears the rings, he arches his back and extends his hips to complete the move.

A well-executed and high dislocate preceding this skill facilitates execution.

This skill may also be executed from a support position. The gymnast swings his legs backward, and when his legs swing forward, he carries his extended arms backward of the vertical and flexes his hips. He straddles his legs outside his arms as he approaches the inverted position, and as he continues to rotate, he lifts his head and shoulders to facilitate this rotation. When his body is parallel to the floor, he releases the rings and "pops an arch" to complete the move.

A half twist can be added to this skill by turning the head and shoulders forcefully in the direction of the twist just as the rings are released.

Double Backward Somersault The gymnast secures a big swing. On the forward swing, as his body passes through the hang position, he flexes his hips vigorously to whip his feet upward, and at the same time he flexes his knees and pulls with his arms. His knees are driven upward forcefully and brought into his chest. As his knees come up between the rings, the rings are released. At this time his head is forward. It remains forward until after the first somersault has been completed. As soon as he releases the rings, the gymnast grasps his lower legs with his hands and pulls to tighten the tuck and thereby shortens the radius of rotation to accelerate the speed of rotation.

Prerequisites: The gymnast should master a backward somersault dismount on the rings and a double somersault on the trampoline before attempting to learn this skill.

Spotting: The move should be spotted first with a hand safety belt. Then it should be hand spotted by two spotters over a double thickness of mats.

HORIZONTAL BAR

Inverted Giant Swing (Eagle) The gymnast begins from an "L" sit on the bar with an undergrip, with the arms fully extended and slightly wider than shoulder width and the back arched. Very likely he got into this position via a forward seat circle. He flexes his hips vigorously to lift his feet over and behind his head to assume a tightly piked position (thighs on the chest), with his shoulders extended rearward to their maximal range without dislocating. His center of gravity is just slightly forward of vertical in order to initiate rotation. He next extends his hips vigorously so that the legs form a straight line with the trunk. At the same time, he holds his shoul-

ders in the fully extended position with his elbows rotated upward. The straight body and extended shoulder positions facilitate achievement of the longest lever possible, which gives him a longer radius of rotation and consequently greater momentum (momentum = mass × velocity—mass is constant—velocity at the toes will be greater when the body is stretched). His legs retain the straight-line relationship with his trunk until he is horizontal or has completed 90° of the rotation. At this point, his hips flex slightly to lead the rest of the body. When he is vertical, at the bottom of his swing, or has completed 180° of rotation, he extends his hips to maximize the "bottoming effect," which will help him get over the top. (At this point, he must retain a tight grip. Spotters should be particularly alert.) As he approaches the horizontal position again, he flexes his hips fully until his thighs are against his chest. If this action is properly timed and the shoulders are held fully extended, the gymnast will be lifted up above the bar. It is during this period of weightlessness that the gymnast turns his hands on the bar from a hang to a support position. The gymnast will then be above the bar, at which time he extends his hips to initiate the next inverted giant swing.

Prerequisites: Forward seat circle and giant swings both directions.

Spotting: This skill should first be attempted in a safety belt. Next, the gymnast can attempt it with two spotters—one directly under the bar who will grasp him around the waist in the event he releases his grip and one about 2 feet to the rear.

German Giant The gymnast begins this skill from a rear support position. The overgrip reverse kip is an excellent means for getting into the starting position since residual momentum after completion of the reverse kip in the legs and shoulders will facilitate moving into the German giant. In the rear support position, the gymnast flexes his hips to bring his extended legs upward and over his head toward the overgrip inlocated handstand position. As his legs move upward, the gymnast leans his extended arms backward slightly in order to counterbalance the weight of the upward moving legs as well as to initiate rotation around the bar. The gymnast next moves into a tightly piked position with his extended arms slightly behind the vertical and with his shoulders extended rearward as far as his shoulder girdle flexibility will permit so that his arms and trunk will be in as nearly a straight-line relationship as possible. He then extends his hips forcefully as he begins his rotation around the bar. At the same time he extends his arms with strong and steady force against the bar. By the time he has rotated 45°, his shoulders and hips are fully extended. He maintains this position until he is near the bottom of the swing, at which time the "bottoming effect" serves as a cue to flex the hips to shorten the radius of rotation to accelerate the speed of rotation. The rapidly upward moving feet and legs give him a feeling of weightlessness as he swings upward. This feeling serves as the cue to rotate his wrists to bring his hands to the top of the bar. Now he has returned to top and may move into another German giant, or just before reaching the top he may "disengage" by bringing his hips and legs between his arms to move into an overgrip handstand position.

Prerequisites: overgrip giant swing, overgrip reverse kip, undergrip giant swing, and a very flexible and strong shoulder girdle.

Spotting: Initial efforts should be made in a safety belt, after which two spotters standing directly under the bar and watching the gymnast's grip very closely can serve by grasping the gymnast around the waist quickly if he loses his grasp. Another spotter (or two) standing 3 feet in front would add additional safety.

Stoop-in Circle Shoot into Inlocated Handstand
The gymnast is circling the bar in an undergrip giant swing. As his body approaches the horizontal in the upward portion of the swing, he flexes his hips slightly and decreases the shoulder angle to shorten the radius of rotation and to thereby accelerate the speed of rotation. This action will produce a feeling of weightlessness as well as place the gymnast in ideal position for the stoop-in. As his body rises above the bar, the gymnast arches his wrists onto the top of the bar into support position. As he approaches the top of the upward swing, the gymnast's body is slightly arched; however, the shoulders are held in a slightly flexed position while the arms press against the bar. At this point the body is about 20° from the vertical. At this moment, the hips

are quickly and vigorously flexed to bring the legs between the arms. This stoop-in action will be completed by the time the gymnast's arms are parallel to the floor. During the stoop-in the shoulder angle decreases. At this point the gymnast endeavors to move his center of weight as far from the bar as he can in order to increase his momentum in the downward swing, which will result in a more effective upward swing.

At the bottom of the swing, the bar will bow downward and then release its energy to lift the gymnast as he circles upward. Throughout the circular swing, from stoop-in to inlocated handstand, the shoulder angle decreases and then goes on to complete hyperextension or as far as the gymnast's shoulder flexibility will permit. Throughout the ascent the gymnast's hips are flexed as fully as his flexibility will permit. As his body rises above the bar and his arms assume a support position, the gymnast vigorously rotates his wrists onto the top of the bar. At the top of the bar, when the skill has been completed, the gymnast's shoulders will be fully hyperextended but without being dislocated, his hips will be fully flexed with his legs fully extended and with his toes opposite his face. His center of gravity will be slightly forward in the direction of execution of the eagle giant to follow.

Spotting: One spotter should stand 1 or 2 feet in front of the bar ready to catch the gymnast by his shoulder and chest in the event he catches his feet on the bar during the stoop-in. Another spotter should stand behind the bar ready to catch the gymnast in the event he loses his grip on the bar during the backward-upward swing.

Prerequisites: Seat rise, undergrip giant swing, stoop vault dismount from a handstand on the parallel bars.

Undergrip Stalder This skill is best initiated from an undergrip giant swing. As the gymnast approaches the bottom of his swing, he decreases slightly the angle of the arms with respect to the trunk (shoulder angle) and at the same time flexes his hips slightly. These actions place his body into position for the beat that occurs at the bottom of the swing when he extends both his hips and shoulders so that his body is in a slightly arched position. These actions also cause the bar to bow downward to a greater degree. Immediately after this action, as his body begins to swing upward and the bar springs upward, he flexes first his shoulders slightly and then his hips to shorten his radius of rotation, which will accelerate his speed of rotation. As his body passes through the horizontal position in its upward swing, he extends his hips to a slightly arched position but maintains the shoulder angle. These actions produce a feeling of weightlessness, which serves as a cue for the rotation of the hands from a hanging to a supporting position. The straddle-in is initiated by a vigorous flexion of the hips when the arms have just passed the upper vertical position. As the gymnast circles forward-downward, the hip and shoulder angles decrease to the extent that his flexibility will allow. His legs should be parallel to his trunk since in this position his center of gravity will be a maximal distance from the bar, which will increase his momentum in the downward swing, resulting in a more effective rise in the backward swing. When the body reaches the bottom of the swing, the hips should be as high above the head as possible. Due to the recoil of the bar and the resultant pull on the arms, which are attached to the body above its center of gravity, the hips will be pulled downward to circle around the shoulders. As the gymnast circles upward around the bar, he must resist the centrifugal force that tends to pull his legs away from his trunk. This is most effectively accomplished by maintaining an adequately decreased shoulder angle (angle of the arms relative to the trunk). As his body rises upward above the level of the bar, the gymnast experiences a feeling of weightlessness. It is at this time that he rotates his hands into a support position; he also begins to extend his shoulders and hips as he pushes downward against the bar. His legs straddle out as wide as his flexibility will permit. Although his trunk and arms move slightly in front of the horizontal as his legs are moving over his head, by the time his legs are over his head his trunk and arms are back along the horizontal line.

Prerequisites: Undergrip giant swing and undergrip seat circle.

Spotting: Two spotters directly under the bar should watch the gymnast's grip carefully to be ready to catch him in the event he releases the bar.

Overgrip Stalder Although there are several ways for moving into the overgrip Stalder, one of the most common is from the overgrip giant swing. As the gymnast approaches the bottom of the swing in the giant swing, his body is slightly arched and his arms are in line with his trunk. Immediately after passing the bottom, he first decreases the shoulder angle and then flexes his hips. As his body approaches the horizontal position in the upward swing, he extends his hips and shoulders. When his arms, trunk, and legs are in a straight-line relationship and his body is about 30° from the vertical, he hyperextends his wrists to bring his hands into a support position. The cue for this action is the feeling of weightlessness. As soon as his hands are in a support position and before he has reached the vertical position, he quickly flexes his hips to straddle his legs outside his arms as narrowly as possible. During the straddle-in, the back should be kept as flat as possible and the arms should push against the bar to facilitate the inward and upward straddling of the legs. As his body rotates downward, he decreases the shoulder and hip angles maximally. His legs are parallel to his trunk. By the time he reaches the bottom of the swing, his hips are directly over his head and his trunk is vertical. As his body rises above the bar, the shoulder and the hip angles increase as he straddles out. The legs should be straddled as wide as possible. From the bottom of the swing through to the handstand, the trunk should be vertical. The gymnast may use either the floor or the ceiling to provide visual cues with regard to body positions.

Prerequisites: Overgrip giant swing, overgrip seat circle, free hip circle into a handstand, and stoop vault dismount from a handstand.

Stalder Hop The Stalder hop is executed in the same manner as the overgrip Stalder except that as the body rises into the handstand position at the completion of the move, the grip is released and the arms are rotated 180° outward with elbows fully extended to catch the bar with an undergrip while still in a handstand position.

This, obviously, requires a considerable upward thrust upon completion of the Stalder.

Prerequisites: Undergrip and overgrip giant swings, swinging reverse pirouette in a handstand on the parallel bars, and a full turn from a reverse grip handstand to a front grip handstand on one parallel bar.

Spotting: Spot with an overhead twisting belt. If such a belt is not available, position two spotters on each side of the uprights. Instruct the two spotters to watch the gymnast's grip.

Straddle Turn Stalder   The gymnast usually executes this move from an undergrip giant swing. As his hips rise above his head upon completing the giant swing, he flexes his hips, straddles his legs, shifts his weight onto his right arm, pivots around this arm after having released the grasp of his left hand, regrasps the bar with his left hand, and brings his left leg over the bar and outside his left arm. Throughout the turn his shoulders remain on the near side of the bar. The hips are held high throughout the turn. After the turn and regrasps have been completed, the gymnast proceeds as in executing an overgrip Stalder.

Backward Uprise Full Turn   This move may be executed from a mixed grip giant swing or a cast In the backward-downward swing, just previous to reaching the vertical position and to accentuate the bottoming effect, the gymnast flexes his hips about 15° and then extends them at the same time, decreasing the shoulder angle by pushing the extended arms downward against the bar. The decrement in the shoulder angle should not be so great that the body rises in a vertical position. At the moment of initiation of the turn, the body should be nearer the horizontal plane than the vertical plane (about 15° to 20° above horizontal). This position will facilitate a bigger and freer forward-downward swing after the regrasp.

The turn is initiated when all parts of the body (the legs being in line with the trunk) are above the bar and the arms are at 75° to the horizontal, by a simultaneous vigorous push-off of the right hand and a turn of the head to the right. The flexed right arm is driven backward with the elbow at shoulder height. During these actions, the left arm serves as a stabilizer by pushing forcefully forward-downward against the bar. The gymnast retains his grasp with the left hand until he can see the bar. The gymnast continues to pull his head and right arm around after the release of the bar. During the turn, the gymnast's legs should remain together and extended and should be in-line with his trunk.

The regrasp should be made with both hands simultaneously. Immediately after the regrasp, the gymnast brings his trunk into a straight-line relationship with his arms in order to facilitate a bigger and freer forward-downward swing.

Prerequisites: Overgrip giant swing, undergrip giant swing, back uprise into a free hip circle, and swan with a full turn into a front drop on the trampoline.

Spotting: Two spotters should stand about 2 feet behind the bar ready to catch the gymnast in the event he misses the regrasp. A twisting belt could be used.

Hecht with a Full Twist: The gymnast executes two undergrip giant swings to gain the necessary momentum. As his body approaches 45° beyond the horizontal near the top of the second giant swing, he gives a tremendous pull with his arms, his left hand leaving the bar slightly before his right so that the left shoulder is slightly forward. This will initiate the twisting action. At this point, his body is slightly arched. The right arm is next thrust forward in front of the body, which at this point is deeply arched and horizontal. At the same time, the left arm is swung to the thigh. At this point, the turn will be one-quarter completed.

To complete the turn, the left arm is next brought above the head while the right arm is swept to the side. At this point the hips are slightly flexed and extended again. Finally, the left arm is drawn to the chest. Before landing, the hips are again slightly flexed to facilitate a controlled landing.

Prerequisites: Undergrip giant swing, overgrip giant swing, front flyaway, rear flyaway, back uprise full turn.

Spotting: Use an overhead twisting belt with the rope wrapped around the bar once to allow for the giant swing rotation.

One-Half Turn (Pirouette) from an Undergrip to an Overgrip Giant Swing We first view the gymnast swinging downward in the overgrip giant swing. (His body actions are the same throughout as in all overgrip giant swings except that he adds the pirouette as he approaches the top of the swing.) As he approaches the bottom of the swing, he flexes his hips and shoulders slightly in preparation for the "beat" at the bottom of the swing. As his body passes between the uprights, he extends his hips and shoulders to secure this "beat." As his swing continues upward and his body approaches the horizontal, he again flexes first his shoulders and then his hips. As his body approaches the top of the swing, he extends his hips and shoulders and at the same time directs his weight to the side of the anticipated pirouette in order to facilitate proper alignment after the turn has been completed. At the same time, he arches his hands to the top of the bar. Before his legs, trunk, and arms are in a straight-line relationship, he initiates the pirouette. The pirouette is completed before his body is vertical. Throughout the turn, his supporting hand presses hard against the bar. The skill is completed with the gymnast in vertical or handstand position on the bar with an overgrip.

Prerequisites: Undergrip and overgrip giant swings, swinging reverse pirouette in a handstand on the parallel bars, and a full turn from a reverse grip handstand to a front grip handstand on one parallel bar.

Spotting: Spot with an overhead twisting belt. If such a belt is not available, position two spotters on each side of the uprights. Instruct the spotters to watch the gymnast's grip.

Free Hip Circle–One-Half Turn Backward into an Undergrip Giant Swing The gymnast is first seen in the handstand position upon completion of the overgrip giant swing. He decreases his shoulder angle to lower his straight body downward. As he does so, his shoulders move forward of the vertical. When his feet have been lowered below his head, his hips flex and his shoulders move behind the vertical. As his feet rotate under the bar, he increases the hip angle while bringing his shoulders backward with arms extended. By the time his hips are under the bar, his legs are at a right angle to his trunk. During

this backward drop, the gymnast's body is well away from the bar in order that he can utilize maximally the "basket effect" to ensure an effortless and fluid ascent. The gymnast's descending body weight will bow the bar downward, and as his body begins to move to the front of the bar, it will bow upward. As it does so, the gymnast increases the shoulder and hip angles while keeping his arms straight. As the gymnast rises above the bar, his body weight is slightly to the left in anticipation of the turn.

As the gymnast's center of gravity moves directly above the bar, he rotates his wrists from a hang to a support position. Just before the shoulders and hips are fully extended, the gymnast initiates the half turn so that during the turn his hips and shoulders continue to extend. The turn should be completed before the gymnast's body has passed the vertical. During the turn, he pushes down on the bar hard with his supporting arm.

Prerequisites: Overgrip and undergrip giant swings, free hip circle to a handstand, and half turn (pirouette) from an overgrip into an undergrip giant swing.

Spotting: Spot under the bar watching the hands after the half turn has been completed to ensure that a secure grip is maintained.

PARALLEL BARS

Cast to a Support Although this skill may be executed from a support position, we see the gymnast starting from a stand between the bars with an inside grip, arms fully extended. He leaps upward between the bars, pushing downward with his extended arms against the bars. As he drops downward between the bars, he flexes his hips fully, rounds his back and stretches his shoulders. All of these actions move his center of weight as far as possible from the center of rotation (his hands) and will increase his angular momentum sufficiently to carry him well above the bars. These actions also increase the "bottoming effect," that is, they ensure a greater rebound from the bars after they bow downward. When his extended arms are passing through the vertical he extends his hips vigorously so that the thrust is at a 45° angle to the bars. At the same time, the gymnast presses down against the bars hard with his extended arms. His hands are pulled off the bars by the upward thrust. He makes the grip change quickly to catch in the support position with his shoulders slightly in front of his hands. After catching, he extends his hips in order to secure a swing for the succeeding move.

Prerequisites: Cast to a hang.

Spotting: The spotter should stand alongside the performer with one hand on his upper back and one on his hips to push him upward between the bars. Needless to say, the spotter should never place his arms between the bars and the performer.

Cast from a Handstand to a Support   The gymnast begins in a handstand position. He stretches his body upward so that his arms, trunk, and legs are in a straight-line relationship. As his body begins to descend, he carries his arms slightly forward of the vertical. However, by the time his body is horizontal, his arms return to the vertical, and as his body drops below the horizontal, his arms move behind the vertical in order to ensure a vigorous descent resulting in a greater rebound and greater thrust (early drop). When his arms are at a 45° angle to the bars, he begins to flex his hips. From this point on, the cast is executed as previously described.

Prerequisites: Handstand and cast from a support to a support.

Spotting: Spot as for a cast to a support.

Cast Half Turn to an Upper Arm Hang   The gymnast executes the cast as previously described; however, as he extends his hips to rise above the bars, he pushes off with his right hand, pulls with his left hand, and twists to his left. He next grasps the left bar with his right hand and then swings his left hand across to grasp the right bar. He completes the thrust with his body fully extended well above the bars in order to have sufficient swing for the succeeding skill.

Prerequisites: Cast from a support to a support.

Spotting: Drape a mat over the bar toward which the twist is being made in order to avoid bruises should the gymnast strike the bar. The spotter should stand alongside the performer on the opposite side.

Peach Basket from a Handstand to a Handstand
The gymnast begins in a handstand position. He stretches his body to remove the arch and to bring his arms, trunk, and legs into a straight-line relationship. He initiates the downward swing bringing his arms only slightly forward of the vertical. However, by the time his body has dropped to the horizontal his arms are vertical. His extended arms move backward of the vertical as his body swings below the horizontal. When his body is at a 45° angle to the bars, he flexes his hips. His hips are maximally flexed by the time he is hanging directly under the bars with his arms vertical. Throughout the drop below the bars, the angle of the arms with respect to the trunk has increased until they are at right angles to the trunk when the arms are vertical below the bars. This position plus the tight pike places the center of weight as far from the hands or center of rotation as possible and ensures a good rebound off the bars after they bow downward, as well as ensuring maximum rotary momentum. At this point, the hips are vigorously extended to shoot the feet directly upward along the vertical line. At the same time, the gymnast attempts to "throw the bars backward behind his head." The hands are pulled off the bar as a result of the vigorous upward thrust and the gymnast quickly changes his grip to catch in or very near the handstand position. At no time during the ascent is the gymnast's trunk below the vertical position.

Prerequisites: Peach basket from a handstand to a support and cast from a handstand to a support.

Spotting: Spot in the same manner as for a cast to a support. Push upward on the near shoulder with one hand from under the bar.

Peach Basket Straddle Cut   Although this skill may be initiated from a stand between the bars with either an inside or an outside grip, we see the gymnast in a cross arm support. The gymnast obtains a slight swing. On the forward swing, when his hips are in front of his hands, he angles his arms backward, and when his hips have dropped below the bar, he flexes his hips. As he drops below the bar, his arms remain fully extended while his shoulders and head are forward. His hips are fully flexed by the time his arms are

30° from the vertical. When his arms reach vertical, he pulls with his shoulders, extends his hips vigorously to shoot upward about 30° above the bars, and pulls his head backward. As his hips reach full extension, his shoulders rise above the bars and his grip is released. He lifts his chest, regrasps the bars, and immediately pushes downward while flexing his hips to quickly execute the straddle cut catch. He may catch with straight arms, in an "L" position, or bend his arms to move into a dip swing and into a forward shoulder roll or into a handstand.

Prerequisites: Uprise straddle cut catch, peach basket from a support, and a support.

Spotting: Spotting is not necessary if the prerequisites have been mastered. Sweatpants or other pants should be worn while learning this skill to prevent abrasions of the legs during the straddle cut as a result of scraping against the bars.

Peach Basket Half Turn to Support Although this move may be executed either as a mount (with inside or outside grip) or from a drop above the bars (with either a late or an early drop), we first see the gymnast in a support with a slight forward swing. His back is slightly arched and his arms are angled slightly forward. Just before his hips reach his hands, he angles his extended arms backward and flexes his hips slightly. A too rapid piking action would cause him to rotate too rapidly. As his body drops below the bars, his head is forward, his shoulders are rounded, his arms are extended and his legs are between his wrists. When his arms are vertical, he extends his hips and pulls his head backward to shoot his body above the bars at about a 30° angle to them. At the same time, he pulls from the shoulders. As the shoulders rise above the bars, he turns his head and shoulders in the direction of the turn and releases the bars to quickly regrasp even before the turn has been completed.

Prerequisites: Peach basket to a support and back uprise with a half turn to regrasp.

Spotting: The spotter should stand alongside the performer with one hand ready to push up on the performer's chest (or back) and the other ready to push up on his legs. He should never place his arms between the performer and the bars. A mat may be dropped over one or

both bars behind the performer's hands to ease the blow in the event he strikes them after the turn.

Forward Somersault to a Regrasp The gymnast has a big swing in a support position. As his body swings backward, he carries his shoulders forward until his arms are about 35° forward of the vertical and his umbilicus is over his hands when his body is horizontal. He releases the bars and then pikes sharply and forcefully so that his trajectory is directly upward. He brings his arms around quickly in the vertical plane (not to the side) to regrasp the bars with his arms extended and behind his hips about 20° behind the vertical.

Prerequisites: Front somersault to an upper arm hang.

Spotting: Spotting this move is difficult. A spotter can stand alongside the performer to spot him from below the bars. The best procedure is to use an overhead belt.

Layout One-Half Turn Forward Somersault The gymnast has a very big forward swing in a support position. When his feet are as high in front as his shoulder flexibility will allow, he pushes off with his right hand to shift his center of gravity over his extended left arm, brings it around to the left, and turns his head to the left. While his legs are still moving upward, he brings his head forward, pikes, and sweeps his right arm toward his legs in the vertical plane to initiate the somersault. Throughout the turn and the initiation of the somersault, the gymnast's left shoulder is directly over his left hand and his left arm is fully extended in order to lend support to his body. He lands on his feet alongside the bars.

Prerequisites: Layout one-half turn dismount (very high) and a piked forward somersault dismount.

Spotting: This move is learned in greatest safety with either a trampoline with a mat on it alongside the parallel bars or mats stacked up to the level of the bars alongside the bars. The gymnast first learns to do a high layout with a half turn into a front drop onto the mats or trampoline. When he can land on his seat in good position and with good control, he can try the move on the parallel bars at their lowest height. He should be spotted for over- or underspin by a spotter standing alongside his anticipated landing spot.

Streuli The gymnast is swinging forward in an upper arm hang. As his feet pass directly under his head, he initiates hip flexion until his legs reach a 45° angle with his trunk by the time his trunk is parallel to the bars. At this time, he extends and lifts his hips, pushes off his hands, and pulls his head backward to lift his shoulders off the bars. As a continuation of the push-off, he brings his hands quickly around to regrasp the bars and continues upward into the handstand position. He extends his arms while he still has upward momentum.

Prerequisites: High front uprise and backward shoulder rolls.

Spotting: The spotter should stand alongside the performer and reach upward between the bars from underneath to push on the performer's near shoulder with one hand and on his hips with the other.

SIDE HORSE

Piked Loop Dismount We see the gymnast executing double leg circles on the left side of the horse before moving into this skill. He pushes off the pommel with his right hand to cause his body to face the horse as it moves past the end. During this phase, his hips are elevated and flexed, his head is up, and his left arm is inclined forward in order to keep his center of weight over his point of support. As his legs clear the end of the horse, he lifts his feet higher than his head by flexing his hips fully. At the same time, he angles his arms backward. He leans slightly to the right to clear the horse and extends his hips after clearing it in order to land in good form and in balance. During this last phase, he maintains contact with the horse with his left hand.

Prerequisites: Double leg circles.

Spotting: Spot from behind the performer ready to catch him under the arms.

Triple Russian The gymnast appears to be executing a triple rear dismount, however, as his legs pass over the horse, he keeps his center of gravity over the center of the end of the horse

by angling his left (supporting) arm to the left and rearward. As his legs swing downward along the side of the horse, he brings his right hand to the end of the horse quickly and angles his arms forward. He pivots around his right arm (which is leaning well forward) to face the horse while his left hand is placed on the horse next to the pommel. Throughout these and the succeeding movements his hips are extended. As his legs swing over the pommels, he shifts his right hand backward next to the pommels. He leans well forward and shifts his left hand to the end of the horse as his body pivots again to face the horse and to complete the move.

Prerequisites: Double leg circles, loops, quadruple rear dismount, (moores.)

Spotting: Unnecessary.

Front Vault Dismount The gymnast is executing double leg circles on the left end of the horse (or has executed a kehre-out from the center to the left end). He pushes his right hand off the pommel and turns his body around his left arm to face the far end of the horse as he quickly brings his right hand to the end of the horse well ahead of his legs. At this point his hips are flexed. He carries his shoulders forward of his hands as his legs whip backward and as his body continues turning. During this portion of the move, the gymnast's abdominal area is against his arms (particularly the right arm) in order to secure added leverage. As he turns around his arms, his legs continue to whip upward until he is in an arched position. This arch is achieved by the time the long axis of his body is at a right angle to the long axis of the horse. To facilitate achievement of this arched position, he must push downward with his arms and avoid carrying his shoulders too far forward of his hands. During the arch, he watches the horse to facilitate stabilization of the upper body. He completes the dismount by bringing his body down along the side of the horse to finish standing to the side of the horse and facing the near end.

In the piked style of front vault dismount, the hips are raised slightly higher when the right hand is moved to the end of the horse. The hips continue to rise as the upper body turns around the arms; the arms and abdominal area do not touch and the fully arched position is achieved later (when the long or vertical axis of the body is almost parallel to the long axis of the horse).

Prerequisites: Loop, tschechenkehre, or German around the end of the horse.

Spotting: Unnecessary.

Reverse Downhill Stockle The gymnast goes into this move from double leg circles or a kehre-in. His legs are circling clockwise. As they pass over the right side of the horse, he flexes his hips, brings his left hip to his left (supporting) forearm, leans his left arm to the left, and lifts his extended right arm upward. After his hips have cleared the end of the horse, he leans his left arm toward the center of the horse and extends his hips. As his legs swing alongside the horse and to the left of his body, he places his right hand down on the end of the horse and leans to his right to bring his legs over the pommels and to complete the move.

Prerequisites: Moore.

Spotting: None required.

Moore Mount The gymnast starts from a stand facing the horse and grasping both pommels with a regular grip. He leaps upward pushing down on the pommels, swings his legs to the left while pivoting around his left arm to face the center of the horse. Next he transfers his right hand to the left pommel as his extended body passes over the left end of the horse. He pivots around his arms to face the horse, flexes, and raises his hips to bring his legs over the left pommel, transferring his left hand to the other pommel to complete the move.

Prerequisite: Moore.

Spotting: None required.

TUMBLING

Russian Front Somersault The gymnast begins with a short run and hops to land on both feet with his arms extended above his head and swinging downward. His legs are angled about 30° behind the vertical and his hips are flexed to about a 45° angle when he lands on his feet. He bends his knees on landing and then extends them as his arms continue swinging backward.

When his arms reach the end of their range of motion, the momentum generated in them is transferred to the gymnast's body and his center of gravity lifts vertically off the mat. However, rotation has already been established since his hips are rising faster than his head. He assists in rotation by bringing his chest to his knees, flexing his knees, grasping his shins, and bringing his head forward. On completing the rotation, the gymnast extends his knees and hips and lifts his head to slow down the speed of rotation and comes out standing erect and in good balance.

The gymnast may do a piked somersault by holding his legs extended and piking tightly. He may also do a "walk-out" from either the tucked or piked somersault by extending first one hip and then the other to land first on one foot and then the other. The "walk-out" somersault can be followed with a round-off, tinsica, front handspring, or aerial. (Girls.)

Prerequisites: Regular front somersault on the mats and Russian front somersault on the trampoline.

Spotting: One spotter should stand alongside the gymnast and place one hand behind his neck to assist in the somersaulting action if necessary. Another spotter should stand alongside the gymnast's anticipated point of landing ready to extend an arm across his chest in the event an overspin appears imminent.

Back Somersault with a Half Twist The gymnast gains the necessary momentum by doing a round-off into a back handspring. He snaps down out of the back handspring with a "blocking action" (body at about a 30° angle in front of the horizontal when his feet contact the mat). This enables him to secure greater height. On take-off, he drives his right arm directly upward, drives his left arm diagonally upward, pulls his head backward while turning it to the right, and pushes backward and slightly to the right against the mat with his feet. These actions will initiate both the somersaulting and the twisting actions. As his body comes up, he brings his legs into a straight-line relationship with his trunk since this position facilitates twisting better than does the arched position. He also whips his left arm to his chest to thereby shorten the radius of rotation, which will accelerate the speed of rotation around his vertical axis. He lands facing the opposite direction. He prepares himself for the landing by bending his knees and hips slightly.

Prerequisites: Layout back somersault on the mats and somersault with a half twist on the trampoline.

Spotting: The best spotting procedure is to utilize a traveling twisting belt. If a traveling belt is not available, a twisting belt should be used. If a twisting belt is not available, a regular belt can be used by wrapping the ropes around the performer's waist so that they will unwind halfway on the round-off and the other half during the twist. This must be figured out carefully by the gymnast and his spotters before trying the skill.

This move can be well spotted by a skilled spotter, who stands to the gymnast's left side and grasps his right hip with his right hand to assist in the twisting action and who places his left hand against the rear of the gymnast's upper legs and pushes to assist in the somersaulting action.

Back Somersault with a Full Twist This move is executed in the same manner as is a back somersault with a half twist except that a more forceful twisting action and a higher lift are necessary. The twisting action is facilitated by bringing the left hand across to the right shoulder instead of across the chest, thus further shortening the radius of rotation and by bringing the legs into a straight-line relationship with the trunk sooner. The right arm is swung backward.

On completion of the full twist, the gymnast extends his arms sideward to slow down the twist and flexes his hips to prepare for the landing.

Prerequisites: Back somersault with a half twist on the mats and a back somersault with a full twist on the trampoline.

Spotting: Same as for the back somersault with a half twist.

Back Somersault with a Double Full Twist This move is executed and spotted in the same manner as a back somersault with a full twist. It should be mastered on the trampoline before being attempted on the mat. It should be spotted

with a twisting belt. This is a difficult move and should be attempted only by advanced tumblers and then only in a twisting belt. Greater twisting force can be secured by throwing the arms upward-sideward on lift-off since this will create a longer lever arm for the twist (but a shorter one for the somersault).

Arabian Front Somersault The gymnast may execute this move from a stand, round-off, or back handspring. We see the gymnast executing it from a back handspring. His feet contact the mat out of the snap down with his body 35° in front of the horizontal to ensure that horizontal momentum will be translated into maximal vertical lift. As he lifts off, he pushes backward and to the left with his feet against the mat and swings his extended right arm directly upward and his extended left arm to the right. By the time he has completed only one-fourth of the somersault, he has completed the half twist so that the last three-fourths of the somersault is a forward somersault. To complete this forward somersault, he brings his chin to his chest, sweeps his arms downward toward his hips and flexes his hips to bring them above and around his head. In learning this move, he should bend his knees to execute the front somersault in tucked position. After he has mastered this, he can attempt the move in piked position by keeping his legs extended. Note that as the gymnast completes the somersault, he lifts his extended arms above his head to slow down the somersault.

Prerequisites: Back somersault with half twist and front somersault.

Spotting: Utilization of an overhead twisting belt would be the best procedure. A twisting belt would be the second-best procedure. Two skilled hand spotters can provide adequate security provided the prerequisites have been satisfied. One spotter should stand to the gymnast's left side and grasp his right hip with his right hand to assist in the twisting action and push with his left hand against the gymnast's thigh to assist in the somersaulting action. The second spotter should stand alongside the gymnast's anticipated point of landing prepared to extend an arm in front of his chest to prevent an overspin.

Double Back Somersault The gymnast executes a round-off and one or two back handsprings to gain maximal momentum. He must secure great height through effective "blocking action," by driving his arms upward very forcefully and springing very forcefully. He must secure a very fast spin by pulling his head back hard and by tucking very tightly. Needless to say, this is a very difficult and hazardous move and should be attempted only by the most skilled gymnasts.

Prerequisites: Layout back somersault, a very high tucked back somersault on the mats and a double back somersault on the trampoline.

Spotting: This move should be learned only in a safety belt utilizing highly skilled spotters. Except in competition, it should be spotted at all times by a highly skilled spotter. As the tumbler completes his first somersault, the spotter lunges forward to one knee with both arms extended, one arm moving in front of the tumbler's chest and the other moving behind his lower legs ready to give added spin.

BIBLIOGRAPHY

Austin, Jeffrey M. "Cinematographical Analysis of the Double Backward Somersault." M.S. thesis, University of Illinois, 1960.

Fortier, Frank, J. "Analysis of the Reverse Lift Forward Somersault." *The Modern Gymnast,* December, 1960.

George, Gerald S. "Anyone for All-Around?" *The Modern Gymnast,* October, 1969.

———. "Horizontal Bar." *The Modern Gymnast,* March, 1970.

———. "Lay-Away Streuli." *The Modern Gymnast,* March, 1971.

Massimo, Joseph L. "Psychology and the Gymnast." *The Modern Gymnast,* March, 1969.

Shurlock, Art. "Let's Go All-Around." *The Modern Gymnast,* August, 1967.

Tonry, Don. "Gymnastic Aids." *The Modern Gymnast,* June-July, 1957.

———. "Parallel Bars." *The Modern Gymnast,* March, 1967.

———. "Something Different." *The Modern Gymnast,* February, 1968.

———. "Something Different." *The Modern Gymnast,* April, 1968.

10

INTERNATIONAL LEVEL SKILLS FOR WOMEN

FLOOR EXERCISE

Yogi Handstand The gymnast starts from a standing position and places her hands on the mat several inches forward from her feet. She brings her chin to her chest, elevates her flexed hips above her head by springing off one or both feet, and angles her arms backward. In the balanced position, the center of weight must be over the hands. The back can be brought nearer the horizontal by angling the arms further backward and by increasing hip flexion. After having held this position for 2 seconds, the gymnast raises one extended leg and brings it around to the mat, pushes with her arms and shoulders, and raises her head to come out in a backbend walk-out position. The yogi handstand position can be learned against a wall.

Prerequisites: Back walkover, handstand, hip flexibility sufficient to permit bringing the trunk to the legs with no bending of the knees.

Spotting: The spotter kneels alongside the performer with one hand under her shoulder and the other under her lower back.

Aerial Cartwheel The gymnast begins with a short run. For the lift-off and to establish rotation, she simultaneously flexes slightly at the hips, swings her right leg upward, springs off her left leg, and lifts her arms up and back. She executes the aerial cartwheel without touching the mats with her hands and lands first on her right foot and then her left. Throughout the move her head is pulled backward. It is important that the forces imparted by the hip flexion, springing leg, swinging leg, and arm action be applied simultaneously. Also, the swinging leg should be held fully extended in order to increase the length of the lever and consequently the momentum generated.

Prerequisites: Cartwheel, one-arm cartwheel.

Spotting: The spotter stands directly behind the point where the gymnast will execute the move. As the gymnast begins to upend, he grasps her at the waist to lift her and at the same time to impart rotary force.

Aerial Walkover The gymnast begins with a short run. To initiate the move, she simultaneously flexes her hips slightly, springs off her right leg, swings her extended left leg up and over her head, and lifts her arms up and backward. She executes the aerial walkover without touching the mat with her hands and lands first on the left foot and then the right. Throughout the move, the head is pulled backward. It is important that the forces imparted by the springing leg, swinging leg, hip flexion, and arm lift be applied simultaneously.

Prerequisites: Front walkover, aerial cartwheel and good back flexibility.

Spotting: The spotter stands alongside the point of execution. As the gymnast initiates the move, the spotter places her near hand on the gymnast's lower back. She uses her other hand to assist in rotation by tapping or pushing on the gymnast's thigh.

Butterfly The gymnast starts from a stand with legs straddled, hips flexed (back parallel to the floor), trunk rotated to the right, head up, and the arms extended to the right in line with the trunk. She swings her arms and trunk to the left forcefully. At the extreme range of this movement, the right foot is pulled off the mat. At this point, she swings her right leg upward to bring it in line with the trunk or slightly above horizontal. At this time, she springs off her left leg and brings it upward to the horizontal plane as the right leg is lowered. She lands on her right foot facing the opposite direction.

Prerequisites: None.

Spotting: None required.

BALANCE BEAM

Back Extension The gymnast starts from a supine position on the beam with her arms stretched above her head and with her hands under the beam. She vigorously flexes her hips to lift them off the beam and to bring her feet above and beyond her head while pulling with her arms. She rolls directly over her head. The hip flexion moves her center of weight higher. During the hip extension she shifts her hands to the top of the beam and pushes strongly downward against the beam. As soon as there is clearance space, she pulls her head backward.

Prerequisites: Backward roll with extension on the mat, handstand on the balance beam.

Spotting: Until the gymnast has mastered this move, two spotters should be provided, one on each side of the beam. The beam should be at its lowest point so that the spotters can grasp the gymnast's thighs in order to assist in the lift and extension. They can also provide support under the gymnast's shoulders and steady the handstand. In the event the gymnast shoots up into the handstand and overbalances, she should tuck her head under, flex her hips and knees, and move into a forward roll onto the beam. The spotters can slow down the drop to the beam in this event. In the event the gymnast shoots into an underbalanced position, the spotters can place an arm under her abdomen to pull her to the side of the beam or slow down the drop if she flexes her hips to land on her feet on the beam.

Valdez The gymnast starts from a position sitting on the beam with the right knee flexed, the right foot on the beam near the hips, the left leg extended forward along the beam, the right hand on the beam behind the buttocks with the hand rotated to the right and the fingers pointed to the left, and the left arm extended horizontally forward. She extends her right leg to lift her body upward and at the same time swings her left leg and left arm upward and over her head while keeping her right arm fully extended in order to better support her weight. She lifts her head and places her left hand on the beam to finish in a crosswise handstand on the beam.

Prerequisites: Crosswise handstand on the beam, valdez on the mat.

Spotting: Two spotters should be used —one on each side of the beam. The spotter on the gymnast's left side places one hand under her left thigh and the other under her left hip to assist the gymnast in the upward thrust. The spotter on the gymnast's right side supports her right arm and grasps her left side as she comes up into the handstand.

Back Somersault Dismount The gymnast starts from a stand on one end of the beam facing inward with her arms extended forward. She rises on the balls of her feet, swings her arms backward, downward, and then upward and over her head as she springs upward and slightly backward pulling her flexed knees to her chest. She grasps her shins momentarily and pulls her head backward to see the mat. She extends her body to land on the mat in good balance on both feet. She may do a swing back somersault in which she goes into a layout (arched) position and then flexes her hips, or she may do the somersault in layout position in which her body is arched throughout the move until just before landing, when she will flex her hips slightly to better absorb the impact of landing.

Prerequisites: The tucked, swing back, and layout somersaults should be learned on the trampoline and the mat before being attempted off the end of the balance beam.

Spotting: One spotter using the hand belt and standing on a table approximately the same height as the beam is utilized to insure that the gymnast does not strike the beam and completes the somersault. This spotter provides lift (if it is necessary) and assists in rotation (if it is necessary) by pushing against the gymnast's buttocks with one hand. Another spotter stands alongside the gymnast's anticipated point of landing ready to prevent overspin by placing one hand on her back.

Front Somersault Dismount The gymnast starts from a stand on the end of the beam facing outward. The toes of her forward foot are curved over the end of the beam. Her arms are extended horizontally forward. She rises on the balls of her feet, swings her arms backward and then downward in the plane of her body as she bends her knees, and then extends her knees forcefully as she drives her flexed arms upward along her body. After her feet have left the beam, she brings her chest downward to her thighs, flexes her knees, and tucks her head. When she has completed the rotation, she opens up to land in good balance on both feet.

Prerequisites: Standing front somersault on the trampoline and diving board.

Spotting: Same as for the back somersault dismount, i.e., one spotter using a belt standing on a table who assists with lift and rotation and another spotter at the anticipated point of landing to check for overspin by placing a hand on the gymnast's chest.

Front Aerial Dismount The gymnast starts from a stand near the end of the beam facing outward. She steps forward with her right foot so

that the toes grip over the end of the beam. Her arms are forward at shoulder height. Simultaneously she springs off the forward leg, swings the rear leg upward and around over her head, and drives her extended arms downward, backward, and around. Her head is pulled backward. Her legs are brought together in the air to ensure a safe landing.

Prerequisites: Aerial walkover on the mat.

Spotting: Spotting procedures are the same as for the front and back somersault dismounts.

Baroni Dismount The gymnast stands near the end of the beam facing outward. She steps forward with her right foot so that her toes grip over the edge of the beam. Simultaneously she springs off her right leg, swings her left leg upward over her head and throws her arms downward in the manner of a round-off. Her head is held backward so as to see the point of landing on the mat at all times. She lands simultaneously on both feet facing the beam and in good balance.

Prerequisites: The baroni on the trampoline and on the mat should be mastered before being attempted off the beam.

Spotting: The spotter should stand on a table and utilize a safety belt with the rope on the near side removed. The other rope should pass either in front of or behind the gymnast in such a manner as to facilitate the turn.

Note: The back and front somersaults, front aerial, and baroni may be done from the center of the beam by directing the thrust to the side of the beam so that the performer will land alongside the beam. These moves should, however, all be learned first from the end of the beam.

"Wendy" Dismount The gymnast starts from a stand at the center of the beam facing the end with her left foot forward. She flexes her hips to place her left hand on the beam as she swings her right leg upward toward the ceiling and springs off her left foot. She swings her right arm around and holds her head pulled backward as she pivots 180° around her left arm while in a handstand position. After completing the turn, she brings her arched body down alongside the beam to land on both feet in good balance facing the end of the beam. The movements of the

"Wendy" are almost identical to those of the one-armed round-off. This move should be done quickly, and the half turn should be completed before reaching the handstand.

Progressions in learning are: (1) on the floor over a line, (2) from the end of the beam, (3) at the center of the beam with a mat draped over the beam, and finally (4) at the center with no mat. When learning the "Wendy" on the floor over a line, the gymnast must tuck her legs under her body (due to lack of height) and should land with her feet next to her left hand. This will ensure completion of the turn and minimize the danger of striking the beam. When practicing the "Wendy" at the end of the beam, a broom handle or other stick could be held loosely against the end of the beam. This would serve to prove to the gymnast that she could clear the beam.

Prerequisites: Round-off and the progressions presented above.

Spotting: The spotter stands to the left side of the beam. She grips the gymnast's left upper arm with her left hand after she has placed it on the beam. She places her right hand on the gymnast's hips or thighs to ensure that she will clear the beam.

UNEVEN PARALLEL BARS

Stem Rise The gymnast starts from a position hanging onto the high bar with a regular grip, arms fully extended, left foot on the low bar with left leg bent, right leg extended vertically with the right toe close to the high bar. She extends her left leg at the knee and hip to spring upward and to bring her hips against the underside of the high bar. The right leg moves upward with the body, but its relationship to the body is not changed. As her hips are brought against the underside of the high bar, she pulls with her arms and flexes her hips to bring her shoulders above the bar and over her arms. At this point, she swings her right leg backward to join her left leg. Throughout the move there are no stops or hesitations. It is a smooth flow of action.

Prerequisites: None.

Spotting: Push upward on the gymnast's near hip with one hand and on her upper back with the other hand.

Front Seat Circle The gymnast starts from a rear support or sitting position on the bar with a reverse or undergrip. She extends her arms to lift her body off the bar while holding her extended legs horizontal. Her hips move upward and backward while her trunk moves closer to her legs (increased hip flexion). She rotates around the bar, at no time allowing her legs to touch the bar during the descent. Throughout the move she holds her legs and arms fully extended. As she comes up over the bar, she thrusts her legs over the bar and places the rear of her upper thighs against the bar.

Prerequisites: Kip and front circle.

Spotting: A spotter can stand to the side of the gymnast and behind the bar to assist in lifting the gymnast's thighs as the circle is initiated and to lift on her hips and back as the move is completed.

Back Straddle The gymnast starts from a stand on the low bar with legs straight and together, left arm extended forward, and right arm rearward gripping the high bar with an under grip. She bends her knees slightly and springs upward and backward straddling her legs wide and lifting them into a straddle "L" position. She pushes downward with her right arm to help lift her body while her left arm moves downward, palm down with fingers flexed in preparation to catch the bar. As her body passes backward over the bar, she releases the grip with her right hand and regrasps the high bar with both hands between her thighs in a regular grip. During the straddle she angles her trunk slightly forward to look for the bar.

In learning this move, if the gymnast finds herself sitting on the bar, she should endeavor to secure a higher jump and a faster and greater rearward movement of her upper body. If she finds her feet grazing the bar during the straddle, she should flex her hips more to raise her legs higher when moving into the straddle "L" position.

Prerequisites: Basic beginning moves.

Spotting: An overhead safety belt is most helpful in learning this move. The gymnast may learn this move over the low bar of the uneven bars by standing on the low parallel bars placed in front of the uneven bars. The spotter's assignment is the same whether the back straddle is done from a stand on the low parallel bars or from the low bar of the uneven bars. She stands behind the high bar and helps to pull the gymnast over the bar and is prepared to catch her in the event of a miss.

Back Straddle over the Low Bar   The gymnast is standing on the low bar, squatting, facing the high bar, and has a regular grip on the high bar with her arms extended. She pulls herself toward the high bar (partial chin-up), pushes her extended legs horizontally away from the bar by flexing her hips, and then drops her legs downward while extending her arms and forcing her chest forward. This forces her body into an arched position and produces a reaction which lifts her hips upward and rearward and lifts her legs upward and forward placing her in a piked position. Her body is moving backward over the low bar in a piked position. She straddles her legs and pushes away from the high bar. As she straddles over the low bar, she grasps it with both hands in a regular grip. She may now move into a free hip circle on the low bar or drop below the bar and move into a glide kip.

Prerequisites: Back straddle, kip, back uprise.

Spotting: One spotter should stand directly behind the gymnast and the low bar prepared to grasp the gymnast by the hips to pull her over the low bar or to catch her in the event she hooks her heels. Another spotter should stand in front of the low bar and far enough to the side of the performer to avoid being hit by the gymnast's straddling legs but near enough to step in in order to prevent the gymnast from striking the low bar after straddling it, by placing a hand on her chest.

Neckspring Dismount   The gymnast is in a thigh rest, that is, with her hips resting against the high bar, her body arched, her arms extended, and her hands gripping the low bar in a regular grip. She tucks her head in toward her chest and bends her arms to lower the back of her neck to the low bar as her extended legs slide down along the high bar. Her hips move into flexion as she lowers herself to the low bar. When her neck is on the bar, she is slightly overbalanced. She extends her hips to swing her legs forward-upward and into an arch while ex-

tending her arms to push herself away from the bar. As she descends toward the mat, she straightens her body to prepare for a balanced landing. Landing with the body weight too far backward is an indication that a more forceful push-off or a deeper arch during flight is called for. Landing with the body weight too far forward can be corrected by pushing off with less force, decreasing the arch in the back, or tightening the hip joints on landing.

Prerequisites: Neckspring on the mat.

Spotting: The spotter should stand in front of the low bar and alongside the gymnast. She should grasp the gymnast's upper arm with one hand and place the other hand under her upper back.

Front Somersault Catch   The gymnast starts from a front support on the low bar facing out. She bends her elbows slightly in order to be enabled to flex her hips to swing her legs first forward and then very vigorously backward. She does not carry her shoulders as far forward as is normal in this movement. As her legs swing vigorously backward and upward, she pushes, or more accurately, springs off her hands, flexes at the hips to bring her trunk up toward her legs, and straddles her legs. Her hips rise above and inside the high bar and her thighs are close to it. She swings her arms between her legs to catch the bar. During and after the catch she increases the hip flexion (tightens the pike).

Prerequisites: Side splits, hamstring flexibility sufficient to place the trunk against the extended legs when in sitting position, free hip circles.

Spotting: This move is most easily spotted with an overhead belt. The bars should be so placed under the belt that the ropes will hang down slightly inside of the high bar. Two hand spotters standing between the bars, one on each side of the gymnast, should be used. These must be experienced people with quick reflexes. They grasp the gymnast's upper arm with one hand and push against her thigh with the other when the legs swing upward toward the high bar. When the gymnast reaches between her legs for the high bar, the spotters help move her arms toward the bar. In the event the gymnast misses the catch, the spotters lift her back or catch her around the waist.

Helen Sjursen, a nationally recognized leader in women's gymnastics, recommends that the low bar be padded or mats draped over it on either side of the hand hold area since sometimes the legs hit this bar after the catch and disengage when they are not straddled wide enough. She also recommends use of a crash pad or several thicknesses of mats between the bars since this will not only make for a softer landing in the event of a miss, but it will also put the spotters higher where they can be more effective.

BIBLIOGRAPHY

Cochran, Tuovi S. *International Gymnastics for Girls and Women*. Reading, Mass.: Addison-Wesley Publishing Co., 1969.

Kjeldsen, Kitty. *Women's Gymnastics*. Boston: Allyn and Bacon, Inc., 1969.

Sjursen, Helen. *Educational Gymnastics—Floor Exercise for Women*. Fanwood, N.J.: H. S. Sjursen, Publisher, 1965.

———. "Front Somey Catch and Spotting." *Mademoiselle Gymnast*, March–April, 1970.

———. "Helen's Corner." *Mademoiselle Gymnast*, September–October, 1967.

———. "Helen's Corner." *Mademoiselle Gymnast*, March–April, 1968.

———. "Helen's Corner." *Mademoiselle Gymnast*, March–April, 1969.

———. "When Is a Back Kip a Back Kip?" *Mademoiselle Gymnast*, May–June, 1970.

11

PUBLICITY AND PUBLIC RELATIONS TO ENLARGE THE EDUCATIONAL ARENA[1]

Gymnastics, like all activities, requires public interest and support if it is to attract participants, if it is to secure the endorsement of school administrators, and if it is to be awarded the funds necessary for its operation. While it is true that enthusiastic and effective teaching is an excellent public relations medium, there can be little question that other publicity media will enhance the growth and acceptance of the sport. The publicizers of football and basketball have been instrumental in making these our most popular American sports. American businessmen have discovered the power of publicity and are making full use of it. It is particularly those who would increase the amount of participation in the lesser known sports such as gymnastics who need to make full use of all publicity media.

Simply defined, publicity is informing as many people as possible about the program in such a way as to enlist their participation and support.

Gymnastics presents a special public relations problem because it encompasses such a variety of activities. It is impossible to present a complete picture of gymnastics or to describe all its benefits in one news article or in one show. This makes it necessary that different messages be delivered in various news articles or programs. And, in order to tell the most people, all publicity media should be used.

Television Gymnastics lends itself well to television. Demonstrations for television shows should be well planned and thoroughly rehearsed. There should be no stage waits while equipment is moved into place or out of the way, nor should there be stage waits while performers move into position. The presentation of skills should be continuous. The skills and routines with greatest spectator appeal should be selected for demonstration. Loss of public interest in and growth of the sport can become the price paid for attempting to protect the "developing personality" of the least skilled children. Some moves, while of less difficulty, may have greater spectator appeal. Colorful costumes should be

[1]Adapted from "Publicity and Public Relations in Gymnastics" by James A. Baley in the *Journal of Health, Physical Education and Recreation,* November, 1961, pp. 27–28.

used. They need not be expensive and can be made by the students or their parents.

Parents should not accompany their children to the television studios. They add to the confusion and tend to make children more anxious and nervous. Many television studios do not have space to accommodate both children and their parents. Students should know in advance precisely where they are to go, what procedures they will follow, and what costumes and equipment to bring.

Several days before his group is scheduled to make a television appearance, the instructor should visit the television station to measure the working area and ceiling height and to make note of any obstacles or unique problems. The group should then rehearse for the show under as nearly identical circumstances as possible.

A different message should be put forth on each show. In the first show, moves on the balance beam and floor exercise might be presented to demonstrate the opportunities inherent in gymnastics for artistic self-expression. Rebound and mat tumbling could be utilized in the second show to demonstrate that gymnastics provides opportunities to develop agility and physical courage. In a third program, the side horse and parallel bars could be used to demonstrate the possibilities for development of perseverance and strength.

With knowledge of gymnastics and a little imagination, the possibilities are limitless. Being an educator, the instructor has the obligation to use care in avoiding exaggeration or misrepresentation. Educators should utilize publicity media to enlarge the educational arena and to more effectively achieve educational goals. Publicity media should not be used to add to the glory of the instructor, the coach, the program, or the school.

Movies and Tapes Movies or video tapes can be produced of activities that are suitable for television and other programs. Such movies can then be used many times, thereby saving money, time, and energy. Tapes about gymnastics can be cut for use by radio stations. Tape-recorded interviews with the students, coach, or champion gymnasts are almost always interesting.

Newspapers Newspaper articles and pictures are important publicity media. The first step in

using news services is to visit the newspaper offices in order to receive instructions from the sports writers. Sports pages have been filled with details concerning football, basketball, baseball, golf, and horse racing, and the sports writers have been quite thoroughly indoctrinated in these activities. Yet, when they are given information and the opportunity, they can develop a thorough appreciation of other worthwhile sports activities.

Newspapers have deadlines that must be met, and these deadlines must be respected. There are specifications concerning the size of typing paper, spacing, and margins that should be learned and adhered to. Some newspapers will want the information in note form and others in story form. In typing the release, one must exercise care with regard to spelling, punctuation, neatness, and the accuracy of facts. Paragraphs should be finished on the page rather than continued to the next page. The story should be complete but not long-winded. Reporters and editors can condense and shorten an article but they cannot fill in with facts which they do not have. Editorializing in news stories is not permissible because opinions and judgments have no place in news stories. Occasionally, an editor will allow a coach or physical educator to write a column under his own name In this instance editorializing is permitted.

Radio A radio presentation is another useful communication medium, but it must contain the quality of vitality. People can be attracted to gymnastic demonstrations by radio presentations that stimulate their curiosity through the painting of word pictures. One can appeal to the listeners' loyalty to school, community, or friends. Interviews with the student participants or the coach are also interesting to many.

Other Media Bulletin boards, posters, student newspapers, and faculty bulletins should be utilized to publicize the gymnastic program within the school itself. Interesting newspaper or magazine articles and pictures of gymnastics can be posted on strategically placed bulletin boards. Stories and pictures of the home group should be prominently displayed. Bulletin boards should be attractive and neat, and the materials should be changed at least once every two or three weeks.

Posters School art departments are often willing to design or to produce posters for a school program. If this is not possible, the posters can be made commercially or by other students. Occasionally, a poster contest can be held in the school. Posters should be eye-catching and stimulating. It is well if they capture a gymnastic movement. The illustrations and the printing on a poster should be large enough to be seen from a distance. A common error is to try to put too much information on a poster.

Faculty Newsletters The faculty news bulletin can be used to inform colleagues of coming events or of progress made, with additional details provided through mimeographed letters or the student newspaper. Mimeographed letters to the faculty can, of course, be overdone. A fine sense of courtesy and consideration is helpful in determining the optimum frequency. Arrangements should be made with the editors and writers of the school newspaper to include the office of the gymnastics coach as a regular stop on their news beat. A regular time and day could be set aside for this purpose so that, for example, every Monday from 10:00 until 10:30 A.M. the coach of gymnastics and the sports writer would meet.

Announcements Announcements of coming events such as home gymnastic meets or gymnastic exhibitions can be prepared, mimeographed, and sent to teachers to be read by them to their classes. These should be brief and not used too frequently since all teachers have a great deal to accomplish in each class period.

Outdoor Practice When weather permits, gymnastic activities can be conducted outdoors. Gymnastics is an interesting activity to watch, and many people will stop to watch the practice sessions and thereby learn more about the activity and develop a greater appreciation of it.

Research The gathering of scientific evidence to substantiate the worth of the program is a part of good publicity and public relations. Needless to say, this research should be carefully done. Research on the effects of participation in gymnastics can also be locally publicized, thereby serving to support the local program.

The endorsement of the program by local physicians or their medical society can also be very helpful. Several pediatricians in Hattiesburg, Mississippi, where the author conducted a Saturday morning tumbling program for children while teaching at the University of Southern Mississippi, recommended participation in this program for many children.

Public relations is much more than just publicity. Public relations is a reflection of the coach's quality of teaching, his relationships with others, and his ideals and principles.

A public relations program has at least four working parts: one reaching out to the community, one going to the students, one to the faculty, and one to the administrator. Three of these parts may be working beautifully for the program, yet the fourth may kill it. All four groups —community, students, colleagues, and the administrator—see the program from somewhat different points of view. To maintain good total public relations it is necessary to understand each group's point of view and needs, and then to appeal to it appropriately.

With regard to the community, the first objective is to stimulate curiosity and a desire to learn more about gymnastics in order to bring the members of the community to the exhibitions and demonstrations. A second objective is to enlist their loyalty, support, and participation. The second objective cannot be realized until the first has been met.

The program exists mainly to serve the students. In order for them to benefit from a gymnastics program, the students must be sufficiently interested to participate. They will do so—if they find the activity enjoyable, ego-satisfying, and personally valuable.

All teachers have programs of their own in which they are primarily interested, and physical educators should not expect their programs to rank first in the interest of their colleagues. Efforts should be made to make colleagues feel as if the gymnastic program is in part theirs— which in truth it must be. Their aid should be enlisted and they should be appropriately recognized.

The administrator is an important person to the program. His support is absolutely essential. Beginning teachers tend to believe that the administrator should be infallible. If they realize that someday they may hold his position, they will realize that he is fallible. He may hunger for public recognition. It doesn't cost a thing to give him this recognition. He may be overburdened, or special interest groups may be exerting pressure on him. The teacher should try to understand the position of the administrator, then keep this understanding in mind when promoting his gymnastics program.

The personal qualities of the coach or instructor of gymnastics are probably the most important ingredients in successful public relations. The coach should have a sincere conviction of the worth of and the need for the activity. He should have a strong desire to serve the students and the community. Finally, he must possess a great deal of energy, for publicity must be done after classes and other primary responsibilities are taken care of.

BIBLIOGRAPHY

Baley, James A. "Public Relations." *Journal of Health, Physical Education and Recreation*, November, 1961.

12

JUDGING AND OFFICIATING[1]

Prior to World War II there were few rules governing gymnastics. Judging usually was done by using the performance of the first performer on the day of competition to set a standard in each event. The officials were selected from persons known to have a knowledge of gymnastics as a result of competitive experience or some association with gymnastics as a teacher, physical educator, or as a fan. As a result, more often than not, there was considerable variation in scores awarded for each competitive performance. Perhaps these discrepancies in evaluation arose from differences in skills performed in different areas of the country. This was even more true on the international level.

Many A.A.U., college, and high school meets were judged by friends of the meet director who agreed to officiate as a favor, even though they had, at best, limited knowledge of the sport.

As the quality of artistic gymnastics improved, judging also improved. Undoubtedly there are many factors responsible for the improvement of judging, but no single factor contributed more to improved judging than the establishment of the Federation of International Gymnastics (F.I.G.), *Code of Points*. The first code of points, written in 1949, established guidelines for evaluating difficulty, combination of exercise, and execution (form). (These criteria are all assigned separate values and judged independently.) Since that time several revisions and improvements have been added. At present the *Code of Points* outlines in great detail not only the exact award for difficulty, combination of exercise, and execution, but also the exact requirements for an exercise in each event. In addition, skills are classified as A, B, and C moves. The A, B, and C classifications of moves (skills) determines the number of points (not to exceed 3.4) to be awarded for the difficulty criterion for the exercise. This system will not permit the exercise to be rated higher in difficulty at the cost of artistic performance. On the other hand, the gymnast cannot lose points he is entitled to for difficulty because of faulty performance. As men-

[1] This chapter was written by Robert Martin, Physical Director at the Jersey City Y.M.C.A. Mr. Martin is a nationally qualified gymnastics judge. He has coached many state high school champion gymnasts.

tioned above, there are three components of the exercise. These are:

1.	Difficulty—total value	3.4 points
2.	Combination—total value	2.6 points
3.	Execution (Form)—total value	4.0 points
	Total Value of Components	10.0 points

Competition is divided into the following categories:

A. Competition 1—dual meet competition
B. Competition 2—team championship competition
C. Competition 3—individual championship competition

The difficulty requirements for Competition 1 states eleven skills must be performed including the start (mount), routine, and finish (dismount). The exercise should comprise:

Four A parts each valued at	.2 points
Five B parts each valued at	.4 points
One C part valued at	.6 points
Total Value	3.4 points

Even though ten parts are counted for value, eleven skills must be shown; if not, .2 points must be deducted from the difficulty score.

Competition 2—Team Championship Competition: The exercise should be comprised of eleven parts as in Competition 1; however, the difficulty requirement differs in that:

Three A parts should be shown at	.2 each
Four B parts should be shown at	.4 each
Two C parts should be shown at	.6 each
Total Value	3.4 points

If, however, eleven skills are not shown, .2 must be deducted for each missing part.

Competition 3—Individual Championship Competition: Again the basic requirement prevails. There must be eleven skills shown in each competitor's exercise with the exception of the vaulting event. The skill requirements are as follows:

1.	Two A parts each valued at	.2
2.	Three B parts each valued at	.4
3.	Three C parts each valued at	.6
	Total Value	3.4

If eleven parts are not shown in the exercise, deduct .2 for each missing part.

In all competition, the exercise of each individual in every event must contain eleven parts (skills); .2 points are deducted for each absent part. If an A, B, or C part is missing, the score of the exercise is decreased by the value of the missing part. For example, if a Competition 1 exercise is performed with three A parts, four B parts and one C part, the judge will deduct .2 for the missing A part, deduct .4 for the missing B part, and, since the exercise contains only eight parts, deduct .6 (3 X .2) for the absence of three of the required eleven parts. Therefore, the total deduction for difficulty will be 1.2, and the overall award for difficulty could not exceed 2.2.

It is important to note that an added A part cannot replace a B part or a C part. However, if 6 B parts are shown and no C part, the total value for six B parts would equal 2.4. Under no circumstances will more than six B parts be credited; however, B parts can replace any number of A parts. (Total value of difficulty may never exceed 3.4.) This of course does not mean every gymnast has to receive 3.4 for his performance. Quite the contrary, it means he will receive the exact award for the amount of A, B, and C parts shown, provided the exercise consists of eleven parts.

COMBINATION OF EXERCISE

In each event the F.I.G. has specified the type of skills that must be performed and the exact penalties for failure to meet the requirements. The total award for combination of exercise is 2.6 points. Therefore, the total deductions under combination of exercise cannot exceed 2.6 points. The *Code of Points* lists specific requirements for the various events as follows.

FLOOR EXERCISE COMBINATION

The exercise must be between 50 and 70 seconds in duration. The entire floor space (20 meters by 20 meters) must be used; the gymnast will be penalized for leaving the area. The exercise must form a rhythmic whole and must include movements of balance, hold parts, strength parts, leaps, kips, and tumbling skills. Basic moves and movement of all parts of the body must conform to gymnastic standards.

Penalties for Faulty Combination

1. Touching the outside area with a part of the body—.1 each time.
2. Touching the outside with support—.2 each time.
3. Sitting, kneeling, or lying outside the area—.3 each time.
4. For additional parts performed outside the area—.1 each time.
5. If the construction of the exercise does not meet the requirements as stated—.3 deducted.
6. Movements that are not generally regarded as gymnastic moves—up to .3 penalty.
7. If the exercise does not have a mount or dismount corresponding to the general quality of the exercise—up to .3 penalty.
8. For no dismount or a poorly executed dismount—.3 to .7 points penalty.
9. If the exercise lacks variety, and skills are repeated more than once—.2 for each repetition.
10. For parts lacking any degree of difficulty or parts with no value—.2 penalty
11. If the C difficulty part is not a moving skill—.2 penalty.

SIDE HORSE

Combination The exercise should be composed predominantly of leg circles. Forward and backward scissors must be executed and one of these must be shown twice consecutively. The entire area of the horse must be worked upon from one side to the other.

Penalties

1. For each intermediate swing (swing between moves)—.3 to .5 points penalty.
2. If all the requirements of the exercise are not met—.3 for each violation.
3. If one part of the horse is not used—.3 for each part not used. (The three parts of the horse are: croup, saddle, and neck.)
4. If the exercise is done only in the saddle—.3 penalty.
5. If the general parts of the exercise

appear to be in one area even though all sides have been worked on—.2 penalty.
6. If the exercise does have double scissors but does not have one forward and one reverse scissors—.3 penalty.
7. If there is only one scissor shown either forward or reverse—.5 penalty.
8. Combinations or skills of the wrong type—.3 penalty.
9. If the exercise does not have a mount or dismount corresponding to the difficulty—up to .3 penalty.
10. If the exercise does not have a real dismount or the dismount is only partly shown—.3 to .7 penalty.
11. If a skill is repeated more than once (that is, if a move is done three times; one repetition is permitted) even though the connecting parts are different—up to .2 penalty.
12. For every connecting part without value (skills not corresponding to the general difficulty of the exercise)—up to .2 penalty.
13. If the C or B part is not constructed to serve the aim of the exercise—up to .2 penalty.
14. For each double-leg circle beyond two—up to .2 penalty.
15. For each set of double-leg circles beyond two on each part of the horse—.2 penalty.

HORIZONTAL BAR

Combination: The exercise shall contain only swinging parts without stops or interruptions. At least one skill must be shown in which both hands release the bar and regrasp simultaneously. The gymnast must execute at least one skill with his back to the bar and one more with either dorsal or cubital grip of the hands. One skill must be shown in which the body rotates around the longitudinal axis (full turn or full twist).

Deductions—Combination

1. For each intermediate swing—.3 to .5 penalty.
2. If the construction does not meet the requirements:
   a. For all strength or hold parts each time—.2 penalty.
   b. If one requirement is missing—.3 penalty.

c. If two requirements are missing—.6 penalty.

3. Movements of the wrong type—each time .3 penalty.

4. If the exercise does not have a mount or dismount corresponding to the general difficulty—up to .3 penalty.

5. If the exercise does not finish with a real dismount or the dismount is only partly shown—.3 to .7 penalty.

6. If a part of the exercise is repeated more than once; (if a move is done three times; one repetition is permissible) even though the connecting parts are different—up to .2 penalty.

7. For every skill that does not correspond to the general difficulty of the exercise—up to .2 penalty

8. If the C and B parts are not constructed to serve the aim of the exercise—up to .2 penalty.

PARALLEL BARS

Combination The exercise must consist of swing, flight, and hold moves. The swing and flight parts should predominate. In addition, one B part either above or below the bars must be shown in which the release of both hands is shown. The C part must be a swinging part. There can be no more than three stop moves. A stop is defined as any skill held for one or more seconds.

Deductions—Combination

1. For each intermediate swing—.3 to .5 penalty.

2. If the C part is not a swinging part—.2 penalty.

3. If the construction of the exercise does not meet the requirements—for each violation deduct .3.

4. Movements of the wrong type—.3 penalty.

5. If the exercise does not have a mount or dismount corresponding to the general difficulty of the exercise—up to .3 penalty.

6. If the exercise is not finished with a real dismount or the dismount is only partly shown—.3 to .7 penalty.

7. If more than two C moves are shown, the swing C parts must predominate. If the swing parts do not predominate—.2 penalty.

8. If a skill is repeated more than once (if a move is done three times; one repetition is permissible) even though the parts before and after are different—up to .2 penalty.

9. For every skill not corresponding to the general difficulty of the exercise—up to .2 penalty.

10. If the C and B parts do not serve the aim of the exercise—up to .2 penalty.

RINGS

Combinations Without swinging of the rings, combined movements of swing, strength, and holds should be shown. There must be at least two handstands of which one must be executed with swing and the other with strength. There must be one strength move commensurate with the general difficulty of the exercise.

Deductions—Combination:

1. For each intermediate swing—.3 to .5 penalty.

2. The construction of the exercise does not meet the requirements:
   a. If the strength part does not correspond to the general difficulty—up to .3 penalty.
   b. If the exercise does not alternate between swing and hold parts—up to .2 penalty.
   c. If there is no swinging or strength handstand—up to .3 for each missing handstand.

3. Skills of the wrong type—up to .3 penalty.

4. If the exercise does not have a mount and dismount corresponding to the general difficulty of the exercise—up to .3 penalty.

5. If the exercise is not finished with a real dismount or the dismount is only partly shown— .3 to .7 penalty.

6. If swing parts do not predominate—.2 penalty.

7. If parts are repeated more than once even though the connecting parts are different—up to .2 penalty.

8. For skills not corresponding to the general difficulty—each time .2 penalty.

9. If the C and B parts are not constructed to meet the aim of the exercise—up to .2 penalty.

FORM AND EXECUTION

Form encompasses the correct postural positions of the body including the head, shoulders, arms, legs, and feet. This aspect of the exercise has the greatest total value (4.0). Deductions are made for unnecessarily bending the arms, legs, or body, opening the legs, arching too much or not enough.

General Deductions—Form and Execution (All Events as Indicated)

1. Shoulders too far forward when body is in support position—up to .3 penalty.
2. Handstands that are not perpendicular or are executed with shoulders too far forward—up to .3 penalty.
3. Turns in handstands in which the body is not perpendicular—up to .3 penalty.
4. Walking in handstands—.1 per step and up to .5 each time.
5. Two or more attempts to arrive in the handstand—.2 to .5 penalty.
6. Interruption of movement in elevation to handstand—up to .3 penalty.
7. Strength parts executed with swing—.3 penalty.
8. Swing parts executed with strength—.3 penalty.
9. If hold moves are not held for at least 1 second—up to .3 penalty.
10. If the hold move is held longer than 3 seconds—up to .2 penalty.
11. Lack of balance in performance or landings—up to .5 penalty.
12. Lack of rhythm or flexibility—up to .2 each time.
13. Gymnastically objectionable movements—up to .3 each time.
14. Mounts onto apparatus too low—.3 penalty.
15. Lack of height in execution of skills—up to .5 each time.
16. Touching the apparatus with parts of the body unnecessarily—.2 to .5 penalty.
17. Interruption of exercise due to poor performance of a skill—.5 to .7 penalty.
18. Falling from the apparatus without letting go—.4 to .8 penalty.
19. Falling from the apparatus with loss of grip—.4 to 1.0 penalty.

Deductions Pertaining to Team and Individuals

Gymnastics by nature is an individual sport in which the performer is responsible for his individual performance. Since no contact with other performers is possible, very few rules are necessary. Of course, the coach, team, and performers are responsible for their own behavior.

Deductions—Individuals

1. Unsportsmanlike conduct by coach, team, or performer—.3 to 1. each time.
2. Coaching or talking to the performer during his performance—up to .2 each time.
3. Failure to comply with regulations regarding gymnastic attire—.3 penalty.
4. Aiding the contestant during his performance—.3 to 1. depending upon the amount of aid rendered.

VAULTING

Although the gymnast has the option of taking two vaults, only one score may count. If he elects to take a second vault, only the score of the second vault shall count. If the second vault is selected from the same category as the first vault, the rating of the vault will be reduced by .5 in addition to all other deductions.

The vault begins with the run, but the run does not count in the scoring. The first step signals the start of the run. The run cannot exceed 20 meters. All vaults must be executed with the momentary support of one or both hands.

If the performer does not attempt the vault due to interference, he shall be given a second chance without penalty. No balks shall be allowed. If a balk occurs on the first attempt, the gymnast may raise his hand and request his second jump, which must count. If a second balk occurs, the gymnast shall receive a score of zero. The different phases of the vaults and their execution must conform to the phases listed by the F.I.G. The first phase (pre-flight) is the portion of the jump after the feet have left the Reuter board and before the hands are placed on the horse. The feet must rise behind the body to a point 30° higher than the head. If this occurs, there is no deduction for pre-flight. However, from a point between where the feet are below the top of the horse to where the feet are 30° above the head a deduction may occur up to 1.0. The second phase, post-flight, occurs after the hands have pushed off the horse. The second phase (post-flight—after pushing off and before landing) must show height and distance. In order to obtain maximum value for the vault, it must be high enough to permit the body to pass through a horizontal position and land one and one-fourth the length of the horse beyond the end of the horse on vaults from the neck, or one length of the horse on vaults executed from the croup.

Long Horse Vault Ratings
Vaults with support of hands on neck:

1.	Straddle	6.7
2.	Squat	6.7
3.	Handstand Pivot Cartwheel	8.7
4.	Stoop—Knees Straight	9.2
5.	Scissor Half Turn	9.2
6.	Giant Cartwheel	9.3
7.	Handspring	9.7 *
8.	Handspring Half Turn	9.7 **
9.	Handspring Full Turn	9.7 **
10.	Handspring Tucked Salto	9.7 **
11.	Yamashita	9.7 *
12.	Yamashita Half Turn	9.7 **
13.	Yamashita Full Turn	9.7 **
14.	Hecht	9.7
15.	Hecht Half Turn	9.7 **
16.	Hecht Full Turn	9.7 **

Vaults with support of hands on croup (near end):

1.	Straddle	7.2
2.	Squat	7.2
3.	Stoop—Knees Bent Then Stretched	8.7
4.	Scissor Half Turn	9.0
5.	Stoop—Knees Straight	9.7
6.	Handspring	9.7 *
7.	Handspring Half Turn	9.7 **
8.	Handspring Full Turn	9.7 **
9.	Yamashita	9.7 *
10.	Yamashita Half Turn	9.7 **
11.	Yamashita Full Turn	9.7 **
12.	Yamashita Front Salto	9.7 **
13.	Hecht	9.7 *
14.	Hecht Half Turn	9.7 **
15.	Hecht Full Turn	9.7 **
16.	Hecht Front Salto	9.7 **

Vaults with exceptional risk are indicated by the asterisk. If these vaults are well executed but have minor faults, some allowance is permitted up to .2 for one-asterisk vaults and up to .3 for two-asterisk vaults. For example, landing with poor balance, or a slight overspin out of a double back somersault shall not be penalized as heavily as landing with poor balance out of a single back somersault.

Zones are marked off at each end of the horse. The zone in which the hands are to be placed must be designated by a white line 3/8-inch wide, 23 5/8 inches from the end. For any vault illegally touching the center zone, a deduction of .5 will be made.

FAMILIES AND CATEGORIES OF VAULTS

Families	Categories		
	Cross or Neck	Twist Half or Full	Extra Saltos
Straddles			
Stoops or Squats	"	"	"
Cartwheels	"	"	"
Hechts (Swans)	"	"	"
Arched Handsprings	"	"	"
Yamashitas (Piked Handsprings)	"	"	"
Backward Saltos	"	"	"

Faults of Execution—Deductions

1. Momentary poor form in holding head, legs, or feet, or separating legs unnecessarily—up to .3 penalty.
2. Poor style (form) during entire vault—.4 to 1.0 penalty.
3. Touching the horse with feet, legs, knees, or other parts of the body—.2 to .5 penalty.
4. Touching the horse during entire vault—.6 to 1.0 penalty.
5. Bent arms in execution of yamashita or handspring—.3 to 1.0 penalty.
6. Bent knees in hecht vault—up to 1.0 penalty.
7. Inadequate body angle during preflight—up to 1.0 penalty.
8. Failure to straighten body before landing—up to .5 penalty.
9. Poor control of vault—up to .5 penalty.

10. Small step or hop upon landing—up to .2 penalty.
11. Several steps or hops when landing —up to .3 penalty.
12. Touching floor with hands when landing—up to .3 penalty.
13. Touching floor with support on hands when landing—.3 to .5 penalty.
14. Landing too close to horse—up to 1.0 penalty.
15. Lack of height in post-flight—up to 1.0 penalty.
16. Too much hip flexion or hip extension when landing—up to .3 penalty
17. Bad direction of vault during flight— up to .3; at arrival on landing—up to .2 penalty; during flight and landing— up to .5 penalty.
18. Touching center zone unnecessarily —.5 penalty.

CODE OF ETHICS

It is important that judges not only have a gymnastic background, but that they have a thorough knowledge of the rules, particularly the F.I.G. Code of Points and the modifications of the associations in which they intend to officiate.

Progress in judging has been continuous and great. Year after year rules are modified and improved. In order to keep pace with this sport, one must attend such clinics as those offered by the United States Gymnastics Federation, The National College Athletic Association, and the United States Gymnastics Judges Association. Gymnastics, like other sports, is always improving and what was new yesterday is old today. To be properly informed one must remain active in participation, research, and development of gymnastics.

An official should not accept any assignment he has not prepared himself for. He should be prompt and well groomed when reporting for an assignment. The judge should be courteous but careful not to socialize freely with the competitors or the coaches. Never should he accept an assignment for an institution by which he is employed, or accept any remuneration beyond his fee for judging, in the way of lodging, travel, or gifts. He should never accept social invitations unless coaches of all participating teams are also invited, nor should he ever evince

particular personal friendship with any coach or competitor.

The competitor's attitude toward judging should be the same as his attitude toward competing. He should be fully aware that in every competition he may at any moment commit an error. This is also true of the judge. It is not feasible to expect every judge to detect every defect of every exercise. This explains why even though the rules for difficulty, combination, and execution are clearly defined, no judges arrive consistently at identical scores. It is very possible for one judge to detect what the other judge has missed. There are over 650 illustrations in the F.I.G. Code of Points governing the value of A, B, and C moves. This is with respect to difficulty only. The judge must commit these to memory. In addition, there are 50 deductions or penalties for execution and combination of exercises. There are approximately only 38 seconds for a performer to execute a minimum of eleven skills. To expect each and every judge to detect every fault and to interpret every move in exactly the same manner is unrealistic. This becomes manifest when it is realized that the range in deduction for a specific error may vary from .1 to 1.0 according to the Code of Points. Since in most cases the deductions range up to .3 and some from .1 to 1.0, other factors have to be considered. Every performer leaves an impression on the official even though there are specific guidelines to follow. Some C moves are more impressive than others. It is unrealistic not to expect this factor to influence a judge. The competitor himself has certain skills he likes to perform more than others. The judge may or may not agree and, when opinion is a factor, inevitably there will be disagreement.

THE F.I.G. CODE OF POINTS

It is impossible for a gymnast to prepare for competition without the guidance of the F.I.G. Code of Points. This judging system is used wherever knowledgeable gymnasts perform— among lower age groups, in high schools, colleges, and in clubs. These rules result in a more uniform method of teaching and evaluating gymnastics. Many organizations have adopted a modified version of the Code of Points. This has

287

been accomplished simply by placing a higher value on A and B moves and by requiring fewer moves in the exercise. However, the value of combination and execution is kept the same. It is therefore advisable for every gymnast and every beginner to obtain the *Code of Points* in order to learn the value of his skills, the requirements of an exercise, and the deductions for omissions and faulty execution. The F.I.G. *Code of Points* may be obtained from the United States Gymnastics Federation, Tucson, Arizona.

SPORTSMANSHIP

Gymnastics, by its nature, presents few problems in sportsmanship. Since it is not a contact sport, there is never any roughness or argument between competitors. Each competitor is responsible for his own individual contribution to the team score. The self-discipline the gymnast must exercise in his training will carry over to his own personal emotional control. Usually, a coach has complete control to the extent that he does not permit the competitor to approach a judge or scorer without his permission. This in itself has a direct bearing on judging. Seldom is it necessary to impose a penalty for unsportsmanlike conduct. When it is necessary, the deduction would range from .3 to 1.0 for each occurrence. A gymnast who displays temper as a result of his own faulty performance, fails to wear a proper uniform, fails to be ready to perform when called, or displays dissatisfaction with a score would be liable for deductions for unsportsmanlike conduct. If it is necessary to penalize a coach for protesting a score too vigorously, or for any other unsportsmanlike conduct, the penalty would be imposed upon the team score.

RELATIONSHIPS BETWEEN JUDGES AND COACHES

In general, gymnasts are about as well behaved as their coaches. The rules are specific in this regard. The coach cannot protest a judge's award without being subject to 0.3 to 1.0 team deduction for each protest. He does, however, have certain rights. He may at any time approach

the judges to make inquiry regarding interpretation of a rule or to indicate he believes the judges erred in placing a value on a degree of difficulty. However, he may not do this without the presence of the opposing coach. It is his right to do this if he adheres to proper procedure. If, after his explanation to the superior judge he continues to dispute the point, he will receive a team penalty for unsportsmanlike conduct. If, in the opinion of the judging panel, they did interpret incorrectly, the coach's complaint will be honored.

SPOTTING AND ASSISTANCE

The acceptability of assisting a performer is the concern of the judges. In floor exercise and side horse, under no circumstances can the performer be assisted by the coach, teammate, or anyone else. As a matter of fact, no one may enter the immediate area of the performer without penalty to the performer. In the long horse, horizontal bar, parallel bars, and ring events, one spotter may be present at the apparatus in case of emergency. He may not give any assistance or even speak to the performer without risk of penalty. Such penalty would be determined by the amount of assistance given and would range from .1 to 1.0. If, in the opinion of a judge, the skill could not have been performed without assistance, the full penalty of 1.0 will be assessed. This rule does not apply to all levels of competition. In many lower age level meets and high school meets, spotting is permitted and even encouraged in the interest of safety; however, the penalty for assistance still prevails.

PREPARING FOR COMPETITION

Just as a gymnast must make himself ready to compete, a judge must also prepare. He must first consider the level of competition he is to judge. Since, as mentioned above, there are often modifications of the F.I.G. *Code of Points*, the judge must acquaint himself with the specific modifications for the contest he is to score. Once the competition starts, the conduct of the meet is in the hands of the superior judge. He is responsible for enforcing all rules and for ensuring that each member of his panel rates the competitors objectively, without prejudice or favoritism. If any judge is consistently out of range in his scores, after due warning the head judge may remove him from the panel.

SPECTATORS

Little can be done to educate spectators on the day of competition. The spectator is often confused when he sees the judges conferring. However, it may be useful to explain the following rules.

In most competitions four officials participate. The highest and lowest scores are discarded and the two middle scores are averaged. If the two middle scores are not in range, the superior judge must see that they are adjusted. When scores of 9.6 or better are awarded, the scores of the judges may not vary by more than .1. Scores of 9.0 to 9.55 may not show a variance of more than .2. Scores 8.0 to 8.95 may not vary more than .3; scores of 6.5 to 7.95, no more than .5; scores of 4.0 to 6.45 no more than .8; all scores below 4.0 no more than 1.0.

HOW TO BECOME A JUDGE

Persons who have been associated with gymnastics either as competitors, coaches, or assistant coaches may become certified officials, if they are willing to commit themselves to a great deal of effort and study. Usually, if an aspiring judge is sincere, he need not be entirely familiar with gymnastic terminology. Gymnastics, like any sport, has its own jargon. For example, the forward salto (the recognized F.I.G. term) is sometimes called the front somy or front flip. The new judge should devote time to learning terminology and to familiarizing himself with the grading and classifications (A, B, or C) of skills.

In addition to this he must learn all the rules and penalties covering combination of exercise and execution. When the candidate has acquired such knowledge, he should attend clinics sponsored by the association for whom he intends to judge. Presently most organizations require that anyone wishing to judge in their association must take a written and a practical test to become certified. This is especially true in high school and intercollegiate leagues.

METHODS OF JUDGING

There are several methods of judging. One is to observe the routine, committing it to memory. This, however, requires an unusual memory and can result in embarrassment if the score awarded is questioned, since many high school and college meets are recorded on closed-circuit television with immediate playback facilities.

The most popular way to judge today is to use symbols for skills. This is something like shorthand writing. In this way the judge may record the entire exercise as it is being performed, listing the deductions for difficulty, technical faults, and breaks in form and execution as he observes the routine. For example, in an exercise missing two B parts he will deduct .8 for difficulty, for three breaks in form he might deduct .3 each time for a total of .9. For lacking two requirements of the combination he would deduct .6. The total deduction would be 2.3 The gymnast's total out of 10 points would be 7.7.

Normally, the higher levels of competition are the easiest to judge because there are fewer deductions. An accomplished gymnast knows the requirements of an exercise and usually makes sure his routine meets these requirements. Therefore, the judge normally need only make deductions for faulty execution and form. On the other hand, in the lower levels of competition, the judge must constantly be on the watch for errors.

13

THE FUTURE OF GYMNASTICS

The future for gymnastics looks bright. There are many reasons for optimism, including the trends toward greater leisure, affluence, congestion, knowledge, mobility, research, and greater use of the communications media.

From the beginning of the Industrial Revolution until the early 1900's, most men began working at age sixteen. Some began earlier. They usually worked twelve hours per day six days each week with little vacation time. The average work week was about seventy hours. By the 1920's, the work week had been reduced to about sixty hours—ten hours per day for a six-day work week. In the 1940's the work week was an average of forty-five hours—eight hours per day for five days and a half day on Saturday. In the 1950's a forty-hour work week was the vogue. Today the average is about thirty-five hours. Some unions have won a thirty-hour work week for their workers. We can be certain that this trend will continue. Scientists, engineers, and motion study experts will continue to devise more efficient methods of production. Computerization and cybernetics will continue to enable man to produce greater amounts with decreasing expenditures of time. Labor unions will continue to press for a greater share of the rewards of this increased productivity for their workers.

An increasing number of people covet leisure more than material rewards. Many of today's youth and an increasing number of adults are critical of our materialism. They are saying that they do not want color TV, big suburban homes, and big cars as much as they want time to enjoy sunsets, music, art museums, a frolic on the beach, and a hobby. Instead of working longer hours to acquire more material things, they want to have more time to enjoy living. There will be increasing pressure to shorten the work week, and it will be shortened.

With a shorter work week, people will have more time to initiate and to sustain a hobby. One hobby that some people will find fascinating will be gymnastics. Former high school and college gymnasts will have time to coach gymnastics, to promote gymnastics, and to participate in and view gymnastic meets. There will be more volunteer and part-time help available to work for gymnastics.

Although the expenditures necessary to initiate a full-blown gymnastic program have been prohibitive to many schools, the costs over a long period are very small. Gymnastic equipment lasts for many years. Parallel bars are not as expendable as shoulder pads. Schools can add a piece or two of gymnastic equipment each year to distribute the cost over a longer period. However, in the years to come, the cost of gymnastic equipment will not be a deterrent to the initiation of a program, because of society's greater affluence. Today many families have their own backyard swimming pool or trampoline. An increasing number will be able to afford these embellishments to the quality of living. People will see that it is a more productive use of their dollar to contribute in tax money to the cost of a trampoline for the school or the community recreation program than to pay the entire cost of the trampoline for use only by family and friends. Furthermore, the school, "Y," or community recreation center will provide a coach or teacher with expertise. An increasing number of elementary, junior, and senior high schools and colleges and universities as well as Y.M.C.A.s, Y.W.C.A.s, Y.M.H.A.s, Y.W.H.A.s, boys clubs, community recreation centers, and private clubs will purchase complete gymnastic equipment and employ either a part- or full-time specialist or coach to teach gymnastics. Many will use volunteer help. These club teams will compete against one another just as high schools are presently doing.

With greater amounts of leisure, people will have more time to read, study, observe, and take advantage of the various communications media. This will lead to greater knowledge, which will result in changed values. Greater knowledge will lead to greater appreciation of the aesthetic qualities in sport and other forms of human movement. People will value less the simplistic combatives and provincial loyalties. Along with increased knowledge, people will come to know more about the wonders of human physiology and anatomy. They will better understand the laws of physics and how they apply to human movement. As a result, they will appreciate more the aesthetic aspects of a well-executed lay-up shot, a back somersault dismount, or the end's sprint, cut, leap, and catch of the football over his shoulder in a perfect synchrony of movement of the legs, arms, eyes, football, passer, and other players. Spectators consequently will appreciate less the brutal aspects of sports, although these will always serve to some extent as a socially approved form of catharsis for feelings of aggression. People will care less who wins or loses because they will see this as a form of provincialism. They will care more for skilled, highly motivated, and enthused performance. This increase in knowledge and change in what people value will enable them to have a greater appreciation of gymnastics because, of all the sports, gymnastics is one of those with great aesthetic appeal.

Like the early Greeks at the pinnacle of their culture, people will appreciate the great beauty of the human body, especially when it is in motion. The Romans during their decadence enjoyed brutal and sadistic exhibitions. All signs today point toward the increasing rejection of the brutal aspects of sports. Legitimate professional wrestling has died. Boxing is dying. Swimming, tennis, golf, modern dance, and gymnastics are growing. Football, even with all the artificial stimuli such as music, bands, cheerleaders, cards, hoopla, and huge expenditures for stadia, films, publicity, athletic scholarships, and scouting is finding it increasingly difficult to sustain attendance. Decreasing numbers of boys are trying out for football teams. These are manifestations of the trend away from enjoyment of the "contact" sports and toward the sports with greater aesthetic appeal and with greater physiological and/or psychological benefits.

One of the greatest boosts to gymnastics occurred when gymnastics events were televised, bringing their beauties into many homes. Before that, many people did not realize the meaning of the word "gymnastics." Some thought that the entire range of gymnastics was limited to head- and handstands, cartwheels, and forward and backward rolls. When they saw double-flyaways, double-twisting somersaults, inverted crucifixes, back somersault dismounts, and other skills, they wanted to learn more of this sport. As more people see more gymnastics on TV, in films, and in pictures in sports pages, more fans will be won over. This movement will pick up momentum as sports editors, television programmers, and film producers begin (belatedly) to recognize its appeal. Gymnastics coaches should make maximal use of these media in order to enlarge the educational arena. They should utilize the media to elicit interest by glamorizing the sport through effective presentation of the highly skilled, especially those of national and international caliber. They should also use the media to show people how champions get to be that way, their training procedures, the progressions they follow, and how they perform beginning and intermediate level skills.

Mobility of people has increased. Today there are more cars, planes, and boats, and people are using them more and more to travel within the city, the state, the country, and internationally. This helps to disseminate ideas. Gymnasts meet and work out with a greater number of other gymnasts and consequently learn new skills (and procedures for learning them) from them. Mobility will continue to increase and gymnasts will learn more from one another. Great numbers travel to Europe and other parts of the world today. More will do so. Many can now attend the Olympic Games. More will do so. This facilitates dissemination of new knowledge and techniques in gymnastics as it does in other areas. The result will be increasing numbers of highly skilled gymnasts, which will force the improvement in skills of those already at the pinnacle.

Congestion in the cities and suburbs will not be relieved. A high density of population militates against the setting aside of land areas for baseball, soccer, football, and tennis, which require considerable space per player. Space will have to be used most efficiently for multistoried buildings for apartments, offices, and factories. There will be less land that does not support a building.

Gymnastics uses space efficiently. Gymnasia can be used year around. Many people can participate in gymnastics in a relatively small space. Ten players can play basketball on a regulation court. One hundred and fifty students could participate in gymnastics in an area this size. Increasingly, athletic directors, physical education directors, and other administrators are going to recognize the space economy of gymnastics. For these reasons, it is predicted that gymnastics will be promoted more enthusiastically by school administrators, particularly in the larger cities.

Some years ago boys and girls were advised to begin gymnastics about sixteen years of age. More recently ten to twelve years as the age of initiation is being advocated. Age group competition in swimming begins at the age of five. Since the A.A.U. initiated age group competition in swimming, the number of competitive swimmers has increased to thousands, perhaps millions. Furthermore, the United States has assumed dominance in the swimming and diving events in the Olympic Games. A great deal of research has been done on swimming; it is receiving more publicity and, ever since A.A.U. age group competition has been initiated, a great many pools have been built in homes, schools, and other institutions, in hotels, motels, and backyards. Thousands, perhaps millions, of parents and relatives of age group swimmers have become fans, supporters, and workers for swimming.

A rather feeble movement has begun in gymnastics to initiate age group competition. This movement should and will gain momentum. When it does, gymnastics will grow by leaps and bounds. It will not grow as fast as has swimming because of the greater need in gymnastics, due to the risk factor, of qualified coaches. These are not available at present in sufficient numbers. Hopefully, the A.A.U. and the Gymnastic Federation will soon vigorously promote age group competition.

Coaches and teachers of gymnastics are seeking answers to many questions. They know that research can provide these answers. Computers have facilitated research. Many more teachers and coaches of gymnastics are pursuing masters or doctoral degrees. To earn these degrees they have to do research studies. They are selecting problems in the coaching and teaching of gymnastics and securing answers to such questions as: (1) How does one predict gymnastic skill? (2) What are the mechanics of a "flifus?" (3) What psychological characteristics are unique to gymnasts? (4) What are the most effective teaching methods for various skills? This trend will continue and intensify and it will lead to more effective teaching and coaching, and to a higher level of skill in a greater number of gymnasts.

The future does indeed look bright for gymnastics. Those beginning to work in this area now can look forward to many happy and satisfying years.

APPENDIX
A

EXHIBITION AND DEMONSTRATION ACTIVITIES

Exhibitions and demonstrations at assembly programs, at PTA meetings, at half time of football and basketball games, for civic groups, before conference and convention groups, and at community affairs are excellent media for eliciting interest in the gymnastic program, and through it, in the total physical education program. When the interest of students, alumni, colleagues, school administrators, and townspeople has been stimulated, the funds and equipment purchases necessary for the conduct of an effective program are much more likely to be forthcoming.

Exhibition and demonstration groups and troupes can serve another even more important function—an educational one. Exhibitions and demonstrations can be presented in such a manner as to make spectators aware of the importance of physical fitness. They can develop in the spectator an appreciation of the beauty of form and movement. They can be so planned, organized, and conducted as to present participants with opportunities to learn and to practice democratic procedures of leadership, followership, cooperation, and appreciation for the unique skills and talents of others. Exhibition troupes provide opportunities for students who possess diversified talents to achieve self-realization.

All of the competitive activities plus singles, doubles, and triples balancing described in Chapters 6, 7, and 8 can be included in an exhibition and demonstration program. Juggling, ladder bouncing, balancing on ladders, vaulting over the Swedish box and elephant, living statuary, pyramid building, mass calisthenics, clown acts, and tumbling off the mini-tramp or springboard can also be included. These will be described below. In addition, singing, dancing, instrumental numbers, magic acts, unicycle riding, and stunts on bicycles can be included to give the exhibition greater variety and broader appeal. The major limitations to the variety of acts are the skills and interests of the students and the desires and energy of the director of the troupe.

LADDER BOUNCING

Ladder bouncing is a relatively simple skill to learn. In a few weeks, a boy who would like to

Ladder bouncing

become a member of the exhibition troupe but who has no particular skill can develop the skill necessary to present a fairly interesting ladder bouncing number.

The student stands on the first or second rung and grips the uprights while the ladder is unsupported. The ladder should angle forward slightly to counterbalance his weight. He balances by pulling the ladder toward himself, by flexing his arms, or by pushing it away by extending his arms. He bounces with the ladder by extending his knees and hips and pulling upward with his arms in the manner of jumping with a pogo stick. In this way, he can hop across the gymnasium floor, in circles, and up and down stairs.

He can "walk" the ladder by shifting his weight from side to side and while balancing in this manner, he can climb up one side and down the other.

LADDER BALANCING

Ladder balancing is a number which is at once spectacular and breathtaking, graceful and beautiful. It is quickly learned, requiring no previous gymnastic training. With proper lighting, costumes, and musical background, it is almost certain to be the high point of any gymnastic or physical education demonstration.

Getting into Position To start, the strongest boy stands in the center of the mat with the ladders lying on the floor to either side of him, their

bases nearest him. The other two men, one on each end of the ladders, lift the tops of the ladders and walk to the center, pushing the ends upward while the bottom man holds the bases down.

In the upright position, the ladders should be angled toward one another about 5° from the vertical and be perfectly aligned from front to rear. The understander or bottom man should stand with his feet apart. He should grasp the rungs to either side of his head with his palms facing him. He secures leverage with each forearm against the rung just below the one he is gripping by flexing or extending his arms.

In climbing to their positions, the middle and top men climb up inside (between) the ladders, mounting from behind the bottom man. They should stay near the center of the ladder and exercise care to pull directly downward rather than backward, making no sudden moves and keeping their bodies in good alignment. In the illustrations, the top and middle men show two different grips that may be used.

The girls climb up the ladders in pairs, one on each side, making their movements in unison. They must keep their weight in close to the ladder and avoid making movements which might give a twist to the ladder. By swinging one leg backward with each step, they add "showmanship" to their performances.

When two of the girls are halfway up, the other two can begin their climb. To give performers a feeling of security while learning, two spotters can be stationed behind the ladders, two in front, and two on each side.

Getting into position

Leg hang

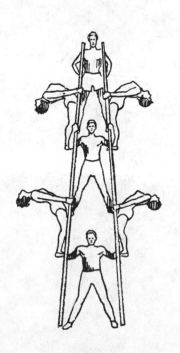

Back arch

The girls should try the following skills on the stall bars before attempting them on the unsupported ladders.

Back Arch In this skill the girls grasp the vertical piece of the ladder directly opposite their hips. Then with their hips against the ladder and their arms held straight, they arch backward as far as possible.

Leg Hang To put themselves into position for the leg hang, the girls, in unison, first place one leg over the rung above the one they are standing on. Then they hook the foot of this leg over the outside of the next lowest rung and move the other foot down one rung.

Finally, they arch backward slowly, and release their hand grip to place their arms into the position illustrated. Their head should be pulled back. They should avoid any sideward motion of their bodies.

Half Eagle To accomplish this skill, the girls stand with their sides toward the ladders and then slowly extend their inside arm and leg to

Half eagle

Full eagle

complete the skill. The trunk should be in a vertical position with little or no arch.

Full Eagle This skill is a continuation of the half eagle, with the men slowly extending their arms to achieve the effect illustrated. It should not be attempted with the girls on the ladders until after the three men can execute the "three spread" with ease and confidence.

"L" The girls should first turn around on the ladders, placing their backs toward the ladder. In turning around, they must exercise great care to keep in close to the ladders with their weight centered. After having completed the turn, they should reach up, one hand at a time, to grasp the rung above their head. They then lift their legs to the horizontal position to complete the move.

"O" The hand grip on the rung is with palms up. While holding onto one rung and standing on another with their back toward the ladder, the girls simply arch out.

Three Spread This skill may be used after the girls have dismounted. The men extend their arms and straddle their legs. After doing the "three spread," the students bring the ladders together

"O"

Three spread

and begin to dismount. The top man comes down first, lowering himself behind the middle man. The middle man comes down next. Both men must keep their weight centered on the ladders. After the top and middle men are down, they should go to the sides of the ladders and "walk" them down in the same manner that they got them up.

VAULTING OVER THE SWEDISH BOX AND ELEPHANT

All of the skills described in Chapter 8 in the section on side horse vaulting can be done over both the Swedish box and the elephant. Because of the added height, these moves when done over the box or elephant are more spectacular, but they also present a greater element of hazard. The moves should be learned over the side horse first, then over the Swedish box, and finally over the elephant. Careful spotting

is required, particularly when the moves are done over the elephant.

There are many methods for presenting a vaulting number. One of the most effective is to have students vault in "rapid-fire" order first over the side horse, then over the Swedish box, and finally over the elephant. They should follow one another at two- to four-foot intervals, doing the same vault over each piece of equipment. After all the students have done all the basic moves, each can finish with his specialty. At this time, they could do the more difficult skills such as handsprings, cartwheels, handstand stoop vaults, hechts, or front somersaults over the box or the elephant. Needless to say, students should have mastered the moves before attempting them in rapid-fire order.

A musical background of marches or college songs and some colorful, eye-catching costumes will embellish the number greatly.

While the skills are executed over the Swedish box and elephant in basically the same manner that they are over the side horse, the greater width and height and the problem of taking off from a springboard or mini-tramp dictate that we make additional comments on each move. We will not, however, present again specific and detailed instructions for each skill.

Courage Vault Very little spring is required to get into the starting position from the springboard or mini-tramp. On dismounting, the student should absorb the impact of landing from the greater height by means of eccentric contraction of the muscles that plantar-flex the feet and extend the knees and hips.

Squat Vault, Straddle Vault, and Stoop Vault A vigorous push from the hands should be made as the feet come forward. The push-off should be from the far bar on the elephant.

Wolf Vault, Flank Vault, and Front Vault The student should avoid too much forward momentum in doing these moves. The hands should be placed on the far bar when doing the wolf and flank vaults over the elephant.

Rear Vault and Rear Vault with a Quarter Turn Very little spring is required to do these moves. Too much spring will result in failure. The extended legs should be lifted, but the hips

Rapid-fire vaulting over the elephant

Dive onto the elephant

Front vault over the elephant

should be kept low, close to the top of the Swedish box or elephant.

High Front Vault The trajectory of the flight should be upward rather than forward in order to get the hips and feet up over the head.

Giant Cartwheel A forceful spring and a high flight are necessary for success. The body should pass through the vertical plane.

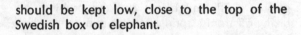

Straddle vault over the elephant

Rear vault over the elephant (front view)

Dive onto the Swedish box

Rear vault over the Swedish box

Stoop vault over the Swedish box

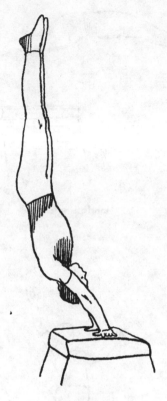

Handspring

Thief Vault The mini-tramp or springboard should be far enough away from the box or elephant to permit the extended forward-swinging leg to avoid striking the piece of equipment. Take-off should be from one foot. The trajectory should be flatter than it is in any of the other vaults.

Neckspring The feet should be kept low until after the hips are over the head. Place the hands on the near bar when doing this move on the elephant.

Handspring A good spring is required. The body should be held extended and in line with the arms while it rotates around the hands.

Handstand Squat, Straddle and Stoop Vaults The student should hold the handstand momentarily before executing the vault. A good spring with a high flight is mandatory in order to get

299

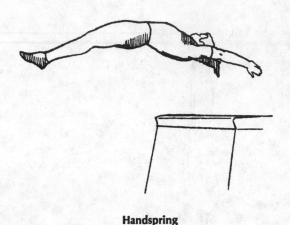

Handspring

Rear vault over the elephant (side view)

Swan vault over the Swedish box

High front vault over the elephant

LIVING STATUARY

into the handstand. Vigorous hip flexion and a good push off the hands are helpful.

Swan Vault A very high spring and a good lift with the arms are essential. The gymnast should not touch the piece of equipment with his hands. His spring alone should enable him to clear the piece with his body arched and his legs extended.

As a means for exaltation of the beauty, form, and grace of the human body, the living statuary number has no peer. Viewing the gilded young men and women gives one a feeling of admiration and awe at the beauty and intricacy which is the human body. The living statuary number is a superlative means for convincing the spectators of the worth of striving for physical fitness.

Giant cartwheel over the elephant

Necessary equipment includes: chemically pure glycerin, which may be purchased at a pharmacy; bronze powder, which may be purchased at a paint store; bathing caps; trunks (rubber, wool, or cotton—in order of suitability); a raised platform; spotlight; and various sports paraphernalia.

The students should cover themselves with the glycerin, smearing it over their entire bodies and trunks with the exception of the areas around the eyes, ears, and genitals. They then rub or pat the bronze powder on their bodies. This should be done in the shower room since it is a messy job.

The glycerin and bronze powder should be removed immediately after the number has been presented. This is easily accomplished with warm water and soap in the shower room.

The students should perform the number on a raised platform 6 to 12 inches high. One to three spotlights may be used. These should be positioned a few feet from the platform and directed upward so that the light strikes the young men at approximately a 60° angle to the floor. This will enhance the appearance of muscular definition since shadows will be created in the depressions, and the high spots will stand out due to the glycerin.

The participants could strike many different poses and representations. Students will enjoy the creative experience of planning and selecting the poses. However, we will make several suggestions for a group of five boys. These follow:

1. Team Sports—batter, football kicker, lacrosse player, basketball player, and hockey player.
2. Combatives—two boxers, two wrestlers, and a fencer.
3. Track and Field—javelin thrower, a baton pass, shot-putter, and discus thrower (or racing start or finish).
4. Gymnastics—handstand, scale, headstand, one-arm half lever, and back bend.
5. Dual Sports—handball, squash rackets, tennis, badminton, or horseshoes.
6. Individual Sports—golf, swimming, archery, weight lifting, and riflery.
7. "The First Man on the Moon."
8. "Victory."
9. "Strife."
10. "Toil."
11. "The Machine Age"—this is a moving statue in which the students can represent such items of machinery as pistons, wheels, etc.

Participants should hold the pose for an agreed length of time. Ten seconds has been the usual time. They should also agree upon the time interval of darkness during which they move into the succeeding pose. The number must be well rehearsed so that the timing between the person operating the spotlights, the performers, and the master of ceremonies is perfect. Performers should be able to find their exact positions in the dark so that the effect is one of balance and harmony. This is achieved in part by proper spacings between the performers and in part by placing the highest pose in the middle and the lowest on the ends. Performers must place their paraphernalia in the same spot each time so that they can find it in the dark. They must also be able to hold their positions without moving.

A musical background is not advised for this number. If it is used, it should be low and subdued.

The comments made by the master of ceremonies during the period while the spotlights are extinguished can help to make the number considerably more effective. Comments should not be made while the spotlight is on the performers. Following are sample introductions for several of the poses.

Team Sports "Team sports are almost a symbol of the 'American Way of Life.' They offer many of us the pleasure of vicarious participation. They offer the participant invaluable lessons in the importance of team work and sportsmanship. Now—'The Living Statues in Team Sports.' "

"The First Man on the Moon"—"Almost everyone witnessed on their TV screen the epical flight to the moon and man's first steps on the lunar surface. These scenes heralded a new phase in man's conquest of his environment. Our living statues would now like to commemorate this historic event."

Statuary should be the closing number of an exhibition.

MASS CALISTHENICS

While many believe that mass calisthenics is out of keeping with the philosophy of promoting individualism that prevails in this country, there is certainly no national philosophy that deprecates improving people's physical fitness status. Mass calisthenics is an excellent means of improving the physical fitness of a large number of people in a short time with no facilities and a minimum of space. Nor does a national philosophy inhibit the ability of people to appreciate the beauty of a sea of humanity all moving in unison. Those who have not experienced participation as a member of a mass calisthenics group will have to take the word of one who has that there is a satisfying feeling, and perhaps a feeling of pride, in being a member of such a group.

Mass calisthenics may be presented in any one of several formations:

1. Line
2. Open square
3. Circle
4. Two or more concentric circles
5. Rectangular
6. Moving

The instructor or a student leader should count cadence while the mass calisthenics number is being rehearsed. However, no one should count when the number is being presented before an audience. The number should be rehearsed and presented with music while each participant maintains his own count.

Any of the moves presented in the floor exercise sections of Chapters 6 and 7 could be incorporated into a mass calisthenics number along with the usual movements used in warm-up exercises such as lunges, sit-ups, push-ups, thrusts, jump-straddles. Tumbling moves could also be utilized. The physical educator or a student leader together with the class can design the routine or sequence of moves so that the creation will become their own.

MINI-TRAMP OR SPRINGBOARD[1]

A fast and an interesting exhibition number can be developed in a relatively short time on the mini-tramp or springboard by students who have not had a great deal of experience in gymnastics. Skills on these pieces of equipment also serve as an excellent activity for physical education classes.

Students should first learn to approach the mini-tramp with a forceful accelerating run, to take off from the floor from one foot, to land on the mini-tramp or springboard with both feet, to take off with the proper lift of the arms, to maintain control and balance during the flight, and to land in balance after doing the move, taking up the impact of landing by bending the knees and hips.

To practice the approach, hurdle, and lift, students should be lined up abreast across the gymnasium floor. They should then practice the three-step approach and hurdle used in diving They should maintain good posture during the approach and accelerate from the start to the hurdle. During the hurdle, the right knee should be pulled upward with the right lower leg held vertically. As they drop downward from the hurdle, they should pull their legs together to land with feet parallel and approximately 6 inches apart. On hitting the imaginary mini-tramp, they should bend their knees and swing their arms downward to the side of their body. To lift off,

[1] All the moves on the mini-tramp which are described in this section may be done by both boys and girls.

they should extend their knees and swing their arms upward with their elbows bent and with their hands passing upward directly in front of their body. They should practice this skill across the gymnasium floor several times.

After the students have mastered the approach, hurdle, and lift-off on the floor, they should try them off the mini-tramp. When they are able to secure a high controlled flight and landing, they can begin to learn various skills. On all of these moves, a spotter should stand directly in front of the mini-tramp or springboard and to one side of the performer.

Jump and Tuck The student draws his knees to his chest with his knees bent and his hips directly under his head during the flight. He then extends his hips and knees for the landing.

Jump and Straddle Toe Touch The student lifts his extended and straddled legs forward to touch his toes with his hands while keeping his hips directly under his head. He should lift his legs to his hands and not drop his trunk to his feet. Having done this, he extends his hips for the landing.

Jump and Jackknife This move is executed in the same manner as a jump and straddle toe touch except that the legs are kept together.

Jump and straddle toe touch

Jump and tuck

Jump and jackknife

Jump and full turn

Swan

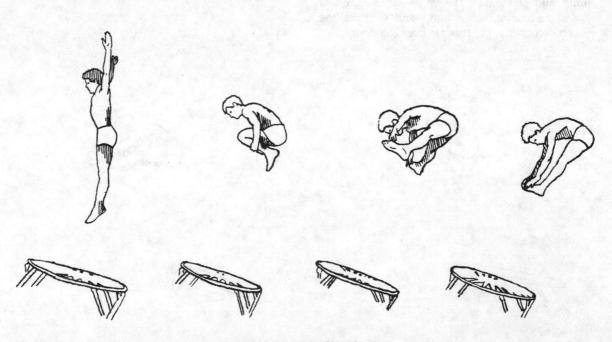

Moves done from a backward jump

Jump and a Half Turn   On take-off, the student turns his head to his left and pulls his right arm across his hips as though swatting a fly on his buttocks. He should keep his body vertical and extended throughout the move. Bending the hips or swinging the arm in too wide an arc will cause the student to move toward the horizontal position.

Jump and Full Turn   This move is executed in the same manner as a jump and half turn except that the student completes a full turn before landing.

Swan   The student leaps upward and into an arched position with his legs extended and his arms angled diagonally upward-sideward to his body. During the flight, his feet should be slightly behind his head; that is, his body should be angled forward from feet to head. Just before landing, he flexes his hips slightly to bring his feet under his body.

Backward Jump   All the preceding moves can also be done from a backward jump. The student should lean them first from a stand on the mini-tramp and later from a run. He should run toward the low end, hit the bed with a slight backward lean and execute the moves as previously described.

Back Somersault   The student starts from a standing position on the mini-tramp. He springs upward with his body slightly arched at the moment he leaves the mini-tramp. He lifts his hips and pulls his head backward, grasps his shins momentarily as he flexes his hips and knees to move into a tucked position, rotates, "kicks" out for the opening, and lands on his feet. The student's initial efforts should be made in a safety belt with two spotters. The spotters should loop the rope of the safety belt around the hand farthest away from the performer and slide the nearest hand along the rope toward the performer as he completes the somersault. After having mastered the move from a standing position, the student should learn it from a run toward the mini-tramp.

Back Somersault in Layout Position   The student starts from a standing position on the mini-tramp. He springs upward lifting his hips hard, pulling his head backward and driving his arms upward and backward to somersault with his body arched and his legs extended. The usual spotting progressions should be followed. These are as follows:

1. In the safety belt with two spotters.
2. In the safety belt with one spotter.
3. Two hand spotters assisting manually.
4. One hand spotter assisting manually.
5. Two spotters ready to assist.
6. One spotter ready to assist.
7. Alone.

Back somersault in layout position

Front somersault

Back Somersaults with Twists The gymnast should learn back somersaults with twists on the trampoline before attempting them off the mini-tramp. After having mastered them on the trampoline, he should learn them on the mini-tramp with a twisting belt before attempting them unsupported.

Front Somersault The mini-tramp is placed in front of the Swedish box with the low end toward it. The student starts from a stand on the box. He jumps onto the bed of the mini-tramp, and as he lifts off, he flexes his hips slightly to cause his hips to be lifted over his head. At the same time, he lifts with his arms and tucks his head and then pulls his arms and trunk downward toward his thighs to move into a tightly tucked position. When he has completed the somersault, he opens up sharply to land on his feet. After the gymnast has mastered the front somersault in the safety belt, he should be hand spotted. In hand spotting, the spotter should stand to the gymnast's right and grasp his right wrist with his left thumb behind it and his fingers in front of it. He should lift and assist during the spin with his right hand by placing it on the gymnast's upper back.

Having mastered the front somersault from a jump from the Swedish box to the mini-tramp, the gymnast should learn the skill from a run.

Baroni The student should master the baroni on the trampoline before attempting it off the

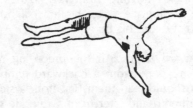

Baroni

mini-tramp. The trampoline is adaptable to front drop and knee drop landings, which are utilized as progressions in learning the baroni on the trampoline. The mini-tramp is not adaptable to these types of landings. The student's initial efforts off the mini-tramp should be made in a safety belt. If the tumbler twists in a counterclockwise direction, the safety belt rope leading from his right hip should cross in front of his body while the rope leading from his left hip should cross behind his body. If he twists in the opposite direction the instructions should be reversed.

Cut-away The student runs toward the mini-tramp and hits the bed with both feet, lifting his hips up behind his body and behind the mini-tramp to execute a front somersault while moving backward to land on his approach side of the mini-tramp. Since the beginner tends to "stall out" due to failure to lift his hips early, the spotter must be prepared to assist with the rotation. He does this by pushing with one hand against the performer's upper back while lifting at his waist with the other hand.

Gainer The student runs toward the mini-tramp and hits the bed to take off from both feet, pushing backward on the bed. He lifts forward and upward with his arms, lifts his feet forward-upward over his head, pulls his head backward, and pulls into a tucked position to execute a back somersault landing on the side of the mini-tramp opposite to his approach side. Initial efforts should be made in a safety belt. The spotter should be prepared to lift the performer and to pull him forward so that he can clear the mini-tramp. He does this by pulling forward and lifting upward with his left hand. He should also be prepared to assist with rotation by pushing upward against the gymnast's hips with his right hand.

APPENDIX B

ORGANIZING AND DIRECTING AN EXHIBITION GROUP

If the physical education teacher has done an effective and enthusiastic job of teaching gymnastics and tumbling in his physical education classes, a number of students will manifest a desire to explore this activity further. They will request permission to practice after school or to form a gymnastic club. The physical educator who sincerely believes in the worth of gymnastics will not deny these requests. This group of students, even if there are only three or four, can serve as the nucleus for an exhibition group that very likely will grow to such numbers that it will become necessary to place limitations upon the numbers.

As soon as this initial group has developed a degree of skill adequate to present a reasonably satisfying demonstration, arrangements should be made to do so. PTA groups always enjoy seeing activities in which their children participate; and school children enjoy watching their friends perform at school assemblies. Because PTA and school assembly groups do not expect a high level of skill, they serve as good "starters" for a demonstration group. After the group has begun to develop more skill and showmanship, arrangements should be made to perform at half times of football and basketball games and before civic groups. At this point in the development of the group, announcements should be made in the school paper and via the bulletin boards that an exhibition troupe has been organized and that interested students are invited to become candidates. This announcement should stress that no previous experience is necessary. As a result of these announcements and of the gain in stature of the activity following the group's appearances at half times of games and at civic affairs, many students will want to join.

With increased numbers it will become advisable to elect officers, to draw up a constitution, and to begin making plans for the "First Annual Home Show of the————Gym Team."

Officers which should be elected include the following:

President
Vice President
Treasurer
Secretary
Historian

A sample of a constitution which served the Gymkana Troupe of the University of Southern Mississippi appears on pages 314–317.

After the various numbers begin to develop several committee chairmen should be elected or appointed by the executive committee. These could include the following:

Stage Committee
Equipment Committee
Music Committee
Publicity Committee
Lighting Committee
Costume Committee
Program Committee
Ticket Committee

It is not only politicians who enjoy being recognized. All of us do. The physical educator should ask the school newspaper to include his office on a reporter's "beat" in order that members of the troupe can be recognized. The chairman or a member of the publicity committee should write the news releases. These should be ready on time in the form desired by the newspaper, grammatically correct, and with correct spelling of names. Demonstrations and exhibitions presented or about to be presented, officers and chairmen elected or appointed, and competition entered all make newsworthy items. The availability of the group for demonstrations should be mentioned during the first year or two, although later on this will become unnecessary.

When groups write requesting a performance by the exhibition troupe, they should be sent a brief description of the various numbers and an agreement form. Samples of those which were used by the Cortland State Teachers College Gymkana Troupe appear on pages 318–319.

A letter should be sent to the parents of the troupe members. In this letter the activities and purposes of the group should be explained and parental permission for the children's participation should be solicited.

In planning for the home show, a "continuity sheet" will be very helpful. During the actual presentation of the exhibition, the continuity sheet is necessary to ensure that lights, music, equipment, costumes, and performers are all coordinated. This continuity sheet should indicate the time each act is to start and finish, the lighting effects, names of personnel and their

costumes, musical background, and all properties needed. It serves as the "cue sheet" for the master of ceremonies, the personnel, the person operating the lights, the wardrobe people, the person operating the record player, and the property men. Every member of the troupe should have a mimeographed copy. A sample copy used by the University of Southern Mississippi Gymkana Troupe is included below.

An exhibition presents an excellent opportunity to educate the spectators about the objectives of physical education, provided the show has a theme that ties all the acts together. The Gymkana Troupe at Cortland State Teachers College, at one of its annual home shows titled "Reverie of Motion," had as its theme the reminiscences of a retired physical educator-coach. The show opened on the scene of an old physical educator-coach who sat in an easy chair looking at a scrapbook and reminiscing about his past experiences in teaching.

As show time approaches, rehearsals should become increasingly disciplined. There should be a rehearsal devoted to perfecting the timing and to "polishing up" each of the numbers. There should be another to work out the details of lighting and costumes, a third to work out the details of music and property manipulation. And there should be a final dress rehearsal to coordinate all the various details.

It is very likely that a successful exhibition troupe will begin to receive requests to perform in cities other than the home town. Some of these may be some distance from the school. During various periods, the gymnastic exhibition troupes of the University of Illinois, the University of Southern Mississippi, Duke University, Springfield College, and Florida State University have all traveled throughout several states presenting exhibitions. The University of Maryland Gymkana Troupe has performed in Alaska and the Aleutian Islands. Many high school groups have traveled extensive distances to perform.

An enthusiastic physical educator must exercise caution in accepting such requests, and if he does accept them, must exercise caution in the conduct of the trip. Chaperones, if not needed in fact, are needed to satisfy parents and particularly faculty members. Parental consent to participate should be secured by the students. Detailed plans and schedules must be made and adhered to. A feeling of pride in representing their school well should be developed in the students. In keeping with this sense of responsibility, students should establish standards of dress and behavior, and enforce them. Properly conducted, the trips can be very valuable educational experiences for the students.

When the exhibition troupe has grown to these proportions, it is time to effect some controls. A limit should be established on the number of out-of-town exhibitions, the total number of exhibitions involving all members of the troupe, and the number of exhibitions in which each student might participate. The total

number of performances of the exhibition troupe might appear excessive and yet no member of the troupe will be overloaded. At many affairs, such as at half times of basketball games, only two or three students might perform at one game while others perform at other games or affairs. The physical educator, however, might easily overload himself. A faculty advisory group should be established. This group should meet at regular intervals to evaluate the program and to advise the director and student officers of the troupe, since they can see the program objectively.

SAMPLE DOCUMENTS OF EXHIBITION GROUPS

SAMPLE SELF-RATING OF SPORTSMANSHIP AND HEALTHMANSHIP FOR CLASSES IN GYMNASTICS

Note:
Rate yourself as honestly as you are able, viewing your performance during the past quarter objectively (as though you were someone else) on the following basis:

5 pts. — always	2 pts. — seldom
4 pts. — usually	1 pt. — almost never
3 pts. — about half of the time	0 pts. — never

This constructive self-analysis will help you to "know yourself" and in that way enable you to discover and to strengthen your weak areas to aid in character development.

	Score
Health Habits:	
Takes a shower after class	_____
Dries hair thoroughly	_____
Wears a clean and appropriate uniform	_____
Always present	_____
Cooperation:	
Promptness—always on time	_____
Coaches other class members	_____
Offers to spot others	_____
Assists in setting up and returning equipment	_____
Conservation:	
Handles equipment with care	_____
Tolerance:	
Appreciates abilities of those who are skilled and has empathy toward those who are unskilled (appreciation for individual differences)	_____
Respects differences of opinion	_____
Courtesy:	
Observes the amenities of social behavior	_____
Personal Direction:	
Effort has been to the limit of his strength and endurance	_____
Has demonstrated self-confidence and courage	_____
Has demonstrated determination	_____
Has learned skills in their progressive order of difficulty	_____
Critical Judgment:	
Has had the courage to discuss courteously with the person in charge procedures that he sincerely feels could be improved upon	_____

Total Points _____
Name _____
Course, hour, and day _____

SAMPLE CONTINUITY SHEET FOR AN EXHIBITION

Time	Name of Act	Lights	Personnel	Costume	Music	Properties
8:00–8:03	Overture by M.S.C. Band	House	Band	Own	Own	Own
8:03–8:05	Presentation of the Flag	Blue spot	M.S.C. Color Guard	Own	"Star Spangled Banner"	Flag
8:05–8:10	Statement of objectives & purposes	House	Dr. James Baley		Fanfare	Public address system
8:10–8:14	"The Buccaneers" (Vaulting)	House	All the men members of the troupe	Jeans cut off below knee, sashes of different colors & bandanas	"Stout-Hearted Men"	Horse, Swedish box, P-Bar, Beat board, Spring board, Mini-tramp, 9 mats
8:14–8:20	"On the Beam" (Balance beam)	Orange spot	Jane Harmon Sandy Mayo	Leotards	"Blue Danube"	Balance beam, two large mats, magnesium
8:20–8:25	"Musical Gymnastics" (Side horse)	White spot	Walt Kerley, Norm Bowne, Joe Sacksteder, Ron Heun	Team uniforms	"Falling in Love"	Side horse, two small mats, magnesium
8:25–8:30	"The Great Grue" (Singles balancing)	Red spot	Merle Grue	Shorts & slippers	"Pomp and Circumstance"	Steps, 3 chairs, pedestal, 4 coke bottles, magnesium
8:30–8:35	"The Apollos" (P-Bars)	House	Ron Edwards, Walt Kerley, Ron Heun, Joe Sacksteder	Team uniforms	"Finlandia"	P-Bars, 3 mats, magnesium
8:35–8:40	"The Bouncing Boy" (Ladder bouncing)	House	Cary Campbell	Slacks, loose shirt, bow tie		Steps, ladder, magnesium
8:40–8:45	"The Jitterbugging Hines" (Dance)	House	Hines school children	Own	Own	4 big mats
8:45–8:53	Poetry of Motion (Floor Exercise)	Purple spot	J. Baley, T. Baley, Sandy Mayo, Ron Edwards, Ron Heun	Boys: shorts, T-shirts Girls: leotards	"Sympathy"	None
8:53–8:59	"The Whirligigs" (Horizontal bar)	House	Merle Grue, Ron Edwards, Walt Kerley, Ron Heun	Team uniforms		Horizontal bar, cables, ropes, stakes, 2 large mats, magnesium
8:59–9:02	"South American Rhythms" (Dance)	Purple spot	Daisy Pinto	Own	"Cordoba"	None

Time	Name of Act	Lights	Personnel	Costume	Music	Properties
9:02–9:10	"Aristocrats of Balance" (Doubles Balancing)	Blue spot	Jane & Norm Ron & Sandy Flo & Cary Ron & Walt	Boys: shorts & shirts Girls: leotards	"Indian Love Call"	2 large mats, magnesium
9:10–9:14	Tumbling Tumbleweeds (Tumbling)	House	Tumbling Tots Tumbling Teens Exhibition Troupe Judy Wills	Boys: shorts & shirts Girls: leotards	"Tumbling Tumble-weeds"	4 large mats, Mini-tramp
9:14–9:17	Family Fun	Green spot	Scotty, Gary, Timmy, and Jimmy Baley and Dr. Baley	Slacks, sport shirts, slippers	"Sonny Boy"	2 mats and magnesium
9:17–9:22	The Sky-Lighters (Ladder Balancing)	Orange spot	Ron Edwards, Merle Grue, Bob Tate, Jane Harmon, Sandy Mayo	Boys: shorts Girls: leotards	"Only a Rose"	Ladders, 4 large mats, magnesium
9:22–9:27	"The Flip-twisters" (Trampoline)	House	Joe Sack-steder, Tim Baley, Jim Baley, Judy Wills	Boys: shorts Girls: leotards	"La Donna Mobile"	Trampoline, 4 mats
9:27–9:35	Egyptian Pyramids (Pyramid Building)	Blue spot	Entire troupe	Boys: shorts Girls: leotards	"Grand Canyon Suite"	4 large mats, magnesium
9:35–9:38	Ronnie Able on Accordian	White spot	Ronnie Able	Formal	Own	Public address system
9:38–9:41	Modern Gymnastics	Red spot	Daisy Pinto	Own	"Carioca"	None
9:41–9:46	The Gym Kids (Mass Calisthenics)	House	Tumbling Tots & Teens	Shirts, shorts, leotards	"Rocking Horse Cow-boy"	None
9:46–9:50	New York at Night (Dance)	Green spot	Mona Watkins	Own	"Tropicana"	None
9:50–9:55	Dixie Darlings (Dance)	House	Miss Jellink and Dixie Darlings	Own	Own	None
9:55–9:58	Living Statues	White spot	Walt Kerley, Ron Edwards, Merle Grue, Cary Camp-bell, Joe Sacksteder	Bathing caps and shorts	"Show and Grace"	Discus, javelin, foot-ball, baseball bat, lacrosse stick, baton, shot put, fenc-ing foil, basketball, glycerin, bronze powder

SAMPLE CONSTITUTION FOR A GYMNASTIC EXHIBITION TROUPE

ARTICLE I *Name and Purpose*

Section 1 This organization shall be known as the Mississippi Southern Gymkana Troupe.

Section 2 It shall be the purpose of the organization:
   a. To promote and maintain an interest in gymnastics and related activities.
   b. To stimulate interest in physical development.
   c. To cultivate an appreciation for beauty, form, and movement.
   d. To cultivate an appreciation for sportsmanship.
   e. To develop greater social and professional cooperation among members.

ARTICLE II *Membership*

Section 1 This organization shall consist of active, alumni, and honorary members.

Section 2 Active membership consists of such bona fide students of Mississippi Southern College, Hattiesburg, Mississippi, who:
   a. Have a quality point ratio of 2.0 for the quarter preceding. Active members with fewer quality points shall be suspended until such time as their quality point ratio equals 2.0.
   b. Active members must attend 75 percent of the meetings and practice sessions—absences of a member deemed excessive by the Executive Council shall result in suspension of membership.
   c. Prerequisites for consideration as an active member are as follows:
      1. Genuine interest in the Troupe, its purposes, and activities.
      2. Participation in one exhibition or demonstration.
      3. Cumulative quality point ratio of 2.0.

Section 3 Honorary memberships in this organization may be conferred by this organization upon any person who through his past or present personal interest has so aided the organization as to merit such consideration—any honorary member shall be entitled to all of the privileges of the organization except voting. Individual may be proposed for honorary membership by any active member. Individuals are elected to honorary membership by affirmative vote of 75 per cent of the active membership. Individuals elected to honorary membership shall receive an appropriate scroll to be conferred at the annual home show.

ARTICLE III *Officers*

Section 1 The officers of this organization shall be: President, Vice-President, Secretary, Treasurer, Publicity Manager, and Equipment Manager. These together with the Faculty Director shall comprise the Executive Council.

Section 2 These officers shall be chosen from the active members of this organization.

ARTICLE IV *Duties of the Officers*

Section 1 It shall be the duty of the President:
   a. To preside at all meetings.
   b. To plan, organize, and conduct all practice sessions with the faculty advisor.
   c. To preside at special meetings of the Executive Council called for the purpose of planning theme and continuity and selecting numbers and performers for all exhibitions and demonstrations.
   d. To call special meetings.

e. To decide all questions of order.

f. To enforce due observance of the Constitution, By-Laws, and rules of order.

g. To appoint all committees not otherwise provided for.

h. To ensure that all members conduct themselves in a manner which will bring credit to our college and to this organization—together with the Executive Council he will take appropriate disciplinary action.

Section 2 It shall be the duty of the Vice-President:

a. In case of vacancy of the President, the Vice-President shall become President and a new Vice-President shall be appointed by the Executive Council subject to approval by the membership.

b. To act as Chairman of the Program Committee.

c. To serve in the absence of the President at meetings of the Executive Council and/or at meetings of the organization.

Section 3 It shall be the duty of the Secretary:

a. To write all communications, announcements, and data of the organization.

b. To report at each meeting of the organization a summary of the minutes of the previous Executive Council meeting.

c. To give notice of all meetings, notify officers of elections, and record the names of all newly elected members.

Section 4 It shall be the duty of the Treasurer:

a. To collect all money from other organizations sponsoring the Gymkana Troupe.

b. To deposit all funds.

c. To make all payments by check and to keep an accurate account of all receipts and expenditures of the organizations.

Section 5 It shall be the duty of the Publicity Manager:

a. To publicize all outstanding accomplishments of the organization to the student newspaper and the press of this and neighboring cities.

b. To ensure that proper publicity for the Troupe and Gym Team is distributed to any appropriate media.

c. To arrange for the printing and distribution of programs for all home shows.

d. To appoint such committees as he may see fit to aid him in the aforementioned duties.

Section 6 It shall be the duty of the Equipment Manager:

a. To see that the required equipment is available at the time and place needed.

b. To turn in to the Executive Council all matters concerning purchasing or replacing of equipment.

c. To repair or arrange for repair and maintenance of equipment.

Section 7 It shall be the duty of the Faculty Advisor:

a. To advise and assist the Executive Council.

b. To assist the Treasurer in the auditing of financial accounts and to countersign all checks written by the Treasurer.

c. To attend the meetings of the Executive Council.

d. To assist the President in matters of organization and leadership.

e. To assist such other officers as is necessary.

ARTICLE V *Election of Officers*

Section 1 Elections:

a. The election of officers shall be held during the fall quarter of the school year, on a

date designated by the Executive Council.
b. The term of office shall be one year.

Section 2 Vacancies:
a. In case of vacancy occurring in any office, with the exception of President and Vice-President, the President shall appoint a successor subject to the approval of the Executive Council.
b. In case of vacancy in the President's Office, the procedure shall be as stated in Article IV, Section 2a.

Section 3 Voting:
a. Nominations for all officers shall come from the floor.
b. Election by secret ballot shall follow.
c. A majority vote of members present at the meeting shall be necessary.
d. New officers shall assume office immediately following announcement of their election.
e. Should an officer resign during the year, the President shall appoint some member to assume the office temporarily and order the secretary to send notice of a special election at the next regular meeting when the vacancy will be filled.

ARTICLE VI *Executive Council*

Section 1 The Executive Council shall consist of the President, Vice-President, Secretary, Treasurer, Publicity Chairman, Equipment Manager, and Faculty Advisor.

Section 2 The President shall call all meetings of the Executive Council whenever he deems it necessary.

Section 3 The Faculty Advisor shall be a faculty member of the Division of Health, Physical Education, and Recreation.

ARTICLE VII *Amendments*

Section 1 Every proposed amendment in alteration of or addition to this Constitution must be handed to the President in writing, who shall present the same to the members of the organization at the next meeting where it may be adopted or rejected by a three-fourths vote of the total active membership. This legislation may be challenged by a written petition to the Executive Council signed by one-fourth of the total active membership.

ARTICLE VIII *Meetings and Quorum*

Section 1 Meetings of the Executive Council or of the active membership shall be held whenever the President deems it necessary.

Section 2 Practice sessions shall be held according to the schedule posted.

Section 3 A quorum shall consist of 50 percent of active members.

BY-LAWS

ARTICLE I *Committees*

Section 1 When necessary, the President shall appoint committees on: music, seating, costumes, membership, social functions, production, and transportation.

Section 2 Committee chairmen shall be selected by the Executive Council.

Section 3 Committee chairmen shall select their own assistants.

ARTICLE II *Awards*

Section 1 All awards shall be awarded by action of a quorum.

Section 2 Two "Best Trouper" awards shall be given at the time of the "Home Show." One for a man performer and another for a woman performer. All active members will cast their votes in sufficient time for the award to be presented at the "Home Show." In addition, two "Best Performer" awards shall be awarded by the Faculty Advisor.

ARTICLE III *Parliamentary Order*

Section 1 Robert's Rules of Order shall be the parliamentary authority on all matters not covered by the Constitution and By-Laws.

ARTICLE IV *Suspension of By-Laws*

Section 1 These laws shall be suspended in case of an emergency by the unanimous vote of all those present at a meeting in which a quorum is present.

ARTICLE V *Responsibility of Members*

Section 1 Members shall be individually responsible for their conduct at all times when representing Mississippi Southern College and the M.S.C. Exhibition Troupe and Gymnastics Team. If necessary, disciplinary action will be taken at the Executive Council.

ARTICLE VI *Social Functions*

Section 1 Social functions will be held in accordance with the plans of the Party Committee.

SAMPLE AGREEMENT BETWEEN SPONSORING GROUP AND
EXHIBITION TROUPE

We would like the Cortland Gymkana Troupe to appear at_____(place)_____

at_____(time)_____on_____(date)_____.

We can pay_____per mile for transportation each way. We could furnish meals for the members of the troupe. We would like a show of_____(time)_____duration. We would like the troupe to follow the demonstration with gymnastic clinic_____(check)_____. Please complete the following to help us to plan appropriately:

Working Area_____   Age Range of Spectators_____

Ceiling Height_____   Probable No. of Spectators_____

Equipment present:_____

    Parallel bars_____   Swedish box_____

    Horizontal bar_____   Tumbling mats (No.)_____

    Rings_____   Record player_____

    Side horse_____   Spotlights_____

    Trampoline_____   Uneven parallel bars_____

    Ropes_____   Balance beam_____

    Springboard_____   Mini-tramp_____

We agree to provide the equipment checked ($\checkmark$) and have assured ourselves of its safe condition.

/s/_____

SAMPLE PUBLICITY RELEASE

BRIEF DESCRIPTIONS OF NUMBERS PRESENTED BY THE CORTLAND GYMNAKA TROUPE

1. *The Collegians:* The entire troupe does a fast, breathtaking (yours as well as theirs) Swedish calisthenic exercise in unison—demonstrating strength, balance, agility, flexibility, power, rhythm, and precision.
2. *The Buccaneers:* All the male members of the troupe demonstrate about fifteen different vaults over the side horse, vaulting box, and elephant in such rapid-fire order that it appears as though they will land on top of one another.
3. *The Balancers:* Several women members of the troupe demonstrate poise and grace while balancing themselves on a balance beam of Olympic specifications.
4. *Baton Twirling:* The pageantry, color, and spirit of one of our most popular sports is kept alive through the long winter months by our whirling, spinning, twisting baton twirlers.
5. *Button's Bouncing Boys (and girls)*: Jay Button leads several members of the troupe in double flips, full twisting front and back flips and all sorts of gyrations, twistings, turnings, and flips on the trampoline.
6. *The Skylighters:* Three men and four women balance themselves on two unsupported ladders while assuming many graceful and difficult positions.
7. *The Aristocrats of Balance:* A man demonstrates strength, balance, and flexibility while a woman demonstrates grace, poise, balance, and courage in a beautiful doubles balancing number.
8. *Living Statuary:* Men gilded in gold depict stirring moments in sports both ancient and modern.
9. *The Iron Dragons:* A triples balancing act which requires the coordinated efforts and synchronized balancing of three people.
10. *Bugs and Batty:* These two satirize and burlesque the efforts of all the other performers throughout the entire presentation.
11. *The Master Builders:* The entire troupe moves from one design of symmetry and balance to another with grace and precision in this pyramid building number.
12. *Silhouette Balancing:* A man and woman (unseen by the audience) execute the well-timed movements of doubles balancing behind a muslin screen, casting graceful silhouettes.
13. *The Tumbling Toreadors:* The men members of the troupe do some fast mat tumbling and hit the springboard to lift themselves into the air before doing flips, gainers, and twists.
14. *The High Flyers:* Both men and women perform on the flying and still rings, performing their moves high over the heads of the onlookers.
15. *The Horsemen:* The Romans devised the side horse in order to teach their soldiers how to mount and dismount. No living horse would tolerate the confusion of agile movement the troupers perform on the modern side horse.

SAMPLE ANNOUNCER'S GUIDE FOR A GYMNASTICS MEET

1:00 P.M.: Warm-ups begin
1:00–2:00 P.M.: Coaches' scratch meeting—Classroom of men's gymnasium
1:45 P.M.: Warm-ups end
2:00 P.M.: Audience rises for National Anthem and contestants march in
2:10 P.M.: Short opening address (welcome to visiting team)

Order of Events

2:10–2:30 P.M.	1. Tumbling (Boys and Girls) Side Horse (Boys)
2:30–2:45 P.M.	2. Trampoline (Boys and Girls) Long Horse (Boys)
2:45–3:15 P.M.	3. Parallel Bars (Boys) Vaulting (Girls)
3:15–3:45 P.M.	4. Horizontal Bar (Boys) Uneven Parallel Bars (Girls)
3:45–4:30 P.M.	5. Floor Exercise (Boys)
4:30–5:00 P.M.	6. Still Rings (Boys) Floor Exercise (Girls)
5:15–5:30 P.M.	7. Presentation of Awards

Note

1. Announce lineup before each event.
   Introduce: "Jones up, Smith on deck," etc.

2. After each routine, call for judges' scores and announce these scores.

3. Announce winners at end of each event.

SAMPLE GYMNASTIC TEAM SCHEDULE

STATE UNIVERSITY OF NEW YORK AT CORTLAND GYM TEAM AND GYMKANA
TROUPE SCHEDULE FOR 1956

Sat.	Dec.	3rd	Elmira "Y" Open House
Fri.	Dec.	9th	Half time—Trampoline
Sat.	Dec.	10th	Half time—Doubles Balancing
Sat.	Jan.	7th	Half Time—"The Edison Airs"—Trampoline
Tues.	Jan.	10th	Homer High School—Assembly Program
Wed.	Jan.	11th	Half time—Parallel Bars
Fri.	Jan.	13th	Half time—Flying Rings
Mon.	Jan.	16th	Swiss Olympic Gymnastic Team
Wed.	Jan.	25th	Elmira "Y" Open House
Wed.	Feb.	1st	Utica High School—Assembly Program
Sat.	Feb.	4th	Gymnastic Meet—Syracuse Turners
Tues.	Feb.	7th	Waverly High School—Assembly Program
Sat.	Feb.	11th	Gymnastic Meet—Springfield College
Wed.	Feb.	15th	Half time—Family Fun
Thurs.	Feb.	16th	Groton Central School—Assembly Program
Fri.	Feb.	17th	Half time—Tumbling
Sat.	Feb.	18th	Rome, N.Y.—Assembly Program
Thurs.	Feb.	23rd	Morning—Scarsdale, N.Y.
			Afternoon—Children's Village, Dobbs Ferry, N. Y.
Fri.	Feb.	24th	Afternoon—Island Tree, Long Island
			Evening—Garden City, Long Island
Sat.	Feb.	25th	Afternoon and Evening—Wesleyan St. School
Fri.	Mar.	2nd	Tully Central School—Assembly Program
Sat.	Mar.	3rd	Half time—Horizontal Bar
Fri.	Mar.	9th	Home Show

SAMPLE GYMNASTIC MEET CHECK LIST #1

I. Prepare in Advance:

_____A. Secure judges
_____B. Secure publicity (*Daily Campus*, TV, radio, wire service)
_____C. Secure scorers' and judges' assistants (15 needed)
_____D. Assign prop men (10 needed)
_____E. Obtain list of entries
_____F. Enter information on score sheets and judges' sheets
_____G. Notify principal and department head
_____H. Make announcer's check sheet

II. Locker Room Arrangements:

_____A. Lockers
_____B. Showers
_____C. Towels

III. Personnel Needed:

_____A. Judges
_____B. Judges' assistants (10)
_____C. Scorers (approximately 6 to 8)
_____D. Prop men (10)
_____E. Announcers (2)

IV. Post-Meet Arrangements:

_____A. Phone results in to newspapers, radio, TV.
_____B. Write up results for morning announcements to students.

SAMPLE GYMNASTIC MEET CHECK LIST #2

Gymnasium Setup

_____A. Set up apparatus
_____B. Set up public address system and record player
_____C. Set up safety mats
_____D. Set up scoring tables (2)
_____E. Chairs needed (approx. 15)
_____F. Set up bleacher seats
_____G. Stop watches (3)
_____H. Magnesium and emery cloth
_____I. Score sheets (made up)

_____J. Judges' sheets
_____K. Tape measure
_____L. Pencils and scratch paper
_____M. Typewriter (1)
_____N. Adding machine (1)
_____O. First aid kit
_____P. Slates, chalk, and erasers
_____Q. Blackboard for scores of each event
_____R. Towels for each team

SAMPLE FLOOR PLAN

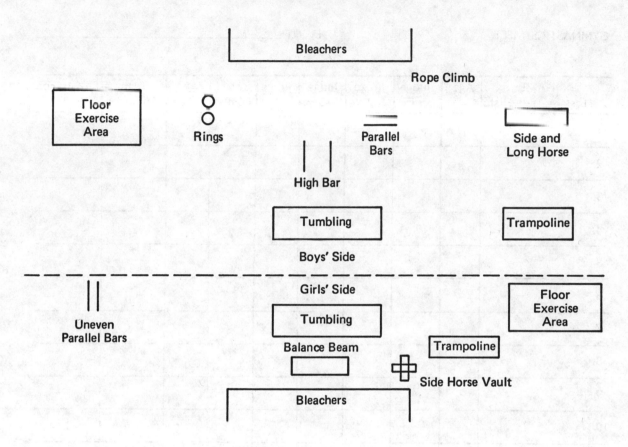

SAMPLE SCORING SHEET

GYMNASTICS MEET   EVENT:_____

	NAME		Age	Judge 1	Judge 2	Judge 3	Judge 4	Total Points	Place	Team Affiliation	Registration Number
	Last	First									
1.											
2.											
3.											
4.											
5.											
6.											
7.											
8.											
9.											
10.											
11.											
12.											
13.											
14.											
15.											
16.											
17.											
18.											

Note: Scratch highest and lowest score and average the remaining two scores.

AN ABSTRACT OF GYMNASTIC RULES THAT CONCERN COMPETITORS IN THE CONNECTICUT GYMNASTIC ASSOCIATION JUNIOR HIGH SCHOOL MEETS

COSTUME
The costume for boys must consist of shirt, trunks or long trousers and gymnastic shoes or slippers. The costume for girls consist of a leotard and gym slippers.

ENTRY FEE
An entry fee of $1 for each event including the all-around event must be paid by all competitors wishing to compete for individual honors.

AWARDS
Regulation medals shall be awarded to first, second, and third place winners. In the event of a tie for first or second place, the meet referee will decide upon the procedure to be used to determine which competitor shall receive the medal. All contestants tying for third place shall receive a medal.

ORDER OF COMPETITION
The competitors shall perform in rotation in the order selected by the committee. No competitor shall be required to perform first in more than one event.

ADMISSION TO THE FIELD OF COMPETITION
Only competitors, judges, scorers, clerks, and those required for maintenance of the apparatus will be admitted on the field of competition. Only those photographers and reporters authorized by the organization sponsoring the meet may be admitted with the approval of the referee.

DURATION OF EXERCISE
Each competitor's exercise shall start from the position of "attention" and shall be judged from the time he begins his combination until he again wholly or in part places his weight upon the mat. An accidental scraping or brushing of the mat shall not terminate the exercise but shall be marked as poor form by the judges.

GUARDING OF THE COMPETITOR
Competitors are permitted to utilize spotters and shall not be penalized for so doing unless it becomes necessary for the spotter to touch and/or assist the competitor in his performance.

FLOOR EXERCISES
Rhythmic movements including elements of balance, strength, flexibility, agility, and tumbling shall be combined into a continuous routine of 50–70 seconds duration. Competitors should attempt to cover as much as possible of the area—which is 39 feet 5 inches by 39 feet 5 inches. This area will be clearly marked by white lines. Girls' floor exercise should be accompanied by music which should harmonize with the movements.

SIDE HORSE
Dimensions are: Length—70.86 inches. Width—13.78 to 14.56 inches. Width between pommels—15.75–17.72 inches. Height to top of pommels—40 inches. The exercise should be continuous, with movements to both sides of the horse and with a reversal of direction. Scissors, single- and double-leg circles, and rear and front vaults may be included.

PARALLEL BARS
Dimensions are: Height—55 inches. Taller gymnasts may elevate the bars 4 inches. The inside width may vary from 14 to 18 inches. Ideally the exercise should include moves above and below the bars, turns, changes, swings, vaults, and balances. Strength moves may be used. A beat board may be used for the mount.

HORIZONTAL BAR

Height—80 to 98 inches. Only swinging and vaulting exercises should be done.

STILL RINGS

Height to point of suspension—18 feet. Rings 80 to 98 inches above the mat. The exercise should consist of swinging, strength, and hold (balance) moves.

LONG HORSE

Dimensions: Same width and length as the side horse but with the pommels removed. Height—40 inches from the floor to the top of the horse at the saddle. The competitor may place the beat board at any distance from the horse he chooses. Each competitor shall apply enough magnesium to his hands (from the tip of the fingers to the heel of the hand) to produce a clearly visible mark on the horse after his vault. A strip of white paint or white tape ¼-inch wide will be used to divide the top of the horse into five areas as indicated:

15.75"	5.9"		5.9"	15.75"

If the marks indicate that any portion of the competitor's hand or hands touched either of the 5.9-inch areas, he shall be penalized by .5 point. On vaults from the neck, the hands must land entirely in the front zone. In vaults from the croup, they must land entirely in the rear zone. In vaults from the saddle, they must land entirely in the central zone. Two clerks shall observe the placing of the competitor's hands and shall notify the judges as to which zone applies. The marking shall be wiped off before the following competitor initiates his vault. The use of any portion of the penalty zones shall lessen the rating by 1.0 point for each zone. Two men shall note the placing of the competitor's hands and report to the scorer. Each competitor may take two trials. The better mark counts. The competitor must attempt the same vault on his second trial. (In the Connecticut Junior Meet we will have two optional vaults.) The competitor must make known his two selection of vaults to the chief scorer before the competition begins.

TABLE OF DIFFICULTY

A—With hands on the NECK
1. Jump, body stretched out, legs stretched sideways (Straddle) — 7.0
2. Jump, by passing over the neck, legs joined and bent (Squat) — 7.5
3. Jump, body straight, legs bent backwards (Sheep vault) — 9.0
4. Jump, body straight, crossing the legs, landing facing right or left (Scissors, with ¼ turn) — 8.5
5. Jump, body straight, crossing legs, land facing back (Scissors, with ¼ turn) — 9.5
6. Jump, body stretched, bending it to pass the straight legs over the neck, stretch body before landing (Stoop or Buecke) — 10.0
7. Handspring (Straight arms) — 10.0
8. Pike Jump (Hecht) — 10.0

B—With hands on the SADDLE
1. Dorsal jump from left to right or to left (Rear vault) — 7.0
2. Jump to handstand, followed by ¼ turn to right arm, putting the left hand on the neck and turn sideways to the left, landing sideways in front of neck—or vice versa (Handspring with ¼ pivoted turn) — 9.0
3. Jump to handstand with a ¼ turn to left during the flight (or to the right) (handstand sideways), and turn sideways to land sideways in front of neck (Giant cartwheel) — 10.0

C—With hands on the CROUP
1. Jump, body straight, legs stretched out sideways (Straddle) — 7.5

2. Jump, legs together and bent forward (Squat)   8.0
3. Jump, legs straight and crossed, facing right or left (Scissors with ¼ turn)   9.0
4. Jump, legs straight and crossed and half a turn, landing backwards, facing the horse,
5. Jump, body straight, legs together and bent backwards, arms sideways (Sheep vault)   9.5
   arms sideways (Scissors with ½ turn)   10.0
6. Jump, body straight, legs bent first, stretched forward during the flight, restretch the
   body before landing (Stoop or Buecke)   10.0
7. Jump, legs straight and crossed, and half a turn backward and a half turn forward,
   landing transversely, back to horse, arms sideways (Scissors with full turn)   10.0

SCORING

Four judges will rate each exercise. Judges do not consult one another, arriving at their scores independently, except in evaluating the first contestant in each event. This is done in order to establish a common reference point. The highest and lowest scores will be eliminated.

All exercises will be scored from 0 to 10 points in tenths of a point. The relative weight given the various aspects of the optional routine shall be as follows:

Difficulty	3.4 pts.	
Combination	1.6 pts.	Value of the exercise
Performance	5.0 pts.	
	10 pts.	

The two elements of the optional exercise will be marked as follows:

Value of the exercise	Points	Performance
No performance	0	No performance
Quite insufficient	1	Very defective
Inferior to average	2	Fair
Average	3	Satisfactory
Good	4	Good
Superior	4.5	Excellent
Perfect	5	Perfect

PERFECT PERFORMANCE

The perfect exercise, which has a right to the highest marks, is one that is presented with elegance, ease, sureness, and confidence, in a rhythm and style well adapted to the nature of the aesthetical exercise, with no fault in the deportment or performance.

DEFECTIVE PERFORMANCE

The defects of performance and style are penalized by deducting a number of whole points or tenths of a point, according to the following directions:

DEFECTS IN GENERAL ELEGANCE

An exercise, although executed without fault, that is done in a rhythm too quick or too slow or with an ill-proportioned display of force, counts less than a perfect exercise. The penalty may be up to 3 tenths of a point.

STOPS, INTERRUPTIONS

1. Without leaving the apparatus. An unprescribed stop entails a deducting of points proportioned to the part of the corresponding exercise; and even a higher penalty if the stop facilitates the following part. Penalty for light cases (hesitation) is 2 tenths; if the interruption is more pronounced, 5 tenths; and in severe cases, up to half the points attributed to the part incorrectly executed.
2. Leaving the apparatus. In cases of leaving the apparatus, if the gymnast wholly or in part places his weight on the mat, the exercise is considered as finished and points are given only for the executed parts (this does not exclude the chance given to a gymnast to repeat a prescribed exercise if he thinks he failed in it).

ADDED MOVEMENTS

If a competitor adds one or several movements, each will be penalized with 3 to 5 tenths. It has to be seen whether the added movements facilitated the performance of the following part, in that case the penalty will be 1 to 5 tenths higher.

MAINTENANCE (HOLDS)

The duration of a prescribed maintenance (hold) (horizontal suspension, handstand, etc.) is usually 2 seconds.

TRAVELING ON THE POMMEL (SIDE) HORSE OR BARS

The traveling on the side horse must be continuous, and with legs stretched. Penalty: Touching the horse, by gliding of feet or legs, 1/10. More severe fault if causing interruption 2/10 to 5/10. Even more severe, i.e. pronounced sitting, 6/10 to 1 point. Touching the floor with one or both feet, without resting the weight of the body on the mat and without leaving of the hands and without noticeable interruption 5/10 to 1 point. On the parallel bars, the deductions are made in the same way. Example: Touching the bars or the floor by gliding, loss of 1/10 to 2/10.

HOLDING OF FEET, ARMS, LEGS, ETC.

Bad holding of toes and head, 1/10 to 2/10. Separating or bending of legs 1/10 to 2/10. Bending of arms 1/10 to 2/10. On the rings, bent handstand or touching of ropes 1/10 to 3/10. Arms bent and touching of ropes 3/10 to 5/10. Horizontal balance, just remarkable or bent arms 2/10 to 5/10. Just remarkable and bent arms, separated support (or above) 6/10 to 1 point. In general, handstands, suspensions or horizontal holds, unstable or not straight holding of body 1/10 to 3/10. Calisthenics: too long a run for handspring or somersault 1/10 to 3/10.

PRESENTATION, LANDING

All exercises must start and finish with good posture. The landing especially must be done with elegance and sureness. Bad posture in the beginning and the finish 1/10 to 2/10. Several steps or jumps 2/10 to 3/10. Landing on the back, knees or hands 5/10 to 6/10.

COMBINATION

Required is an exercise, well combined, presenting original parts or connections, a good start and a finish of value. The essential part must be connected with elegance, without additional balancing, nor repetitions, nor too easy parts relating to the general required difficulty. The optional exercise must differ clearly from the prescribed exercise and bring a different combination, especially in the start and finish. However, including one or the other part of the latter does not necessarily constitute a fault of combination, if the combinations before and after are different.

Penalties:

1. Unnecessary swinging, parts or combinations of no value, broken swings 1/10 to 3/10.
2. Combinations not conforming with the type of exercise meant for the apparatus 2/10 to 5/10.
3. If the duration of the floor exercise does not correspond with the time limit of 50 to 70 seconds, it will be penalized, but the judges will refrain from too pedantic a reasoning, because the too short exercise will have less difficulty and the too long one is usually due to faults in the execution. Loss from 1/10 to 3/10 maximum.
4. Maximum of loss for defective combinations: 2 points.

DIFFICULTY

The judge must watch that the difficulty exists in the essential parts as well as in the combinations. Besides, the judge must have a good knowledge of all elements that could possibly enter in a combination of movements. It is important that the judges can see the difficulty with knowledge of the cause and that they can get the most exact idea of all that could develop in that domain of difficulty. The task is difficult. The judges must have a great deal of practice and be able to see quickly and rightly.

EXECUTION

Special attention should be given to ease and perfect technique. The exercise must be adapted to the ability of the gymnast in difficulty and combination. Too difficult exercises that the gymnast can hardly or only incompletely master will be severely marked, because in artistic gymnastics the gymnast should be able to control his body with elegance and sureness.

RATING

To determine the mark, one can proceed in two ways:

1. By adding the points given for each of the two elements, that is:

Value: maximum difficulty with one fault in combination, therefore 5 less 0.2 =   4.8

Performance: general miss in elegance = − .2
incorrect performance = − .7
Therefore, 5 less (.2 + .7) = 5 − .9 =   4.1

                                                   Mark   8.9

2. By giving the exercise a maximum corresponding to its value (in case of perfect performance) and by then deducting faults in the performance. Example:

Value: maximum difficulty (fault in combination)   9.8

Faults in performance: general miss of elegance = − .2
incorrect performance = − .7
Therefore total deduction = 9.8 − .9 =   Mark   8.9

TUMBLING

Tumbling shall be limited to three routines of not over two minutes' duration. The mats or mat shall be no less than 60 feet in length. Touching the floor on either side of the mat will be regarded as poor form and the judges will deduct points accordingly. A contestant shall not be penalized for tumbling off the ends of the mats. He shall be permitted to leave the ends of the mats to secure a running start. Balance (or held) moves are not to be included in tumbling routines.

TRAMPOLINE

Each competitor shall perform two routines of ten bounces each with a ten second rest between the two routines. The competitor may take any number of preparatory bounces previous to his first moves in each routine. However, counting the first move as the beginning of the series, the performer shall be permitted ten contacts with the bed in each routine. Judges shall deduct points for poor planning for moves done after the tenth bounce. Routines must begin and end on the bed. One bounce is required after every somersault. A timer shall count (loudly enough that all can hear) the number of contacts with the bed. He shall also count off the seconds during the ten second rest period between routines. A minimum of six spotters (two on each side and one on each end) are mandatory. If a performer leaves the trampoline or is prevented from leaving the trampoline by his spotters, his routine is considered terminated at that time. Girls shall do only one ten-bounce routine with no rest period.

UNEVEN PARALLEL BARS

The height of the upper bar shall be between 6 feet 8 inches and 7 feet 2 inches, measured from the top of the bar to the floor. The height of the lower bar shall be between 4 feet and 4 feet 6 inches. The measurement between the bars shall be 14½ to 16 inches. Exercises shall be primarily swings with grasps and regrasps as the performer changes from bar to bar. Movements should be continuous and vigorous with a minimum of temporary balances. A beat board may be used on the mount.

BALANCE BEAM

The height of the beam shall be between 2 feet 6 inches and 3 feet 9 inches, measured from the top of the beam to the floor. The length of the beam shall be 16 feet 4 inches. The width of the beam at the top shall be 4 inches. The routine must be lively and continuous while avoiding monotony of rhythm. Steps, runs, jumps, turns, and dance movements (from ballet, contemporary and folk dancing) may be used in addition to rolls, acrobatic moves, and some balance positions. Moves in the erect, sitting, and lying positions should all be included. Sustained positions should not predominate. A beat board may be used on the mount. The exercise should last from 1 to 1½ minutes.

SIDE HORSE VAULT

The height of the horse shall be 36 inches measured from the top of the horse at the saddle to the floor. A Reuther board will be used. The competitor's hands must contact the horse. The landing should be well controlled and without jar. The vault will be judged by the length of the flight and the execution and control of the body throughout the vault. Each contestant shall be permitted two trials on each of the two optional vaults. The best will count. Contestants must report their selections previous to the initiation of competition.

TABLE OF DIFFICULTY

Vaults	Rating
Squat	3.5
Squat, 90 degree turn	4.0
Squat, 180 degree turn	4.5
Wolf vault (squat rt., left sideleg)	4.5
Wolf vault (squat rt., left sideleg), 90 degree turn right	5.0
Wolt vault (squat rt., left sideleg), 90 degree turn left	5.5
Wolf vault (squat rt., left sideleg), 180 degree turn without holding	5.5
Straddle	6.5
Straddle, 90 degree turn	7.0
Flank vault	7.0
Rear vault	7.0
Front vault	7.0
Window vault	7.0
Stoop (bent hip)	7.0
Neckspring	7.5
Headspring	8.0
Straddle, 180 degree turn	8.0
Squat archway (layout)	8.5
Bent arm handspring	8.5
Flank, 90 degree turn outward	8.5
Bent arm handspring, 90 degree turn	9.0
Stoop archway (layout)	10.0
Straddle archway (layout)	10.0
All straight-arm handstands	10.0

    1. handspring   4. handstand straddle
    2. handstand, 90 degree turn-off   5. handstand stoop
    3. handstand to cartwheel   6. handstand squat

Vaults	Rating
Cartwheel	10.0
Swan	10.0
Swan straddle	10.0

GENERAL REGULATIONS

1. No contestant shall be required to perform first in more than one event.
2. Except in the floor exercise, all contestants shall be permitted a spotter. However, contestants needing assistance will be penalized.
3. The contestant shall be entirely responsible for her own music in the free exercise event.
4. Girl contestants falling off the uneven parallel bars or balance beam may continue the exercise if the interruption was less than three seconds. Points will, however, be deducted.
5. Personal injuries should be reported to the meet director.

6. Contestants demonstrating lack of emotional control, indicating dissatisfaction in any manner with the score awarded them by the judges or seeking unfair advantage will be barred from further competition in that meet. The involved officials and the meet director will make this decision. Coaches are requested to present models of exemplary behavior for their children.

REFERENCES

Amateur Athletic Union of the United States Gymnastics Yearbook, 1956, official rules (men and women): pp. 64, 66–69.

Gymnastics Guide, June 1963—June 1965, with official rules and standards, edited by Dorothy MacLean, The Division for Girls' and Women's Sports: pp. 71–72.

APPENDIX C

SUPPLIERS OF GYMNASTIC EQUIPMENT

Name and Address	Specialty
American Athletic Equipment Co. Box 111 Jefferson, Ia. 50129	Equipment
American Playground Device Co. P.O. Drawer 2599 Anderson, Ind. 46011	Equipment
Atlas Athletic Equipment Co. Dept. M., 2339 Hampton Ave. St. Louis, Mo. 63139	Mats
Bickmore Acrobatic Company 16526 Sherman Way Van Nuys, Calif.	Circus equipment
Crons Gymnastic Specialties 41 Broadway Astoria, Long Island, N.Y. 11103	Gym clothes and accessories
Frank Endo 12200 So. Berendo Ave. Los Angeles, Calif. 90044	Shoes, handgrips, pants, suspenders, rings, chalk, films
Gymnastic Aides Northbridge, Mass. 01534	Charts and manuals
Gymnastic Associates, Ltd. 2210 Beaconsfield Ave. Montreal, Quebec, Canada	Equipment
Gymnastic Supply Company 247 W. Sixth St. San Pedro, Calif. 90733	Mats, equipment
Gym Master Company 3200 So. Zuni St. Englewood, Colorado 80110	Equipment
International Gymnastic Materials 3256 W. North Ave. Chicago, Illinois	Uniforms, handguards, slippers
Jayfro Corp. P.O. Box 400 Waterford, Conn. 06385	Equipment
Marcy Gym Equipment 1736 Standard Ave. Glendale, Calif. 91201	Equipment
Modern Gymnast Magazine Sundby Publications 410 Broadway Santa Monica, Calif. 90401	
Nissen Corporation Cedar Rapids, Ia. 52406	Equipment
Olympia Mat Mfg. Co., Inc. 9051 Del Mar Ave. Montclair, Calif. 91763	Mats
Olympic Products 269 E. Argyle St. Valley Stream, Long Island, N.Y.	Uniforms

Port a Pit   Crash pads
P.O. Box C
Temple City, Calif. 91780

Sedlinger Trampoline Co.   Trampolines
P.O. Box 2
Garland, Texas 75040

Sundby Publications   Movies
P.O. Box 777
Santa Monica, Calif. 90406

Shreveport Gymnastic Supply Co.   Gym clothes and
P.O. Box 5374   accessories
Shreveport, La. 71105

Universal Resilite   Gym pants
12 No. Cottage St.
Valley Stream, N.Y. 11580

Don Wilkinson   Photos
1013 8th Ave.
Greeley, Col. 80631

Zwickel Gymnastic Tailors   Uniforms
P.O. Box 309
Jenkintown, Pa. 19048

INDEX

NOTE: Individual moves are listed in progressive order of difficulty rather than alphabetically.